COMPARATIVE POLITICAL THEORY

COMPARATIVE POLITICAL THEORY

AN INTRODUCTION

Edited by
Fred Dallmayr

*(in consultation with
Wm. Theodore de Bary,
Roxanne L. Euben, and
Anthony J. Parel)*

First published in 2010 by
PALGRAVE MACMILLAN®
in the United States—a division of St. Martin's Press LLC,
175 Fifth Avenue, New York, NY 10010.

Where this book is distributed in the UK, Europe and the rest of the world,
this is by Palgrave Macmillan, a division of Macmillan Publishers Limited,
registered in England, company number 785998, of Houndmills,
Basingstoke, Hampshire RG21 6XS.

Palgrave Macmillan is the global academic imprint of the above companies
and has companies and representatives throughout the world.

Palgrave® and Macmillan® are registered trademarks in the United States,
the United Kingdom, Europe and other countries.

ISBN: 978–0–230–61862–6 (hardcover)
ISBN: 978–0–230–61863–3 (paperback)

Library of Congress Cataloging-in-Publication Data

Comparative political theory : an introduction / edited by Fred
Dallmayr.
    p. cm.
Includes bibliographical references and index.
ISBN 978–0–230–61862–6—ISBN 978–0–230–61863–3
    1. Political science. 2. Political science—Philosophy. 3. Comparative
government. I. Dallmayr, Fred R. (Fred Reinhard), 1928–

JA71.C5655 2009
320.01—dc22   2009006278

A catalogue record of the book is available from the British Library.

Design by Newgen Imaging Systems (P) Ltd., Chennai, India.

First edition: April 2010

10 9 8 7 6 5 4 3 2 1

Printed in the United States of America.

To those willing to learn everywhere

CONTENTS

Part Four   East Asian Political Thought

PREFACE

This book is an introduction to a new field of scholarly inquiry, a subfield of political science called "comparative political theory." The assumption guiding this book is that, in all or most societies throughout history, there has been some thinking or theorizing about politics, about the right and wrong ways, and the proper and improper ways of conducting public life in a community. Yet, at least as far as the practice in the United States is concerned, the teaching of political theory has been confined almost exclusively to the so-called Western "canon," that is, the tradition of political thought stretching roughly from Socrates to Marx or Nietzsche. No doubt, this is an immensely rich tradition and college students should be exposed to it and learn about its subtle nuances, its arguments and counterarguments, its points and counterpoints. However, in our age of rapid globalization, confinement to this canon is no longer adequate or justifiable. In our time, when the winds of trade spread not only goods but also ideas and cultural legacies around the globe, confinement to the Western tradition amounts to a parochial self-enclosure incompatible with university studies.

Globalization, to be sure, is only a very broad umbrella conception, which, by itself, does not explain the upsurge of the new kind of inquiry. In addition and as a backdrop to globalization, a number of other events or developments have conspired to make room for comparative political theory. Of major importance in this context was the demise of the Soviet Union in 1989 and thus of the cold war era during which the entire globe was dominated by two competing ideologies, liberalism and communism—ideologies that both were equally disinterested in nuanced cultural or civilizational distinctions. With the demise of this totalizing dichotomy, new perspectives or paradigms of inquiry were liberated or unleashed, a development that gave rise to such initiatives as multiculturalism, identity politics, postcolonial and gender studies, and even (what Gilles Kepel called) the "revenge of God." This upsurge was accompanied by a host of new intellectual and philosophical currents, like postmodernism, deconstruction, neo-Nietzscheanism, and neo-pragmatism.

The importance of comparative and cross-cultural studies was made clear to many observers barely a few years after the collapse of the Soviet Union by the publication of Samuel Huntington's article "The Clash of Civilizations?" in 1993. The merit of Huntington's essay was that it shifted the focus of global analysis from the Westphalian paradigm of sovereign nation-states to the "fault lines" existing between cultures and civilizations. The downside of his article was that he treated civilizations on a par with traditional, monolithic nation-states—and thus neglected precisely what is most valuable about cultures and civilizations: the fact that they are storehouses of accumulated learning and possess the ongoing capacity to learn afresh and transform themselves in the light of new experiences.

In large measure, comparative political theory—like comparative philosophy and comparative humanities—is an attempt to prove Huntington's thesis wrong. Of course, no one can rule out the possibility of cultural clashes or conflicts; but the thesis cannot be allowed to become a "self-fulfilling prophecy." In lieu of the Huntingtonian scenario, comparative inquiry places the emphasis on cross-cultural encounters, mutual learning, and (what has been called) "dialogue among civilizations." It so happens that, in 1999, the Iranian President Khatami proposed the idea of such a dialogue in a speech to the General Assembly of the United Nations; and the Assembly took up the idea and proceeded to designate 2001 as the "Year of the Dialogue Among Civilizations." The idea of such dialogue is significant for comparative political theory, which, like every comparative study, has to rely on cross-cultural questioning, dialogue, and perhaps contestation. Its urgency was underscored by the dramatic events of September 11 and the subsequent invasion of Iraq—events under whose shadow the world still lives today.

One particularly distinctive aspect of comparative political theory needs to be noted: as a subfield of political theory or political philosophy, it concentrates not so much on governmental structures and empirical political processes (the concern of "comparative politics") but rather on ideas, perspectives, and theoretical frameworks as they have been formulated in the past, and continue to be articulated today, in different parts of the world. In choosing this focus, comparative political theory places itself in large measure in the context of what modern political philosophy calls "civil society," a realm that forms a bridge between the strictly "private" and strictly "public" domains of life. Proceeding in this manner, practitioners can garner support from the American philosopher John Dewey, when he wrote about modern democracy: "Democracy is more than a form of government; it is primarily a mode of associated living, of conjoint communicated experience." Comparative political theorists proceed on the assumption or hope that something like a global civil society is emerging, making room for mutual learning and the cultivation of better understanding about ideas, aspirations, and practices.

The present text is a collection of essays seeking to introduce (mainly) college students to the field of comparative political theory. The assumption of the editor is that such students either have had a course dealing with the "canon" of Western political thought or else are taking such a course in tandem with a broader comparative class. Many of the chapters in this book make reference to leading Western thinkers, such as Plato, Aristotle, Machiavelli, Hobbes, and Locke. If teachers in the comparative class find that many of their students are not, or not sufficiently, familiar with these

Western thinkers, it will be incumbent on them to provide a brief background. After all, comparative political theory necessarily includes in its ambit comparisons between "Western" and "Eastern" thinkers, as well as between Indian and East Asian or between Islamic and African theoretical perspectives.

As an "Introduction" designed for a typical one-semester course, the book cannot possibly cover the wide field of global ideas throughout the ages. To make the undertaking feasible, I decided to focus on three main civilizational contexts (sometimes called "non-Western" contexts): the Islamic, the Indian, and the East Asian. Unfortunately, this focus leaves important other regions out of account, such as the African and Latin American. The choice was guided not by evaluative but by purely pragmatic considerations (what can be done in one semester). The present volume is organized in the form of a tour or journey: a journey leading from the more familiar to the less familiar, from the more proximate to the more distant. The journey starts from the Islamic civilization—a choice based on the fact that, as part of the so-called "Abrahamic" religions, Islam is closer than other cultures to the Western canon. The tour then proceeds to India or the Indian subcontinent and finally leads to East Asia (mainly China and Japan).

In each case, attention is given to both ancient or classical traditions and to modern and contemporary intellectual developments. This is also customary in the Western canon where Plato may be compared or contrasted with Machiavelli and Aristotle with Hobbes. To be sure, in the case of cross-cultural comparison, a special peculiarity needs to be noted: the historical trajectories of different cultures are not synchronized; hence the European Middle Ages do not neatly map onto a corresponding "medieval" period in India or Asia. Another, still more important feature needs to be kept in mind: cultures are linguistic and semantic frameworks whose ingredients are correlated in a particular, culture-specific order. There is no assurance that the coordination of semantic elements will carry over from place to place. The following are some examples. In the Western canon, the domains of philosophy (reason) and religion (faith) have over time become separated and today are often seen as opposites. This is by no means the case in "Eastern" traditions where philosophy and religion are often intimately linked. This is why, in the study of "non-Western" societies, religion must play a much larger role than would be customary in the West. Similarly culturally specific are the relation between private and public spheres of life and the respective weight accorded to ethical virtue and freedom. Finally, and perhaps most importantly, "politics" does not signify the same thing or occupy the same semantic status across cultures. This means that comparative study has to concentrate not on isolated terms but on broader semantic clusters or fields.

As an introduction to comparative political theory, this book is concerned primarily with ideas rather than historical details. Still, to understand the ideas, some historical background is needed. Hence, the introductions to the respective parts of the book offer a condensed historical information. Each part of the study contains at the end a selective bibliography that should allow students to explore more deeply a given topic. At this point I want to express my deep gratitude to the consulting editors, Professors deBary, Euben, and Parel, whose advice at many stages in the preparation of this book was invaluable. Now, let the journey begin.

October 2008   Fred Dallmayr

PERMISSIONS

The chapter by Ira R. Lapidus. "The Golden Age: The Political Concepts of Islam" has been reprinted with the permission of SAGE Publications.

The chapter by Mushin Mahdi, "Alfarabi" has been reprinted with the permission of the University of Chicago Press.

The chapter by Roxanne L. Euben, "A View Across Time: Islam as the Religion of Reason" has been reprinted with the permission of Princeton University Press.

The chapter by John L. Esposito, "Contemporary Islam: Reformation or Revolution?" has been reprinted with the permission of Oxford University Press.

The chapter by Youssef Choueiri, "The Political Discourse of Contemporary Islamist Movements" has been reprinted with the permission of the Perseus Book Group.

The chapter by Bhikhu Parekh, "Some Reflections on the Hindu Tradition of Political Thought" has been reprinted with the permission of SAGE Publications India.

The chapter by K. J. Shah, "Of *Artha* and *Arthashastra*" has been reprinted with the permission of SAGE Publications India.

The chapter by Thomas Pantham, "The Socio-Religious and Political Thought of Rammohun Roy" has been reprinted with the permission of SAGE Publications India.

The chapter by Anthony Parel, "Gandhi and the Emergence of the Modern Indian Political Canon" is reprinted with the permission of The Review of Politics.

The chapter by R. C. Pillai, "The Political Ideas of Jawaharlal Nehru" is reprinted with the permission of SAGE Publications India.

The chapter by Tu Weiming, "The Value of the Human in Classical Chinese Thought" has been reprinted with the permission of State University of New York Press.

The chapter by Ronald C. Keith, "Law and Society in Confucian Thought" has been reprinted with the permission of Lexington Books.

The chapter by Daniel A. Bell and Hahm Chaibong, "The Contemporary Relevance of Confucianism" is reprinted with the permission of Cambridge University Press.

The chapter by José I. Cabezón, "Buddhist Principles in the Tibetan Liberation Movement" is reprinted with the permission of State University of New York Press.

The chapter by Wm. Theodore de Bary, "East Asia and the West: Catching Up with Each Other" has been reprinted with the permission of Harvard University Press.

PART ONE

COMPARATIVE POLITICAL THEORY AND CULTURAL COMPARISON

INTRODUCTION

As indicated in the Preface, comparative political theory involves an effort of cross-cultural learning, of acquiring the ability to move, translate, and interpret across different (though by no means monolithic) cultural traditions. To this extent, comparative study cannot be monological, but has to be dialogical and perhaps polylogical. This means that practitioners in this field have to be at least bilingual and perhaps multilingual. This aspect also forms the background of the chosen phrase "comparative political theory." As we know, some theorists would prefer a more ambitious title like "global political theory" or "universal political philosophy." Without completely dismissing such preferences, the editor and his consultants have decided to cling to their title for a simple reason: the absence of a global or universal language. If there were such a language, no effort of translation and cross-cultural interpretation would be needed. Under present circumstances there is also the danger of hypostasis: that a certain hegemonic language would arrogate to itself the epithets of "global" or "universal," thereby marginalizing all other languages and cultures.

In terms of methodology, comparative political theory proceeds mainly through the interpretation of texts, utterances and practices, which in turn are embedded in a distinct life-form or cultural way of life. By relying on interpretation, it necessarily invokes the resources of interpretation theory or "hermeneutics," a theory which holds that interpreting or interpretive understanding is basically a dialogical enterprise. This means that, in approaching and interrogating other cultures, the interpreter is himself or herself called into question—with the result that the attempt to understand alien cultures usually entails also a new or revised self-understanding. On the basis of this revised self-understanding, new questions are then put forth, triggering a new round of deepened understanding and self-understanding. In addition to the resources of hermeneutics, comparative study relies on the teachings of language theory, linguistics, and philology—all of which fine-tune the mind to the demands of careful exegesis. Beyond the confines of textual interpretations, comparative political theorists will often find helpful the insights of comparative anthropology as well as the lessons derived from geographical area studies and the participatory involvement in concrete life-worlds.

In large measure, academic philosophy has been way ahead of political theory in moving into the area of comparative study. A particularly instructive text is the volume edited by philosophers Gerald Larson and Eliot Deutsch titled *Interpreting across Boundaries: New Essays in Comparative Philosophy*. Indian philosopher Daya Krishna has contributed to this volume an important chapter called "Comparative Philosophy: What It Is and What It Ought to Be." In his essay, Krishna first of all takes exception to the claim that only Western philosophy (including political philosophy) is "philosophy" in the proper sense—a claim that elevates the Western canon to a spurious "universal" status. In addition to debunking a hegemonic universalism,

Krishna also takes aim at cultural "relativism," based on a supposed "incommensurability" of cultures, which would undermine comparative inquiry altogether. For Krishna, comparative philosophy has to focus on both similarities and differences, but initially keep differences clearly in mind. Proceeding in this way, he writes, comparative study helps "to enrich oneself with the awareness of an alternative possibility of thought." Thus, comparative philosophy "has the chance to function as a mutual liberator of each philosophical tradition from the limitations imposed upon it by its own past."[1] In a similar vein, comparative philosopher Henry Rosemont Jr., in a chapter "Against Relativism," undercuts a complacent cultural relativism, fashionable in some quarters, without endorsing the pretense of Western universality. The proper path for him is to search for "homoversal" (perhaps better "transversal") principles and conceptions, which allow us to navigate between cultures without diminishing their richness.[2]

Perhaps the most instructive chapter in the volume is by Spanish-Indian philosopher Raimon Panikkar, entitled "What Is Comparative Philosophy Comparing?" Like Daya Krishna, Panikkar argues against the equation of comparative philosophy with a "universal" doctrine based on a "One-World" formula, against what he calls "the monomorphism of a monolithic reality." By ignoring differences, this equation nips comparison in the bud before it can even get started. For Panikkar, comparative philosophy is a philosophical inquiry dealing with different philosophical traditions and frameworks. In his view, there are five major types of such inquiry, not all of which are equally valid or helpful. One is a "transcendental" approach. It starts from a priori premises and adopts an Archimedean standpoint, thereby subsuming all other forms of reflection under its own schema. For Panikkar, this approach shortchanges differences while elevating itself to the status of a metaphilosophy. A second approach is "formal-structural" and concentrates on the invariant features—the governing syntax or algebra—underlying all cultures. Again, the approach is too far removed from concrete semantic contents to lead very far. A third option is linguistics or linguistic analysis, which, although valuable in many respects, tends to stop at the level of formal rules without entering into deeper philosophical inquiry. A fourth option is "a certain phenomenological method." Although finding an advance in this approach, Panikkar chides some phenomenologists for focusing too much on private consciousness at the expense of the study of texts and shared life-forms. A fifth approach—the one favored by Panikkar—is called "dialogical" or "imparative" philosophy.[3]

In opposition to the transcendental or Archimedean perspective, dialogical philosophy places itself in the midst between cultures, approaching them laterally rather than from the top down. The approach is also called "imparative," from the Latin *imparare*, meaning to learn. In Panikkar's words, we choose "the name of 'imparative philosophy' in order to stress an open philosophical attitude ready to learn from whatever philosophical corner of the world, but without claiming to compare philosophies from an objective, neutral, and transcendent vantage point." To adopt a learning attitude means to accept the existing plurality of philosophies as well as the "pluralism" of life-worlds. However, wedded to reflective inquiry, comparative study does not allow pluralism to degenerate into a shallow relativism inclined to celebrate not difference but indifference. To quote Panikkar again:

> Imparative philosophy does not pretend to possess a fulcrum outside time and space and above any other philosophy from which to scrutinize the different human philosophical perspectives.... [But] it is constitutively ready to

question its own most basic foundations if this is requested by any other philosophical school. Nothing is nonnegotiable.[4]

Comparative philosophers have not been alone in exploring and clarifying the "method" of comparative inquiry. Less frequently, political theorists have also pursued this line of inquiry, usually adding their own accents or preferences. Among an older generation of political theorists mention must be made especially of Eric Voegelin and Leo Strauss. In examining cross-cultural currents especially during the so-called "ecumenic age," Voegelin discovered certain ideational parallels or analogues—what he called "equivalences"—between cultural traditions, parallels which, falling short of identities, allow for a degree of pluralism. In terms of approach, Voegelin preferred the accent on "consciousness" (Panikkar's fourth approach), supplementing it with some normative-transcendental principles.[5] A similar approach was followed by Leo Strauss, though with a distinctive interpretive twist. In studying the texts of another tradition—say, the texts of the Islamic philosopher al-Farabi—Strauss considered it important not to cling to the texts alone, but to penetrate to the intention of the author or what the author wanted to convey in a given text.[6] This approach—the search for the author's mind (*mens auctoris*)—was a prominent feature of nineteenth-century interpretation theory or hermeneutics, and it continues to attract numerous followers. There are at least two difficulties, however, with this approach. The first is the problem of access. Especially in the case of authors far removed from us in time and space, it appears nearly impossible to enter and decipher an author's mind or consciousness with any degree of confidence. This problem is compounded by another aspect. Even if we could reliably access the inner mind, there is no neat coincidence of intention and text. As part of a complex system of linguistic signifiers, texts often say more or other things than what the author had in mind. Hence, the meaning of texts cannot readily be fixated by resort to states of mind.[7]

The essay by Fred Dallmayr titled "Beyond Monologue: For a Comparative Political Theory" (see below) elaborates in greater detail on the historical background and contemporary motivations of comparative political theory. The main emphasis of the essay, however, is on the pioneering work of some recent and contemporary political theorists as well as on the future directions and implications of this kind of study. The essay might fruitfully be read in conjunction with another essay by Kenneth Schmitz (not included in this volume), which tackles a difficult but crucial theoretical problem, namely, how it is possible to think together and reconcile "The Unity of Human Nature and The Diversity of Cultures."[8] Schmitz offers a useful definition of "culture," which should be kept in mind throughout subsequent readings: culture, he says, is "the distinctive ensemble of more or less stable and general ways in which a community and its members act, an integer of customs, values and traditions, usually bound together by a common language and often by common group memories." Within this ensemble of features, politics is concerned with organizing and giving direction to the affairs of the community (which can happen in diverse ways). Like Daya Krishna and Rosemont, Schmitz is critical of both a sham universalism and a radical heterogeneity of cultures: in the first case there is no need for, in the second no possibility of comparison.

In his essay, Schmitz distinguishes also usefully between "plurality" and "pluralism." While the former refers simply to the factual coexistence of cultures, pluralism means a mutual engagement and learning experience among them. Schmitz lists two main factors explaining the diversity of cultures: first, the need for survival

(Latin *esse*), which may employ different methods and resources; and second, the search for meaning and well-being (Latin *bene esse*), which involves ethical dispositions, historical experiences, imagination, memory, and the like. The most important question raised by Schmitz is this: Given the great diversity of cultures, how can humanity be said to exhibit commonality? He discusses several modes of commonality, finding both family resemblances and the use of analogical language insufficient. Invoking both Aristotle and Hegel, he settles in the end in favor of a concrete or "contextual" commonality achieved through cross-cultural interaction and dynamic participation in the fostering of humanity across cultural borders. In his words, what is needed is the engagement to cultivate

> the positive opportunities the *space between* offers us: the opportunity to sift what is essential and what is best and best loved in one's own culture, to sift it from what needs eradication, correction and development, and to respect that process in others....The exchange calls for listening as well as speaking, for we are being called to venture out into relatively unexplored seas, into unknown space between the cultures, in which we must recognize the freedom of others to contribute to what can only be the *joint* building up of the unity-in-diversity of humankind.

NOTES

1. Daya Krishna, "Comparative Philosophy: What It Is and What It Ought to Be," in Gerald J. Larson and Eliot Deutsch, eds., *Interpreting Across Boundaries: New Essays in Comparative Philosophy* (Princeton, PA: Princeton University Press, 1988), pp. 79–80, 83.
2. Henry Rosemont, Jr., "Against Relativism," in *Interpreting Across Boundaries*, pp. 68–69.
3. Raimundo Panikkar, "What Is Comparative Philosophy Comparing?," in *Interpreting Across Boundaries*, pp. 118, 121–127.
4. Panikkar, pp. 127–130.
5. See Eric Voegelin, "Equivalences of Experiences and Symbolization in History," *Philosophical Studies*, vol. 28 (1981), pp. 88–102; also his *Order and History*, vol. 4: *The Ecumenic Age* (Baton Rouge: Louisiana State University Press, 1974).
6. Compare Leo Strauss, *Persecution and the Art of Writing* (Glencoe, IL: Free Press, 1952).
7. This is the gist of Jacques Derrida's arguments in *Speech and Phenomena*, trans. David B. Allison (Evanston, IL: Northwestern University Press, 1973), and *Writing and Difference*, trans. Alan Bass (Chicago, IL: University of Chicago Press, 1978).
8. See Kenneth Schmitz, "The Unity of Human Nature and the Diversity of Cultures," in George F. McLean and John Kromkowski, eds., *Relations Between Cultures* (Washington, DC: Council for Research in Values and Philosophy, 1991), pp. 305–322.

BEYOND MONOLOGUE: FOR A COMPARATIVE POLITICAL THEORY[1]

Fred Dallmayr

Over four decades ago, Leo Strauss concluded one of his essays famously by stating that political science "fiddles while Rome burns."[2] The basic aim of the phrase was to stir the profession from the prevailing slumber of positivism or behavioralism, or from a certain mindlessness induced by random data gathering. At the same time, and perhaps more specifically, the phrase was meant to be a clarion call to fellow political theorists to recapture the Socratic élan of their enterprise: the task to unravel the meaning and moral direction of political life. Many things have happened since Strauss penned his essay; but its timeliness has not diminished. In the wake of 9/11 and the ensuing global repercussions, his phrase has acquired still greater relevance, prompting the question whether political science—and political theory in particular—is properly attentive to the "burning" issues of our time, that is, properly responsive to the Socratic challenge of critical political inquiry. In an effort to foster such responsiveness, the present chapter advances a proposal addressed chiefly to political theorists, but with implications for the entire profession: the proposal to replace or supplement the rehearsal of routinized canons with a turn to global, cross-cultural, or "comparative" political theorizing. In the following discussion, I first offer some reasons or motivations why the turn seems appropriate today. Next I discuss a variety of theoretical or philosophical inspirations buttressing or undergirding the turn. Finally I explore its broader political implications.

Before proceeding further, let me briefly sketch my sense of cross-cultural or comparative political theory (whose contours will emerge more fully in subsequent discussions). By this term I mean a mode of theorizing that takes seriously the ongoing process of globalization, which entails, among other things, the growing proximity and interpretation of cultures or the emergence of (what Marshall McLuhan called) the "global village." In contrast to hegemonic or imperialist modes of theorizing, the term implies that the language or idiom of the emerging "village" (or global civil society) cannot be monopolized by one segment of its population. Differently put, shared meanings and practices—to the extent that this is possible—can only arise from the lateral interaction, negotiation, and contestation among different, historically grown cultural frameworks. This, in turn, means that the basic approach favored by comparative political theory is dialogical or "hermeneutical" (the latter term signifying reliance on mutual interpretation).[3] Given this orientation, practitioners of comparative theorizing necessarily have to be multilingual as well as trained in good translation practices—although the vast terrain of cross-cultural comparison imposes limits on the range of linguistic competence.[4] Basically, practitioners need to steer a course between the stance of narrow area specialists and that of abstract generalists: while the former slight the "theoretical," the latter miss the "comparative" component of comparative political theory. In terms of prominent contemporary approaches, comparative theorizing clearly departs from (what is commonly called) "formal theory," a perspective that imposes a general or universal "form" on diverse phenomena, thereby disclosing its indebtedness to the universalist claims of the European Enlightenment.

SOME CONTEMPORARY MOTIVATIONS

There are many reasons supporting the turn to comparative political theory. Ineluctably, one of these reasons is 9/11. At its annual meeting in the fall of 2001, the program of one of the leading professional organizations featured a panel with the topic "What Is Political Theory?" The panel attracted a large audience—and appropriately so. Panelists included leading practitioners of the field in America and their comments offered thoughtful and well-informed reflections on many topics in the long history of political thought. Nevertheless, despite these undeniable qualities, the panel also revealed a deep-seated professional bias or what one may call an intellectual inhospitability: By limiting themselves to familiar theories of the Western "canon" (from Plato to Rawls), panelists inadvertently paid tribute to what Samuel Huntington had termed the "West's" exclusion of, or predominance over, the "rest."[5] Barely ten days after the meeting 9/11 happened—with consequences we are still trying to unravel today. Surely, one of the things dramatically revealed on that day was the vulnerability of America: the fact that the country is inexorably part and parcel of our globalizing world—which cannot help but have serious professional and theoretical consequences. Witnessing the rapid sequence of the above events, a senior practitioner of political theory (like myself) was bound to recall Leo Strauss' words of several decades ago regarding a certain "fiddling" of (otherwise well-intentioned) professionals.

To be sure, 9/11 was only a particularly striking symptom nested in a host of complex global developments. Like a sudden bolt of lightning, the event illuminated the contours of a rapidly changing and disturbing international landscape. Roughly contemporaneously with event, many parts of the world witnessed episodes of genocide and ethic cleansing—on a scale that belied facile assumptions of shared standards. In their combined effect, episodes of this kind laid siege to the fragile fabric of international "order," which had prevailed since World War II. At the same time, the rapid expansion of global markets challenged or eroded the traditional structure of nation-states around the world—a challenge that carried in its wake the emergence of new forms of global economic hierarchy or inequality.[6] Partly as a result of these changed conditions, national independence or "liberation" movements were often forced into retreat, being eclipsed by the upsurge of a multitude of postcolonial and neocolonial modes of tutelage and subservience. What became increasingly clear to thoughtful observers of these changes was the need to imagine and cultivate new cross-cultural or intercivilizational bonds or arrangements, this time grounded in the active engagement and participation of cultures and people "on the ground," that is, in the juncture of local and global concerns.[7]

The dramas of the age were bound to intrude in due course into academia. Although often shielded by ivory tower conventions, many academic disciplines were ready to follow and keep pace with the unfolding cross-cultural and globalizing scenario. Without question, the leader in this respect was the discipline of anthropology, a field committed since its beginnings to far-flung ethnological and ethnographic studies. Ever since Edward Tylor's work on "primitive cultures" and Malinoski's journey to the Trobriand Islanders, hosts of cultural anthropologists have been eager to immerse themselves in the rich tapestry of cultural idioms and traditions around the globe. In exemplary fashion, methodological guideposts for these studies—above all the methods of field interviews and "hermeneutical" under-standing—were articulated by a number of leading practitioners, including Clifford Geertz and Marshall Sahlins.[8] Building on these precedents, other human sciences were poised to follow suit, sometimes adding a more political edge. Under the impact of postcolonialism and the upsurge of global communications networks, new fields of academic inquiry were launched, including the fields of "culture studies" and "post-colonial studies" dedicated to the examination of the interconnection and contestation between Western and non-Western societies in our time.[9] As one should not forget, broad cross-cultural perspectives have also been fostered for some time by practitioners of "religious studies," sometimes yielding a rich harvest of inter-religious comparisons.[10] All these academic and nonacademic developments combined were bound to put pressure also on "political science," an enterprise ini-tially launched as a strictly Western (or American) discipline. The first upshot of this pressure was "comparative politics," a subfield conducted along empirical lines and largely wedded to Western conceptual models. Eventually, however, political theo-rists were placed under the same pressure and hence compelled to reconsider "canon-ical" attachments.

PHILOSOPHICAL SOURCES OF INSPIRATION

When turning to political theory, a certain peculiarity needs to be noted. Although attentive to some of the motivations discussed so far, political theorists are ultimately bound to be persuaded only by properly theoretical arguments, chiefly by arguments provided by recent and contemporary philosophy. As it happens, twentieth-century European and Anglo-American philosophy is replete with guideposts pointing in the direction of a more cross-cultural orientation, that is, an opening of the "West" toward the "rest." Prominent among these guideposts or sea-changes are the so-called "linguistic turn" (the turn from ego consciousness to language) associated with Ludwig Wittgenstein and a host of subsequent philosophers; "phenomenol-ogy" (the study of the meaning of phenomena) launched by Edmund Husserl; "hermeneutics" (interpretation theory); and facets of "pragmatism" and postmodern "deconstruction" (both aiming at the critique of traditional metaphysical premises). What is common to these different orientations is a certain dissatisfaction with mod-ern Western egocentrism (stylized in Descartes' *ego cogito*) and its corollary of Eurocentrism. Sometimes all the mentioned sea changes converge in a philosophical work, which is preeminently true of the work of Martin Heidegger. The very starting point of Heidegger's philosophy—his formulation of human existence as "being-in-the-world"—places him at odds with Cartesian metaphysics by inserting the "think-ing ego" immediately into a world context composed of societies, fellow beings, and nature. The method adopted in his *Being and Time* was explicitly described as a "hermeneutical phenomenology," that is, as an interpretive study of human world experience. Over the years, his intellectual trajectory was marked by growing con-cern with the wider world context, now taking the form of globalization, and with the role of language in cross-cultural understanding. After World War II he collaborated with a Chinese scholar in the translation (not completed) of the *Tao*

Te Ching. Subsequent decades saw him preoccupied with the progressive "Europeanization" or standardization of the globe under the aegis of Western technology. In response, his writings urged a new "planetary thinking," which, though nurtured by local cultural idioms, would transcend hostile parochialisms through dialogical engagement.[11]

Heidegger's initiative was pursued and fleshed out by his student and associate Hans-Georg Gadamer, probably the leading philosopher of "dialogue" in recent times. Gadamer's accent from the beginning has rested on hermeneutics, that is, the endeavor to gain understanding through an intensive dialogue or encounter between reader and text, between self and other, between indigenous traditions and alien life forms. Truth or insight, from this vantage, cannot be garnered by a retreat into neutral spectatorship or a "view from nowhere," but only through a concrete existential engagement—an engagement where familiar assumptions (or "pre-judices") are brought to bear, and allowed to be tested, against unfamiliar perspectives and practices in a shared search for meaning. This approach was famously outlined in Gadamer's *Truth and Method*, which presented interpretation no longer as an optional academic methodology but as constitutive ingredient of human existence and human inquiry. The more concrete cross-cultural and multicultural implications of this view were subsequently developed in a number of writings, especially in a volume titled *The Legacy of Europe*, which sought to extricate Europe (or the West) resolutely from the straitjacket of "Eurocentrism," presenting it instead as the emblem of multicultural diversity ready for new learning experiences in a globalizing age.[12]

As it happens, Heidegger's and Gadamer's teachings have been well received and creatively re-interpreted by numerous thinkers in East Asia, India, and the Muslim world. A good example of creative reception is the Indian philosopher J. L. Metha. Raised in India and trained initially at Banares Hindu University, Mehta later spent considerable time in Europe and America where he gained a thorough knowledge of Western philosophy, and especially of the works of Heidegger and Gadamer. Repeatedly, he acknowledged the significance of their thought—not for the sake of passive imitation but of creative renewal. As he wrote at one time: "For all non-Western civilizations, however decrepit or wounded, Heidegger's thinking brings hope, at this moment of world history, by making them see that . . . they are now free to think for themselves, in their own fashion." For Mehta, as for his Western mentors, the task of contemporary philosophy, especially planetary philosophy, was neither to discard all indigenous traditions in favor of the supremacy of Western modernity, nor to become entrenched in traditional parochialisms and sequestered worldviews; nor was it a matter of forging a hasty fusion or confusion shortchanging reciprocal questioning. In his words again: what is required is "no facile compromise or reconciliation, miscalled 'synthesis'" but rather "a relentless exposure to the tension between the scientific consciousness [of the West] and the legacy of the [cultural and religious] past"; only in this way is it possible to "learn to address the right questions to our religious tradition and be rewarded by answers truly adequate to our present situation."[13]

To be sure, Heideggerian impulses have not been alone in fostering a philosophical sea change; they were fruitfully assisted by developments in language philosophy and French phenomenology and deconstruction. In the former domain, Wittgenstein's later writings contextualized human reason and the subject of cognition (*cogito*) by making them a function of grammar and of multiple "language games." The implications of this move were developed still more resolutely by the Russian linguist Mikhail Bakhtin whose idea of "heteroglossia" underscores the need for multilingual dialogues between (only partially translatable) idioms and cultural frameworks.[14] In the French context, Jacques Derrida's work points in a similar direction; his key notion of *différance* (radical self-difference), in particular, is meant to unsettle rigidly self-contained identities or invariant meaning structures. Drawing out the political implications of this notion, his book *The Other Heading* urges a basic repositioning of Europe or the West in the world, a repositioning that would replace its role as "capstone" or headmaster by a different "heading" more hospitable to cross-cultural learning.[15] In recommending this change, the book endorses the legacy of his older compatriot, Maurice Merleau-Ponty, whose reflections on language and culture urgently deserve to be remembered today. As for Derrida, the task for Merleau-Ponty was to resist the lure of a privileged or hegemonic spectatorship and to engage rather in the labor of concrete "lateral" interactions. As he wrote in a text on modern social science: "How can we understand someone else without sacrificing him to our logic or it to him?" Preferring to assimilate reality quickly to our ideas, (Western) social science has tended to proceed "as if it could roam over the object of its investigations at will . . . [as] an absolute observer." As an antidote to this approach, Merleau-Ponty proposed an alternative path to the universal: "no longer the overarching universal of a strictly objective method, but a sort of lateral universal which we acquire through ethnological experience and its incessant testing of the self through the other person and the other person through the self."[16]

All the mentioned initiatives combined paved the way to a properly "comparative" philosophizing on a cross-cultural or intercivilizational plane. The challenge of such a mode of philosophizing was well understood and confronted by J. L. Mehta when he tried to compare Heidegger's thought with the complex tradition of Indian Vedanta. In such an attempt, he realized, abstract metaphysical concepts and categories need to be put aside or at least "sublated" for the goal of "setting free, bringing into view and articulating in contemporary ways of speaking . . . the matter of thinking which, in what has actually been realized in thought, still remains unsaid and so unthought in the tradition of the East."[17] Parallel arguments can be found in the writings of the Spanish-Indian scholar Raimundo Panikkar. In an instructive essay titled "What is Comparative Philosophy Comparing?" Panikkar attacked a widespread tendency to submerge comparison in the categories of a hegemonic and supposedly "universal" metaphysics. Under such auspices, he noted, comparative studies are integrated into "the thrust toward universalization characteristic of Western culture," its desire to exert control "by striving toward a global picture of the world." A basic endeavor of his essay was to debunk this pretense: "Comparative philosophy cannot accept a method that reduces all visions to the view of one single philosophy" or meta-philosophy. As an alternative Panikkar delineated what he termed a "dialogical" or else "imparative" mode of philosophizing [see Introduction above]. Such a mode of philosophizing, he observed, reflects an attitude "which is convinced that we cannot escape taking a stand somewhere when we philosophize" and that such a limitation makes our theorizing "relative to similar enterprises undertaken from different angles." The proper method to be pursued, in Panikkar's view, is a "diatopical hermeneutics," that is, a mode of interpretation required when the difference to be negotiated is "the distance between two (or more) cultures which have independently developed in different spaces (topoi) their own forms of philosophizing and ways of reaching intelligibility."[18]

COMPARATIVE POLITICAL THEORY

Despite their political connotations, philosophical guideposts of this kind have reached political scientists and theorists only with some delay. Apart from other complicating factors, this delay may have something to do with the nature of academic political science, or at least with its mainstream self-image. In the view of many practitioners, the subject matter of political science is power and its exercise in a collective arena—and nothing else. Given this privileged focus, the same practitioners tend to be attracted or attached to what are called the "corridors of power"— which nowadays are located chiefly in the West. Even students of international politics, including global development, preponderantly share the same outlook. In light of this disciplinary orientation, it is not entirely surprising that many of the pioneering efforts in the direction of a comparative political theory have been launched by practitioners located at, or hailing from, the periphery of the "corridors of power."

A good case in point is the Canadian-Indian political theorist Anthony Parel. Having immersed himself in his earlier years in a thorough study of Western political thought (with a focus on Aristotle, Aquinas, and Machiavelli), Parel subsequently shifted his research toward comparative or cross-cultural inquiries, paying special attention to (East) Indian traditions. Corroborating this shift, he soon cleared a path for himself and other practitioners by (co-)editing the very first book in this field of inquiry: *Comparative Political Philosophy: Studies Under the Upas Tree* (1992). As he noted in introducing his book, scholarship in political theory has preponderantly come to mean the study of modern Western political thought—on the assumption that modern Western texts are "products of universal reason itself." In our contemporary context, however, this assumption has become dubious. In fact, Parel found "mounting evidence" suggesting that Western claims of universality are being "questioned by other cultures, or at least by significant representatives of these cultures"—a questioning which renders comparative political theorizing today "both opportune and intellectually satisfying." In terms of the text, the phrase "comparative political philosophy" meant an approach that takes seriously "the validity of cultural pluralism and philosophical pluralism," which does not amount to an endorsement of relativism or radical incommensurability. Although acknowledging the distances between cultural frameworks, comparison in Parel's view has to explore not only existing differences but also possible overlaps or similarities—what (following Eric Voegelin) he terms "equivalences." Thus, it is possible to discover fruitful resemblances by comparing, for instance, "the Aristotelian *politikos* and the Confucian *junzi*, Indian dharma and the pre-modern Western notion of 'natural justice,' the Islamic prophet-legislator and the Platonic philosopher-king." Paying heed both to equivalences and differences is bound to enrich scholarship, by being able both to "deepen one's understanding of one's own tradition and engender understanding and respect for the traditions of others."[19]

A parallel foray beyond mainstream "canons" was undertaken roughly at the same time by the Korean-American political theorist Hwa Yol Jung. Relying in part on Continental philosophy and in part on the work of the historian Hayden White, Jung introduced the notion of a "differential" or "diatactical" mode of theorizing (where "diatactics" means a concrete-experiential form of encounter). As he wrote (in 1989), modern Western thinking has tended to be monological and "logocentric" (centered on the *cogito*), thereby allowing a detached and "disembodied reason" to generate the specters of ethnocentrism and Eurocentrism.

To counteract these specters, diatactics champions a "new, lateral way of interpreting culture, especially an alien culture, based on the principle of *difference* in the Heideggerian sense of both *Differenz* and *Unterschied* (i.e., heterology)." More recently, Jung has spelled out further the implications of this approach in a volume titled *Comparative Political Culture in the Age of Globalization*. The basic aim of the volume is again to "decenter" or call into question the "canonization" of the modern West, its "narcissistic or hegemonic" self-image that privileges Europe or the West as "cultural, scientific, religious and moral mecca and capital of the world." Casting his cultural net very wide—from the Latin American thinker Enrique Dussel to the Vietnamese Thich Nhat Hanh—Jung now links comparative study with a "relational ontology" or a conception of "interbeing" according to which everything must "inter-be" or be "inter-connected to everything else" in the world. Employing such terms as "transtopia" and "transversality," his study credits comparative theorizing with overcoming the twin dangers of "ethnocentric chauvinism" and "faceless universalism," as well as the dead-ends of "Orientalism" and "Occidentalism."[20]

Another major impulse promoting "transversal" studies comes from the Canadian political theorist Charles Taylor. Deeply rooted in the Hegelian tradition—creatively reinterpreted—as well as in recent philosophical hermeneutics, Taylor's work has given a powerful boost to cross-cultural or "multicultural" studies highlighting dialogical encounter and recognition. As he writes in a famous study on that topic: a crucial feature of human life is "its fundamentally dialogical character" manifest in the fact that "we define our identity always in dialogue with, sometimes in struggle against, the things our significant others want to see in us." Without shortchanging the modern ideas of individual freedom and equality, Taylor finds it desirable to supplement the liberal "politics of equal dignity" with a sturdy "politics of difference," which—in lieu of an abstract "difference blindness"—seeks to "maintain and cherish distinctness," that is, the "potential for forming and defining one's own identity, as an individual and as a culture." As one should note, multiculturalism from his perspective does not imply an "anything goes" relativism nor a "melting pot" confusion, but rather an open-minded learning process across boundaries: "an admission that we are very far away from that ultimate horizon from which the relative worth of different cultures might be evident."[21] Relying on these premises, Taylor has engaged in comparative inquiries on many levels: focusing not only on relations between Anglophone and Francophone political cultures in his native Canada, but also on broader East-West comparisons—for example, on the different usage of the "language of rights" between Western liberals and Asian Buddhists. As he writes thoughtfully in the latter context, proper cross-cultural comparison arises not from an exodus from the past but from a willingness to engage in mutual learning: "Contrary to what many people think, world convergence will not come through a loss or denial of traditions all around, but rather by creative reimmersions of different groups, each in their own spiritual heritage, traveling different routes to this goal."[22]

In the field of multiculturalism, one of the most significant contributions is owed to the British-Indian political theorist Bhikhu Parekh. Like Anthony Parel, Parekh devoted his early career to a sustained immersion in Western political thought, giving particular attention to the works of Jeremy Bentham, Michael Oakeshott, and Hannah Arendt. Like Parel again, he subsequently broadened his horizons, shifting his focus to the legacy of Gandhi and to issues of postcolonialism and multiculturalism. His book, *Rethinking Multiculturalism: Cultural*

Diversity and Political Theory, is a path-breaking text in this field. Apart from probing discussions of such topics as the meaning of "culture," the relation between pluralism and universalism, and the appropriate structure of a multicultural society, the book offers valuable observations on comparative political theorizing along dialogical or hermeneutical lines. Such theorizing, he states, has to recognize the interplay of three aspects or factors: "the cultural embeddedness of human beings, the inescapability and desirability of cultural diversity and intercultural dialogue, and the internal plurality of each culture." Together with Panikkar and Gadamer, Parekh remonstrates against the adoption of a privileged "view from nowhere," which distances and neutralizes all cultural differences: "The common good and the collective will that are vital to any political society are generated not by transcending cultural and other particularities, but through their interplay in the cut and thrust of a dialogue."[23]

The preceding survey of political theorists cannot and does not claim to be exhaustive; given the vast scope of the cross-cultural domain every account necessarily has to be selective. Yet, my presentation would be seriously remiss if it did not refer at least briefly to other significant contributions. Among an older generation of theorists, mention must surely be made of two prominent thinkers: Leo Strauss and Eric Voegelin—the former because of his attentiveness to the great Muslim philosopher al-Farabi; the latter because of his notion of "equivalences" and his study of the "ecumenic age."[24] Partly following Strauss's lead, Islamic political philosophy of the classical age has been the central focus of Charles Butterworth whose writings on al-Farabi and Ibn Rushd have established standards of scholarly excellence in this field. In turn, Butterworth's example has inspired a number of younger theorists dedicated to the exploration of the connection between modern and contemporary Islam and Western democratic theory.[25] As in the case of academic philosophy proper, Western political theorists today can find resonance and responsiveness in virtually all non-Western contexts. Thus, to take up the example of Islam again, important contributions to comparative political theorizing can be found in the works of the Moroccan Muhammad al-Jabri, the Iranian Abdolkarim Soroush, and many others.[26] In the Indian context, comparative theory can find valuable dialogue partners in such thinkers as Rajni Kothari, Ashis Nandy, Rajeev Bhargava, and Thomas Pantham.[27] In the East Asian context, a lively dialogue is already ongoing among such theorists as Daniel Bell, Chaibong Hahm, Joseph Chan, and numerous others. Similar comments could be made about Africa and Latin America.[28]

CRITICAL QUERIES AND BROADER IMPLICATIONS

As a result of the initiatives sketched so far, comparative political theory has been steadily gaining momentum, emerging as a viable field or subfield in the professional discipline. A number of publication outlets are available today, making the enterprise attractive especially to younger scholars.[29] At this point, some critical queries might be addressed, before turning to broader implications. To obviate misunderstanding, it seems desirable to comment first of all on the vexed issue of "universalism" (repeatedly alluded to in the preceding discussion). Comparative or cross-cultural study is often taken to task for favoring a parochial "identity politics" and thus betraying the idea of universalism or the aspirations to "universality" inherent in modernity. The charge is unfounded or at least misdirected. To be sure, being attentive to diverse traditions or life-forms, comparative study valorizes difference or "otherness" (including what Taylor calls a "politics of difference"); but this is far removed from parochialism. Actually, one might claim that cross-cultural comparativists are genuine or better universalists. This claim can be buttressed by the simple test question: *who* is universal or *whose* conception of universalism is really universal? Anyone who asserts to be universal and thus monopolizes universalism, by this very act necessarily excludes others from his/her monopoly (thereby undermining the very idea of universalism). Shunning monopolistic or monological gestures, all we can plausibly and truthfully do is to "aspire" to universality in our different ways; but to do this we surely need to take others and their aspirations seriously, which requires dialogue and empathetic attentiveness.

The point of comparative political theory, in my view, is precisely to move in the direction of a more genuine universalism, and beyond the spurious "universality" traditionally claimed by the West and the Western canon—and also by some recent intellectual movements. The idea of "universal feminism" is a case in point. Clearly, the idea makes no sense unless we believe that women make some difference, that we need to listen to women in order properly to aspire to universality. But women make a difference in different ways. As the great feminist congress in Beijing demonstrated, "universal feminism" cannot be monopolized by Western (especially American) women. Western women, it became clear, need to listen to Asian women, to African women, and Muslim women etc.; that is, they have to take otherness seriously and hence cannot pretend to speak for all others universally. This is ultimately a deep defense and justification of global democracy: no one can speak universally for everybody. It is also a defense of "deliberative" democracy, and especially of what Iris Marion Young has called "communicative" democracy, where communication makes room for the rich diversity of idioms.[30]

In this context, another critical query arises: Is cross-cultural communication entirely benign and are there not limits to understanding, especially limits to the desirability and willingness to understand? The answer to the latter part of this query surely has to be in the affirmative. Every effort at understanding encounters limits or dimensions of difference, which need to be respected. Moreover, there are cultural differences, which, though understandable, may yet be unacceptable. Nearly every culture contains features which are repugnant to a critical observer, even a sympathetically inclined observer. In non-Western societies, features that are usually lifted up as particularly obnoxious and horrifying are untouchability, female infanticide, and female circumcision. As it seems to me, practices of this kind are indeed horrible and unacceptable. Here, several points should be noted. First of all, horror is not a monopoly of the "East" but can also be found abundantly in Western, so-called "Judaeo-Christian" civilization (witness the crusades, the Inquisition, world wars, holocaust, and Hiroshima), which should hardly lead to a wholesale rejection of that civilization. Next, dialogue as sketched above is not necessarily harmonious or consensual but includes challenge and critical contestation. Thus, faced with appalling features, comparativists are not condemned to silence. The central issue here is whether critique proceeds from a presumed self-righteousness or hegemonic arrogance, or else from a shared engagement and a willingness to undergo a *mutually* transforming learning process. Basically, I agree on this point with Taylor's argument that different cultures have a "presumptive" worth in their favor which can be defeated, and with Amy Gutmann's distinction between mere tolerance and genuine respect.[31]

Turning to broader implications and benefits: From the angle of political theory, one of the main benefits of comparative study is its tendency to rekindle the critical élan endemic to political philosophy since the time of Socrates and Plato but likely to

be curbed or throttled by canonization. Moving from the domain of habitual familiarity in the direction of the unfamiliar is likely to restore the sense of "wondering"
(*thaumazein*) extolled as pivotal to philosophizing by the ancients. To the extent that
Western modernity today functions as the dominant standard, comparative theorizing in many ways re-opens the "battle between the ancients and the moderns"—a
battle which curiously criss-crosses or intersects with the difference between East and
West. What is at issue here is not a nostalgic return to a pristine past, but a willingness
to undergo cross-temporal and cross-cultural interrogation and questioning. As Parel
remarks: being focused on the presence of the present, modernity has "subverted the
classical and medieval traditions" in the West, while also attempting to "subvert the
political philosophies of other cultures as well." This observation is seconded by
Merleau-Ponty who writes, referring to fashionable evolutionary models celebrating
Western superiority or "maturity": "The Orient's 'childisness' has something to teach
us, if it were nothing more than the narrowness of our adult ideas."[32]

Beyond narrowly academic confines, comparative theorizing has wider ramifica-
tions by sustaining a critical political outlook—what Parekh calls a "radically critical
perspective" on society. In our time, political liberalism has achieved virtually canonical status, edging out of the way nearly all competing ideologies or perspectives; moreover, under the auspices of market "neo-liberalism," its canonization has become
globalized. The point here is not to disparage liberalism's original intent, its "critical
and emancipatory thrust" (in Parekh's words): that is, its role as a liberating agent free-
ing people from unquestioned dogmas and oppressive political structures.[33] However,
something happens when an initial inspiration is transformed into an "established"
creed or doctrine. At this point, instead of preserving its élan, the original critique or
mode of critical questioning is in danger of turning into an answer or unquestioned
dogma. Differently put, liberty changes from a liberating promise into a vested status
or privileged possession. Only a rekindling of questioning—along temporal and cross-
cultural lines—can provide an antidote to this danger of congealment.[34]

In terms of long-range political vision, comparative political theorizing places itself
on the side of global democratic cooperation over against oligarchic or imperial control, the side of dialogical interaction over against hegemonic unilateralism and
monologue. The dangers of the latter are evident both in academic studies and in
global politics. In the academic domain, Charles Taylor long ago exposed the consequences of unilateral ethnocentrism: the tendency to interpret "all other societies in
the categories of our own" and finally to erect the "Atlantic-type polity" into the
zenith of politics.[35] In the political arena, Albert Camus' warning remains memorable
when he writes that "dialogue on the level of mankind is less costly than the gospel
preached by totalitarian [and other hegemonic] regimes in the form of a monologue
dictated from the top of a lonely mountain. On the stage as in reality, monologue
precedes death."[36] For his part, Hans-Georg Gadamer has pleaded in favor of a "politics of dialogue and phronesis (practical wisdom)," aiming at the creation of a "new
world order of human solidarity."[37] Such a politics, it seems to me, might yet salvage
our earth from the ravages of genocidal mayhem and nuclear disaster. In supporting
such a politics, political science as a discipline might escape the lure of "fiddling" and
become a valuable participant in the effort to build a just global peace.

NOTES

1. This essay was first published in *Perspectives on Politics*, vol. 2, No. 2 (2004),
   pp. 249–257.

2. Leo Strauss, "An Epilogue," in Herbert J. Storing, ed., *Essays on the Scientific Study of Politics* (New York: Holt Rinehart and Winston, 1962), p. 327.

3. See in this respect the chapters "Dialogue among Civilizations: A Hermeneutical Perspective" and "Conversation Across Boundaries: E Pluribus Unum?" in my book *Dialogue among Civilizations: Some Exemplary Voices* (New York: Palgrave/Macmillan, 2002), pp. 17–30, 31–47.

4. In my view, practitioners should be well familiar with at least one major non-European language. Familiarity of this kind will sensitize them to the intricacies of language and to the problems of translation (without obviating, of course, the need and the benefits of translation).

5. See Samuel P. Huntington, "The Clash of Civilizations?" in *Foreign Affairs*, vol. 72 (Summer 1993), especially the section "The West versus the Rest," pp. 39–41. As used in the present pages, terms like "West" and "non-West" should always be read in quotation marks, to avoid the temptation to essentialize their meaning.

6. On this point see the chapter "Globalization and Inequality" in my *Dialogue among Civilizations*, pp. 67–84; also Richard Falk, *Predatory Globalization: A Critique* (Cambridge, UK: Polity Press, 1999).

7. See, e.g., Johan Galtung, *The True Worlds: A Transnational Perspective* (New York: Free Press, 1980); Elise Boulding, *Building a Global Civic Culture: Education for an Interdependent World* (Syracuse, NY: Syracuse University Press, 1988); also my *Alternative Visions: Paths in the Global Village* (Lanham, MD: Rowman and Littlefield, 1998).

8. See Clifford Geertz, *The Interpretation of Cultures: Selected Essays* (New York: Basic Book, 1973); Marshall D. Sahlins, *Culture and Practical Reason* (Chicago: University of Chicago Press, 1978); also James Clifford and George Marcus, eds., *Writing Culture: The Poetics and Politics of Ethnography* (Cambridge, MA: Harvard University Press, 1986).

9. See, for example, Herbert I. Schiller, *Culture Inc.* (New York: Oxford University Press, 1989); Andrew Benjamin et al., eds., *Postcolonial Cultures and Literatures* (New York: P. Lang, 2002); Alfred J. Lopez, *Posts and Pasts: A Theory of Postcolonialism* (Albany, NY: SUNY Press, 2001); Bill Ashcroft, Gareth Griffith, and Helen Tiffin, *Postcolonial Studies: The Key Concepts* (New York: Routledge, 2000); Gayatri C. Spivak, *The Post-Colonial Critic* (London: Routledge, 1990).

10. See Huston Smith, *The World's Religions* (New York: Harper Collins, 1991); Harold Coward, ed., *Hindu-Christian Dialogue: Perspectives and Encounters* (Maryknoll, NY: Orbis Books, 1990); Heinrich Dumoulin, *Christianity Meets Buddhism*, trans. John C. Maraldo (LaSalle, IL: Open Court, 1974); Ninian Smart, *Buddhism and Christianity: Rivals and Allies* (Honolulu: University of Hawaii Press, 1993); Osman Bakar and Cheng Gek Nai, eds., *Islam and Confucianism: A Civilizational Dialogue* (Kuala Lumpur: University of Malaya, 1997).

11. See Martin Heidegger, *Being and Time*, trans. Joan Stambaugh (Albany, NY: SUNY Press, 1996); pp. 30–34; *The Question of Being*, trans. William Kluback and Jean T. Wilde (New York: Twayne, 1958), pp. 106-107; *On the Way to Language*, trans. Peter D. Hertz (New York: Harper and Row, 1971); also Paul Shih-yi Hsiao, "Heidegger and Our Translation of the *Tao Te Ching*," in Graham Parkes, ed., *Heidegger and Asian Thought* (Honolulu: University of Hawaii Press, 1987), pp. 93–103.

12. See Hans-Georg Gadamer, *Truth and Method*, 2nd rev. ed., trans. Joel Weinsheimer and Donald G. Marshall (New York: Crossroad, 1989); and his *Das Erbe Europas: Beiträge* (Frankfurt-Main: Suhrhamp, 1989).

13. See J. L. Mehta, *Philosophy and Religion: Essays in Interpretation* (New Delhi: Manoharlal Publishers, 1990), p. 31; and *India and the West: The Problem of Understanding* (Chico, CA: Scholars Press, 1985), p. 124.

14. See Mikhail Bakhtin, *The Dialogical Imagination*, ed. Michael Holquist (Austin, TX: University of Texas Press, 1981).

15. See Jacques Derrida, "Différance," in *Margins of Philosophy*, trans. Alan Bass (Chicago: University of Chicago Press, 1982), pp. 1–27; and *The Other Heading: Reflections on Today's Europe*, trans. Pascale-Anne Brault and Michael B. Naas (Bloomington, IN: Indiana University Press, 1992).

16. Maurice Merleau-Ponty, "From Mauss to Claude Lévi-Strauss," in Signs, trans. Richard C. McCleary (Evanston, IL: Northwestern University Press, 1964), pp. 115, 120.

17. J. L. Mehta, "Heidegger and Vedanta: Reflections on a Questionable Theme," in Parkes, ed., *Heidegger and Asian Thought*, pp. 28–29.

18. Raimundo Panikkar, "What Is Comparative Philosophy Comparing?" in Gerald J. Larson and Eliot Deutsch, eds., *Interpreting Across Boundaries: New Essays in Comparative Philosophy* (Princeton: Princeton University Press, 1988), pp.116–118, 125–130, 132–134.

19. See Anthony J. Parel, "The Comparative Study of Political Philosophy," in Parel and Ronald C. Keith, eds., *Comparative Political Philosophy: Studies Under the Upas Tree* (New Delhi: Sage Publications, 1992; new ed., Lanham, MD: Lexington Books, 2003), pp. 11–14.

20. See Hwa Yol Jung, *The Question of Rationality and the Basic Grammar of Intercultural Texts* (Niigata: International University of Japan, 1989), pp. 14, 48–49; and *Comparative Political Culture in the Age of Globalization: An Introductory Anthology* (Lanham, MD: Lexington Books, 2002), pp. 2, 8, 13–14.

21. See Charles Taylor, "The Politics of Recognition," in Amy Gutmann, ed., *Multiculturalism and "The Politics of Recognition"* (Princeton: Princeton University Press, 1992), pp. 32–33, 40–42, 73.

22. Taylor, "Conditions of an Unforced Consensus on Human Rights," in Joanne R. Bauer and Daniel A. Bell, eds., *The East Asian Challenge for Human Rights* (Cambridge, UK: Cambridge University Press, 1999), pp. 143–144.

23. Bhikhu Parekh, *Rethinking Multiculturalism: Cultural Diversity and Political Theory* (London: Macmillan, 2002), pp. 338–340.

24. See especially Muhsin Mahdi, "Alfarabi," in Leo Strauss and Joseph Cropsey, eds., *History of Political Philosophy* (Chicago: Rand McNally, 1963), pp. 160–180; Eric Voegelin, *Order and History*, vol. 4: *The Ecumenic Age* (Baton Rouge: Louisiana State University Press, 1974); and his "Equivalences of Experience and Symbolization in History" in *Philosophical Studies*, vol. 28 (1981), pp. 88–102.

25. See Charles E. Butterworth, *Alfarabi: The Political Writings* (Ithaca, NY: Cornell University Press, 2001); *Averroes' Middle Commentaries on Aristotle's Poetics* (Princeton: Princeton University Press, 1986); Butterworth and I. William Zartman, eds., *Between the State and Islam* (New York: Cambridge University Press, 2001). Among younger scholars in this field, see especially Roxanne L. Euben, *Enemy in the Mirror: Islamic Fundamentalism and the*

Limits of Modern Rationalism (Princeton: Princeton University Press, 1999).

26. See especially Muhammed Abed al-Jabri, *Arabic-Islamic Philosophy: A Contemporary Critique*, trans. Aziz Abassi (Austin: University of Texas Press, 1999); Abdolkarim Soroush, *Reason, Freedom, and Democracy in Islam: Essential Writings of Abdolkarim Soroush*, trans. and ed. Mahmud Sadri and Ahmad Sadri (New York: Oxford University Press, 2000). Compare also Abdulaziz Sachedina, *The Islamic Roots of Democratic Pluralism* (New York: Oxford University Press, 2001). On Soroush see also my "Islam and Democracy: Reflections on Abdolkarim Soroush," in *Dialogue among Civilizations*, pp. 167–184.

27. See, for example, Rajni Kothari, *State against Democracy: In Search of Humane Governance* (Delhi: Ajanta, 1988); *Rethinking Development: In Search of Humane Alternatives* (New York: New Horizons Press, 1989); Ashis Nandy, *The Intimate Enemy: Loss and Recovery of Self under Colonialism* (Delhi: Oxford University Press, 1983); *Traditions, Tyranny and Utopias* (Delhi: Oxford University Press, 1987); Rajeev Bhargava, ed., *Secularism and Its Critics* (New York: Oxford University Press, 1998); Thomas Pantham, *Political Theories and Social Reconstruction* (New Delhi: Sage Publications, 1995).

28. See, for example, Daniel A. Bell and Chaibong Hahm, eds., *Confucianism and the Modern World* (Cambridge, UK: Cambridge University Press, 2003); Joseph Chan, ed., *Political Theory in China* (2001; in Chinese). Compare also Enrique D. Dussel, *The Invention of the Americas*, trans. Michael D. Barber (New York: Continuum, 1995); Paulin J. Hountondji, *The Struggle for Meaning: Reflections on Philosophy, Culture and Democracy in Africa* (Athens, OH: Ohio University Center, 2002); Emmanuel C. Eze, *Postcolonial African Philosophy: A Critical Reader* (Cambridge, MA: Blackwell, 1997).

29. See especially the series of books entitled *Global Encounters: Studies in Comparative Political Theory* which I edit for Lexington Books (an imprint of the Rowman and Littlefield Publishing Group). Starting with *Border Crossings: Toward a Comparative Political Theory* (1999), the series (comprising already nineteen volumes) brings together scholars and intellectuals from around the globe in a kind of global public discourse.

30. See Iris Marion Young, *Inclusion and Democracy* (New York: Oxford University Press, 2000), pp. 62–64. Compare also Seyla Benhabib's plea for "the creation and expansion of deliberative discursive multicultural spaces in liberal democracies," in *The Claims of Culture: Equality and Diversity in the Global Era* (Princeton: Princeton University Press, 2002), p. 101.

31. See Amy Gutmann, "Introduction," and Charles Taylor, "The Politics of Recognition," in *Multiculturalism and "The Politics of Recognition,"* pp. 21–22, 66–68, 72–73.

32. Merleau-Ponty, "Everywhere and Nowhere," in Signs, p. 139; Parel, "The *Comparative Study of Political Philosophy*," in Parel and Keith, eds., Comparative Political Philosophy, pp. 13–14.

33. Parekh, *Rethinking Multiculturalism*, pp. 339–340.

34. In this context, one can also not forget a frequent complicity of "liberal" regimes in forms of illiberal oppression: chiefly complicity in colonial and imperialist ventures predicated on "white man's burden" and "*mission civilisatrice.*"

35. Taylor, "Interpretation and the Sciences of Man," *Review of Metaphysics*, vol. 25 (1971), p. 34.

36. Albert Camus, *The Rebel*, trans. Anthony Bower (New York: Alfred A. Knopf, 1956), p. 284.

37. See Thomas Pantham, "Some Dimensions of the Universality of Philosophical Hermeneutics: A Conversation with Hans-Georg Gadamer," *Journal of Indian Council of Philosophical Research*, vol. 9 (1992), p. 133.

PART TWO

ISLAMIC POLITICAL THOUGHT

INTRODUCTION

In terms of political ideas and institutions, the Islamic world—more than any other "non-Western" region—has suffered from a great deal of stereotyping and summary indictments. Today, the labels frequently pinned on Muslims, even by half-way educated people in the West, are "fundamentalist," "fanatic," or "terrorist." What such labels blithely forget is that Western culture exhibits its own share of fundamentalism and fanaticism. How can one forget the long and bitter religious wars, and especially the Thirty Years War as a result of which European society was nearly decimated? And how can one forget the slaughter of the Huguenots in France, and the (partly religiously motivated) genocide of indigenous peoples in the New World? And how ignore that "terrorism," in the contemporary sense, was inaugurated by the "Reign of Terror" during the French Revolution? Another summary labeled often applied to the "Orient," and especially to Islamic societies, is that of "Oriental despotism." Ever since the onset of modernity, Western thinkers have been fond of distinguishing between "Occident" and "Orient" in terms of "free" and "unfree," or enlightened and despotic regimes. But how can we forget the despotism of Henry VIII, Louis XIV, not to mention Hitler and Mussolini?[1]

Both prudence and fairness dictate to discard such summary labels—without, of course, condoning cases of fanaticism or terrorism wherever they may occur. Approached from a more dispassionate angle, the political history of Islamic societies is highly diversified and complex, and so are the political ideas or theories informing that history. In the course of historical development, one finds benign and less benign forms of political rule, and more or less free types of political regimes. This is precisely the aspect that renders Islamic traditions comparable with other traditions—something which would be impossible if they were separated by an unbridgeable gulf. The possibility of comparison extends beyond regime types to the level of political imagination, informal structures, and social customs. Sociology teaches that before the rise of formal collective structures (like city states, states or empires), people tended to be gathered in clans or tribes that typically were ruled by patriarchs or chieftains. This was also the case in pre-Islamic Arabia, which was fragmented into numerous tribes—one of the most prominent being the Quraish tribe in Mecca. As in many other parts of the world, pre-Islamic people had a kind of "natural" religion characterized by animism, fetishism and (what has been called) "poly-daemonism." After the rise of Islam, this entire prehistory has been called the period of "ignorance" (*jahiliyya*).

As is well known, the religion of Islam was brought to the people in Arabia by Prophet Muhammad (570–632 A.D.) who was a poor relative of the large and wealthy Quraish tribe. He started out as a shepherd boy, but later married Khadija, a business woman, with whom he remained happily married until her death twenty years later. This is not the place to recount the story of Muhammad's life and accomplishments. A few points, however, need to be lifted up for better understanding. Muhammad is considered, and considered himself, a "prophet" (*rasul*) in the great Jewish tradition.

By all accounts, he was a modest, unassuming, and saintly man—but he was not seen, nor did he see himself, as "divine" or as an incarnation of God. Herein lies a major difference from Christianity: like Jews, Muslims do not recognize the divinity of Christ (despite a recognition of his saintly quality as a prophet). This is only one of the differences between the three "Abrahamic religions." Although all three are called "religions of the book," the books in question differ, in content and style. The Hebrew scriptures present mainly the history of the Jewish people, together with reflections and hymns of praise, and were written by rabbis and learned men throughout many centuries. The Christian "Bible" is an account of the life and death of Jesus, written by some devoted followers in the early centuries of the Christian era. By contrast, the Muslim book—called the *Qur'an* (recitation)—does not at all tell a story and was not written by Muslims. In fact, in orthodox Islamic belief, the *Qur'an* was not even written by Muhammad, but is a text revealed to him by God through the angel Gabriel in successive revelations after 610 A.D. Thus, in contrast to the other sacred texts, the *Qur'an* speaks mostly in the first voice—the voice of God, offering instructions, admonitions, and guidance. Subdivided into chapters (*suras*), the text can be read almost like a series of poems, "divine" poems.[2]

To some extent, the charge of "Oriental despotism" is based on the very meaning of "Islam," which is "surrender." However, as one should note well, surrender here does not denote submission to earthly rulers or potentates, but to God alone—a God who, throughout the *Qur'an*, is called "most benevolent, ever merciful" (that is, the opposite of despotic). Such surrender is actually an ingredient in all religions. As William James has noted: "When all is said and done, we are in the end absolutely dependent on the universe; and into sacrifices and surrenders of some sort . . . we are drawn pressed as into our only permanent positions of repose."[3] Even more pointedly, comparative theologian Huston Smith observes that, surrendering oneself to Allah, means "to be freed from other forms of slavery [or bondage]—ones that are degrading, such as slavery to greed, or to anxiety, or to the desire for personal status." To render the meaning still clearer, Smith suggests construing surrender as "commitment," a term which implies "moving toward rather than giving up. In this reading, Islam emerges as a religion that aims at total commitment, commitment in which nothing is withheld from the Divine."[4]

Urging surrender to God alone, Islam not only shuns despotism and autocratic rule but is at least potentially compatible with democracy (depending upon how democracy is defined). After the final defeat of the Meccans, the Prophet established a simple administrative regime far removed from ostentatious displays of power. In the words of Huston Smith again: "As the supreme magistrate, he continued to lead as unpretentious a life as he had in the days of his obscurity. He lived in an ordinary clay house, milked his own goats, and was accessible day and night to the humblest in his community."[5] In formulating policies, the Prophet relied on consultation (*shura*) with an inner circle of followers who, in turn, consulted or communicated with the larger Muslim population. As it seems, every effort was made to achieve as broad a consensus (*ijma‘*) as possible. In large measure, this practice continued during the period of the Prophet's four immediate successors (*caliphs*): Abu Bakr, Umar, Uthman, and 'Ali. Because of their adherence to the Prophet's example, the four are also called the "righteous (or rightly guided) Caliphs" (*rashidun*). However, power struggles and contests for supreme position were not absent during this period: with the exception of Abu Bakr, all righteous caliphs were assassinated after a short rule. The assassination of 'Ali, husband of the Prophet's daughter Fatima, by a disgruntled soldier in 661 led to the splitting off of a faction of believers (*shi‘a*) from the larger community.

Ever since that time one distinguishes between Sunnis, followers of the general tradition (*sunna*), and Shi'i or Shiites, followers of 'Ali.

During the time of the early caliphs, Islam expanded rapidly throughout Arabia, the Near East and North Africa, and as far eastward as Persia and India. After the death of 'Ali, Sunni Islam was organized into several larger empires or caliphates: the Ummayyad caliphate (661–750) centered in Damascus; the 'Abbasid caliphate (750–1258) centered in Baghdad, and later—after the Mongol invasions—the Ottoman Empire (1453–1919) and the Moghul Empire in India (1495–1858). Shi'a Islam flourished mainly in Persia (Safavid Empire, 1501–1732) and parts of what today is Iraq, Pakistan, and Lebanon. Instead of paying tribute to caliphs, Shiites acknowledged the authority of Imams, with many of them holding that the twelfth Imam after 'Ali (*al-Mahdi*) went into hiding to return at a later point. The vast expansion of Islam brought Muslims in contact with older civilizational traditions (like the Babylonian, Persian, and Indian), many of which boasted high accomplishments in philosophy, literature, science, and the arts. The contact inevitably encouraged a kind of syncretism or accommodation whereby Islamic teachings were enriched and also complicated through novel accretions.

This syncretism was especially pronounced in the case of the 'Abbasid caliphate where Baghdad emerged as the center of a pluralistic culture with dazzling splendor. During the reign of successive enlightened caliphs, all the humanities and sciences were able to flourish in an unprecedented manner, due partly to the establishment of great universities, such as al-Azhar in Cairo (972) and Nizamiyya in Baghdad (1065) as well as a vast network of schools (*madrasas*). The 'Abbasid period also saw the flowering of Islamic philosophy represented by such great thinkers as al-Farabi (870–950), Ibn Sina (Avicenna, 980–1037), and Ibn Rushd (Averroes, 1126–1198). The great issue for these thinkers was how to reconcile Islamic faith with non-Islamic Greek philosophy, especially the teachings of Plato and Aristotle. A similar tension emerged among Muslim theologians, with some privileging faith (Asharites) and others making some room for human reason (Mutazilites). An important development was also the creation of several schools of law offering detailed interpretations of Islamic law (*shari'a*). A further captivating aspect was the cultivation of a mystical, inner-directed faith (Sufism) by such thinkers and poets as al-Ghazali (1058–1111), Ibn 'Arabi (1165–1240), and Jalal al-Din Rumi (1207–1273).

The destruction of Baghdad by the Mongols (in 1258) put an end to 'Abbasid rule, but not to an open-minded Islam friendly to the sciences and humanities. An outstanding example during the ensuing "time of troubles" was the work of Ibn Khaldun (1332–1406), sometimes called the founder of historical sociology. Born in Tunisia, Ibn Khaldun led a very turbulent life, moving first to Spain, then back to North Africa, and finally to Cairo where he became Grand Qadi (judge) of the "Maliki" school of law. While on a mission to Damascus, he was trapped in the city besieged by the Mongol ruler Timur (Tamerlane); managing to escape he returned to Cairo. Ibn Khaldun is most famous for his *Prologomena* (*Muqaddimah*), which was meant as an introduction to a larger work called "Book of Examples" (*Kitab al-'Ibar*). In his writings he explored the reasons for historical change, focusing on the tensions between nomadic tribes and settled communities, with the invasion of the nomadic Mongol tribes being a primary impulse. A central aspect of his work is the discussion of the meaning of community or solidarity (*'asabiyya*) and how the latter can be maintained in different contexts.

The first two essays reprinted below examine developments from the beginning of Islam to the time of troubles. In his essay "The Golden Age: The Political Concepts of Islam," Ira Lapidus distinguishes between two "golden ages" or early paradigms for Islamic political regimes: "prophetic theocracy" and "imperial Islamic society." The first paradigm extends mainly from the beginning of the Prophet's rule (622 A.D., year of the emigration or *hijra* to Medina) to the end of the rule of the righteous caliphs (661). The second paradigm refers especially to the Ummayyad and 'Abbasid caliphates and the later Ottoman Empire. While, during the first period, religion and political rule were closely unified, the second period witnessed a steady differentiation between the role of clerics and the power of bureaucrats and military leaders. Lapidus discusses a number of important jurists and political thinkers during the second period, such as al-Mawardi (985–1058) and Ibn Taimiyya (1263–1328) who consigned religion to an ideal-normative realm, while treating political power as a coercive instrument to combat corruption. Lapidus also classifies contemporary Muslim countries based on the degree to which they imitate the first or second paradigm (leaving out such important countries like Malaysia and Indonesia). One clearly can take exception to some of Lapidus's categories. The notion of "prophetic theocracy" sidelines some of the egalitarian (and potentially democratic) features of the early period. The paradigm of an "imperial society," on the other hand, lumps together too many different historical stages, neglecting the very slow differentiation between politics and religion over the centuries.

Lapidus's essay may be fruitfully compared with another paper by Charles Butterworth titled "Political Islam: The Origins" (not included in this volume).[6] In his paper, Butterworth discusses first of all the difference between the modern West and Islamic traditions. In the modern age, he notes, Western political thought has become secularized, insists on the separation of church and state, and no longer recognizes or upholds "divine right"; it also accords primacy to freedom over virtue. By contrast, Islamic civilization during the "golden ages" was more holistic or integrated—although a loosening of the initial unity was undeniable during the "imperial" period. The paper comments on al-Mawardi who reflected on the desirable qualities of a caliph, and on the relation between political rule and religious faith. Butterworth gives major attention to the leading Muslim philosophers of the time. Greatly influenced by Plato, al-Farabi divided the study of politics into two domains: the practical-mundane sphere (the Platonic cave) and the higher theoretical sphere of general "ideas." In his study *The Political Regime*, he queried whether it was preferable to have a philosopher or a prophet as ruler, settling the issue by opting for a prophet-philosopher. More influenced by Aristotle, the Persian Ibn Sina focused on the nature of political community, the nature of law, and also on the qualities of a virtuous caliph. In turn, the Andalusian Ibn Rushd—likewise under Aristotelian influence—tried to defend philosophy against narrow clerical attacks. He also distinguished between religious and philosophical discourses in terms of different linguistic genres (what today we may call "language games").

In his essay on "Alfarabi" (reprinted below), Muhsin Mahdi places the emphasis on al-Farabi's persistent endeavor to correlate and harmonize the teachings of Islam with classical Greek philosophy, especially the works of Plato. Special attention is given to his reflections on the "virtuous regime" seen as the fulfillment and realization of human excellence and virtue. The best regime in his view is characterized by the conscious striving for moral perfection, the clear distinction between virtues and vices, and the concerted effort of rulers and citizens to teach and learn about this distinction. Leading up to this supreme model are a number of defective political regimes: "ignorant" regimes where people do not know the distinction of good and evil (harking back to the time of *jahiliyya*); "immoral" regimes where people do have some knowledge of virtue but always act otherwise; and "erring" or confused regimes where some good principles are overshadowed by their opposites. As Mahdi shows, al-Farabi devoted much thought to the character of the supreme ruler (in a "virtuous city"), distinguishing between the Platonic ruler-philosopher and the Islamic ruler-prophet. The two types correspond to two eminent human faculties: reason and imagination. For al-Farabi, the best ruler would be one able to combine both faculties, thus representing a "perfect human being." Mahdi also comments on the role of law in al-Farabi's thought and on his views on education, warfare, and democracy.

As indicated before, following the time of troubles Muslim societies managed to regroup slowly and consolidate into larger imperial structures: chiefly the Ottoman, Moghul, and Safavid empires. The beginnings of Ottoman rule can be traced back to 1299; but its status as imperial power dates basically from the conquest of Byzantium or Constantinople in 1453. Under the leadership of some great Sultans, like Suleiman the Magnificent (1520–1566), the Ottomans extended their dominion over most of the Near East, Egypt, North Africa, and even the Balkans; they laid siege to Vienna in 1529 and 1683. Significantly, the Ottoman rulers retained the title of "caliphs" (recognized by all Sunni Muslims). The Moghul rule in India and South Asia (1495–1858) was established by descendants of the Mongol invaders Timur and Jenghis Khan who by that time had converted to (Sunni) Islam. Among the great Moghul emperors one must mention Akbar the Great (1556–1605) who encouraged interfaith discussions and a kind of multiculturalism in India, and also Shah Jahān (1627–1666) who built the Taj Mahal and also the Red Fort and Great Mosque in Delhi. The Safavid Empire in Persia (1501–1732) was the center of the Shiite tradition by endorsing "Twelver Shiism" or "*Imamiyya*." Some Safavid rulers actually claimed to be spokesmen for the "hidden Imam" (a claim challenged by more orthodox clerics). Among the most famous rulers was Shah Abbas I (1587–1629).

Starting in the early seventeenth century, European powers began to make inroads into the Islamic world. In 1609, the British East India Company was established and over the two succeeding centuries managed to acquire political power able to challenge the Moghul rule. Other European powers, like the French and Portuguese, also established footholds in India and the Middle East. By 1828, the British Parliament began legislating for the Indian subcontinent. Following a revolt by Indian soldiers (Sepoy mutiny), the last living Moghul ruler was deposed by the British in 1858 and India became formally a part of the British Empire (the "jewel in the crown"). Similar developments occurred in the Near East and North Africa where Ottoman rule was steadily challenged or eroded by Europeans. Egypt was invaded by Napoleon in 1798–1801 and subsequently succumbed increasingly to French and British (direct or indirect) control. In 1882, a revolt by an Egyptian ruler, Pasha Ahmed 'Arabi, was crushed by British troops.

The progressive advances of Western colonialism and imperialism exerted a profound influence on Muslim culture and political thought. By its very nature, modern Western culture—shaped by science, rationalism, secularism, and individualism—constituted a challenge to the more traditional and "holistic" worldview still present in the Islamic world. The reaction to this Western challenge took mainly three forms—and, as will be shown, a similar scenario unfolded in other "non-Western" contexts as well. The first reaction is that of radical rejection or negation: the "gifts" brought by the West are considered worthless and both religiously and ethically corrupting. This reaction will subsequently be called "rejectionism" or "radical traditionalism" (which sometimes, though not always, may take the form of a militant or aggressive "Islamism"). The second type is that of quick surrender or assimilation: the "gifts" of the West are welcomed as liberating and perhaps superior, while native traditions are discarded. This option will be called "assimilationism" or "radical modernism." The third possibility involves a compromise or negotiation: some of the "gifts" of the West are accepted provided they are integrated with beneficial elements of a reformed tradition. This option will be called "moderate traditionalism" or "reformism."[7]

Despite occasional overlaps, the three types of reactions have basically alternated in dominating Islamic thought during the past 200 years, and still do so today. Given that the first inroads of the West were often military in nature, the initial response in many parts of the Muslim world tended to be "rejectionist." An early form of radical traditionalism was Wahhabism, initiated by Muhammad ibn 'Abd al-Wahhāb (1703–1787) in the later eighteenth century in Arabia. In the following century, the Wahhabi movement spread to the Middle East, North Africa, and even India. The leaders of the movement branded all who disagreed as heretics or apostates (*kuffar*), thereby justifying the use of force and even "holy war" (*jihad*) against opponents. In some areas controlled by Wahhabis, there was a religious police (*mutawiun*) rigidly enforcing religious law (*shari'a*). After a period of decline, Wahhabism experienced a revival in the twentieth century and is assumed to provide ideological support to militant or terrorist forms of rejectionism.

The encounter with the West, however, did not always lead to vehement opposition. Especially when Western policy shifted from military confrontation to educational and economic methods, the reaction in Muslim societies was often one of compromise or accommodation, that is, of moderate traditionalism or reformism (called *salafiyya*). Such reformism was particularly strong in Egypt and the near East. Among the leading reformers of the nineteenth century were the Egyptians Jamal al-Din al-Afghani (1837–1897) and Muhammad 'Abduh (1849–1905). The basic aim of the reformers was to combine the best the West had to offer with the best of the Islamic tradition. Thus, they embraced the modern Western emphasis on reason and science and also some educational innovations; at the same time, they also tried to preserve the core of traditional Islamic philosophy and theology, properly interpreted. In valorizing reason and upholding a balance between knowledge and faith, the outlook of the reformers actually harkened back to the classical age of Islamic philosophy, the time of al-Farabi and al-Ghazali. For this reason, the period is also designated as Islamic "Renaissance" (*Nahda*). Both al-Afghani and 'Abduh invoked the broad horizons of the "golden age" to justify their ambitions vis-à-vis reactionary clerics. The latter were sufficiently irritated to force al-Afghani into temporary exile in Paris. 'Abduh was spared this fate and even became the Grand Mufti of Egypt. Contemporary defenders of a moderate Islam often point to the nineteenth century example of "*salafiyya*," while also noting some of its shortcomings (such as a certain shallowness in combining reason and faith).[8] A parallel development to reformism in Egypt was the so-called *Tanzimat* movement in the Ottoman empire, a movement aiming mostly at constitutional and legal reform.

In her essay, "A View Across Time: Islam as the Religion of Reason," Roxanne Euben discusses the arguments of reformism under the (ambivalent) title of "Islamic modernism." She puts the emphasis mainly on al-Afghani and 'Abduh, but also mentions some followers like Rashid Rida. As she points out, al-Afghani pursued a dual aim (which in the end was one): to counter and combat European imperialism and, at the same time, to embrace some Western rationalist methods and scientific innovations for the purpose of strengthening Islamic culture and society. Actually, for him, reason was by no means a European monopoly, but was a major feature of classical Islamic philosophy, now in need of renewal. Both reactionary clericalism and secular rationalism, in his view, were misguided because both stipulate a gulf between reason and faith; the proper path to follow was a Luther-style reformism. For 'Abduh, the linkage was even closer because both reason and revelation are divine gifts: "God has sent down two books: one created, which is nature, and one revealed, which is the *Qur'an*." Reason, for 'Abduh, meant the exercise of critical judgment on the basis of available evidence, but an exercise that has to respect Qur'anic teachings and injunctions. Reason is particularly important whenever revealed scripture is silent or unclear; in this case, interpretation (*ijtihad*) has to do its creative work. In the concluding pages of her essay (not included here), Euben points to the aftermath of reformism: the upsurge of radical modernism, on the one side, and the rise of radical "fundamentalism" or rejectionism, on the other. The major figures mentioned in the "fundamentalist" camp are the Egyptian Sayyid Qutb (1906–1966), the Pakistani al-Maududi (1903–1980), and the Iranian Ayatollah Khomeini (1900–1989).

In the twentieth century, moderate traditionalism or reformism was succeeded initially by a powerful upsurge of radical modernism. In part, this upsurge had to do with World War I and the ensuing destruction or dismantling of the Ottoman Empire in 1919. Following the establishment of the Turkish Republic, President Kemal Pasha Ataturk embarked on a process of rapid modernization or Westernization, by replacing the Islamic *shari'a* with the Swiss civil code, exchanging the Arabic script for Western script, and abolishing the traditional "fez" in favor of the European hat. The most dramatic innovation, however, was the abolition of the caliphate in 1924. A strong modernizing trend emerged also in Persia/Iran where the Pahlavi dynasty (1925–1979) supported a full-fledged program of Westernization in the fields of science, industry, and education. As in Turkey, the Pahlavi policies always faced the opposition of both moderate reformers and radical rejectionists or "Islamists," with the latter sometimes using the term "Westoxification" to denounce the modernizing program. Following the demise of the Ottoman Empire, many formerly Ottoman territories were placed under a European "mandate system" sponsored by the League of Nations. In these areas too, strong modernist tendencies emerged, chiefly in the form of the adoption of Western political ideologies, such as liberalism, socialism, Marxism, and nationalism. The most ambitious political movements in the Middle East were Panarabism and the Ba'th Party, which promoted a form of democratic socialism.

The spirit of modernism persisted throughout World War II and well into the cold war era. By the end of the war, most former League of Nations mandates in the Middle East were transformed into independent nation-states. At the same time, a new state was created in what was formerly Palestine: the state of Israel (whose creation had been promised by the British in the so-called Balfour Declaration of 1917). The catch-words of the time were nation-building and development, together with such ideological programs as nationalism and socialism borrowed from the West. These catch-words were most vigorously implemented in the successor state of the Ottoman Empire, Turkey, but also found many adherents in other Muslim countries. As mentioned, Persia/Iran was steadily modernized under the Pahlavi kings: Reza Khan (1925–1941) and Muhammad Reza (1941–1979). In Egypt, a British-sponsored monarchy (1922–1952) was succeeded by a Republic of which Gamal 'Abd al-Nasser became President (1954–1970) pursuing such policies as Arab socialism, nationalization of the Suez Canal (1956), and a short-lived merger with Syria. Elsewhere, a modernizing monarchy was established in Jordan (1949); following a British-sponsored monarchy, a secular Republic was proclaimed in Iraq (1958) dedicated to a left-leaning Panarabic program. In Northern Africa, Libya gained independence from Italy in 1951; Tunisia established an independent Republic in

1955, ending its status as a French protectorate; and after a bitter struggle Algeria seceded from France (to which it had belonged) in 1962, under such left-leaning leaders as Ben Bella and Boumedienne.

The momentum of modernizing nation-building began to falter in the later part of the twentieth century. Many factors account for this decline or change of political climate. In his essay, "Contemporary Islam: Reformation or Revolution?" John Esposito lists a number of these factors. For one thing, modernization and secularization (or Westernization) always appealed only to a small Western-educated elite, while failing to penetrate into, and successfully persuade, the larger masses of the population. More importantly, the programs championed by the nation-builders did not produce the tangible benefits they had promised. With the pursuit of economic development, there came a new division between the rich and the poor, a gulf intensified by widespread corruption and mismanagement. Faced with the slogans of modernization, many ordinary people became alienated and experienced a loss of identity. As Esposito indicates, by far the most important event accounting for the shift in political climate was the Arab-Israeli war (the so-called "Six-Day War") of 1967, which exposed the political and military disarray of the new Muslim nation-states. In addition to this defeat, Esposito mentions the Lebanese civil war and the Pakistan-Bangladesh civil war a few years later. All these factors combined prompted the upsurge of a new countermodern or anti-Western climate: the upsurge of Islamic "fundamentalism" or what Esposito calls "Islamic revivalism" or else "militant Islam." This new outlook gained an initial boost in the Egyptian-Israeli war of 1973; it found its most radical expression in the Iranian revolution of 1978–1979, a revolution directed against modern forms of corruption and "Westoxification" and dedicated to the restoration of religious piety, ethical conduct, and social justice. Esposito also points to the side- and after-effects of the revolution: the fact that, in its aftermath, militant Islamism emerged from a limited sectarian creed into a broad political movement.[9]

This movement is by no means devoid of theoretical self-awareness or sophistication. In his essay, "The Political Discourse of Contemporary Islamist Movements," Youssef Choueiri singles out for attention the three political thinkers mentioned before: Sayyid Qutb, al-Maududi, and Ayatollah Khomeini. As Choueiri shows, there is considerable overlap between their theories despite the fact that the first two are Sunni Muslims and the third a Shiite. All three thinkers are opposed to key modern Western ideas or ideologies like democracy, liberalism, nationalism, and socialism (or Marxism). All these ideas are seen as a new form of "ignorance" (*jahiliyya*) and paganism. At least in the case of Qutb, the same verdict of paganism also extends to classical Greek and traditional Islamic philosophy; all three are resolute in rejecting the reformism (*salafiyya*) of the nineteenth century. In the case of democracy, there is a certain ambivalence as democratic elections may sometimes serve as a gateway to Islamic rule. The most objectionable feature of democracy, in the eyes of many (though not all) Islamist thinkers, is the idea of popular sovereignty, which directly contradicts God's absolute supremacy and power. The Marxist notion of a dictatorship of the proletariat suffers from the same defect as popular sovereignty. Capitalism is criticized for its glorification of private self-interest and the use of usury—aspects that are vastly inferior to the Islamic practices of almsgiving and religious taxes (*zakat*). Regarding political leadership, Qutb and Maududi favor a kind of "Muslim vanguard" willing and able to wage war (*jihad*) against corrupt secular regimes, while Khomeini opted for a quasitheocracy headed by a leading jurist.

As one should note, radical Islamism (or reactionary traditionalism) is only one strand in a welter of political ideas and movements in the contemporary Islamic world. This aspect is obscured by the widespread "war on terrorism" rhetoric that privileges and, in a way, plays into the hands of Islamic extremism. Though often sidelined by the media, there are other strands, particularly the strand of moderate traditionalism or reformism. It is chiefly this strand of reformism that harbors the promise of a peaceful negotiation or reconciliation between the modern West and Islam (no such reconciliation, of course, is needed in the case of secular modernizers in the Muslim world). Negotiation or accommodation is particularly crucial with respect to democracy. In an essay titled "Islamicist Utopia and Demcracy" (not included in this volume), Lahouari Addi delineates one path that might lead to such a compromise.[10] The animus of Addi's essay is directed against the radical Islamists discussed by Choueiri; this kind of Islamism, he observes, inevitably blocks the way to democracy because of its dedication to religious/clerical supremacy. What has to happen to facilitate accommodation is a certain "privatization" of faith. Departing from secular modernizers, however, Addi is willing to grant to religious faith an ethical and spiritual authority in civil society outside government. As he writes:

> Modernity does not require the separation of religion and politics or the marginalization of religion as a precondition. Nobody has the right to prevent the mosque from condemning corruption and arbitrariness or emphasizing the duty to assist widows and orphans. It is even desirable for the mosque to have moral authority in society, in order to appeal to the preservation of human values.

Negotiation and reconciliation, of course, always demand two sides. It is not sufficient for Muslim reformers to offer an olive branch to Western democracy; they must also be welcomed and supported by people in the West instead of being demonized and thrown together into one pot with radical Islamists and *jihadists*. This requires a cooling down of the rhetoric on all sides and the exercise of good judgment and political prudence (what Aristotle called "*phronesis*"). Muslim reformers stand on solid ground. They can appeal to the legacy of nineteenth century reformism (*salafiyya*) and beyond that to the great tradition of Islamic philosophy, which brought together Islam and Greek philosophy during the 'Abbasid period. Since the West benefited so enormously from the revival of Greek learning accomplished by Muslim thinkers in the Middle Ages, it certainly behooves intellectuals in the West today to remember that common bond and to offer their sympathy to the heirs of al-Farabi and Ibn Rushd today.

NOTES

1. On "Oriental despotism" see Karl August Wittfogel, *Oriental Despotism: A Comparative Study of Total Power* (New Haven, CT: Yale University Press, 1957), and Patricia Springborg, *Western Republicanism and the Oriental Prince* (Austin, TX: University of Texas Press, 1992).
2. An exception is the first Sura, which is a prayer offered by the faithful to God (similar to the Lord's Prayer). The idea that the *Qur'an* exists authentically in God's mind accounts for a certain literalism and widespread (though not universal) aversion to interpretation (*ijtihad*). As mentioned in the Preface, there are certain difficulties when the focus of reading is placed on the author's mind or intention (*mens auctoris*); the difficulties are intensified if the author is claimed to be God. Even more than in ordinary texts, there is the problem of access to "mind." There is also the problem of confining divine revelation to one language, here Arabic, as spoken at a certain time and in a certain place.

3. William James, *The Varieties of Religious Experience* (New York: Macmillan, 1961), p. 57.

4. Huston Smith, *The World's Religions: Our Great Wisdom Traditions* (New York: Harper Collins, 1958), p. 238. Traditionally, Islamic "surrender" rests on five pillars: the creed (*shahada*) simply stating that there is no God but God and that Muhammad is his messenger; daily prayers (*salat*); fasting (*sawm*) during the month of Ramadan; alms-giving (*zakat*); and (if possible) pilgrimage to Mecca (*hajj*). Some people add as a sixth pillar struggle (*jihad*), which basically means moral struggle, and only in some instances armed struggle. In addition to the *Qur'an*, Muslims generally acknowledge the authority of the collected "sayings of the Prophet" (*hadith*).

5. Smith, *The World's Religions*, p. 229.

6. See Charles E. Butterworth, "Political Islam: The Origins," in Charles E. Butterworth and I. William Zartman, eds., *Political Islam*, in *The Annals*, vol. 524 (November, 1992), pp. 26–37.

7. The three types of reaction are discussed by a number of writers, though often under different labels. Thus, Robert J. Holton distinguishes between "homogenization," "polarization," and "hybridization" where the first term corresponds to the option of assimilation/radical modernism, the second term to rejectionism, and the last term to middle-of-the-road reformism. See Holton, *Globalization and the Nation State* (London: Macmillan, 1998). On the other hand, Jung In Kang differentiates between three strategies: "assimilation," "reversal," and "syncretism." In his words: "In the assimilative strategy, the periphery accepts the universal and superior status of the center, accommodates institutions, practices, values and cultures of the center, and thereby seeks to assimilate/integrate itself to the center....In contrast, the reverse strategy refuses to assimilate, seeks to maintain and stress the differences, and furthermore reverses their evaluation and transvalues the attributes of the periphery from symbols of particularism and inferiority to those of universality and superiority....[Finally] the syncretic strategy selectively takes some elements of the center and periphery, and then seeks to synthesize them." See Kang, "Beyond Eurocentrism: Reexamining Cultural Discourse Strategies to Overcome Eurocentrism in the Context of Polycentric Multiculturalism," *Korean Political Science Review*, vol. 38 (2004), pp. 183–200. Kang also mention a "deconstructive" strategy whose character, however, remains elusive.

8. As one should note, nineteenth-century "*salafiyya*" can and should be differentiated from a broader, moderate traditionalism or "salafism" harking back to the example of the "*salaf*," the earliest and most pious Muslims.

9. As one should remember, radical Islamism has a longer tradition reaching back to the rise of Wahhabism in the eighteenth century. In Egypt, radical Islamism was inaugurated by Hassan al-Banna (1905–1949), founder of the Muslim Brotherhood. President Nasser was assassinated by a Brother in 1970.

10. See Lahouari Addi, "Islamicist Utopia and Democracy," in Charles E. Butterworth and I. William Zartman, eds., *Political Islam*, in *The Annals*, vol. 524 (November, 1992), pp. 120–130.

The Golden Age: The Political Concepts of Islam[1]

Ira M. Lapidus

The Islamic revival is once again of urgent importance. Now, in the midst of a worldwide Muslim struggle over the role that Islam should play in contemporary societies, we are faced with compelling questions: How much does this revival reflect the desire to return to a golden age of Muslim past? How much is it a contemporary phenomenon? Indeed, what is the Islamic and, in particular, the Middle Eastern political heritage, and what is its impact in the present?

The Middle Eastern Islamic heritage provides not one but two basic constellations of historical society, two golden ages, two paradigms, each of which has generated its own characteristic repertoire of political institutions and political theory. The first is the society integrated in all dimensions, political, social, and moral, under the aegis of Islam. The prototype is the unification of Arabia under the leadership of the Prophet Muhammad in the seventh century. The Prophet brought together the Meccans who left their home to join his community, the Medinans who accepted Islam, individual Arabians who emigrated to Medina, fractions of clans, converts made among the aristocratic families of Mecca, and various tribes in western Arabia; he unified a disparate and fragmented population into a single community. The Prophet functioned, on the one hand, as an economic and political leader and, on the other, as an exemplar of individual righteousness and morality. In this community, no distinction was made between religion and religious authority and the state and secular authority.[2]

The concept of an undifferentiated political religious community was carried over from the Prophet to the early caliphs. The Rashidun, who ruled from 632 to 660 A.D., did not inherit the Prophet's capacity to receive revelation, but their authority to implement and execute revealed law was considered as great as his authority to pronounce it.[3] Most Muslims, though for different reasons, believe that the first civil war (656–660 A.D.), brought this authority to an end and that ever after the office of the caliphate was corrupted. The Shiites believe that it fell into the hands of inappropriate successors, for only 'Ali and the Family of 'Ali could rightfully be caliphs; the Sunnites accept the actual historical succession but believe that later rulers were secular, self-serving kings—neither true caliphs nor true representatives of the community bequeathed by the Prophet.

Nonetheless, this image of the Prophetic community has inspired ever-renewed movements to restore the wholeness of the *umma* (community of Muslims). Shiites and Kharijites have struggled to restore the leadership of the rightful Iman. Repeatedly, Sunnite reformers have risen up to overthrow corrupt governments and

set up a state committed to an Islamic morality. Sufi heroes have attempted to establish their authority, acting self-consciously in imitation of the Prophet. These reformers, like the Prophet himself, commonly found their supporters in tribal or other
factionalized societies. Like the Prophet, they attempted to integrate individuals,
families, clans, lineages, and clientele groups into a unified body. Such movements
include, in North Africa, the Fatimids, the Almoravids, the Almohads, and the Sa'di
and Alawite dynasties in Morocco; the Safavid dynasty in Iran; and, throughout the
Muslim world, Berber Zawaya lineages, Evliadi among Turkomans, and Sufi-led
movements such as the Sanusiyya. All of these movements exemplify the impulse to
recreate, under religious leadership, the ideal community exemplified in the first
golden age of Islam.[4] Nowadays, neo-Islamic movements, still inspired by the same
underlying concept, take up the old ideal. Now this ideal, however, is supported not
by tribal and rural communities but by the urban petite bourgeoisie, petty traders,
craftspeople, bazaaris, and mobile and sometimes deracinated students.

THE SECOND GOLDEN AGE

The second historical paradigm is the imperial Islamic society, built not on Arabian
or tribal templates but on the differentiated structures of previous Middle Eastern
societies. With the advent of Islam, Middle Eastern societies had already been
organized into differentiated tribal, state, and church institutions. After the Arab
conquests, the early caliphate underwent a similar differentiation. Tribal armies
were displaced by newly recruited client forces who were expected to be more
dependent upon, loyal to, and obedient to their rulers, and tribal chiefs were replaced
by administrative cadres drawn from the conquered populations. At the same time,
the caliphate was transformed from the charismatic succession to the religious
authority of the Prophet into an imperial institution and a regime governed not by
religious norms but by the laws of political survival. As the caliphate took on an
increasingly secularlized political identity, the religious heritage of the Prophet
came to be embodied in his companions and their disciples and successors, scholars, and holy men. Eventually, the caliphs retained only a nominal role as the official representatives of Islam and the official fount of state and religious authority,
while the Muslim populace came to be organized into schools of law, theological
sects, Shiite communities, Sufi lineages, and brotherhoods representing the legacy
of the Prophet.

Such religious groups were commonly independent of state regimes. Most with-
drew from participation in government and were concerned with community solidarity, worship, education, law, personal morality, and the upholding of the symbols
of Islam. While religious scholars maintained their aspiration for an ideal society in
which state and community were integrated as in the time of the Prophet, they were
not actually committed to bringing it about in practice. In return for state support,
they commonly legitimized reigning governments and taught acceptance and submission to the common people.

By the eleventh century, Middle Eastern states and religious communities were
highly differentiated. States were officially committed to the defense and patronage
of Muslim worship, education, law, and *jihad*, but they were not inherently Islamic
institutions. It was widely recognized that these states operated on the basis of non-
Islamic legitimation. Conquering regimes, be they Arab or Turkish, looked back to
tribal ancestry as the basis of dynastic legitimacy. By the cultivation of local languages,
poetic traditions, architectural motifs, musical themes, and cultic practices, Middle

Eastern states asserted independence from Islam and identified themselves as cosmopolitan, imperial, and patrimonial regimes legitimated by non-Muslim civilization.[5]

Thus, despite the common statement that Islam is a total way of life defining
political as well as social and family matters, most Muslim societies did not conform
to this ideal. They were in fact built around separate institutions of state and religion.
The separation of state and religion yields a second image of the golden age of Islam.
This image is embedded in the Ottoman empire; it is an image of a world-conquering
empire, establishing the dominion of Islam over all peoples and fulfilling the Islamic
"providence" or "manifest destiny" to rule the world. This was a golden era of security, preeminence, and world domination. This was a golden age also because the
Ottoman empire upheld the true practice of Islam. It was the protector and patron,
indeed the organizer and master, of the scholars and holy men who managed Muslim
education, Muslim legal and judicial affairs, and Muslim worship.[6]

The practical tradition of separation of state and religion also generated a sociopolitical theory. Muslim political theorists, such as al-Baqillani, al-Mawardi, and
Ibn Taimiyya, devised a theory of the caliphate that symbolized the ideal existence
of the unified *umma*, while at the same time allowing for historical actualities. The
conclusion of their theorizing was that the state was not a direct expression of
Islam but a secular institution whose duty it was to uphold Islam. The community
of scholars and holy men were the ones who truly carried on the legacy of the
Prophet.[7]

In this tradition, the realm of Islamic authenticity lies within the soul of the individual and in the relations of individuals to each other within small communities.
This is the Islam that sees holiness and religion as incompatible with state power.
Politics are expected to be violent and corrupt. The control of the state is justified
only by conquest; obedience is legitimated by the need to submit, to minimize further warfare, and to prevent anarchy in society, but the state cannot embody a religious ideal. This renunciation of political utopianism may help explain some cases of
acquiescence to patrimonial regimes and the relative weakness of democratic or other
secular utopian movements in the present-day Middle East.

THE NON-ISLAMIC POLITICAL HERITAGE

This second paradigm allows for a differentiated nonreligious concept of political
authority. Alongside the Islamic concept of the caliph as the upholder of Islam,
there is a concept of political rationality inherently valid in its own terms as a
source of political behavior. This level of political thinking is expressed in the
Persian political heritage in which the ruler is the shadow of God on earth and
bears a divine authority independent of religion. He both upholds order and serves
as a moral example to his subjects. Rulership and statehood, in a sense, serve a
religious purpose apart from Islam and apart from the spokesmen of the religious
establishment.[8]

Furthermore, behind the formal and literary concepts of the state and the ruler,
there were also working assumptions, axioms, and premises about the nature and
organization of political power that did not reach the level of formal theory but are
nonetheless crucial to understanding Middle Eastern politics. One is that state power
is not an expression of the total society but rather the prerogative of certain individuals or groups. Control of the state belonged to certain families, tribes, dynasties,
or military castes. Not only did some groups rule over others, but elites and subjects
were of a totally different standing. Government was the prerogative of the one and

not of the other. In Middle Eastern societies, there was a caste-like bifurcation
between the military elite and the subject population.[9]

A further assumption of Middle East political systems was that, within the ruling
elite and between the ruling elite and the various segments of the subject population,
the exercise of political power was organized through networks of clients and retain-
ers. These networks were bound together by subjective obligations, such as the oath
of allegiance or gratitude, rather than by legal or other formal, institutional, or hierarchical considerations.[10]

Between rulers and subjects, political power was brokered by intermediary notables. For example, in the Mamluk empire of Egypt and Syria, state-appointed governors cultivated local notables, appointed them to offices, contributed to their
religious and charitable causes, and organized public works in return for cooperation
in maintaining public order and facilitating taxation. The governors similarly cultivated ties with youth gangs, fraternities, and the populace of town quarters.[11] In
Middle Eastern societies with a strong tribal component, Sufis played the intermediary role. Muslim holy men—sometimes charismatic teachers, sometimes the custodians of local shrines, sometimes the members of holy lineages, sometimes affiliated
with brotherhoods—facilitated the selection of tribal chiefs, mediated disputes,
organized long-distance trade, and otherwise helped in the administration of rural
populations.[12]

Thus we have not one but two paradigms, two concepts of the Muslim golden
age. One looks to a unified state and society under the leadership of the caliph,
whose authority extends to all realms of personal and public concern. This is the
integralist conception of Islam. The second, in both its classic and Ottoman versions,
tacitly recognizes the institutional division between the structures of state and religion. In this paradigm, Muslims look to the religious sphere for personal and communal fulfillment, to Islam as a personal and social ethos and not a concept or
institution of the political regime. Finally, the differentiation of state and religion
allows for an imperial and secular notion of the state and for the incorporation of
Middle Eastern but not Islamic institutions and concepts into the theory, legitimation, and operation of political regimes....

NOTES

1. This is part of an essay first published in Charles E. Butterworth and I. William
   Zartman, eds., *Political Islam*, in *The Annals*, vol. 524 (November 1992).
2. W. Montgomery Watt, *Muhammad at Mecca* (New York: Oxford University Press,
   1953); *Muhammad at Medina* (New York: Oxford University Press, 1955).
3. Patricia Crone and Martin Hinds, *God's Caliph* (New York: Cambridge University
   Press, 1986).
4. On revivalist movements, see Ira M. Lapidus, *A History of Islamic Societies* (New
   York: Cambridge University Press, 1988), pp. 257–259, 563–568; John Voll,
   Islam: Continuity and Change in the Modern World (Boulder, CO: Westview
   Press, 1982); Fazlur Rahman, *Islam* (Chicago: University of Chicago Press,
   1979), pp. 193–224.
5. Lapidus, *History of Islamic Societies*, pp. 137–180; A.K.S. Lambton, *Theory and
   Practice in Medieval Persian Government* (London: Variorum Reprints, 1980);
   H. Busse, *Chalif und Grosskönig, die Buyiden im Iraq* (Beirut: Franz Steiner
   Verlag, 1969).

6. On the Ottoman empire, see Halil Inalcik, *The Ottoman Empire: The Classical Age, 1300–1600* (London: Weidenfeld & Nicolson, 1973); H.A.R. Gibb and Harold Bowen, *Islamic Society and the West* (New York: Oxford University Press, 1954, 1957).

7. Yusuf Ibish, *The Political Doctrine of al-Baqillani* (Beirut: American University Press, 1966); al-Mawardi, *Les Statuts gouvernementaux*, trans. E. Fagman (Algiers: Adolph Jourdan, 1915); Ibn Taymiya, *Ibn Taymiya on Public and Private Law in Islam* (Beirut: Khayats, 1968); Henri Laoust, *Essai sur les doctrines socials et politques de Takid-Din Ahmad b. Tamiyya* (Cairo: L'Institut française d'archéologie orientale, 1939).

8. On Persian political theory, see E.I.J Rosenthal, *Political Thought in Medieval Islam* (New York: Cambridge University Press, 1958); al-Jahiz, *Le livre de la couronne*, trans. Charles Pellat (Paris: Société d'édition "Les belles lettres," 1954); Nizam al-Mulk, *The Book of Government or Rules for Kings*, trans. H. Darke, 2nd ed. (London: Routledge & Kegan Paul, 1960); Kai Ka'us b. Iskandar, *A Mirror for Princes: The Qabus Nama*, trans. Reuben Levy (New York: E.P. Dutton 1951).

9. On the rulers and the ruled, see Gibb and Bowen, *Islamic Society and the West*, passim.

10. For example, see Roy Mottahedeh, *Loyalty and Leadership in an Early Islamic Society* (Princeton, NJ: Princeton University Press, 1980).

11. Ira M. Lapidus, *Muslim Cities in the Later Middle Ages*, 2nd ed. (New York: Cambridge University Press, 1984).

12. On the social and political functions of Sufism, see Lapidus, *History of Islamic Societies*, pp. 168–172, 254–257, 261–264. For further examples, see V.N. Basilov, "Honour Groups in Traditional Turkmenian Society," in *Islam in Tribal Societies: From the Atlas to the Indus*, ed. A.A. Ahmed and D.M. Hart (London: Routledge & Kegan Paul, 1984), pp. 220–243; Julia Clancy-Smith, "Saints, Mahdis and Arms: Religion and Resistance in Nineteenth-Century North Africa," in *Islam, Politics, and Social Movements*, ed. Edmund Burke and Ira M. Lapidus (Berkeley, CA: University of California Press, 1988), pp. 60–80; Charles C. Stewart with E.K. Stewart, *Islam and Social Order in Mauritania* (New York: Oxford University Press, 1973).

Alfarabi[1]

Muhsin Mahdi

Alfarabi (al-Fārābī), circa 870–950 A.D., was the first philosopher who sought to confront, to relate, and as far as possible to harmonize classical political philosophy with Islam—a religion that was revealed through a prophet-legislator (Muhammad) in the form of a divine law, that organizes its followers into a political community, and that provides for their beliefs as well as for the principles and detailed rules of their conduct. Unlike Cicero, he had to face and solve the problem of introducing classical political philosophy into a radically different cultural atmosphere; unlike Augustine he did not have a relatively free sphere of this-worldly life in the organization of which classical political philosophy could apply unchallenged, but had to face and solve the problem of the conflicting claims of political philosophy and religion over the whole of a human's life.

The importance of Alfarabi's place in the history of political philosophy consists in his recovery of the classical tradition and in making it intelligible within the new context provided by the revealed religions. His best-known writings are political works concerned with the political regimes and the attainment of happiness through political life. They present the problem of the harmony between philosophy and Islam in a new perspective—that of the relation between the best regime, in particular as Plato had understood it, and the divine law of Islam. His position in Islamic philosophy corresponds to that of Socrates or Plato in Greek philosophy in so far as their chief concern may be said to be the relation between philosophy and the city. He was the founder of a tradition that looked to him, and through him to Plato and Aristotle, for a philosophic approach to the study and understanding of political and religious phenomena. His works inspired men like Avicenna, Averroes, and Maimonides. They admired him as their "second teacher" after Aristotle, and he was the only postclassical thinker whose authority commanded their respect alongside that of the ancients.

DIVINE AND POLITICAL SCIENCE

There are a number of striking resemblances between many of the fundamental features of Islam and the good regime envisaged by classical political philosophy in general, and by Plato in the *Laws* in particular. Both begin with a god as the ultimate cause of legislation and consider correct beliefs about divine beings and the world of nature as essential for the constitution of a good political regime. In both, these beliefs should reflect an adequate image of the cosmos, make accessible to the citizens at large (and in a form they can grasp) the truth about divine things and about the highest principles of the world, be conducive to virtuous action, and form part of the equipment necessary for the attainment of ultimate happiness. Both consider the functions of the founder and legislator, and after him of his successors in the leadership of the community, of absolutely central importance for its organization and preservation. Both are concerned with the giving and the preserving of divine laws. Both are opposed to the view that mind or soul is derivative from body or is itself bodily—a view that undermines human virtue and communal life—and to the timorous piety that condemns man to despair of the possibility of ever understanding the rational meaning of the beliefs he is called upon to accept or of the activities he is called upon to perform. Both direct the eyes of the citizens to a happiness beyond their worldly concerns. Finally, both relegate the art of the jurist and that of the apologetic theologian to the secondary position of preserving the intention of the founder and of his law, and of erecting a shield against attacks.[2]

Alfarabi's important political works (*The Virtuous City, The Virtuous Religion*, and *The Political Regime*) are a meeting ground between Islam and classical political philosophy where these affinities, and not possible differences or conflicts, occupy the foreground. By laying the stress on such affinities, and by encouraging or even forcing both Islam and philosophy each to take a step in the direction of the other, he intends to make visible the common elements in both and to encourage and guide his Muslim reader to understand the characteristic features of classical political philosophy. This is revealed first of all in the very style of these works and in the way in which they are composed. Stylistically, they bear as much resemblance to legal codes as to philosophic treatises. They consist mainly of positive statements about the attributes of God, the order of the world, the place of man within it, and how a good society is to be organized and led. Following a pattern common to Plato's *Laws* and the Koran, many of these statements are preceded by preludes preparing the way to the promulgation of sound laws for regulating the conduct of rulers and prescribing the beliefs and the actions of the citizens. Although not philosophic or political treatises or specific legal promulgation, in the strict sense, these works contain the results of philosophic and political investigations presented in a practically useful way—as a basis for formulating a plan to order a good political regime. They are works whose form and intention could be readily understood by a Muslim reader committed to the acceptance of a true view of the world at large and to obedience to laws that promote virtue and lead to ultimate happiness. But they also conform to the intention of classical political philosophy in that they aim at presenting a rational and persuasive account of the world, couched in terms understandable to the citizens. They perform an important practical task in so far as they indicate by their appearance the possibility of a rational understanding that does not destroy, but preserves and explains, the beliefs and actions prescribed by the revealed law and they achieve a preparatory task inasmuch as they indicate the direction in which such a rational understanding can be sought.

Alfarabi's political works form a new genre of writing in Islamic political literature. With habitual caution, he discreetly abstains from directly quoting, expounding, or even referring to the Koran, Muhammad, or specifically Islamic religious issues. Yet the first impressions that Alfarabi's works leave on his readers are unmistakable: the author intends to enable his coreligionists, and indeed all communicants of revealed religions, to see the wide area of harmony that exists between their divine law and the practical intention of classical political philosophy. These readers could now see in their divine law a practical fulfillment of the doctrines of the most prominent wise men of antiquity. They could turn to the study of these philosophers, not merely for the limited purpose of defending their own beliefs and practices, or the negative purpose of assuring themselves that rational understanding is powerless before the higher authority of revelation and the divine law, but for rising above the slavish state of blind believers and for penetrating into the secret intentions of revelation and the divine law—to enlighten themselves, through the understanding of the most respectable tradition of human wisdom, about the wisdom of their religion. Alfarabi gives them in these works the possibility of gaining a new attitude toward the study of the works of Plato and Aristotle. He also encourages them to cease considering these philosophers as the originators of a foreign tradition that might undermine their beliefs and social virtues, a tradition that they ought to study with a view to refuting and combating it. He makes them see that this tradition belongs to them no less than to the Greeks, and that they must make it their own because it is concerned with matters closest to their minds and hearts. They are made to hope for a fuller understanding of their highest political and religious concern—the things that constitute the essence of their religion and their way of life, distinguish them from their heathen ancestors, and give them their unique claim to superiority over other communities.

THE VIRTUOUS REGIME

The central theme of Alfarabi's political writings is the virtuous regime, the political order with the realization of human excellence or virtue as a guiding principle. He conceives of human or political science as the inquiry into "man" in so far as he is distinguished from other natural beings and from divine beings, seeking to understand his specific nature, what constitutes his perfection, and the way through which he can attain it. Unlike other animals humans are not rendered perfect merely through the natural principles present in him, and unlike divine beings they are not eternally perfect but need to achieve perfection through the activity proceeding from rational understanding, deliberation, and choosing among the various alternatives suggested to him by reason. The initial presence of the power of rational knowledge, and of the choice connected with it, is man's first or natural perfection, the perfection he is born with and does not choose. Beyond this, reason and choice are present in humans to use for realizing their end or the ultimate perfection possible for their nature. This ultimate perfection is identical with the supreme happiness available to him. "Happiness is the good desired for itself, it is never desired to achieve by it something else, and there is nothing greater beyond it that man can achieve."[3]

Yet happiness cannot be achieved without being first known, and without performing certain orderly (bodily and intellectual) activities useful or leading to the achievement of perfection. These are the noble activities. The distinction between noble and base activities is thus guided by the distinction between what is useful for, and what obstructs, perfection and happiness. To perform an activity well, with ease, and in an orderly fashion requires the formation of character and the development of habits that make such activities possible. "The forms and states of character from which these [noble] activities emanate are the virtues; they are not goods for their own sake but goods only for the sake of happiness."[4] The distinction between virtue and vice presupposes knowledge of what human perfection or happiness is as well as the distinction between noble and base activities.

The virtuous regime can be defined as the regime in which humans come together and cooperate with the aim of becoming virtuous, performing noble activities, and attaining happiness. It is distinguished by the presence in it of knowledge of human's ultimate perfection, the distinction between the noble and the base and between the virtues and the vices, and the concerted effort of the rulers and the citizens to teach and learn these things, and to develop the virtuous forms or states of character from which emerge the noble activities useful for achieving happiness.

The attainment of happiness means the perfection of that power of the human soul that is specific to man, of his reason. This in turn requires disciplining the lower desires to cooperate with and aid reason to perform its proper activity and also acquiring the highest arts and sciences. Such discipline and learning can be accomplished only by the rare few who possess the best natural endowments and who are also fortunate to live under conditions in which the requisite virtues can be developed and noble activities performed. The rest of humans can only attain some degree of this perfection; and the extent to which they can attain that degree of perfection of which they are capable is decisively influenced by the kind of political regime in which they live and the education they receive. Nevertheless, all the citizens of the virtuous regime must have some common notions about the world, humans, and political life. But they will differ with regard to the character of this knowledge, and hence with regard to their share of perfection or happiness. They can be divided broadly into the following three classes: (a) The wise or the philosophers who know the nature of things by means of demonstrative proofs and by their own insights. (b) The followers of these philosophers who know the nature of things by means of the demonstrations presented by the philosophers, and who trust the insight and accept the judgment of the philosophers. (c) The rest of the citizens, the many, who know things by means of similitudes, some more and others less adequate, depending on their rank as citizens. These classes or ranks must be ordered by the ruler who should also organize the education of the citizens, assign to them their specialized duties, give their laws, and command them in war. He is to seek, by persuasion and compulsion, to develop in everyone the virtues of which he is capable and to order the citizens hierarchically so that each class can attain the perfection of which it is capable and yet serve the class above it. It is in this manner that the city becomes a whole similar to the cosmos, and its members cooperate toward attaining happiness.

The virtuous regime is a nonhereditary monarchical or an aristocratic regime in which the best rule, with the rest of the citizens divided into groups that (depending on their rank) are ruled and in turn rule—until one arrives at the lowest group that is ruled only. The sole criterion for the rank of a citizen is the character of the virtue of which he is capable and that he is able to develop through his participation in the regime and obedience to its laws. Like the regime itself, its citizens are virtuous, first, because they possess, or follow those who possess, correct similitudes of the knowledge of divine and natural beings, human perfection or happiness, and the principles of the regime designed to help man attain this happiness; and, second, because they act in accordance with this knowledge in that their character is formed with a view to performing the activities conducive to happiness.

Once the main features of the virtuous regime are clarified, the understanding of the main features and the classification of all other regimes become relatively simple. Alfarabi divides them into three broad types. (a) The regimes in which citizens have had no occasion to acquire any knowledge at all about divine and natural beings or about perfection and happiness. These are the *ignorant* regimes. Their citizens pursue lower ends, good or bad, in complete oblivion of true happiness. (b) The regimes in which citizens possess the knowledge of these things but do not act according to their requirements. These are the *wicked* or *immoral* regimes. Their citizens have the same views as those of the virtuous regime; yet their desires do not serve the rational part in them but turn them away to pursue the lower ends pursued in ignorant regimes.

(c) The regimes in which citizens have acquired certain opinions about these things, but false or corrupt opinions, that is, opinions that claim to be about divine and natural beings and about true happiness, while in fact they are not. The similitudes presented to such citizens are, consequently, false and corrupt, and so also are the activities prescribed for them. These are the regimes that have been led astray or the *erring* regimes. The citizens of such regimes do not possess true knowledge or correct similitudes, and they too pursue the lower ends of the ignorant regimes. The regimes in error may have been founded as such. This is the case with the regimes "whose supreme ruler was one who was under an illusion that he was receiving revelation without having done so, and with regard to which he had employed misrepresentations, deceptions, and delusions."[5] But they may also have been originally virtuous regimes that had been changed through the introduction of false or corrupt views and practices.

All these types of regimes are opposed to the virtuous regime because they lack its guiding principle, which is true knowledge and virtue or the formation of character leading to activities conducive to true happiness. Instead, the character of the citizens is formed with a view to attaining one or more of the lower ends. These ends are given by Alfarabi as six, and each of the general types mentioned above can be subdivided according to the end that dominates in it. (a) The regime of *necessity* (or the *indispensable* regime) in which the aim of the citizens is confined to the bare necessities of life. (b) The *vile* regime (oligarchy) in which the ultimate aim of the citizens is wealth and prosperity for their own sakes. (c) The *base* regime the purpose of whose citizens is the enjoyment of sensory or imaginary pleasures. (d) The regime of *honor* (timocracy) whose citizens aim at being honored, praised, and glorified by others. (e) The regime of *domination* (tyranny) whose citizens aim at overpowering and subjecting others. (f) The regime of *corporate association* (democracy) the main purpose of whose citizens is being free to do what they wish.

THE PHILOSOPHER-KING AND THE PROPHET-LEGISLATOR

To combine divine and political science is to emphasize the political importance of sound beliefs about divine beings and about the principles of the world. We saw that both Islam and classical political philosophy are in agreement concerning this issue. Muslims believed that the primary justification of their existence as a distinct community was the revelation of the truth about divine things to Muhammad, and that, had he not come to them with his message, they would have continued to live in misery and uncertainty about their well-being in this world and the next. It was also because of such considerations that Plato thought that kings must become philosophers or philosophers kings. Once the quest for the best regime arrives at the necessity of combining divine and political science, it becomes necessary that the ruler should combine the craft of ruling with that of prophecy or of philosophy. The ruler-prophet or the ruler-philosopher is the human being who offers the solution to the question of the realization of the best regime, and the functions of the ruler-prophet and of the ruler-philosopher appear in this respect to be identical.

Alfarabi begins his discussion of the supreme ruler with the emphasis on the common function of the ruler-philosopher and the ruler-prophet as rulers who are the link between the divine beings above and the citizens who do not have direct access to knowledge of these beings. He is the teacher and guide "who makes known" to the citizens what happiness is, who "arouses in them the determination" to do the things necessary for attaining it, and "who does not need to be ruled by a man in anything at all."[6] He must possess knowledge, not need any other man to guide him, have excellent comprehension of everything that must be done, be excellent in guiding all others in what he knows, have the ability to make others perform the functions for which they are fit, and have the ability to determine and define the work to be done by others and to direct such work toward happiness. These qualities evidently require the best natural endowments, but also the fullest development of the rational faculty. (According to Aristotelian psychology as Alfarabi presents it in his political works, the perfection of the rational faculty consists of its correspondence to, or "union" with, the Active Intellect.) The supreme ruler must be a man who actualizes his rational faculty or who is in union with the Active Intellect.

> This man is the true prince according to the ancients; he is the one of whom it ought to be said that he receives revelation. For man receives revelation only when he attains this rank—that is, when there is no longer an intermediary between him and the Active Intellect.... Now because the Active Intellect emanates from the being of the First Cause [God], it can for this reason be said that it is the First Cause that brings about the revelation to this man through the mediation of the Active Intellect. The rule of this man is the supreme rule; all other human rulerships are inferior to it and are derived from it.[7]

This supreme ruler is the source of all power and knowledge in the regime, and it is through him that the citizens learn what they ought to know and to do. As God or the First Cause of the world directs everything else, and as everything else is directed toward Him, "the case ought to be the same in the virtuous city: in an orderly fashion, all of its parts ought to follow in their activities in the footsteps of the purpose of its supreme ruler."[8] He possesses unlimited powers and cannot be subjected to any human being or political regime or laws. He has the power to confirm or abrogate previous divine laws, to enact new ones, and "to change a law he had legislated at one time for another if he deems it better to do so."[9] He alone has the power to order the classes of people in the regime and assign to them their ranks. And it is he who offers them what they need to know.

For most people, this knowledge has to take the form of an imaginative representation of the truth rather than a rational conception of it. This is because most people are not endowed, or cannot be trained to know divine things in themselves, but can only understand their imitations, which should be made to fit their power of understanding and their special conditions and experience as members of a particular regime. Religion is such a set of imaginative representations in the form of a divine law, legislated for a particular group of men, and necessitated by the incapacity of most men to conceive things rationally and their need to believe in the imitations of divine beings, and of happiness and perfection, as presented to them by the founder of their regime. The founder must then not only present a rational or conceptual account of happiness and the divine principles to the few, but also adequately represent or imitate these same things for the many. All the citizens are to accept and preserve that with which he entrusts them: "the ones who follow after happiness as they cognize it and accept the [divine] principles as they cognize them are the *wise men*; and the ones in whose souls these things are found in the form of images, and who accept them and follow after them as such, are the *believers*."[10]

Thus far Alfarabi identifies the ruler-prophet and the ruler-philosopher. They are both supreme rulers absolutely, and both have absolute authority with regard to legislating beliefs and actions. Both acquire this authority in virtue of the perfection of their rational faculty, and both receive revelation from God through the agency of the Active Intellect. Wherein, then, does the ruler-prophet differ from the ruler-philosopher?

The first and primary qualification that the ruler of the virtuous regime must possess is a special kind of knowledge of divine and human things. Now, man possesses three faculties for knowledge: sensation, imagination, and reason (both theoretical and practical), and these develop in him in that order. Imagination has three functions: (a) It acts as a reservoir of sensible impressions after the disappearance of the objects of sensation. (b) It combines sensible impressions to form a complex sensible image. (c) It produces *imitations*. It has the capacity to imitate all nonsensible things (human desires, temperament, passions) through sensible impressions or certain combinations of them. When later the rational faculty develops, and man begins to grasp the character, essence, or form of natural and divine beings, the faculty of imagination receives and imitates these rational forms also, that is, it *represents* them in the form of sensible impressions. In this respect, imagination is subordinate to the rational faculty and depends on it for the "originals" that it imitates; it has no direct access to the essence of natural and divine beings. Further, the limitations that it fabricates are not all good copies: some may be more true and nearer to the originals, others defective in some respects, and still others extremely false or misleading copies. Finally, only the rational faculty that grasps the originals themselves can judge the degree of the truth of these copies and of their likeness to the originals. The rational faculty is the only faculty that has access to the knowledge of divine or spiritual beings, and it must exercise strict control to insure that the copies offered by the imaginative faculty are good or fair imitations. It may happen in rare cases that this imaginative faculty is so powerful and perfect that it overwhelms all the other faculties, and proceeds directly to receive or form images of divine beings. This rare case is the case of prophecy:

> It is not impossible that man, when his imaginative power reaches utmost perfection, should receive in his waking hours from the Active Intellect...the *imitations* of separate [immaterial] intelligibles and all other noble [sacred] beings, and to view them. By virtue of the intelligibles he had received, he will thus have [the power of] prophecy about divine things. This, then, is the most perfect stage reached by the power of imagination and the most perfect stage at which man arrives by virtue of his imaginative power.[11]

The description of the nature of prophecy thus leads to the distinction between the faculty of imagination and the rational faculty. It explains the possibility of prophecy as the perfection of the faculty of imagination, and that imagination can almost dispense with the rational faculty and receive the images of divine beings directly and without the latter's mediation. There are two powers by means of which man can communicate with the Active Intellect: his imagination and his rational faculty or his intellect. When he communicates with it by means of his imagination, he is "a prophet who warns about what will happen and who informs about what is taking place now"; while when he communicates with it by means of his rational faculty he is "a wise man, a philosopher, and has complete intelligence."[12]

It would appear then that the ruler-prophet and the ruler-philosopher both can be said to possess the qualification of knowledge required for being the supreme ruler of the virtuous city; or that two kinds of equally virtuous regimes are possible, one ruled by a prophet without philosophy and the other ruled by the philosopher without prophecy. Yet in his political writings Alfarabi does not even consider the possibility of a virtuous regime ruled by a prophet who does not possess a developed rational faculty. The distinction between prophecy and philosophy is a psychological distinction, and it is useful for understanding the nature of prophecy and philosophy respectively. But in discussing the quality of knowledge required by the supreme ruler, Alfarabi is explicit in demanding the perfection of both faculties: the supreme ruler is not called a perfect prophet or a perfect philosopher, but a "perfect human being." To begin with the philosopher, even his philosophy or the wisdom he is seeking remains incomplete so long as he does not possess perfect mastery in imitating the rational or theoretical knowledge in his possession in order to teach it to the young or to present it to the multitude. This lack becomes an essential defect when he is faced with the task of governing a city and educating it. His very quality as philosopher (that is, as one who devotes himself to theoretical knowledge irrespective of its use in, or relation to, the city) disqualifies him as a ruler. He cannot be a *ruler*-philosopher without the power of imagination of which the prophet is the most accomplished representative.

As to the prophet, while his imaginative power seems to make him particularly fit for ruling, the workings of his imagination do not enjoy the benefit of rational control: he lacks the constant check of the degree of truthfulness or verisimilitude of the imitations produced by his powerful imagination, a function that only the rational faculty can perform. The best ruler for the virtuous city must therefore be a ruler-philosopher-prophet. Alfarabi does not say whether Muhammad the prophet was also a philosopher, but he requires the combination of prophecy and philosophy, or the exercise of the imaginative and the rational powers, in the supreme ruler of the virtuous city. Philosophy or wisdom is indispensable for ruling a virtuous city. "If it should happen at any time that wisdom has no share in ruling, and [the ruling authority] fulfilled all other conditions, the virtuous city remains without a prince, the ruler who takes care of the business of this city will not be a prince, and the city will be exposed to perdition. Thus if it does not happen that there should exist a wise man to associate with him, then after a time the city will surely perish."[13]

LAW AND LIVING WISDOM

Wisdom or philosophy is an indispensable condition for the founding and survival of the virtuous city. Prophecy, on the other hand, is indispensable for founding a virtuous city but not for its survival. In enumerating the qualities of the supreme ruler or the founder of the virtuous city, Alfarabi stipulates the coincidence of excellent rational and prophetic faculties. This requirement is imposed by the composition of the virtuous city as a political community, that is, the fact that it must be made up of two broad groups: (a) the few who are philosophers or can be addressed through philosophy, and who can be taught the theoretical sciences and hence the true character of divine and natural beings as they are; (b) the many who (because they lack the necessary natural endowments or have no time for sufficient training) are not philosophers, who live by opinion and persuasion, and for whom the ruler must imitate these beings by means of similitudes and symbols.

While the few can be made to grasp rationally the meaning of human happiness and perfection and the rational basis or justification of the virtuous activities that lead to man's ultimate end, the many are incapable of such understanding and have to be taught to perform these activities by persuasion and compulsion, that is, by explanations that could be understood by all the citizens regardless of their rational capacity, and by prescribed rewards and punishments of an immediate tangible kind. The supreme ruler teaches the few in his capacity as philosopher, and he presents similitudes and prescribes rewards and punishments for the many in his capacity as prophet. To be believed and practiced by the many, these similitudes and prescriptions should be formulated by the prophet, and accepted by the citizens, as true, fixed, and permanent; that is, the citizens should expect definite rewards and punishments for belief and unbelief, and for obedience and disobedience. The prophetic faculty culminates, then, in laying down laws concerning both the beliefs and the practices of the many, and the prophet who assumes this function becomes a prophet-legislator. The rational faculty, in contrast, culminates in teaching the theoretical sciences to the few. In his summary of Plato's *Laws*, Alfarabi also understood Plato to say that these virtuous few "have no need for fixed practices and laws at all; nevertheless they are very happy. Laws and fixed practices are needed only for those who are morally crooked."[14]

It is only as viewed by the subjects that laws are fixed and are of unquestionable divine authority. We saw that the supreme ruler of the virtuous regime is the master and not the servant of the law. Not only is he not ruled by any man, he is also not ruled by the law. He is the cause of the law, he creates it, and he abrogates and changes it as he sees fit. He possesses this authority because of his wisdom and his capacity to decide what is best for the common good under given conditions; and conditions can arise under which the changing of the law is not only salutary but indispensable for the survival of the virtuous regime. In so doing, he must be extremely cautious not to disturb the faith of the citizens in their laws, and should consider the adverse effect that change has on attachment to the law. He must make a careful appraisal of the advantage of changing the law as against the disadvantage of change as such. Thus he must possess, not only the authority to change laws whenever necessary, but also the craft of minimizing the danger of change to the well-being of the regime. But once he sees that changing the law is necessary and takes the proper precautions, there is no question as to his authority to change the law. Therefore, so long as he lives, the rational faculty rules supreme and laws are preserved or changed in the light of his judgment as philosopher.

It is this coincidence of philosophy and prophecy in the person of the ruler that insures the survival of the virtuous regime. As long as rulers who possess these qualities succeed each other without interruption, the same situation prevails.

> The successor will be the one who will decide about what was left undecided by his predecessor. And not this alone. He may change a great deal of what his predecessor had legislated and make a different decision about it when he knows this to be best in his own time—not because his predecessor had committed a mistake but because his predecessor decided upon it according to what was best in his own time, and the successor decides according to what is best for a later time. Were his predecessor to observe [the new conditions] he would have changed [his own law] also.[15]

The coincidence of philosophy and prophecy is extremely rare, and chance may not always favor the virtuous regime with the availability of a man who possesses all the necessary natural endowments and whose training proves successful. Thus the question arises as to whether the virtuous city can survive in the absence of a man with all the qualifications required in the supreme ruler, and particularly those of philosophy and prophecy. Granting that the best possible arrangement demands the existence of all these qualifications in one man who must rule, can the regime originated by such a ruler survive at all in his absence? The only qualification that Alfarabi is willing to drop in *The Virtuous City* is prophecy, and then only if provisions are made for the presence of proper substitutes for prophetic legislation. These substitutes consist of (a) the body of laws and customs established by the "true princes," and (b) a combination of new qualities in the ruler that make him proficient in the "art of jurisprudence," that is, knowledge of the laws and customs of his predecessors, willingness on his part to follow these laws and customs rather than change them, the capacity to apply them to new conditions by the "deduction" of new decisions from, or the "discovery" of new applications for, established laws and customs, and the capacity to meet every new situation (for which no specific decisions are available) through understanding the intention of previous legislators rather than by the legislation of new laws or by any formal change of old ones. So far as the law is concerned, this new ruler is a jurist-legislator rather than a prophet-legislator. He must, however, possess all the other qualities, including wisdom or philosophy, that enable him to discern and promote the common good of his regime at the particular period during which he rules.

In the event that no single human being should exist who possesses all these qualifications, then Alfarabi suggests a third possibility: a philosopher and one other man (who possesses the rest of the qualities, except philosophy) should rule jointly. Were even this to prove unobtainable, he suggests finally a joint rule of a number of men possessing these qualifications severally. This joint rule does not, however, affect the presence of the required qualifications but only their presence in the *same* man. Thus the only qualification whose very presence may be dispensed with is prophecy. The substitutes for prophecy are the preservation of old laws and the capacity to discover new applications for old laws. To promote the common good and preserve the regime under new conditions as these emerge, neither the coincidence of philosophy and prophecy in the same man, nor the coincidence of philosophy and jurisprudence, proves to be an indispensable condition. It is sufficient to have philosophy in the person of a philosopher who rules jointly with another man or a group of men who possess, among other things, the capacity to put old laws to new uses. Unlike prophecy, philosophy cannot be dispensed with, and nothing can take its place. Unlike the absence of prophecy, the absence of philosophy is fatal to the existence of the virtuous regime. There is no substitute for living wisdom.

WAR AND THE LIMITATIONS OF LAW

In addition to philosophy and prophecy (or else proficiency in the art of jurisprudence), there is a third and indispensable qualification that must be present in the ruler of the virtuous regime or in one of the group that rule it jointly: that is, daring and warlike virtue. This qualification is required for carrying out the ruler's responsibility as the supreme educator of all the citizens, that is, to form and improve their moral character. Since not all men can be convinced, or aroused to perform virtuous activities, by means of persuasive and passionate speeches, the method of persuasion or consent is not sufficient. As the father does with his children and the schoolteacher with the young, so the ruler has to use force and compulsion with those who, out of nature or habit, cannot be educated or persuaded to obey the law spontaneously. Hence the ruler needs to employ two groups of educators: a group that educates the citizens by persuasion and by means of arguments; and a warlike group to compel the lazy, the wicked, and the incorrigible to obey the laws by force. The supreme ruler, or the rulers, should lead, direct, and supervise the activities of both groups. To command the second group, he or they should possess a daring nature and excel in the art of war.

The nature and the extent of the compulsion and force to be applied within a certain regime depend on the character of the citizens: the more virtuous they are, the less need there is to apply force. But there are cases where the ruler may have to conquer a whole city and force it to accept his virtuous or divine law, or where the use of force would considerably shorten the time required to establish his law while the issue of persuasion is too uncertain and its prospects too remote. Compulsion is legitimate inside the regime with regard to those citizens who are of intractable natures or bad habits, and with respect to a whole city as a prelude to the establishment of a new divine law where it is lacking. Physical force, overpowering, or war is a "fundamental element" of the law and one of the basic "preludes" for establishing it. Alfarabi seems to favor not only defensive war but offensive war also; and he speaks of the war conducted by the ruler of the virtuous regime as a just war and of his warlike purpose as a virtuous purpose.

Further, while like Plato and Aristotle, Alfarabi considers the "city" the first or smallest unit that constitutes a political whole and in which man can attain his political perfection, unlike them he does not seem to consider the city also the largest possible unit in which a virtuous regime can be expected to flourish. Instead, he speaks of three "perfect" human associations: the largest in size is the association of all men in the entire inhabited world; the intermediate is the association of a nation in a portion of the inhabited world; and the smallest is the association of the inhabitants of a city in a portion of the land inhabited by a nation. If we combine his teaching about just or virtuous war and conquest with the idea of a perfect human association extending over the entire inhabited world, we can be led to the conclusion that Alfarabi deliberately modified the teachings of Plato and Aristotle on an important issue with the intention of supplying a rational justification for the Islamic concept of holy war whose aim was to propagate the divine law everywhere on earth; that he favored a war of civilization whereby a more advanced nation justifies the conquest of more backward nations; or that he preached the idea of a universal or a world state. These conclusions must now be examined in the light of Alfarabi's views on war and the character of the law.

He mentions two extreme views regarding war. The first is the view that to overpower and dominate others is the natural state of man and that war is therefore the only universally just course of conduct. The second is that the natural state of man is universal peace and peaceful coexistence is therefore the only just course of conduct. This latter view can in turn have the corollary that only in defensive war, war forced upon one by the unnatural conduct of a warlike enemy, is there a just cause for taking up arms. These are according to him the views of the inhabitants of the "ignorant and erring cities" that are opposed to the virtuous regime.[16] They give rise to two types of regimes, "tyrannies," and "peace-loving regimes." The latter are not considered sufficiently important; and their view, though mistaken, is evidently not dangerous. At any rate, he does not list them as a main subdivision of the regimes opposing the virtuous regime which is partly due to the fact that, unlike war, peace is not one of the main "ends" pursued by men but a means to other ends, such as pleasure or gain.

War, conquest, the overpowering and enslaving of others, and tyranny over them, is, in contrast, one of the supreme ends pursued by men. It gives rise to the "tyrannical regime" in which men associate with each other, practice warlike activities, frame their laws, and order their regime with the main purpose of enslaving each other or other regimes. They do not enslave and kill to attain other ends, but to satisfy a supreme end common to all of them, "the love of tyranny." Indeed, the bad regimes pursuing other ends, such as wealth, honor, or pleasure, are in many cases transformed into tyrannies when these other ends are attained. The satisfaction of these desires seems to free the citizens of bad regimes to pursue the highest evil of "ignorant and erring" regimes, that is, the view that "tyranny is the good." War as an end in itself is for Alfarabi the supreme vice that can have no place in the regime whose end is the supreme virtue.

Having made use of the advantages of war and compulsion to establish his divine law and to suppress the wicked and the incorrigible, the ruler of the virtuous regime must return to promote friendship among the citizens and to the peaceful work of persuasion and free consent. To persuade the majority of citizens, he has to produce similitudes of divine and natural beings, and of virtue and happiness, that are adequate in respect of their proximity to the original forms of these things, but that are also adequate with respect to those who are to be persuaded by them. The similitudes should bear some relation to the nature, past experience, and habits of the citizens. Unlike the business of war, peaceful persuasion requires the legislator to make concessions to the character of the ruled, the degree of their preparation for virtuous laws, differences among them, and the extent to which the citizens can be improved. These are prelegal conditions that he does not create but must presuppose and that he cannot change except to a limited extent and then only gradually.

Further, the legislator cannot produce similitudes and utilize persuasive methods designed to meet the peculiar nature and habits of each individual citizen; the law cannot treat each man as a case by himself. General beliefs and practices must be prescribed for all the citizens and must correspond to their distinctive character as a group. Now, what is adequate for one group and hence just with regard to them may be inadequate for another group and hence unjust with regard to them. To legislate for all men with respect to "human nature" or what they all have in common will mean being unjust to most if not to all men. Therefore, if it is the case that the inhabited world is divided into nations and cities, and this division is based not on arbitrary but on natural distinctions or distinctions that are somehow related to nature, such distinctions could form the limits within which general beliefs and practices that are both effective and just could be prescribed.

Alfarabi qualifies his statement about the three perfect associations (the city, the nation, and the association of all men in the entire inhabited world) with the observation that the association of all men in the entire inhabited world is divided into nations. "Nations are distinguished from each other by two natural things—natural make-up and natural character—and by something that is composite (it is conventional but has a basis in natural things), namely, language."[17] These distinctions are the product of geographical differences among the various parts of the earth (temperature, foodstuff, and so on) that in turn influence the temperament of their inhabitants. But although they constitute the nation as a natural unit, these natural national similarities are not a sufficient political bond for the sake of which the members of a nation should like each other or dislike other nations. The proper objects of like and dislike are the perfections or the virtues, and these are not given by nature but by the Active Intellect, by science, and by legislation. The nation is in turn divided into cities or city-states that are distinguished by their regimes and laws.

Only the city is likened by Alfarabi to the perfect living body. The organs of the living body do not simply cooperate toward a common end; they have different ranks, each of which is perfect when it performs its proper function (be that a sub-ordinate or a superior one), and all of which are ruled by the most perfect organ. Applied to the nation and the association of all men in the entire inhabited world, this similitude would require the subordination of cities to each other, and of nations to each other, according to their degree of perfection. Yet Alfarabi never speaks of such subordination as being legitimate except within a single city; and the cities opposed to the virtuous city are not investigated with a view to being subordinated to a virtuous city but to being transformed into such a city. A virtu-ous nation is not a group of cities ruled by a virtuous or perfect city, but the nation "*all* of whose cities *cooperate* regarding the things by which happiness is attained"; and the association of all men in the entire inhabited world is virtuous "only when the nations in it *cooperate* to achieve happiness."[18] The virtuous community of all men presupposes virtuous nations, and the virtuous nation in turn presupposes virtuous cities.

The consideration of the specific character and function of the prophetic faculty and of the divine law points to the conclusion that religion should be particularly sensitive to the limitations imposed by the natural and conventional differences among nations and cities. If a religion or divine law is not spurious, obscurantist, or fanatic, it does not promote but suppresses and transcends the ends pursued in igno-rant regimes (including tyranny), and substitutes for them the end that can be pur-sued only through the belief in adequate or salutary similitudes of divine and natural beings, and through commands and prohibitions that promote virtue and happiness among a particular group ready for its message. It must therefore abandon the end of the tyrannical regime whose aim is absolute and universal tyranny and restrict the use of force to the extent to which it is necessary to establish a new regime and sup-press the wicked and the incorrigible inside that regime. Otherwise, it will be forced to legislate beliefs and practices that can be accepted and performed by all men, that is, to lower its standards to conform to the natural capacity of the overwhelming majority of men rather than uphold the ones that help a relatively good city or nation to achieve true virtue or happiness. The alternative aim of promoting virtue or hap-piness among the best or the elect in every city and nation is ruled out because this is not the proper function of religion but of philosophy. We recall Alfarabi's distinc-tion between the functions of prophecy and philosophy in the virtuous regime. The few who are endowed with rare natures and are given proper training are offered, not similitudes, but theoretical knowledge of the divine and natural beings themselves, and of virtue and happiness, while the beliefs and practices legislated in the divine law aim at the many.

Now, the natural and quasinatural distinctions among cities and nations need not form a barrier against the transmission of theoretical knowledge. Such knowl-edge presupposes the presence of a tradition of theoretical inquiry and of rare indi-viduals; but once these conditions are fulfilled, it can be freely transplanted from one city to another and from one nation to another. The universal community of the superior men of every city and nation or of the uncrowned kings of humanity is not a community of believers in a particular set of dogmas. It is the community of lovers of the one and true wisdom. By its very nature, according to Alfarabi, a reli-gion cannot provide the basis for such a community. Religion arises because of the incapacity of the many to understand the true character of beings and of human happiness. It remedies this situation by presenting them with similitudes that take into account the limitations of their understanding and their natural and conven-tional characteristics as a distinct group. Also, because the true principles of nature and true political principles are invariable, they are inflexible and cannot themselves be adjusted to the degree of understanding and the particular character of a distinctive political group. Similitudes, in contrast, may be adjusted for this purpose because they can be nearer to, or remote from, reality. In addition, there can be a number of good similitudes of the same reality. These similitudes are all good or virtuous if they succeed in making the members of the particular political groups for which they are designed good or virtuous. "Consequently, there may be a number of virtuous nations and a number of virtuous cities whose religions are different."[19] Alfarabi's approach to religion leads to a philosophic science of divine laws. By presenting divine laws, jurisprudence, and theology as parts of political science, he points to the possibility of a neutral discussion of all religions or "sects" and of the features common to them all.

DEMOCRACY AND THE VIRTUOUS REGIME

Of the six regimes opposed to the virtuous regime, the first and the last, that is, the regimes of necessity, and democracy, occupy the privileged position of supplying the most solid and the best starting point for the establishment of the virtuous regime and for the rule of virtuous men. The regime of necessity (as the counterpart of the city of the pigs in Plato's *Republic*) offers the opportunity for introducing a virtuous regime among citizens who are not as yet corrupted by the love of money or honor, by indulgence in pleasures, or by the desire for glory. But since all of these exist in democracy, it is not clear at first sight what contribution democracy could make to the virtuous regime.

Following Plato's description (*Republic* VIII), Alfarabi sets down the first principle of democracy (that is, of pure democracy, or of extreme democracy, as Aristotle calls it) as freedom, and he calls the democratic regime also the "free" regime. Freedom means the ability of everyone to pursue anything he desires, and that he should be left alone to do anything he chooses in the pursuit of his desires. The second principle is equality, which means that no man is superior to another in anything at all. These two principles define the basis of authority, the relation between the ruler and the ruled, and the attitude of the citizens to each other. Authority is justified only on the basis of the preservation and promotion of freedom and equality. Whatever the accomplishments of the ruler, he rules only by the will of the citizens, however unaccomplished he or they may be: he must follow their wishes and cater to their whims. The citizens honor only those who lead them to freedom and to the achievement of whatever makes possible the enjoyment of their desires, and those who preserve that freedom and make it possible for them to enjoy their different and conflicting desires, and who defend them against external enemies. If such men can perform these functions and still remain themselves content with the bare necessities of life, then they are considered virtuous and are obeyed. The rest of the rulers are functionaries who perform services for which they receive adequate honors or financial remunerations; and the citizens who pay them for these services consider themselves, because of this, superior to these rulers whom they support. Such also is the case of those whom the public lets rule either because it takes a fancy to them or because it wants to reward them for a service rendered by their ancestors. Despite these differences, a close investigation of the democratic regime shows that, ultimately, there are really no rulers and ruled; there is one supreme will, which is that of the citizens; and the rulers are instruments serving the desires and wishes of the citizens.

Unlike the other five regimes, there is no single or dominating end desired or wished for by the citizens of the democratic regime. They form innumerable groups, similar and dissimilar, with a variety of characters, interests, aims, and desires. So far as ends are concerned, democracy is a composite regime: various groups, aiming at the ends characterizing the other regimes, exist side by side and pursue different ways of life; they form a conglomeration in which the different parts are interwoven with each other; and they are free to fulfill their distinct aims independently or in cooperation with others.

Because the democratic regime makes possible, preserves, protects, and promotes every kind of desire, all kinds of men come to admire it and consider it as the happy way of life. They come to love democracy and to love to live in it. A great number migrate to it from different nations, and residents and foreigners meet, mix, and intermarry. The result is the greatest possible diversity of natural character, upbringing, education, and ways of life; yet every type of man is encouraged, or allowed, to achieve what he desires as far as his capacity admits. A fully developed democratic regime presents a colorful spectacle of infinite diversity and luxury.

But this means that, of all the regimes opposed to the virtuous regime, the democratic regime contains the greatest amount and variety of good and evil things; and the more it expands and becomes perfect, the more the goodness and the evil it contains. It will therefore also contain a number of the parts of the virtuous city. Alfarabi mentions in particular the possibility of the rise of virtuous men, and of the presence of wise men, rhetoricians, and poets (that is, men who deal with demonstrative science, persuasion, and imitation) in all kinds of things. If the regime of necessity contributes citizens uncorrupted by unessential desires and pleasures, the democratic regime, most of whose citizens are corrupted by luxury, offers the highly developed sciences and arts essential for the establishment of the virtuous regime. And in the absence of the virtuous regime in which these sciences and arts have the best opportunity to develop in the right direction, the democratic regime is the only regime that provides ample opportunity for their development and allows the philosopher to pursue his desire with relative freedom.

NOTES

1. This is a chapter first published in Leo Strauss and Joseph Cropsey, eds., *History of Political Philosophy* (Chicago, IL: University of Chicago Press, 1981).
2. Alfarabi, *The Enumeration of the Sciences*, ed. Osman Amine (2nd ed.; Cario: Dār al-Fikr al'Arabī, 1949), v; *The Virtuous Religion*, MS, Leiden, Cod. Or. No. 1002, fols. 53*v*–54*v*.
3. *The Virtuous City*, ed. Fr. Dieterici (Leiden: Brill, 1895), p. 46; cf. *The Political Regime* (Hyderabad: Dā'irat al-Ma'ārif al-'Uthmāniyyah, 1345 A. H.), pp. 42–45, 48.
4. *Virtuous City*, p. 46; cf. *Political Regime*, pp. 43–44.
5. *Virtuous City*, p. 63; cf. *Political Regime*, p. 74.
6. *Political Regime*, pp. 48–49.
7. Ibid., pp. 49–50.
8. *Virtuous City*, pp. 56–57; cf. *Political Regime*, pp. 53–54.
9. *Political Regime*, pp. 50–51.
10. Ibid., p. 56.
11. *Virtuous City*, p. 52.
12. Ibid., pp. 58–59.

13. Ibid., p. 61.

14. *Plato's Laws*, ed. Franciscus Gabrieli (London: Warburg Institute, 1952), p. 41.

15. *Virtuous Religion*, fol. 54r.

16. *Virtuous City*, pp. 75–80.

17. *Political Regime*, p. 40.

18. *Virtuous City*, p. 54.

19. *Political Regime*, p. 56; *Virtuous City*, p. 70.

A View Across Time: Islam as the Religion of Reason*

Roxanne L. Euben

In my work I have approached Sayyid Qutb as a political theorist because, I have argued, his own preoccupations with the moral foundations of political authority are the preoccupations of political theory as a field, and, moreover, his political thought is significantly shaped by the experience of Western colonialism and cultural influence. In emphasizing this kind of context for Qutb's work, I have tried to illustrate an approach that, to borrow and perhaps subvert Clifford Geertz's language about interpreting culture, works to expose what is familiar in the unfamiliar without denying its particularity.[1] Within the proposed framework of comparative political theory, such exposure is potentially double, for it simultaneously provides a window into the world of Islamic fundamentalism and holds a mirror up to our own world. Yet at the same time that Qutb's perspective on "the modern condition" illuminates the extent to which modern ideas we value are experienced and redefined in other cultures, the cultural syncretism of Qutb's thought blurs the boundaries between Islam and the West. In this way, his work comes to seem less a perspective of radical difference than a different perspective on what it does and must mean to live in the modern world.

Yet the attempt to expose familiarity in unfamiliarity risks orienting Qutb's thought, and the agenda of Islamic fundamentalists more generally, in terms of "our" concerns: the very paradigm of familiarity inevitably measures Qutb's intelligibility in terms of his accessibility, or inaccessibility, to Western worlds of meaning. This is a concern despite the fact that those worlds of meaning have substantially framed Qutb's own political thought. In the following discussion, then, I contrast nineteenth-century Islamic "modernist"[2] arguments for the compatibility of Islam and reason with Qutb's insistence that such arguments are both false and corrosive to Islamic authenticity. Indeed, in *Signposts along the Road* and *The Islamic Conception and Its Characteristics*, Qutb explicitly repudiates such arguments as an apologia for Western dominance, and therefore as a prescription for further decay rather than renewal. For Qutb contends that the emphasis on the importance of reason in Islam, and arguments for the compatibility of modernity and Islam, rationality and revealed law, are simply poorly masked attempts to justify Islam against both the obscurantism of Islamic scholars and attacks from Western and Eastern secularists.[3] The underlying premise and implication of such apologetics, Qutb argues, is that Islam is on trial because it is somehow "guilty" and therefore in need of exoneration.[4] This defensive posture is a position not of strength and certainty but of powerlessness. As we have seen, while Qutb does not eschew the exercise and importance of human reason for understanding aspects of the world, he is outraged by the claim that reason and scripture are equally important for knowledge and guidance when it is self-evidently true that

> [divine revelation] came down to be a source which human reason must consult, to be the standard in terms of which all judgments, knowledge and concepts of human reason are evaluated, and to correct the deficiencies and distortions produced by reason. There is, no doubt, congruence and harmony between the two but on this basis alone: the absolute supremacy of divine revelation over human reason, not a posited equality or commensurability between them.[5]

What has alternately been called Islamic "modernism," Islamic reformism, or at times referred to by the term *salafiyya*—a word deriving from the Arabic root meaning "predecessors" or "forebears"—provides a point of sharp contrast to Qutb's rejection of rationalist ambitions to understand human nature and purposes.[6] In general, Islamic modernism refers to an intellectual stream of nineteen-century Islamic thought that took shape in the shadow of the slow decline of the Ottoman Empire and the expansion of European political and economic power. Such thought posited a golden age in the earliest generations in Islamic history and sought simultaneously to revive and reform Islam in the image of that golden age,[7] thereby providing a bulwark against the encroachments of Western imperialist and colonialist power upon a decaying Islamic community. This historical and political context had also shaped a prior generation of Muslim intellectuals—writers such as Rifa'a Badawi Rafi' al-Tahtawi (1801–1873) and Khayr al-Din Pasha (1820s to 1889)—yet at that time, the disparity in power had not yet lent what Sharabi calls a "menacing aspect" to European growth. For this earlier group of Muslim thinkers, European ascendence was "less of a threat and more of a promise."[8]

Thus, although the gradual but steady growth of European influence in the workings of the Ottoman Empire in particular had been a matter of concern among Muslim intellectuals for some time, in the mid-1800s "they had not yet become so great as to constitute the central problem of political life, and the main problem was still what it had been for the Ottoman writers of the seventeenth and eighteenth centuries—internal decline, how to explain and how to arrest it."[9] The years 1875–1882 radically altered that landscape: by 1877 Russia had attacked Turkey, Tunisia was occupied by the French four years later, and by 1882 Egypt was occupied by the British. "The problem of inner decay still exercised men's minds," Hourani observes, "but there was grafted on to it a new problem, that of survival: how could the Muslim countries resist the new danger from the outside?"[10] Although Islam had always moved through repeated cycles of renewal and reform, what distinguished the modernist movement of the late nineteenth century from earlier attempts at Islamic "purification" was its profound engagement with the external threat posed by Europe.[11]

The movement is perhaps most closely associated with the work of Muhammad 'Abduh (1849–1905), but it arguably includes, or was significantly presaged by, the anti-imperialist philosophy and activism of 'Abduh's sometime collaborator, Jamal al-Din al-Afghani [al-Asabadi] (1839–1897).[12] For many scholars of Islam, the influence of Afghani and 'Abduh is an established fact, and the importance of their political thought and activism for understanding subsequent developments in Middle Eastern politics is undisputed. For example, Charles C. Adams cites approvingly biographers who have described 'Abduh as "one of the creators of modern Egypt" and "one of the founders of modern Islam";[13] Badawi calls Afghani the Socrates of the Islamic Reformist school; and Wilfred C. Smith argues that it was Afghani who first stressed the "Islam-West" antinomy, and the first important figure with "nostalgia for the departed earthly glory of pristine Islam."[14]

Since the 1960s, however, a number of scholars have challenged the standard account of Afghani and 'Abduh as pioneering Islamic reformists, casting doubt upon their sincerity and emphasizing their failure systematically or significantly to reformulate Islamic doctrine.[15] Yet even these critics portray Afghani and 'Abduh as inaugurators of Islamic revival broadly understood. For example, a leading scholar on Afghani, Nikki Keddie, notes that while some scholars have exaggerated Afghani's direct influence over subsequent movements and ideologies in the Middle East, and that Afghani in fact wielded little political influence during his lifetime, it is also true that "Afghani was one of the first influential figures to try to restate the Muslim tradition in ways that might meet the agonizing problems brought by the growing encroachments of the West in the Middle East."[16] Sylvia Haim concurs in her overview of Arab nationalism by stating that Afghani offered the most "significant" and "influential" defense of Islam and can be credited with transforming Islam into an ideology. She concludes: "His political activity and teaching combined to spread among the intellectual and official classes of Middle Eastern Islam a secularist, meliorist, and activist attitude toward politics, an attitude the presence of which was essential, before ideologies such as Arab nationalism could be accepted to any degree."[17] The lively and unceasing debate over the significance, impact, and originality of both thinkers and their work assures, and indeed presupposes, their importance in Islamic political thought.

As this analysis takes Qutb's criticisms of Islamic modernism as a point of departure for examining arguments of the modernists themselves, this chapter does not attempt an analysis of Afghani's and 'Abduh's lives and thought in full, nor does it aspire to be a full account of Islamic modernism. Lastly, this analysis cannot stand in for a genealogy: indeed, it is one of the paradoxes of the contemporary Islamist movement that while 'Abduh is explicitly rejected as the modernist who "let reason in the back door," as it were, Afghani is celebrated as a great anti-imperialist defender of Islam, an argument that, as we shall see, privileges some of his writings over others.[18] As with my analysis of Qutb, I approach Afghani's and 'Abduh's thought with a particular set of purposes: to highlight the extent to which these responses to the challenge of Western cultural and political power are premised upon the assumption that rationalism not only is compatible with Islamic teachings but is actually enjoined by such teachings when rightly—which is to say rationally—understood.

Afghani and Islamic Philosophy

The father and mother of science is proof, and proof is neither Aristotle nor Galileo. The truth is where there is proof, and those who forbid science and knowledge in the belief that they are safeguarding the Islamic religion are really the enemies of that religion. The Islamic religion is the closest of religions to science and knowledge, and there is no incompatibility between science and knowledge and the foundation of the Islamic faith.[19]

Any analysis of Jamal al-Din al-Afghani's political thought, no matter how carefully delimited, immediately encounters the difficulty of locating him, both geographically and intellectually. Afghani wanted it known that he was born and raised as a Sunni Muslim in Afghanistan, but it has been persuasively established that he was most likely born into a family of sayyids (descendants of the prophet) in Asadabad, Iran, near Hamadan in 1839. Thus he was raised and educated as a Shiite Muslim at home until he was ten, when he continued his religious education in Tehran and in the shrine cities of Iraq.[20] Afghani's Iranian origins are for Elie Kedourie a sign of the duplicitousness and manipulation that tarnishes not only his life but his intellectual agenda as well. In contrast, M. A. Said Badawi argues that given the historical tensions between Sunnis and Shiites, Afghani's pan-Islamic commitments necessitated a Sunni identity.[21]

The confusion surrounding his origins is only exacerbated by the complex interplay of his intellectual, political, and religious commitments. For example, he apparently made different arguments to different audiences. Consequently, much of the secondary literature on Afghani is preoccupied with determining the "real" versus the merely strategic in Afghani's writings. Nikki Keddie has argued in several books, including a seminal biography, that Afghani's reputation as a pioneering Islamic reformer obscures the extent to which his commitment to Islam often served rather than shaped his political interest in strengthening the Muslim world against Western power.[22] Kedourie goes as far as portraying Afghani as an almost Machiavellian figure whose commitment to Islam was entirely utilitarian. Kedourie further argues that examination of both the substance and function of Afghani's and 'Abduh's shifting Islamic commitments reveals a heterodoxy tantamount to irreligiosity.[23]

While it is difficult if not impossible to determine definitively in retrospect what Afghani "really believed," it is possible to argue that his political writings are consistently characterized by the tension that defined his life: the repudiation of Western imperialism in all its forms and the conviction that Western rationalist methods and the technological and scientific expertise they produced were necessary for political strength and for the survival of the Islamic community. Afghani's anti-imperialism in particular is a remarkably consistent thread in his life: after a childhood in Iran, Afghani spent most of his peripatetic life agitating for pan-Islamism[24] and against European imperialism. His first recorded political activities are in India, where he apparently moved from Iran in 1855–1856. It was in India that his exposure to British imperialism had a profound effect, and in India, he came into his first direct contact with the sciences and mathematics of Europe. Afghani came to Afghanistan for the first time in 1866 and appears on the political scene in his late teens already as a decidedly anti-imperialist, anti-British activist. In what was to become a pattern in his life, Afghani was expelled from Afghanistan in 1868 when the new Amir of Afghanistan grew suspicious of him. He made his way to Istanbul by 1869 and found favor with the reformer and leader Ali Pasha. But he was expelled on the grounds of heresy in 1870 after he delivered a public lecture drawing upon his training in Islamic philosophy and comparing prophecy to philosophy, "the highest of crafts."[25]

The arguments of this lecture, as well as those of his other writings on philosophy, illustrate the centrality of Afghani's conviction that the decay of the Muslim *umma* (community) and its manifest weakness in relation to European ascendence are inextricably tied the neglect of science and philosophy. In contrast to Qutb's insistence that to be truly Muslim means acknowledging the limits of human reason in matters metaphysical and moral, for Afghani the survival of Islam depends not on the repudiation of rationalism but on the employment of it against the real enemy: imperialism. Thus while Qutb argues that the intrusion of ancient philosophy and rationalism inaugurated a corruption of Islam completed by the aggressive secularism

of the Enlightenment, Afghani attributes the decay of Islam to the negation and
neglect of reason and philosophy, both of which are transhistorical imperatives for
knowledge.

Afghani thus seeks to disentangle the prevailing equation of rationalism and the
West so that the free exercise of reason appears neither inimical to Islamic truths nor
tantamount to Westernization. Toward this end, Afghani's "Lecture on Teaching
and Learning" (delivered in Calcutta in 1882) establishes a distinction between the
power of science and the power of particular cultures or nations whose successes
have been facilitated by science. As science and philosophy are the means by which
human beings obtain truths about the world, such truths and the methods used to
obtain them are not the product of the West but of human endeavor generally. The
subject of science is universal, and the truths it reveals are self-evident. All wealth
and riches are products of these universal truths, truths that encompass not only the
functioning of nature and human nature, but, by extension, the requirements for
living and living well.[26] This means that scientific truths do not now reside in
European culture any more than they did in Egypt or Phoenicia at the pinnacle of
their civilizational strength. Science, constituted and guided by the ultimate science,
philosophy, is the source of real power in the world. Thus, according to Afghani,
"There was, is, and will be no ruler in the world but science."[27] Although rationalism
is currently associated with Western culture, Afghani insists that Islam has contributed substantially to the evolution of human rationality and that, in addition, the
very universality of rational methods and the truths they produce belies construc-
tions of Islam as inherently incompatible with rationalism.[28]

Thus Afghani contends that "real" Islam encourages the use of reason, even or
especially when interpreting scripture to guide human action. Doing so, moreover,
is the precondition to both truth and the strength of the Islamic community. But,
Afghani argues, Muslim scholars have insisted on dividing up the world into "Muslim
science" and "European science," not understanding that "science is that noble
thing that has no connection with any nation.... [E]verything that is known is
known by science, and every nation that becomes renowned becomes renowned
through science. Men must be related to science, not science to men."[29] For Afghani,
to bifurcate science in this way entails the claim that Islam is incompatible with self-
evident knowledge. Because this knowledge is both the precondition to and expression of any culture's wealth and power, such bifurcation not only positions Islam in
opposition to truth, but also condemns Islam to decay and weakness.

> [A] science is needed to be the comprehensive soul for all the sciences, so that
> it can preserve their existence, apply each of them in its proper place, and
> become the cause of the progress of each one of those sciences. The science
> that has the position of a comprehensive soul and the rank of a preserving force
> is the science of *falsafa* or philosophy, because its subject is universal. It is
> philosophy that shows man human prerequisites. It shows the sciences what is
> necessary. It employs each of the sciences in its proper place.... That commu-
> nity without the spirit of philosophy could not deduce conclusions from these
> sciences.[30]

For Afghani, scientific knowledge and the philosophy that governs its discovery
progress over time and flourish in different places and cultures at different moments
in history. In emphasizing an understanding of knowledge as dynamic and evolutionary, Afghani challenges the view that there is in the universe a fixed sum of

knowledge, a "solid and immobile" mass to be acquired "not by analysis, induction and experiment but by the simple amassing of what already existed or, at most, by deductive reasoning from accepted axioms."[31] This evolutionary view of knowledge underlies his contention in the "The Benefits of Philosophy" that the *umma* needs philosophy because it is the precondition not only to scientific knowledge but also to moral development. For in *The Refutation of the Materialists* Afghani argues that men (women are not mentioned) are by nature cruel, greedy, and ignorant, and that the closer they are to their true nature, the closer they are to animals.[32] Given human nature, then, morality reflects an arduous and ongoing battle against the pull of bestial nature, a battle in which habit and education are therefore crucial.[33] Insofar as philosophy facilitates the exercise of reason, it broadens the scope of human thought from mere instinct to reflection and insight, thereby making possible the emergence not only of virtue but of civilization itself. Philosophy is thus what distinguishes human beings from animals.

If philosophy is the crux of human development, moral and scientific, what, then, is the point of religion for Afghani? His arguments in this regard must be situated in the context of his political activities for, as Kedourie persuasively argues, Afghani's paramount concern with imperialism often relegated Islam to secondary significance, both in thought and practice, as the means to political, economic, and scientific mastery of the material world. Indeed, it is often noted that Afghani seemed willing to work anywhere, with anyone—sultan, despot, or colonialist—who would advance his anti-imperialist objectives. After Afghani was expelled from Istanbul for his lecture on philosophy, for example, he began an eight-year stay in Cairo, living on a government pension arranged by Riaz Pasha, whom Hourani dubs a "minister of liberal views."[34] During this time, Afghani became the center of a group of young Egyptian intellectuals, including Muhammad 'Abduh, drawn to Afghani's anti-imperialism and his use of Islamic philosophy to render Islam compatible with scientific, technological, and political progress. Initially on good terms with the heir to Egypt's monarchy, Afghani was deported to India in 1879, once Tawfiq wrested power from his profligate father with the help of British and French intervention.

After a time in India and Paris, Afghani visited London in 1885 at the invitation of Wilfrid Blunt, a highly placed Englishman sympathetic to Irish, Arab, and Indian nationalist aspirations. Through Blunt's auspices, Afghani negotiated with British statesmen in an unsuccessful attempt to encourage the British to leave Egypt. In an echo of the circumstances that marked many of Afghani's previous "departures," Blunt eventually asked him to leave his house when two of Afghani's friends argued somewhat violently there. Afghani then went to Iran, Russia, and then back again to Iran, where he served as adviser to Shah Nasir al-Din. But the shah eventually expelled Afghani for his involvement in the Tobacco Uprising of 1890–1891, a mass protest against the shah's concession of a monopoly over the Iranian tobacco industry to a British company.[35] Afghani then traveled to Istanbul at the request of the Ottoman Sultan Abdulhamid, but soon incurred the sultan's enmity and distrust by expressing support for an Arab caliphate, an implicit challenge to Ottoman authority. Moreover, one of Afghani's Iranian disciples had killed the Shah of Iran in 1896, arguably at Afghani's urging; not surprisingly, this contributed to Abdulhamid's growing sense that Afghani posed a danger to his authority. Anxious to retain a measure of control over Afghani's political activities, the sultan denied him permission to leave Istanbul several times. Afghani spent the final years of his life in Istanbul, a virtual prisoner at the sultan's court, until he died of cancer in 1897.

It was after his expulsion from Egypt that Afghani returned to India for two years and wrote one of the rare documents of his views on religion, *The Refutation of the*

Materialists. In this attack on a growing group of Westernizing modernists in India called the *neicheris*, or "followers of nature," Afghani emerges perhaps for the first time as a staunch defender not only of the integrity of the Muslim community but of Islam per se against the challenges of the unorthodox and Muslims overly imitative of the West. In the introduction, Afghani states that religion is a crucial link in the development of knowledge, in the advance of civilization, and in the very possibility of morality. Indeed, evoking the language of disease and cure that characterizes Qutb's assessment of modernity, Afghani has been quoted as saying that "every Muslim is sick, and his only remedy is in the Qur'an."[36] Although Afghani readily acknowledges the defects of Islam, he insists that such defects are not inherent, but rather are the products of current understanding and practice. For Afghani, an understanding of the true Islam means recognizing that the achievements of philosophy are not defined in opposition to the truths of religion. Religion in general, and Islam in particular, has facilitated the transformation of human beings from ignorance and savagery to knowledge and civilization, and it has done so by encouraging the free exercise of human reason. Proper reading reveals the extent to which rationalist methods and philosophical truths are not only encouraged by, but actually contained in, the Qur'an and the traditions. The Qur'an and the Prophet exhort Muslims by word and example to pursue "knowledge, wisdom, learning, reflection, thought, and insight" and include moral guidance entirely in keeping with the truths of philosophy. With the Qur'an, Allah "planted the roots of philosophical sciences into purified souls, and opened the road for man to become man.... [T]he Precious Book was the first teacher of philosophy to the Muslims."[37] Religion properly understood both enjoins and makes possible human perfectibility. This capacity is "the greatest deterrent to men rending each other to pieces like tearing lions, raging wolves, and biting dogs. It is the greatest obstacle keeping men from having the low and base qualities of animals. It is the best incentive for intellectual activity and the use of man's mental faculties. It is the most influential factor in purifying souls of impure vices.[38]

In tying religion not only to moral but also to scientific progress, Afghani makes religion essential to human survival and advancement, and hence to "modernity" itself. In this view, modernity and Islam properly understood are mutually constitutive. Indeed, Afghani affirms the superiority of Islam to all other religions because Islam rightly understood is absolutely unique in exhorting believers to exercise their reason and prohibiting them from "blind submission."[39] This suggests that Afghani's objection to Muslim scholars is not that they bow to divine authority but that they misinterpret such authority and its truths as antithetical to the philosophical reasoning and insight that are necessary to all progress, scientific, political, and moral. Moreover, in *Refutation of the Materialists*, Afghani asserts that the Enlightenment makes exactly the reverse mistake: the *philosophes* posited an opposition between reason and revelation only to resolve the contradiction in favor of reason. In this way reason became linked to the negation of divinity, religion, and custom. For Afghani, then, both traditional Muslim scholars and Enlightenment philosophers are misguided because they either accept or advance a false opposition between rationalism and religion. By contrast, Luther's reformism, which Afghani claims has simply drawn on Muslim examples, demarcates a "third way," or, more accurately for Afghani, the only way:

[T]he members of each community must found their beliefs, which are the first things written on the slates of their minds, on certain proofs and firm evidence. In their beliefs they must shun submission to conjectures and not be content with mere imitation (*taqlid*) of their ancestors. For if man believes in things without proof or reason, makes a practice of following unproven opinions, and is satisfied to imitate and follow his ancestors, his mind inevitably desists from intellectual movement, and little by little stupidity and imbecility overcome him—until his mind becomes completely idle and he becomes unable to perceive his own good and evil; and adversity and misfortune overtake him from all sides....[40]

'ABDUH AND THE THEOLOGY OF UNITY

"The light of this Glorious Book which used to be followed by science no matter where it went, East or West, must inevitably return to its full splendor and rend the veils of error. It will return to its original place in the hearts of Muslims, and will take shelter there. Science will follow it, for it is its only friend, its sole support."[41] Unlike Afghani's work, which is less theology or political theory than political and social criticism, Muhammad 'Abduh's work is theological and philosophical in nature. This distinction is perhaps the reason why Qutb singles out 'Abduh—and his student, Rashid Rida—in his most direct criticisms of Islamic modernism. Yet any analysis of 'Abduh's modernism must attend to Afghani's profound influence upon it. For like Afghani, 'Abduh aims at revitalizing Islam as a resource for moral and communal strength to meet the challenge of modern developments and European power. 'Abduh, like Afghani, seeks to delineate an understanding of Islam not as it is currently practiced, but as it is when rightly understood. And, like Afghani, 'Abduh criticizes believers who eschew reason and rationalists who repudiate Islam for failing to understand that the true Islam is the religion of reason. Thus for 'Abduh and for his sometime collaborator, Islam is the "first religion to address human reason, prompting it to examine the entire universe, and giving it free rein to delve into its innermost secrets as far as it is able. It did not impose any conditions upon reason other than that of maintaining the faith."[42]

Yet unlike Afghani's literal and figurative homelessness, 'Abduh's life and thought were defined by a commitment not only to Islam generally but also to the politics of his native Egypt. There is no mystery surrounding 'Abduh's origins or the substance of his education: he was born in 1849 in an Egyptian Delta village to a family of the peasant class.[43] Like Qutb, 'Abduh memorized the Qur'an at an early age, and when he was only thirteen years old he was sent to the Ahmadi mosque at Tanta to continue his religious training. Unhappy with what he saw as the impenetrable methods of instruction he encountered there, 'Abduh ran away on two separate occasions and hid for several months with various uncles. Ultimately, he fell under the influence of a paternal uncle, Shaykh Darwish Khadr, trained in Islamic Sufism. Through sheer persistence Khadr initiated him into the Sufi approach to Islamic instruction and practices. 'Abduh then voluntarily returned to Tanta deeply committed to and infused with Islamic mysticism.[44] Fired by love of religious instruction, 'Abduh continued his traditional religious education at al-Azhar from 1866 to 1877, graduating with the degree of *alim*.

It was during this time at al-Azhar, in 1869, that 'Abduh first met Afghani and became a fervent disciple. 'Abduh was in the midst of his studies in traditional Islam, yet he found in Afghani a fellow traveler, one who both led him to greater engagement with worldly affairs and exposed him to the works of the Islamic philosophers. 'Abduh's association with Afghani was to cause him great trouble over the course of his life. There was, for example, a tension between the traditionalism of his teachers at al-Azhar and the more heterodox influences encouraged by Afghani. Consequently al-Azhar authorities attempted to withhold 'Abduh's teaching license, although he was eventually granted the license through the intercession of the university rector. After obtaining his degree, 'Abduh began teaching at al-Azhar and in 1878 was appointed a teacher at Dar al-'Ulum, the newly founded "modern" teaching college that both Hasan al-Banna and Qutb would attend more than thirty years later. Yet when Afghani was expelled from Egypt in 1879 by the new Khedive, 'Abduh was fired from Dar al-'Ulum and ordered into retirement because he was a known associate of Afghani.

After his dismissal from Dar al-'Ulum, in the early 1880s, 'Abduh became an active critic of the growing European influence in Egyptian politics and of the corruption of a ruling elite that had increased Egypt's dependence upon foreign powers. A supporter of and key player in the nationalist opposition to the Egyptian monarchy, 'Abduh was imprisoned and then tried along with other nationalists by Khedive Tawfiq, who had been restored to power by the British. 'Abduh was sentenced by the court to three years of exile from Egypt, forbidden to return without the permission of the Khedive. In 1884 'Abduh went to Paris at Afghani's invitation. There he collaborated with his radical mentor in producing revolutionary articles against British imperialism and became embroiled in Afghani's anti-British intrigues.

It was during this exile from Egypt that 'Abduh gave a series of lectures in Beirut—updated and given again at al-Azhar—that were later revised and published by his student Rashid Rida as *Risalat al-Tawhid* [The Theology of Unity] in 1897. In this text, perhaps his most famous, 'Abduh argues that Islam, properly understood, starts from the premise that reason is a feature of human nature, and human nature is created by God. Consequently, reason is no less a gift from God than is revelation: "God has endowed us with senses and implanted in us faculties that we employ in all their dimensions entirely as a gift of God."[45] As both revelation and reason are divine creations, a contradiction between the laws of God expressed in the Qur'an and tradition and those of God embodied in the natural world is an impossibility.[46] Those who infer an essential enmity between Islam and the exercise of critical reason from the history of Islamic practice have mistaken a debased Islam for the true faith. The "real" Islam has never ceased to exhort Muslims to use their reason. Thus Islam cannot be antithetical to the fruits of human reason, the discoveries of modern science. Indeed, 'Abduh argues that the Qur'an and tradition encourage the pursuit of knowledge of the material world as the means necessary for survival and well-being, and actually anticipate sciences such as modern astronomy and studies of the Earth's resources. As 'Abduh notes, "God has sent down two books: one created, which is nature, and one revealed, which is the Qur'an. The latter leads us to investigate the former by means of the intelligence which was given to us. He who obeys, will become blessed; he who turns away, goes toward destruction."[47]

Like Qutb, 'Abduh argues that Islamic law is part of the divine universal law that is also embedded in physical and biological phenomena. But while Qutb emphasizes the dark mystery that constitutes the core of the divine will, 'Abduh argues that the inherent rationality of such laws makes reason not only an appropriate but a necessary means by which human beings may know (most of) them.[48] Indeed, reason is the human faculty that enables us to distinguish between true and false beliefs, and by which we may obtain awareness, if not full understanding, of the divine truths necessary for living and living well.

Religion is a general sense for investigating the means to happiness that are obscure to reason. Reason is the ultimate authority in the recognition of this sense and the uses for which it was given; it also [establishes the necessity of] obedience to the beliefs and rules of conduct that religion reveals. How can reason be denied its due in this matter, for it is reason that examines the evidence for this sense in order to arrive at its knowledge and that it is given by God?[49]

Moreover, the Islamic exhortation to exercise reason encourages a healthy skepticism toward, rather than an unquestioning obedience to, the authority of tradition. Adopting Afghani's evolutionary view of knowledge, 'Abduh avers that simple precedence in time is insufficient to establish precedence in knowledge or ability. Thus the exhortation to reason about the world precludes the uncritical acceptance of dogma (*taqlid*, or blind imitation) on the authority of tradition, or the submission to logical contradictions against the clear weight of sense-evidence.[50]

In arguments like these, 'Abduh most clearly defines reason in terms of what it is not: reason is posited as the opposite of imagination without evidence, tradition without proof, suspension of intellectual reflection, and adherence to unexamined dogma and credulous superstition.[51]

Islam reproaches leaders of religions for simply following in the footsteps of their forebears, and for their adherence to the plans of their ancestors....Thus it liberates the power of reason from its fetters, releasing it from enslavement to blind imitation of tradition. Islam has restored reason to its kingdom, a kingdom in which it reigns with judiciousness and wisdom, deferring to God alone and conforming to His sacred law. There are no limits to the possible pursuits within its domain, and no end to the extent of the explorations possible under its banner.[52]

Reason thus means the exercise of critical judgment on the basis of logical and empirical proof. Importantly, though his understanding of reason is clearly indebted to Afghani, and by extension to the Islamic philosophers and their Greek masters, it is also more than slightly reminiscent of the ways in which reason came to be defined in modern European thought in opposition to the authority of the clergy, the pull of habit and tradition, and the suspension of critical judgment they were thought to presuppose. In this connection, it is instructive to note that European political, social, historical, and educational thought would increasingly influence his thinking in later life; he would come to display a particular affinity for, among others, his friend Herbert Spencer, whom he cites when arguing that spiritual and material progress are dialectically intertwined, and that such interaction is the motor for civilizational advancement.[53] As Hourani argues:

His intellectual problems were those of Islamic thought but they were also those of nineteenth century Europe, in particular the great debates about science and religion....Islam seemed to him to be a middle path between the two extremes: a religion fully consistent with the claims of the human intellect and the discoveries of modern science, but safeguarding the divine transcendence....Islam indeed was the religion of human nature, the answer to the problems of the modern world.[54]

In 'Abduh's understanding of reason, we thus see a complex amalgamation of influences usually understood as Western and Islamic. Like the *philosophes*, 'Abduh defines reason in opposition to blind authority and to all inherited truths; yet unlike the *philosophes* and like Afghani, he does not oppose reason to faith in divine truths.

While Afghani's commitment to Islam as a source of political solidarity at times superseded all other considerations, 'Abduh was consistently and particularly attentive to the costs and dangers that unchecked reason posed for those religious truths that are beyond human comprehension. His anxieties in this regard place him closer to Qutb than to Afghani. As a result, 'Abduh insists upon the relevance and role of reason in the "true Islam" but also carefully delineates its limits. In every passage where 'Abduh celebrates the rationalism of Islam, he concludes with a crucial, if vague, qualification: the imperatives of reason must be in conformity with Islamic law, its exercise guided by the aim of maintaining rather than undermining faith. This repeated qualification implicitly suggests, first, that 'Abduh is intent on granting to religion the ultimate power to determine truth, and, second, that there is a constant danger that reason will overreach itself, and in so doing transgress the principles of faith and destroy the purchase of Islamic truth. 'Abduh thus exhorts believers to exercise their critical faculties in accordance with the injunctions of the Qur'an and tradition, but also admonishes rationalists to attend to the limits of rational inquiry. Toward the latter end, 'Abduh establishes levels of knowing, or kinds of truths: those that are accessible to human understanding, those that are entirely inaccessible, and those that require confirmation by an authority other than reason. For example, reason can lead to belief in the existence of God, an understanding of some of his attributes, awareness of the afterlife, distinctions between good and evil, and the authority of prophecy. Reason can thus lead human beings to accept the authority of revelation whose truths are therefore consistent with the products of rational inquiry. Such revelation—disclosed by the Prophet whose authority has been established by reason—provides the means to accept truths that reason cannot reach. But, 'Abduh cautions repeatedly that reason cannot penetrate such unknowable concepts as God's essence and the essences of nature and human nature, which are, by definition, beyond human comprehension. In language reminiscent of Qutb, 'Abduh argues that pursuit of the unknowable is not only fruitless but transgressive of the precepts of faith:

> As for speculation about the essence of the Creator, on the one hand, it is an attempt to probe that which is forbidden to human reason; on the other hand, the pursuit of His essence is beyond the grasp of human faculties. These pursuits are foolish and dangerous, foolish because they are a search for that which is unattainable, dangerous because it amounts to a strike against faith in that it is an attempt to define that which cannot be defined, and an attempt to limit that which has no limits....[55]

Despite the political activism that marked the earlier stage of his life, 'Abduh's later work tends to resign such explicitly political matters to God's will, instead taking up the prior task of developing the methods by which such arguments can be made.[56] This reticence may be informed by his journey from radical-in-exile to appointment later in life as Grand Mufti of Egypt. For after six years of exile, 'Abduh was pardoned by the Khedive and returned to Egypt in 1888 with the help of influential British supporters. Upon his return, he was appointed to the bench of one of the "Native Tribunals," a court that administered a jurisprudence based on the French code.[57] Again with the help of British influence, in 1889 he was appointed Grand Mufti of Egypt—the highest institutional religious authority in Egypt—an office he would hold until his death in 1905. In assuming this position, 'Abduh became the most influential authority in Egypt on matters of religious law, his *fat-was* (legal opinions) "authoritative and final."[58] It may be, as Kedourie argues, that 'Abduh's tenure as Grand Mufti was devoid of innovation and marked by a traditionalism peculiar given the heterodoxy of his early religious beliefs and the radicalism of his political commitments, both of which he had at one time shared with Afghani:

> The rebel of the eighteen-seventies, the subversive journalist of the eighteen-eighties, was thus indebted for his exalted position to the despotism of the Khedivial Government which the British occupant was endeavouring to tincture with some benevolence. It remains to add that successive annual reports…record with unfailing regularity the absolute failure to effect any substantial reform in the religious courts. Abduh's appointment thus added one more link to the long chain by which the Muslim Institution was shackled into utter subservience to the Ruling Institution.[59]

NOTES

* This is a chapter, excerpted from Roxanne L. Euben, *Enemy in the Mirror: Islamic Fundamentalism and the Limits of Modern Rationalism* (Princeton, NJ: Princeton University Press, 1999).

1. Clifford Geertz, "Thick Description: Toward an Interpretive Theory of Culture," in *The Interpretation of Cultures* (New York: Basic Books, 1973), p. 14.

2. I place "modernism" within quotation marks here to signal the ways in which what is called Islamic "modernism" is not an uncomplicated embrace of the ideas and processes constitutive of what we in the West identify as modernity, but rather reflects a complex and eclectic amalgamation of Western ideas and reinterpreted Islamic traditions. For all future references, then, modernism is meant to signal this syncretism.

3. Sayyid Qutb, *The Islamic Conception and Its Characteristics* (Cairo: Dar al-ʿArabiyya, 1962), pp. 17–24.

4. Qutb, *Signposts along the Road* (Beirut: Dar al Shuruq, 1991), pp. 159–160.

5. Qutb, *The Islamic Conception and Its Characteristics*, p. 20.

6. There is some terminological confusion, however. For example, Muhammad 'Abduh's student, Muhammad Rashid Rida (1865–1935) is more often referred to as the leader of the *salafiyya* movement in contradistinction to the modernist school. By contrast, Sylvia Haim argues that Afghani and 'Abduh "inaugurated" the *salafiyya* movement, but that Rashid Rida was its "undoubted intellectual leader" (*Arab Nationalism: An Anthology*, [Berkeley: University of California Press, 1962], p. 20). Other scholars have described Afghani or 'Abduh as the "founders" or the center of Islamic modernism or revival; still others have argued that the *salafiyya* project unites the work of 'Abduh and Rida. Moreover, Lapidus persuasively argues that there is a difference between Islamic modernism and Islamic reformism: Islamic reformism should be identified with the 'ulama', Islamic modernism should be associated with Muslim elites and intellgentsias (*A History of Islamic Societies*, [Cambridge: Cambridge University Press, 1988], pp. 560–570). What is clear is that Afghani, 'Abduh, and Rida are all central to nineteenth-century Islamic revival, a conclusion echoed by M. A. Said Badawi's *The Reformers of Egypt* (London: Croom Helm, 1978), and in keeping with al-Azmeh's suggestion that *salafiyya* can be regarded as a generic term that captures

the call to "return to the Koran and the salutary example of pious epigones (the *salaf*)" (*Islams and Modernities*, [London: Verso, 1993] p. 87, n. 1). Yet adding to the confusion are the ways in which Afghani's and 'Abduh's ideas subsequently influenced a diverse array of movements and people: as Anouar Abdel Malek argues, 'Abduh's ideas, for example, simultaneously influenced Mustafa Kemal's (Atatürk) National Party, the renovation of al-Azhar, and Rashid Rida's "fundamentalism" (Abdel Malek, *Egypt: Military Society* [New York: Random House, 1960], p. 202).

7. Such a Golden Age of Islam is generally identified as the time from the Prophet Muhammad through the period of the "Rightly Guided Caliphs" (621–661).

8. Hisham Sharabi, *Arab Intellectuals and the West: The Formative Years* (Baltimore: Johns Hopkins University Press, 1970), p. 27.

9. Albert Hourani, *Arabic Thought in the Liberal Age: 1798–1939* (Cambridge: Cambridge University Press, 1983), p. 103.

10. Ibid., 104.

11. Sharabi, *Arab Intellectuals and the West*, 31.

12. The modernist school has also encompassed, among others, the more conservative political thought of Muhammad Rashid Rida. Yet while Afghani, 'Abduh and Rida all strove for a revitalization of Islam, only Rida interpreted such revival as, in Haim's words, a "puritanical revival of strict Islamic practices and religious fervor; it was for this reason that [like Qutb] he was a Hanbalite, following the strictest of the four schools of Islamic law, and that he later cast his lot with the Saudi and the Wahhabi revival" (Haim, *Arab Nationalism*, p. 21). Thus I focus on Afghani and 'Abduh in the interests of exploring the diversity of views grouped under the umbrella of "Islamic revival."

13. Hourani, *Arabic Thought in the Liberal Age*, p. 130; B. Michel et le Cheikh Moutstapha 'Abdel Razik, *Cheikh Mohammed 'Abdou: Rissalat al-Tawhid* (Paris, 1925), p. xlii, cited by C. C. Adams, *Islam and Modernism in Egypt* (New York: Russell & Russell, 1933), p. 2.

14. W. C. Smith, *Islam in Modern History* (Princeton, NJ: Princeton University Press, 1957), pp. 47–51.

15. Sharabi, in his *Arab Intellectuals and the West*, and Hasan Rida exemplify the literature extremely skeptical both of the intellectual powers of Afghani and 'Abduh, and of the substantive merit of their work (Rida, "Les discussions sur le système social prennent l'aspect de controverses grammaticales," *L'Égypte nassèrienne* [Paris, 1964], cited by Sharabi, p. 35). Among the texts that challenge their sincerity are Elie Kedourie, *Afghani and 'Abduh* (London: Frank Cass, 1966), and Nikkie Keddie, *An Islamic Response to Imperialism* (Berkeley: University of California Press, 1968) and *The Root of Revolution* (New Haven, CT: Yale University Press, 1981).

16. Keddie, *An Islamic Response to Imperialism*, p. 96, 3.

17. Haim, *Arab Nationalism*, pp. 6, 10, 15.

18. Abdallahh Laroui outlines the Enlightenment spirit of Afghani's reformism in *Islam et modernité*. al-Azmeh notes the irony in the ways contemporary Islamic fundamentalism has "resurrected the Romanticism of Afghani and re-established him as the fount of authenticity and its main proponent and, indeed, its idol" (*Islams and Modernities*, p. 54).

19. Afghani, "Lecture on Teaching and Learning," in *An Islamic Response to Imperialism*, p. 107. I have relied on Keddie's excellent translation of this and Afghani's other works from the original Persian.

20. Most of these biological details are drawn from Hourani's *Arabic Thought in the Liberal Age* and Keddie's two seminal works on Afghani: *An Islamic Response to Imperialism*, and *Sayyid Jamal al-Din "al-Afghani": A Political Biography* (Berkeley, CA: University of California Press, 1972).

21. Badawi, *The Reformers of Egypt*, p. 7.

22. Keddie, *Sayyid Jamal al-Din "al-Afghani,"* and *An Islamic Response to Imperialism*. A similar argument is also made by Haim in *Arab Nationalism*.

23. Kedourie, *Afghani and 'Abduh*. By contrast, Keddie avoids the charge of "unbelief," preferring to refer to Afghani, for example, as an "Islamic deist."

24. Although the term "pan-Islamism" was originally coined by Turkish Young Ottomans, Afghani is credited with spreading its call for superseding sectarian, class, and territorial divisions to unify all Muslims in a single community capable of recapturing the greatness and strength of Islamic civilization in its heyday.

25. Although there is no surviving text of the talk, Keddie infers its content from various responses and commentaries (*An Islamic Response to Imperialism*, p. 17).

26. "Lecture on Teaching and Learning," pp. 104–105.

27. Ibid., p. 102.

28. The argument that Islam had contributed substantially to what is now European knowledge was made by earlier writers such as Tahtawi and Khayr al-Din, who argued that the adoption of "Western knowledge" constituted not imitation but reclamation.

29. Ibid., p. 107.

30. Ibid., p. 104.

31. H.A.R. Gibb, *Modern Tends in Islam* (Chicago: University of Chicago Press, 1947), p. 65.

32. Afghani, "Refutation," *An Islamic Response to Imperialism*, p. 140.

33. Afghani, "Commentary on the Commentator," *An Islamic Response to Imperialism*, pp. 126–127.

34. Hourani, *Arabic Thought in the Liberal Age*, p. 109.

35. Keddie, *Roots of Revolution*, p. 66.

36. Muhammad al-Makhzumi, *Khatirat Jamal al-Din al-Afghani al-Husayni* [Thoughts of Jamal al-Din al-Afghani al-Husayni] (Beirut, 1931), 88, cited by Sharabi, *Arab Intellectuals and the West*, p. 26.

37. Afghani, "The Benefits of Philosophy," *An Islamic Response to Imperialism*, pp. 110, 113–114.

38. Afghani, "Refutation," *An Islamic Response to Imperialism*, p. 142.

39. Here Afghani posits a dubious contrast between the inherent rationality of Islam and the irrationality of Christianity, which has at its core the worship of the Trinity.

40. Ibid., p. 171.

41. 'Abduh, *al-Islam wa al-Nasraniyya* [Islam and Christianity], (Cairo: Al-Manar, 1905), p. 149.

42. 'Abduh, *Risalat al-Tawhid* (hereafter referred to a *The Theology of Unity*), (Cairo: Dar al-Ma'arif, 1966), p. 176. All translations from this work are my own, from the original Arabic.

43. These biographical details are drawn from C. C. Adams's *Islam and Modernism in Egypt*; Hourani's *Arabic Thought in the Liberal Age*; Kedourie's *Afghani and 'Abduh*; and Badawi's *The Reformers of Egypt*.

44. 'Abduh's first book, in 1874, was a reflection on mysticism entitled *Risalat al-Waridat* (Mystic Inspirations).

45. 'Abduh, *Theology of Unity*, p. 143.
46. Ibid., pp. 83–84.
47. Muhammad 'Abduh, *Al-Manar*, pp. vii, 292, cited in C. C. Adams, *Islam and Modernism in Egypt*, p. 136.
48. 'Abduh, *Theology of Unity*, pp. 18–32.
49. Ibid., p. 122.
50. Ibid., pp. 143–152.
51. Ibid., pp. 26–32.
52. Ibid., p. 147.
53. Adams, *Islam and Modernism in Egypt*, pp. 95, 197.
54. Hourani, *Arabic Thought in the Liberal Age*, pp. 143–144.
55. 'Abduh, *Theology of Unity*, p. 55.
56. Rida, *Tarikh al-Ustadh al-Imam al-Shaikh Muhammad 'Abduh*, 1:11–12, cited in Malcolm H. Kerr, *Islamic Reform* (Berkeley: University of California Press, 1966), p. 109.
57. Adams, *Islam and Modernism in Egypt*, p. 69, n. 4.
58. Ibid., p. 79.
59. Kedourie, *Afghani and 'Abduh*, pp. 38–39.

CONTEMPORARY ISLAM:
REFORMATION OR REVOLUTION?[1]

John L. Esposito

Much of the reassertion of religion in politics and society has been subsumed under the term *Islamic fundamentalism*. Although *"fundamentalism"* is a common designation, in the press and increasingly among academics, it is used in a variety of ways. For a number of reasons it tells us everything and yet, at the same time, nothing. First, all those who call for a return to foundational beliefs or the fundamentals of a religion may be called fundamentalist. In a strict sense this could include all practicing Muslims, who accept the Quran as the literal word of God and the Sunnah (example) of the Prophet Muhammad as a normative model for living.

Second, our understanding and perceptions of fundamentalism are heavily influenced by American Protestantism. *Webster's Ninth New Collegiate Dictionary* defines the term *fundamentalism* as "a movement in 20th century Protestantism emphasizing the literally interpreted Bible as fundamental to Christian life and teaching." For many liberal or mainline Christians, the term "fundamentalist" is pejorative or derogatory, being applied rather indiscriminately to all those who advocate a literalist biblical position and thus are regarded as static, retrogressive, and extremist. As a result, fundamentalism often has been regarded popularly as referring to those who are literalists and wish to return to and replicate the past. In fact, few individuals or organizations in the Middle East fit such a stereotype. Indeed, many fundamentalist leaders have had the best education, enjoy responsible positions in society, and are adept at harnessing the latest technology to propagate their views and create viable modern institutions such as schools, hospitals, and social service agencies.

Third, "fundamentalism" is often equated with political activism, extremism, fanaticism, and anti-Americanism. Yet while some engage in radical religiopolitics, most, as we shall see, work within the established order.

Perhaps the best way to appreciate the facile use of "fundamentalism" and its inadequacy (the many faces and postures of fundamentalism) is to consider the following. This term has been applied to the governments of Libya, Saudi Arabia, Pakistan, and Iran. Yet what does that really tell us about these states other than the fact that their rulers have appealed to Islam to legitimate their rule or policies? Muammar Qaddafi has claimed the right to interpret Islam, questioned the authenticity of the traditions of the Prophet Muhammad, silenced the religious establishment as well as the Muslim Brotherhood, and advocated a populist state of the masses. The rulers of Saudi Arabia, by contrast, have aligned themselves with the *ulama* (clergy), preached a more literalist and rigorous brand of Islam, and used religion to legitimate a conservative monarchy. Qaddafi's image as an unpredictable, independent supporter of worldwide terrorism stands in sharp relief beside the low-key, conservative, pro-American King Fahd. Similarly, contrast the foreign policy of the clerically run Shii state of Iran with the military, lay regime (1977–1988) which implemented Pakistan's Islamic system (*nizam-i-Islam*) under Gen. Zia ul-Haq. Iran under the Ayatollah Khomeini was highly critical—even condemnatory—of the West, often at odds with the international community, and regarded as a radical terrorist state, while Pakistan under the Islamically oriented Zia ul-Haq was a close ally of the United States who enjoyed warm relations with the West and the international community and was generally regarded as moderate.

I regard "fundamentalism" as too laden with Christian presuppositions and Western stereotypes, as well as implying a monolithic threat that does not exist; more fitting general terms are "Islamic revivalism" or "Islamic activism," which are less value-laden and have roots within the Islamic tradition. Islam possesses a long tradition of revival (*tajdid*) and reform (*islah*), which includes notions of political and social activism dating from the early Islamic centuries to the present day.[2] Thus I prefer to speak of Islamic revivalism and Islamic activism rather than of Islamic fundamentalism.

THE RESURRECTION OF RELIGION: MODERNIZATION AND DEVELOPMENT THEORY CONFOUNDED

Just as European imperialism and colonialism has been based upon and legitimated by a modernity that was Western in its origins and forms, so too the development of non-Western regions including the Muslim world was based upon a theory of modernization that equated development with the progressive Westernization and secularization of society. In particular, secularization was regarded as a sine qua non for modernization: "Political development includes, as one of its basic processes, the secularization of polities, the progressive exclusion of religion from the political system."[3] Both the indigenous elites, who guided government development programs in newly emerging Muslim states, and their foreign patrons and advisers were Western-oriented and Western-educated. All proceeded from a premise that equated modernization with Westernization. The clear goal and presupposition of development was that every day and in every way things should become more modern (i.e., Western and secular), from cities, buildings, bureaucracies, companies, and schools to politics and culture. While some warned of the need to be selective, the desired direction and pace of change were unmistakable. Even those Muslims who spoke of selective change did so within a context that called for the separation of religion from public life. Western analysts and Muslim experts alike tended to regard a Western-based process of modernization as necessary and inevitable and believed equally that religion was a major hindrance to political and social change in the Muslim world.

The conceptual world that resulted was one of clear dichotomies: tradition versus change, fundamentalism versus modernism, stagnation versus progress and development. Science and technology were seen as powerful aids in this process of secular development. However, the reality proved to be far different from the ideal. Modernization as Westernization and secularization remained primarily the preserve of a small minority elite of society. Most important, the secularization of processes and institutions did not easily translate into secularization of minds and culture. While a minority accepted and implemented a Western secular worldview, the majority of most Muslim populations did not internalize a secular outlook and values.

Daniel Crecelius's perceptive observation regarding Egypt, long regarded as among the more modern Muslim societies, ran counter to the prevailing wisdom but proved true for most Muslim countries:

> Most studies on the process of modernization or secularism recognize the necessity for all systems by which man lives, the psychological and intellectual, no less than the political and economic, to undergo transformation.. We do not find this change in Egypt, whether at the level of the state or society, except among a small minority of Westernized individuals. Traditional beliefs, practices, and values reign supreme among Egypt's teeming village population and among the majority of its urban masses. It should be emphasized that adherence to tradition is not confined to any single class or group of occupations, but is characteristic of a broad spectrum of all Egyptian social classes.[4]

For many, the contemporary revival of Islam challenged the received wisdom and seemed to deal a death blow to reason and common sense. The most forceful manifestations of the Islamic resurgence have occurred in the more advanced and "modernized" (seemingly secular) countries of the Muslim world such as Egypt, Iran, Lebanon, and Tunisia. In a very real sense, Islamic revivalism has often been seen and experienced as a direct threat to the ideas, beliefs, practices, and interests of Muslim secular elites as well as Western governments and multinational corporations. The clash of worldviews has reinforced the Western tendency to see Islamic activism as extremism and fanaticism, as an antimodern return to the past rather than the projection of an alternative vision for society. Because it does not conform to modern secular presuppositions, to the West's most cherished beliefs and values, Islamic activism is regarded as a dangerous, irrational, and counter-cultural movement.

Yet Islamic organizations have attracted the educated and professional (teachers, engineers, lawyers, scientists, bureaucrats, the military). Many of the leaders of Islamic organizations are graduates of major universities from faculties of medicine, science, and engineering. Modern technology has been harnessed by conservative clergy and political activists alike to organize and mobilize mass support as well as disseminate their message of religion and sociopolitical activism. The widespread use of radio, television, audio and videocassettes, computers, and fax machines has made for a more effective communication of Islam nationally and transnationally. Thus technology and communications have purveyed not simply a modern secular culture but also a revitalized and, at times, transnational Islam. Religious leaders, who were initially resistant, have come to depend upon modern technology. Village Muslims no longer live in relatively isolated worlds solely dependent upon their local religious leaders for knowledge of Islam. Television, radio, and audiocassettes now expose them to a diversity of voices (preachers) and messages or interpretations of Islam. Just as Christian televangelists can now preach their messages not just to those in their parishes but to audiences from rural Oregon to New York City and to peoples throughout the world, so too modern science and technology have been harnessed to preach the message of Islam. Whereas in the past people were limited by the realities of time and space and of language and government censorship, today Muslims throughout the world have available to them inexpensive translations and recordings of Islamic materials. They can be broadcast legally or easily shipped across borders, as witnessed by the spread of the writings and sermons of Khomeini throughout Iran during the Shah's rule, or the availability of the writings and

cassettes of popular preachers and activists throughout the world. Thus modernization has not simply led to progressive secularization but instead has been a major
factor in the resurgence of Islam in Muslim societies.

THE ISLAMIC RESURGENCE

Islam reemerged as a potent global force in Muslim politics during the 1970s and
1980s.[5] The scope of the Islamic resurgence has been worldwide, embracing much
of the Muslim world from the Sudan to Indonesia. Heads of Muslim governments as
well as opposition groups increasingly appealed to religion for legitimacy and to
mobilize popular support. Islamic activists have held cabinet-level positions in
Jordan, the Sudan, Iran, Malaysia, and Pakistan. Islamic organizations constitute
the leading opposition parties and organizations in Egypt, Tunisia, Algeria, Morocco,
the West Bank and Gaza, and Indonesia. Where permitted, they have participated in
elections and served in parliament and in city government. Islam has been a significant ingredient in nationalist struggles and resistance movements in Afghanistan,
the Muslim republics of the former Soviet Central Asia, and Kashmir, and in the
communal politics of Lebanon, India, Thailand, China, and the Philippines.

Islamically oriented governments have been counted among America's staunchest
allies (Saudi Arabia and Pakistan) and most vitriolic enemies (Libya and Iran). Islamic
activist organizations have run the spectrum from those who work within the system—
such as the Muslim Brotherhoods in Egypt, Jordan, and the Sudan—to radical revolutionaries like Egypt's Society of Muslims (known more popularly as Takfir wal-Hijra,
Excommunication and Flight) and al-Jihad (Holy War), or Lebanon's Hizbullah (Party
of God) and Islamic Jihad, which have resorted to violence in their attempts to overthrow prevailing political systems.

Yet to speak of a contemporary Islamic revival can be deceptive, if this implies that
Islam had somehow disappeared or been absent from the Muslim world. It is more
correct to view Islamic revivalism as having led to a higher profile of Islam in Muslim
politics and society. Thus what had previously seemed to be an increasingly marginalized force in Muslim public life reemerged in the seventies—often dramatically—as
a vibrant sociopolitical reality. Islam's resurgence in Muslim politics reflected a
growing religious revivalism in both personal and public life that would sweep across
much of the Muslim world and have a substantial impact on the West in world
politics.

The indices of an Islamic reawakening in personal life are many: increased attention to religious observances (mosque attendance, prayer, fasting), proliferation of
religious programming and publications, more emphasis upon Islamic dress and values, the revitalization of Sufism (mysticism). This broader-based renewal has also
been accompanied by Islam's reassertion in public life: an increase in Islamically
oriented governments, organizations, laws, banks, social welfare services, and educational institutions. Both governments and opposition movements have turned to
Islam to enhance their authority and muster popular support. Governmental use of
Islam has been illustrated by a great spectrum of leaders in the Middle East and Asia:
Libya's Muammar Qaddafi, Sudan's Gaafar Muhammad Nimeiri, Egypt's Anwar
Sadat, Iran's Ayatollah Khomeini, Pakistan's Zia ul-Haq, Bangladesh's Muhammad
Ershad, Malaysia's Muhammad Mahathir. Most rulers and governments, including
more secular states such as Turkey and Tunisia, becoming aware of the potential
strength of Islam, have shown increased sensitivity to and anxiety about Islamic
issues. The Iranian Revolution of 1978–79 focused attention on "Islamic

fundamentalism" and with it the spread and vitality of political Islam in other parts of the Muslim world. However, the contemporary revival has its origins and roots in the late 1960s and early 1970s, when events in such disparate areas as Egypt and Libya as well as Pakistan and Malaysia contributed to experiences of crisis and failure, as well as power and success, which served as catalysts for a more visible reassertion of Islam in both public and private life.

THE EXPERIENCE OF FAILURE AND THE QUEST FOR IDENTITY

Several conflicts (e.g., the 1967 Arab-Israeli war, Chinese-Malay riots in Malaysia in 1969, the Pakistan-Bangladesh civil war of 1971, and the Lebanese civil war of the mid-1970s) illustrate the breadth and diversity of these turning points or catalysts for change. For many in the Arab and broader Muslim world, 1967 proved to be a year of catastrophe as well as a historic turning point. Israel's quick and decisive defeat of Arab forces in what was remembered as the Six-Day War, the Israeli capture and occupation of the Golan Heights, Sinai, Gaza, the West Bank, and East Jerusalem, constituted a devastating blow to Arab/Muslim pride, identity, and self-esteem. Most important, the loss of Jerusalem, the third holiest city of Islam, assured that Palestine and the liberation of Jerusalem would not be regarded as a regional (Arab) issue but rather as an Islamic cause throughout the Muslim world. The defense of Israel is dear to many Jews throughout the world. Likewise, for Muslims who retain a sense of membership in the transnational community of believers (the *ummah*), Palestine and the liberation of Jerusalem are strongly seen as issues of Islamic solidarity. As anyone who works in the Muslim world can attest, Israeli control of the West Bank, Gaza, and Jerusalem as well as U.S.-Israeli relations are topics of concern and bitter debate among Muslims from Nigeria and the Sudan to Pakistan and Malaysia, as well as among the Muslims of Europe and the United States.

The aftermath of the 1967 war, remembered in Arab literature as the "disaster," witnessed a sense of disillusionment and soul-searching that gripped both Western-oriented secular elites as well as the more Islamically committed, striking at their sense of pride, identity, and history.[6] Where had they gone wrong? Both the secular and the Islamically oriented sectors of society now questioned the effectiveness of nationalist ideologies, Western models of development, and Western allies who had persisted in supporting Israel. Despite several decades of independence and modernization, Arab forces (consisting of the combined military might of Egypt, Jordan, and Syria) had proved impotent. A common critique of the military, political, and sociocultural failures of Western oriented development and a quest for a more authentic society and culture emerged—an Arab identity less dependent upon the West and rooted more indigenously in an Arab/Islamic heritage and values. Examples from Malaysia, Pakistan, and Lebanon reflect the turmoil and soul-searching that occurred in many parts of the Muslim world.

Because Islam is often equated with the Middle East, we tend to forget that the largest Muslim populations are to be found in Asia (Indonesia, Pakistan, Bangladesh, and India). Asia too proved to be a major theatre for the growth of Islamic revivalism. In Southeast Asia, Chinese-Malay communal riots in Kuala Lumpur in 1969 signaled that growing Malay Muslims lagged behind the more prosperous urban-based Chinese (non-Muslim) minority. In response to charges that the Chinese enjoyed disproportionate economic and educational advantages, a perceived threat to Malay status and identity, the Malaysian government responded by implementing an affirmative action-like plan (*bhumiputra*, sons of the soil) of incentives and quotas to strengthen Malay Muslim life. Greater emphasis on Malay identity, language, values, and community contributed to the attraction and growth of Islamic revivalism in a culture where many regard it as axiomatic that to be Malay is to be Muslim.

The Pakistan-Bangladesh civil war in 1971 changed the map of South Asia when the Islamic Republic of Pakistan, established in 1947 as a Muslim homeland, lost its eastern section. The loss of East Pakistan and its recreation as Bangladesh raised serious questions about the nature (or perhaps better, the failure) of Pakistan's Islamic identity and ideology. At the same President Zulfikar Ali Bhutto, a secular socialist, for economic and strategic reasons increasingly appealed to Islam in the 1970s to establish Pakistan's ties with its oil-rich Arab/Muslim brothers in the Gulf states, who offered economic aid, and revenue in the form of wages of Pakistani military and laborers hired to work in the Gulf. This tilt toward the Gulf unleashed a process in which Islam moved from the periphery to center stage as both the government and the opposition used it to legitimate their competing claims and to gain popular support.

In Lebanon the Shii Muslims, long a minority in a Christian-dominated system, increasingly called for greater political representation and socioeconomic reforms to better reflect demographic changes which had resulted in a Muslim majority. A charismatic religious leader, Imam Musa Sadr, appealed to Shii identity, history, and symbols to organize and mobilize members of the Shii community into what in the mid-seventies would become the Movement for the Dispossessed, more commonly known today as AMAL. In the aftermath of the Iranian revolution, Lebanon would see the rise of more radical Islamic groups such as Hizbullah (Party of God), equally concerned with issues of identity and power.

The forms that the Islamic revival has taken have varied almost infinitely from one country to another. However, there are recurrent themes: a sense that existing political, economic, and social systems had failed; a disenchantment with, and at times a rejection of, the West; a quest for identity and greater authenticity; and the conviction that Islam provides a self-sufficient ideology for state and society, a valid alternative to secular nationalism, socialism, and capitalism.

The experience of failure triggered an identity crisis which led many to question the direction of political and social development and to turn inward for strength and guidance. The Western-oriented policies of governments and elites appeared to have failed. The soul-searching and critique of the sociopolitical realities of the Arab and Muslim world, which followed the 1967 war and the crises in Pakistan, Malaysia, and Lebanon, extended to other Muslim areas, embraced a broad spectrum of society, and raised many questions about the direction and accomplishments of development. More often than not, despite the hopes aroused by independence, the mixed record of several decades of existence was a challenge to the legitimacy and effectiveness of modern Muslim states. A crisis mentality fostered by specific events and the general impact and disruption of modernity spawned a growing disillusionment, a sense of failure.

Politically, modem secular nationalism was found wanting. Neither liberal nationalism nor Arab nationalism/socialism had fulfilled its promises. Muslim governments seemed less interested and successful in establishing their political legitimacy and creating an ideology for national unity than in perpetuating autocratic rule. The Muslim world was still dominated by monarchs and military or ex-military rulers, political parties were banned or restricted, and elections were often rigged. Parliamentary systems of government and political parties existed at the sufferance of rulers whose legitimacy, like their security, depended on a loyal military and secret police. Many were propped up by and dependent upon foreign governments and multinational corporations as well.

Charges of corruption and of concentration and mal-distribution of wealth found a ready reception as one looked at individual countries and the region. The disparity between rich and poor was striking in urban areas, where the neighborhoods and new suburbs of the wealthy few stood in stark contrast to the deteriorating dwellings and sprawling shantytowns of the many. The vast chasm between rich and poor was even more pronounced between Arab oil states, which ironically tended to be among the least populated countries (Kuwait, Saudi Arabia, the Emirates) and the greater number of poor, densely populated countries (Egypt, Syria, Pakistan, Bangladesh). Both Western capitalism and Marxist socialism were rejected as being part of the problem rather than the solution, as having failed to redress widespread poverty and mal-distribution of wealth. Capitalism was regarded as the system of special interests and new elites that produced a society more driven by materialism and conspicuous consumption than concern for equity and social justice. Marxism was dismissed as a godless alternative which struck at the heart of religion, substituting the material for the spiritual. Young people in particular found themselves in a world of shattered dreams that offered a dim future. In many countries idealism, study, and hard work were rewarded by unemployment or underemployment, housing shortages, and a lack of political participation that increased the sense of frustration and hopelessness.[7]

Socioculturally and psychologically, modernization was seen as a legacy of European colonialism perpetuated by Western-oriented elites who imposed and fostered the twin processes of Westernization and secularization. Just as dependence on Western models of development was seen as the cause of political and military failures, so, too, some Muslims charged, blind imitation of the West and an uncritical Westernization of Muslim societies which some called the disease of "Westoxification" led to a cultural dependence which threatened the loss of Muslim identity. The resultant process of secular, "valueless" social change was identified as the cause of sociomoral decline, a major contributor to the breakdown of the Muslim family, more permissive and promiscuous societies, and spiritual malaise.

The psychological impact of modernity, and with it rapid sociocultural change, cannot be forgotten. Urban areas had undergone physical and institutional changes, so that both the skylines and the infrastructure of cities were judged to be modern by virtue of their Western profile and facade. To be modern was to be Western in dress, language, ideas, education, behavior (from table manners to greetings), architecture, and furnishings. Urban areas became the primary locations and showplaces for work and living. Modern governments and companies as well as foreign advisers and investors focused on urban areas, so that the results of modernization only trickled down to rural areas. Rapid urbanization therefore meant the migration of many from outlying villages and towns. The hopes of the poor for a better life were often undermined by the realities of poverty in urban slums and shantytowns. Psychological as well as physical displacement occurred. Loss of village, town, and extended family ties and traditional values were accompanied by the shock of modern urban life and its Westernized culture and mores. Many, swept along in a sea of alienation and marginalization, found an anchor in religion. Islam offered a sense of identity, fraternity, and cultural values that offset the psychological dislocation and cultural threat of their new environment. Both the poor in their urban neighborhoods, which approximated traditional ghettos in the midst of modern cities, and those in the lower middle class who took advantage of the new educational and job opportunities of the city and thus experienced culture shock more profoundly and regularly, found a welcome sense of meaning and security in a religious revivalism. Islamic organizations' workers and messages offered a more familiar alternative which was consistent with their experience, identified their problems, and offered a time-honored solution.

Finally, American ignorance of and hostility toward Islam and the Middle East, often critiqued as a "Christian Crusade" mentality influenced by Orientalism and Zionism, were blamed for misguided U.S. political-military policies: support for the "un-Islamic" Shah of Iran, massive military and economic funding of Israel, and the backing of an unrepresentative Christian-controlled government in Lebanon.

These crises and failures reinforced a prevailing Muslim sense of inferiority, the product of centuries of European colonial dominance, which left a legacy of both admiration of Western power, science, and technology and resentment of Western dominance, penetration, and exploitation.[8] The failures of the modern experience stood in sharp contrast to an Islamic ideal which linked the faithfulness of the Islamic community with worldly success, as witnessed by the memory of a past history in which Islam was a dominant world power and civilization.

FROM FAILURE TO SUCCESS

During the 1970s, Islamic politics seemed to explode on the scene, as events in the Middle East (the Egyptian-Israeli war and the Arab oil embargo of 1973, as well as the Iranian Revolution of 1978–79) shocked many into recognition of a powerful new force that threatened Western interests. Heads of state and opposition movements appealed to Islam to enhance their legitimacy and popular support; Islamic organizations and institutions proliferated.

In 1973 Egypt's Anwar Sadat initiated a "holy war" against Israel. In contrast to the 1967 Arab-Israeli war that was fought by Gamal Abdel Nasser in the name of Arab nationalism/socialism, this war was fought under the banner of Islam. Sadat generously employed Islamic symbols and history to rally his forces. Despite their loss of the war, the relative success of Egyptian forces led many Muslims to regard it as a moral victory, since most had believed that a U.S.-backed Israel could not be beaten.

Military vindication in the Middle East was accompanied by economic muscle, the power of the Arab oil boycott. For the first time since the dawn of colonialism, the West had to content with and acknowledge, however begrudgingly, its dependence on the Middle East. For many in the Muslim world the new wealth, success, and power of the oil-rich countries seemed to indicate a return of the power of Islam to a community whose centuries-long political and cultural ascendance had been shattered by European colonialism and, despite independence, by second-class status in a superpower-dominated world. Most of the oil wealth was located in the Arab heartland, where Muhammad had received the revelation of the Quran and established the first Islamic community-state. The largest deposits were found in Saudi Arabia, a self-styled Islamic state, which had asserted its role as keeper of the holy cities of Mecca and Medina, protector of the annual pilgrimage (*hajj*), and leader and benefactor of the Islamic world. The House of Saud used its oil wealth to establish numerous international Islamic organizations, promote the preaching and spread of Islam, support Islamic causes, and subsidize Islamic activities undertaken by Muslim governments.

No event demonstrated more dramatically the power of a resurgent Islam than the Iranian Revolution of 1978–79. For many in the West and the Muslim world, the unthinkable became a reality. The powerful, modernizing, and Western-oriented regime of the Shah came crashing down. This was an oil-rich Iran whose wealth had been used to build the best-equipped military in the Middle East (next to Israel's) and to support an ambitious modernization program, the Shah's White Revolution. Assisted by Western-trained elites and advisers, the Shah had governed a state that the United States regarded as its most stable ally in the Muslim world. The fact that a revolution against him and against the West was effectively mounted in the name of Islam, organizing disparate groups and relying upon the mullah-mosque network for support, generated euphoria among many in the Muslim world and convinced Islamic activists that these were lessons for success to be emulated. Strength and victory would belong to those who pursued change in the name of Islam, whatever the odds and however formidable the regime.

For many in the broader Muslim world, the successes of the 1970s resonated with an idealized perception of early Islam, the Islamic paradigm to be found in the time of the Prophet Muhammad, the Golden Age of Islam. Muhammad's successful union of disparate tribal forces under the banner of Islam, his creation of an Islamic state and society in which social justice prevailed, and the extraordinary early expansion of Islam were primal events to be remembered and, as the example of the Iranian Revolution seemingly verified, to be successfully emulated by those who adhered to Islam. Herein lies the initial attraction of the Iranian Revolution for many Muslims, Sunni and Shii revolt against impiety, oppression, and injustice. The call of the Ayatollah Khomeini for an Islamic revolution struck a chord among many who identified with his message of anti-imperialism, his condemnation of failed, unjust, and oppressive regimes, and his vision of a morally just society.

By contrast, the West stood incredulous before this challenge to the Shah's "enlightened" development of his seemingly backward nation, and the resurrection of an anachronistic, irrational medieval force that threatened to hurtle modern Iran back to the Middle Ages. Nothing symbolized this belief more than the black-robed, bearded mullahs and the dour countenance of their leader, the Ayatollah Khomeini, who dominated the media, reinforcing in Western minds the irrational nature of the entire movement.

EXPORTING THE REVOLUTION

The success of the Iranian Revolution fired the imagination of the Muslim world and made Muslim governments tremble. Postrevolutionary Iran influenced Islamic activists throughout the world. In the aftermath of the revolution, delegations of Muslim leaders came from North America, the Middle East, and Southeast Asia to Teheran to congratulate Khomeini. Sunni as well as Shii activist organizations, extending from Egypt (the moderate Muslim Brotherhood and radical al-Jihad) to Malaysia (ABIM, or the Malaysian Youth Movement, and the militant PAS) drew inspiration from the example of Iran. The Iranian Revolution provided lessons "to awaken Muslims and to restore their confidence in their religion and their adherence to it, so that they may assume the reins of world leadership of mankind once again and place the world under the protection of the esteemed Islamic civilization."[9] The Iranian Revolution served as a reminder that Islam is a comprehensive way of life that regulates worship and society: "It is religion and state, governance and politics, economics and social organization, education and morals, worship and holy war."[10]

Long-quiescent Shii minority communities in Sunni-dominated states like Saudi Arabia, the Gulf, and Pakistan aggressively asserted their Shii identity and rights and were emboldened to express discontent with ruling regimes. At the same time, threatened Muslims rulers increasingly branded their Islamic opposition as Khomeini-like or accused Iran of exerting undue influence on their domestic politics.

Gulf rulers were particularly nervous about the appeal of Iran's revolutionary example and rhetoric. In Iraq, where Shii constitute 60 percent of the population, the government of Saddam Hussein, a nominally Sunni Muslim ruler, was shaken by eruptions in the Shii cities of Karbala, Najaf, and Kufa (June 1979). Khomeini denounced Saddam Hussein as an atheist and called for the overthrow of his regime. Saddam Hussein countered by vilifying Khomeini and appealing to Iran's minority Arab population to revolt. The government suspected Iranian influence within Iraq's Shii activist groups—in particular, in the Islamic Call Society (al-Dawa) and the newly formed (1979) Mujahidin.[11] The Ayatollah Muhammad Baqir al-Sadr, one of Iraq's most prominent and influential Shii activist clerics, who had befriended Khomeini during his exile in Iraq, welcomed Iran's revolution and Khomeini's Islamic government. Saddam Hussein acted decisively. Shii leaders were arrested. Baqir al-Sadr, who had declared Iraq's Baathist regime un-Islamic and forbidden any dealings with it, was executed (April 1980), and al-Dawa was outlawed. In an atmosphere in which both Iraq and Iran played upon centuries-long Arab-Persian and Sunni-Shii rivalries and hostilities, the situation deteriorated. In September 1980 Iraq invaded Iran, initiating a war that would last eight years.

Khomeini was particularly critical of the Saudi and Gulf governments. He denounced them as "un-Islamic" monarchies, disdainfully characterizing their military and economic ties with the United States as "American Islam." Audiotapes of Khomeini and revolutionary leaflets were smuggled into these Sunni-dominated states, and daily Arabic broadcasts from Teheran were explicit in their critique and their agenda:

> The ruling regime in Saudi Arabia wears Muslim clothing, but it actually represents a luxurious, frivolous, shameless way of life, robbing funds from the people and squandering them, and engaging in gambling, drinking parties, and orgies. Would it be surprising if people follow the path of revolution, resort to violence and continue their struggle to regain their rights and resources?[12]

The worst fears of Gulf rulers and of the West—that Iran's Revolution would prove contagious—seemed to be coming true in the first years after the revolution. In November 1979 Saudi Arabia was rocked by two explosive events. On November 20, as Muslims prepared to usher in the fifteenth century of Islam, the Grand Mosque at Mecca was seized and occupied for two weeks by Sunni militants who denounced the Saudi monarchy. Khomeini's accusation that Americans had been behind the mosque seizure led to attacks against American embassies and the destruction by fire of the American embassy in Islamabad, Pakistan.

While still reeling under the seizure of the Grand Mosque, on November 27, the house of Saud saw riots break out among the 250,000 Shii Muslims in the oil-rich Eastern Province (Al-Hasa) where Shii constitute 35 percent of the population.[13] Pent-up emotions and grievances among Shii, who felt discriminated against by their Sunni rulers and cheated by an unfair distribution of oil wealth and government services, had exploded earlier in the year in response to Iran's revolution and the triumphant return of Khomeini.

Events in the early 1980s did nothing to lessen concern among governments in the Gulf, the wider Muslim world, and the West. Statements by the ruling ayatollahs in Iran, who called for an aggressive, expansionist policy, exacerbated the situation. President Khamenei called upon prayer leaders from forty countries to turn their mosques into houses of "prayer, cultural and military bases [to]...prepare the ground for the creation of Islamic governments in all countries."[14] The Iran-Iraq war, which officially began with Iraq's invasion of Iran on September 22, 1980, inflamed relations between Iran and its neighbors. The Gulf states organized the Gulf Cooperation Council (GCC) and threw their substantial financial support to Iraq. Khomeini called upon the GCC to "return to the lap of Islam, abandon the Saddam Hussein regime in Baghdad, and stop squandering the wealth of their people."[15]

During the same period, Bahrain and Kuwait were also threatened by Shii unrest.[16] In 1981 the government of Bahrain foiled an Iranian-inspired coup by the Shii Front for the Liberation of Bahrain. Kuwait, 30 percent of whose population is Shii, was hit by car bombings of the American and French embassies (1983) and was forced to crack down on Shii unrest in 1987 and 1989.

Iran frequently used the annual *hajj* to Mecca to propagate its revolutionary message. The Ayatollah Khomeini and other senior clerics rejected the Saudi claim to be the keepers of the holy sites and maintained that the *hajj* had a rightful political dimension. Iranian pilgrims, displaying posters of Khomeini and chanting slogans against the United States, the Soviet Union, and Israel, clashed with Saudi security in June 1982. The tensions continued during subsequent years and climaxed in 1987 when more than 400 people were killed in a confrontation between Iranian pilgrims and Saudi security forces.

Despite these sporadic disturbances and government fears of massive unrest, Iran's export of its revolution proved in the end to be surprisingly unsuccessful in rallying Iraqi Shii as well as the populations of the Gulf states. By and large, most Iraqi (Arab) Shii were swayed more by nationalist than religious ties to their (Persian) co-religionists in Iran. Pockets of Shii militancy in the Gulf states did not translate into significant revolutionary movements. To thwart their growth, governments successfully used a combination of carrot and stick, addressing socioeconomic grievances while increasing security and imprisoning and deporting dissidents.

Lebanon provides the clearest and boldest example of the direct impact of Iran's Revolution. After the revolution, Iran sent a contingent of its Revolutionary Guards to Lebanon who influenced the development of Shii militant organizations there, in particular Hizbullah and al-Jihad, supplying training, material, and money. In contrast to the more moderate Shii AMAL, which fought for a more representative reapportionment of power within the existing state structure, the goal of Iranian-inspired organizations was the eventual creation of an Islamic state. Iran was suspected of attempting to further that end through everything from bombings of Western embassies to car bomb attacks and the taking of hostages.

FROM THE PERIPHERY TO THE CENTER: MAINSTREAM REVIVALISM

While the exploitation of Islam by governments and by extremist organizations has reinforced the secular orientations of many Muslims and cynicism in the West, a less-well-known and yet potentially far-reaching social transformation has also occurred in the Muslim world. In the 1990s, Islamic revivalism has ceased to be restricted to small, marginal organizations on the periphery of society and instead has become part of mainstream Muslim society, producing a new class of modern-educated but Islamically oriented elites who work alongside, and at times in coalitions with, their secular counterparts. Revivalism continues to grow as a broad-based socioreligious movement, functioning today in virtually every Muslim country and transnationally. It is a vibrant, multifaceted movement that will embody the major impact of Islamic revivalism for the foreseeable future. Its goal is the transformation of society through the Islamic formation of individuals at the grassroots level. Dawa (call) societies work in social services (hospitals, clinics, legal-aid societies), economic projects (Islamic banks, investment houses, insurance companies), education (schools, childcare centers, youth camps), and religious publishing and broadcasting. Their common programs are aimed at young and old alike.

A more pronounced Islamic orientation is now to be found among the middle and lower classes, educated and uneducated, professionals and workers, young and old, men, women, and children. A new generation of Islamically oriented leaders have appeared in Egypt, the Sudan, Tunisia, Jordan, Iran, Malaysia, Kuwait, Saudi Arabia, and Pakistan. Islamic activists have become an accustomed part of the political process, participating in national and local elections, scoring an impressive victory in Algeria's municipal elections, emerging as the chief opposition parties or groups in Egypt, Tunisia, and Jordan, and serving in cabinet positions in the Sudan, Jordan, Pakistan, Iran, and Malaysia.

For many who have nurtured visions of Islamic activism as the work of a small band of radicals and terrorists, the reality of Islam's strength, its expanding spheres of influence in mainstream politics and society, are both bewildering and menacing. How is one to make sense of the growth and prominence of Islamic activism in much of the Muslim world? What are the roots of the Islamic resurgence? Is Islamic fundamentalism simply a form of religiously motivated terrorism and extremism? If so, why does it enjoy such widespread support? Why is Islam so prominent in Muslim politics? Where and how has Islam been reasserted in politics and society? Why has Islamic revivalism proved to be so strong in those countries long regarded as among the most Westernized—Egypt, Lebanon, Iran, and Tunisia? How could Saddam Hussein, the most secular and un-Islamic of leaders, have appealed to Islam in the 1991 Gulf War? Finally, to what extent is there an "Islamic threat"?

NOTES

1. This is the first chapter in John L. Esposito, *The Islamic Threat: Myth or Reality?* (New York: Oxford University Press, 1992).
2. John O. Voll, "Renewal and Reform in Islamic History: *Tajdid and Islah*," in John L. Esposito, ed., *Voices of Resurgent Islam* (New York: Oxford University Press, 1983); Nehemiah Levtzion and John Voll, eds., *Eighteenth-Century Renewal and Reform in Islam* (Syracuse, NY: Syracuse University Press, 1987).
3. Donald Eugene Smith, ed., *Religion and Modernization* (New Haven, Conn.: Yale University Press, 1974), p. 4.
4. Daniel Crecelius, "The Course of Secularization in Modern Egypt," in John L. Esposito, ed., *Islam and Development: Religion and Sociopolitical Change* (Syracuse, NY: Syracuse University Press, 1980), p. 60.
5. For studies of the Islamic resurgence see Yvonne Y. Haddad, John O. Voll, and John L. Esposito, eds., *The Contemporary Islamic Revival: A Critical Survey and Bibliography* (New York: Greenwood Press, 1991); John L. Esposito, *Islam and Politics*, 3rd ed. (Syracuse, NY: Syracuse University Press, 1991); John

L. Esposito, ed., *Islam in Asia: Religion, Politics and Society* (New York: Oxford University Press, 1987); James P. Piscatori, ed., *Islam in the Political Process* (Cambridge: Cambridge University Press, 1983); and Nazih Ayubi, *Political Islam: Religion and Politics in the Arab World* (London: Routledge, 1991).

6. See John J. Donohue, "Islam and the Search for Identity in the Arab World," in Esposito, ed., *Voices of Resurgent Islam*, ch. 3; Ali Merad, "The Ideologization of Islam in the Contemporary Arab World," in Alexander S. Cudsi and Ali E. Hillal Dessouki, eds., *Islam and Power* (Baltimore, Md.: The Johns Hopkins University Press, 1981), ch. 3; Yvonne Y. Haddad, "The Arab-Israeli Wars, Nasserism, and the Affirmation of Islamic Identity," in John L. Esposito, ed., *Islam and Development: Religion and Sociopolitical Change* (Syracuse, NY: Syracuse University Press, 1980), pp. 118–120.

7. Philip S. Khoury, "Islamic Revivalism and the Crisis of the Secular State in the Arab World," in I. Ibrahim, ed., *Arab Resources: The Transformation of a Society* (London: Croom Helm, 1983), pp. 213-34; Ayubi, *Political Islam*, pp. 164–174; Henry Munson, *Islam and Revolution* (New Haven, Conn.: Yale University Press, 1988), ch. 9.

8. James P. Piscatori, *Islam in a World of Nation States* (Cambridge: Cambridge University Press, 1986), p. 26.

9. The Islamic (Student) Association of Cairo University, "Lessons from Iran," in John J. Donohue and John L. Esposito, eds., *Islam in Transition: Muslim Perspectives* (New York: Oxford University Press, 1982), p. 246.

10. Ibid., p. 247.

11. See Michael C. Hudson, "The Islamic Factor in Syrian and Iraqi Politics," in James P. Piscatori, ed., *Islam in the Political Process* (Cambridge: Cambridge University Press, 1983), pp. 86ff.

12. Jacob Goldberg, "The Shii Minority in Saudi Arabia," in Juan R. I. Cole and Nikki R. Keddie, eds., *Shiism and Social Protest* (New Haven, CT: Yale University Press, 1986), p. 243.

13. William Ochsenwald, "Saudi Arabia and the Islamic Revival," *International Journal of Middle East Studies* 13:3 (August 1981): 271, 276–77; Joseph Kechichian, "The Role of the Ulama in the Politics of an Islamic State: The Case of Saudi Arabia," *International Journal of Middle East Studies* 18:1 (February 1986): 56–68; James P. Piscatori, "Ideological Politics in Saudi Arabia," in Piscatori, *Islam in the Political Process* (Cambridge: Cambridge University Press, 1983), p. 67.

14. Shaul Bakhash, *The Reign of the Ayatollahs: Iran and the Islamic Revolution* (New York: Basic Books, 1984), pp. 234–235.

15. Delip Hiro, *Iran Under the Ayatollahs* (London: Routledge and Kegan Paul, 1985), p. 340.

16. Joseph Kostiner, "Kuwait and Bahrain," in Shireen T. Hunter, ed., *The Politics of Islamic Revivalism* (Bloomington, IN: Indiana University Press, 1988), pp. 121ff.

The Political Discourse of Contemporary Islamist Movements[1]

Youssef Choueiri

The second Gulf war afforded various Islamist movements a rare opportunity to put some of their ideas into practice. After all, it was Saddam Hussein who throughout the crisis espoused and expounded various fundamentalist themes and ideas. The slogan *Allahu akbar* ("God is Great") was decreed to be inscribed on the Iraqi flag. The confrontation itself was invariably depicted as being between belief and unbelief, faith and atheism, and good and evil. The slogan of *jihad*, the hallmark of contemporary fundamentalism, pervaded all the statements, speeches, and announcements made by the Iraqi president or broadcast on his behalf. Arab nationalism, the official ideology of the regime, figured as a subtext needing constant decoding, or at best, an anomalous survival in the context of a new terminology. Allusions to the early career of the Prophet were made, analogies drawn, and lessons to be learned reiterated in the best traditions of fundamentalist discourse. The world was thus divided into two diametrically opposed camps: the believers and unbelievers (or infidels). As a matter of fact, anyone familiar with the vocabulary and terminology of Islamic fundamentalism would have detected an unmistakable transformation in the theoretical and political analysis of the Iraqi regime.

The rhetoric of fundamentalist notions made it possible for a whole host of Islamic movements to rally to Baghdad's cause. Some Islamist movements, such as the Islamic Liberation Party (Hizb al-Tahrir al-Islami), called on Saddam to declare himself the new Caliph of all Muslims. Various Islamic activists visited Baghdad to declare their allegiance and full-hearted support.

Although it is not my intention to analyze the political background of such a transformation, it remains of direct relevance to the long-term prospects of Islamic fundamentalism in the Arab world as a whole. To simplify matters, one could put forward the following propositions: During the past decade, Saddam Hussein's policies and strategy have dealt Islamic fundamentalism a double blow. During the Iran-Iraq War (1980–1988) he succeeded to a large extent in discrediting the viability of Khomeinism as a revolutionary or alternative force. His adoption of an openly Islamic rhetoric throughout the Gulf crisis served, as it turned out, to weaken the credibility of all other Sunni groups. Whereas his relatively efficient military performance against Iran deprived Shi'ite fundamentalism of its potential influence and appeal, Saddam's defeat in his reincarnation as an Islamic fundamentalist robbed the Arab Islamic parties of their opportunity to assert themselves or gain direct power. Both in his victory and defeat Islamic fundamentalism suffered moral and political losses.

It is perhaps appropriate at this juncture to highlight the complex and varied nature of the political forces that proclaimed their support of Iraq. Nevertheless, one cannot escape the conclusion that the ideological battle assumed Islamic dimensions, forcing secular, nationalist, and other trends to adjust their pronouncements in the same direction.

The hard core of the pro-Iraq alliance, the Islamist movements and parties in the Arab world, may be divided into three groups or categories: The first includes radical groups that consider themselves in a permanent state of war. These groups condemn democracy both as a means of attaining power and a process of government. Relying on the theoretical analysis of Sayyid Qutb, the Egyptian Muslim Brother, their perception of democracy makes its application a direct violation of God's sovereignty. The desires and opinions of secular majorities, it is contended, represent an outright usurpation of divine laws. Democracy implies human agents devising their own legislation. The legislative exclusiveness of God (*hakimiyya*) is inseparable from the question of doctrine. To these groups, Islam has ceased to exist outside their immediate circles. Humanity as a whole has therefore reverted to the age of ignorance (*jahiliyya*). Consequently, multiparty politics and all practices that derive their legitimacy directly from a sovereign electorate are rejected. The nation is not entitled to legislate at will. Or, as Sayyid Qutb explains, "Muslim scholars confuse the act of exercising power with that of its source." In other words, people do not possess, nor do they delegate, the right of sovereignty. Rather, they implement what God has legislated in accordance with His exclusive authority. In this sense, Islam must first be restituted, and then the discussions of technical procedure, such as elections, can proceed. Political power has to be gained before all other considerations. The Egyptian Jihad (al-Jihad al-Islami) organization is the most prominent representative of this trend.

Democracy is seen in the same light as Arab nationalism, secularism, and socialism and considered a manifestation of Western decadence and corruption. The immediate enemy, however, remains the local political elite rather than external forces such as Zionism or imperialism.

The second category includes movements and parties such as the Muslim Brethren of Jordan and the Islamic Front in Algeria. These parties represent a political trend that accepts the means and practices of multiparty politics and democratic institutions without an equal acceptance of democracy as a permanent process or the ultimate form of government. Their acceptance of multiparty politics does not, therefore, constitute an integral part of their ideological aim. This aim remains an Islamic state, which by its very nature excludes non-Islamic platforms and ideas. It seems that the willingness of some Arab governments to tolerate, implicitly or explicitly, the presence of an Islamic trend, be it a party or a movement, which is the case in Egypt, grants this trend the opportunity to take advantage of a situation in which certain Arab regimes are pursuing open-door policies in both the economic and political fields. These Islamist parties are then the strange bedfellows of democracy: Their sympathies embrace its immediate advantages, while they remain skeptical of its ultimate aims.

The third category has been officially deprived of the implicit or explicit legality of our second category. This is the case of the Renaissance Party (al-Nahda) led by Rashid al-Ghannushi in Tunisia, and the Syrian Muslim Brethren (al-Ikhwan al-Muslimun Suriyya). These two organizations have been banned in both Syria and Tunisia and judged by the officials of these two countries to be terrorist bands bent on violence and destruction. The public pronouncements of the Tunisian and Syrian Islamic fundamentalists are sometimes designed to highlight the peaceful and democratic credentials of their struggle; their resort to violence is often attributed to the harsh treatment meted out to their members at the hands of the security forces. However, ideologically and politically, Tunisian and Syrian fundamentalism is virtually indistinguishable from the first category. There is, moreover, factional strife within these movements and a tendency to rely on outside forces in order to change the political structure in their respective countries.

By and large, these three trends share a number of common ideological features that lend their discourse a coherence of tactics and strategy. This discourse is fundamentally opposed of Islamic reformism and its main representatives, particularly Mohammad 'Abduh, Rashid Rida, and Ibn Badis. Thus, democracy is either excluded at the outset or tolerated as one of the available means to attain exclusive political control. The Islamic fundamentalist belief in God's sovereignty goes hand in hand with the doctrine of *jihad* as the sixth pillar of Islam. This entails a method of armed struggle, coupled with an assertion of Islam as a religion that has to be ultimately embodied in a totalitarian state.

Islamic radicalism postulated the restoration of Islam as an eminently political endeavor. Consequently, other activities, such as elections, demonstrations, and propaganda campaigns, were subordinated to this overriding idea. Its other hallmark is the belief that the method of struggle must be commensurate with the goal of and direct relevance to its realization.

In this sense, an Islamic state can only be brought about by waging *jihad*, or armed struggle in its widest connotations, and under the leadership of a dedicated, well-organized elite. This triad—the state, armed struggle, and a revolutionary organization—is reminiscent of Leninist forms and arguments perfected at the turn of the twentieth century. These forms, however, do not necessarily imply a convergence of content or ultimate aims.

The discourse of contemporary Islamic radicalism derives its possibilities and rules of formation from the writings of three Muslim thinkers and activists: Abu al-A'la al-Maududi (d. 1979), Sayyid Qutb (d. 1966), and Ayatollah Khomeini (d. 1989). This chapter is devoted to an initial exposition of the main themes of their texts as the unique founders of this particular "discursivity."[2]

GOD'S SOVEREIGNTY

This concept seeks to go beyond the mere affirmation of the existence of God in order to assert His authority in the daily life of His creatures and servants. Hence, the universe is judged to be one single organic unity, both in its formation and movement.[3] The unity of the universe mirrors the absolute oneness of God. The Qur'an is the word of God. It is seen by Sayyid Qutb as a divine symphony with its rhythmical tones, reverberations, and movements of climax.

Islam is then a manifestation of a harmonious cosmic order that conveys its fixed order in the similar messages handed down to a chain of prophets extending from Adam to Muhammad. Without God's guidance, the human intellect swims in the sea of the unknown.[4] Consequently, *jahiliyya*, or pagan ignorance, becomes "a psychological state which rejects God's guidance, and a system that refuses to conduct its affairs according to God's commands." Moreover, such a rejection leads "to inevitable deviations, entailing misery, destruction and suffering."[5]

Jahiliyya is bound to lift its head whenever people's hearts are devoid of a divine doctrine and their lives cease to be governed by legal injunctions derived from this doctrine. It also has the same characteristics, irrespective of time and place. Humanity today is living a second *jahiliyya*, more sinister in its implications than the *jahiliyya* of pre-Islamic days.[6]

THE POLITICAL DISCOURSE OF CONTEMPORARY ISLAMIST MOVEMENTS

Human life is therefore a battle of moral and religious values. Those who forsake God and become atheists turn into "brutish animals." In other words, without spiritual beliefs human beings cannot be differentiated from beasts and savage creatures.[7] Seen in this light, European history consists of a connected series of *jahiliyyas*: Hellenism, the Roman Empire, the Middle Ages, the Renaissance, the Enlightenment, and the French Revolution. It is no wonder that modern European colonialism is pronounced to be "a perverse appetite of a pagan society."[8]

Thus, Islam is "knowledge"; all other ideologies and theories are mere "opinions," in the Aristotelian understanding of these two terms. This is all the more so since Islam accords with nature and represents an authentic reproduction or representation of a harmonious universe. The universe is the visible book of God, and the Qur'an is His recited word. Moreover, just as Islam is a method that remains permanent in its fundamentals and constituent parts, so is man's essence. All alterations and developments associated with man's life do not change his nature. Such a premise becomes self-evident when faith is shown to be instinctive, whereas atheism is a transient and false phase.[9]

Whereas human reason is limited by space and time, divine revelation is universal and absolute. Islam, as a result, has an independent existence outside the actual conditions of any generation of Muslims.[10] Nevertheless, the cosmic order, regulated by God, places man on this earth to be His functionary and lieutenant.

Rituals (*'ibadat*), such as praying and fasting, form an integral part of the wider domain of human transactions and politics (*mu'amalat*). As a matter of fact, all human activities have to be performed as acts of worship.[11] This view is adopted not only to preserve Islam but also to make it more amenable to change. Hence, institutions or practices that could no longer be revived, such as slavery, are explained away as having been temporary devices created to deal with a transient and transitional situation.[12]

In Qutb's exegesis, the Qur'an is treated like another cosmos, possessing its structures, harmonious components, and complementary functions. Both teem with their stars and planets, seas and rivers, plants and animals, human beings, angels, and jinns. Furthermore, the Qur'an resonates with that mysterious and hidden silence that emerges out of a vast firmament. At that moment, grains of sand and bright stars merge into each other in an embrace of cosmic love.[13]

Nevertheless, God's attributes—divinity, lordship, omnipotence, omnipresence, and omniscience—reiterated by Qutb, al-Maududi, and Khomeini—are directly dependent for their elaboration on Islamic theology and Greek philosophy. This is a paradoxical state of affairs since these two disciplines were not integrated into the main doctrinal corpus of Islam until almost two centuries after its emergence. It is also ironic that Qutb often stigmatized these two disciplines and called upon the members of his well-disciplined vanguard to reject them as intellectual distortions developed under the influence of pagan currents of thoughts.

Aristotle asserts that man is a political animal by nature. Contemporary Islamic thought appropriates this notion and amalgamates it in its contention that holds the sound instinct of man to be essentially religious. The apparent contradiction is then obliterated or sublated by redefining religion to encompass all aspects of life, particularly its focal political organization.

POLITICS AND DEMOCRACY

In contemporary Islamic thought, democracy is denuded of its neutral connotations and descriptive attributes. Like socialism, it is considered to rest on a comprehensive worldview. Being an expression of a philosophical substructure, it cannot be confined to administrative procedures. Its adoption is automatically accompanied by its wider domain and conclusions.

To Qutb, the general characteristics of a political system are governed by one predominant feature. It is this particular feature that authorizes the relative position and function of all the other elements. In addition, the dominant feature is itself conditioned by a deeper and more comprehensive theory. Institutions and their attendant theoretical justifications are therefore mere manifestations of an interrelated organic entity.

The dominant feature of liberal democracy is the concept of majority rule and the sovereignty of the people, whereas that of communism is the dictatorship of the proletariat, which is basically the absolute authority of a single party. In an Islamic polity, *shura* (mutual consultation) is the essential quality that defines the criteria of selecting the leader of the community (the Imam), members of a consultative assembly, and the executive officials of the state.[14]

In a democratic system, it is a small minority that controls the levers of power and wealth. This minority conceals its real aims behind a number of political cultural facades. These facades serve to divert attention away from the actual wielders of power, on the one hand, and subject the entire society to a consistent operation of indoctrination and brainwashing, on the other. All social classes are thus in the grip of a few thousand usurers who own and run the principal financial companies and credit banks.[15]

Under communism, the party bosses, acting in the name of the proletariat, use the state apparatus to unleash a reign of terror, placing all society under a system of constant surveillance. Common ownership becomes synonymous with the supremacy of the state, which is in turn under the absolute control of the party machine. Although usury is prohibited, the exaltation of production and the satisfaction of materialistic needs lead to depravities and emotional vacuity. Similarly, capitalism's sole aim is to lend money at exorbitant rates of interest. Capital, labor, land, and the market are thus dominated and manipulated by Jewish usurers, according to this view. This is the epitome of a parasitic system that is alien to the insistence of Islam on productive work and useful goods. Hence, Islam singles out licit and illicit activities. It acknowledges private ownership of property but restricts its scope. All members of society are de jure shareholders of wealth, since it is originally bestowed by God on man. God has created all things and is consequently the owner of His own creation, including wealth and property. Man is a trustee of God and engages in certain economic activities, exerting his productive labour according to divine injunctions.[16]

Whereas capitalism is built on usury, the Marxist socialism on the abolition of private property, Islam has its system of social solidarity, mutual obligations, and security. It restricts private property without abolishing it. This is accomplished by the collection of the religious tax known as *zakat*. Levied on incomes, property, and fixed capital, its rate varies between 3 and 20 percent. Its main purpose is to eliminate

poverty and economic misery.[17] Except for its insistence on the prohibition of direct
interest-earning, an Islamic economic system is an "enlightened" form of capitalism.
According to al-Maududi, its hallmark is the way it eradicates extravagance in spend-
ing, hoarding, and accumulation. The prevention of accumulation consists in hand-
ing over the surplus income to the needy and less fortunate. Should moralistic
promptings and Islamic ethics fail to curb individual tendencies of greed and rein-
vestment of capital, legal limitations would become operative. Lending for the sake
of earning interest on accumulated savings is thus strictly prohibited. However, joint
ventures and investment in industry are considered lawful, provided no usurious
transactions are involved. If accumulation of wealth does occur, the state would have
the right to levy an annual percentage rate on the accumulated sum and spend it on
welfare benefits. This is the *zakat* system prescribed by the Qur'an. A public treasury
or exchequer has therefore to be set up in order to cater to the needs of the poor and
the unemployed. These procedures eliminate the necessity of taking out insurance
policies or keeping deposit accounts in banks—the two evil features of capitalism.
Moreover, the social agency of *zakat* produces an additional bonus: It restores
"a proper balance between production and consumption" by improving the purchasing power of the less fortunate sections of society, as well as obviating the need to
export surplus production to other countries.[18]

The diffusion of wealth, designed to prevent its concentration in a few hands, is
also the aim of the Islamic law of inheritance. According to this legal rule, all near
and distant relatives of a deceased person are entitled to well-defined shares in his
legacy. By excluding primogeniture, the circulation of wealth is thus assured in a
process of full equity and as part of God's wisdom.[19]

NATIONALISM

The idea of the oneness of God and of His exclusive sovereignty is meant to reinstate
Islam as a political system. Whereas secular nation-states implement their own laws
and consider religion a spiritual affair or a national heritage, Islamic fundamentalism, particularly in its Sunni branch, condemns the pagan connotations of nationalism. According to al-Maududi, Qutb, and Khomeini, the underlying strength of
Islam is its universal doctrine. Its basis, ever since its inception, denotes a sublime
endeavor that dissociates itself from nationalist notions of race, color, and language.

Qutb, for example, points out that the Arabs did not succeed in "conquering
kingdoms and destroying thrones" until they had become oblivious, for the first
time in their history, of their Arab identity. They suppressed their national and racial
chauvinism, thinking of themselves as being nothing else but Muslims. Today as in
the early days of Islam, the only valid and legal division in all societies is that between
"the Party of God" (Hizb Allah) and "the Party of Satan" (Hizb al-Shaytan).[20]

Hence, individuals do not become human and proper members of society except
as believers and Muslims. This concept was of particular relevance to the identity of
the Arabs, given the fact that they occupy a distinctive position in Islam as its founders and propagators.

To al-Maududi, the concept of both the nation and nationalism is as old as human
civilization. However, the Qur'an does not justify or commend the bond of nationalism, be it linguistic, racial, economic, or territorial. Moreover, the Prophet
Muhammad combated the nationalist fanaticism of the Arabs in order to pave the
way for the universalist mission of Islam. The only differentiation that was then
allowed revolved around belief and unbelief, polytheism and monotheism, atheism

and Islam. All other differences were relegated to the background or obliterated altogether.[21] Qutb often spoke disparagingly of "inferior and brutish" human beings who adopt secular or nationalist ideologies. He rejected Arab nationalism out of hand, ridiculing its narrow and sterile theoretical basis. God's choice of Arabia as the cradle of His final message had nothing to do with the nationalist qualities of its inhabitants. He did so for reasons connected with the absence of "state structures and political coercion in the Arabian Peninsula." In other words, Arabia was simply a more convenient conduit to receive and nurture the prophetic message.[22]

Qutb goes on to point out that the Arabs today have nothing to offer the world except their religion. In all other fields—literature, arts, sciences, industrial production, and social philosophy—they have been overtaken by others. Without Islam, the Arabs would be worthless and useless. Thus, each nation has a special mission in life and particular skills: The Greeks and the Germans are noted for their philosophical investigations; the British excel in scientific discoveries and empire-building; and the Japanese are known for their mass-production and technological products.[23]

As for Khomeini, Islamic history is reduced at his hands, apart from the brief period of the Prophet's career, 610–632 A.D., to a span of five years, which is the duration of the reign of the fourth caliph, 'Ali b. Abi Talib (656–661 A.D.). Consequently, apostasy took place in Islam at an early stage and persisted down to the twentieth century. To him, "the age of ignorance" (*jahiliyya*) set in with the advent of the Ummayyad dynasty in 661. The most prominent factor in the degeneration of Islam was the adoption of Arab nationalism:

> Unfortunately, true Islam lasted for only a brief period after its inception. First the Ummayyads and then the Abbasids inflicted all kinds of damage on Islam.... The process was begun by the Ummayyads, who changed the nature of government from divine and spiritual to worldly. Their rule was based on Arabism, the principle of promoting the Arabs over all other peoples which was an aim fundamentally opposed to Islam and its desire to abolish nationality and unite all mankind in a single community, under the aegis of a state indifferent to the matter of race and color.[24]

LEADERSHIP AND JIHAD

Contemporary Islamic thought, particularly in its radical variety, accords political struggle and power the most pivotal function in its strategy as a whole. It is essentially an elitist conception of politics. It projects life as a vital force imbued with an instinctive drive. Hence, direct action becomes the substitute for detailed programs and compensates for lack of material power. Whereas Qutb called for the emergence of "a Muslim vanguard," composed of resolute individuals and turning itself into "a living organism," Khomeini directed all his efforts toward recruiting a new corps of young clerics and students of religion who would dedicate their lives to political action. He also affirmed the permanent role of the men of religion in his state as well as the absolute rulership of the jurist.

To al-Maududi, the question of leadership takes priority over all other political issues, for the leaders of society decide its general development and value system. Thus states dominated by corrupt and immoral politicians mold all institutions and the citizenry in their own image. By contrast, a pious and God-fearing political elite is bound to impart its virtues to various sectors of the population. The quintessence of human life is undoubtedly manifested in political leadership. The central task of an Islamic revolutionary party is to topple idolatrous governments and wrest power from their representatives. It is, in al-Maududi's analysis, a religious obligation incumbent on the community as a whole. The establishment of a virtuous Imamate is required by divine law in order to embody moral values in society at large.[25] Moreover, the distinguishing marks of a human being are nobility of character and high moral standards. Morality has always been the decisive factor in winning or losing a battle. A compact group, armed with the moral ideals of Islam, must therefore be formed, regardless of the material resources it has at its disposal. A well-organized, self-disciplined, hardened group, relying on faith and material power, is bound to overcome its enemies. Islam is simply "the manifestation of belief in action."[26]

Qutb adopted al-Maududi's idea of political struggle, singling out the latter's lecture on "Jihad in Islam" as one of the most valuable theoretical contributions to contemporary Islamic thought. In that lecture al-Maududi called for the establishment of an "International Revolutionary Party" in order to wage jihad against tyrannical governments. Its members were called "the functionaries of God" and their duty would consist in wiping out "oppression, mischief, strife, immorality, high-handedness and unlawful exploitation from the world by force of arms."[27]

Perhaps Qutb's most important legacy to Islamic activists was his system of classifying societies according to well-defined criteria. This system provided Islamic movements a tool of analysis with which they could clearly identify their task. Since he thought that the task of these movements was no less than the reenactment of the two phases of the Prophet's career, it would be useful at this stage to give a brief account of the Meccan and Medinan phases so as to be able to gauge Qutb's contemporary contribution.

The first Islamic state in history, and irrespective of its rudimentary organization, came into being through a process of peaceful means. The Meccan phase (c. 610–622 A.D.) was confined to a series of warnings and admonitions directed at the pagan Arabs, particularly the wealthy members of al-Quraysh, Muhammad's tribe. This led to a series of provocative reactions on the part of the Prophet's opponents. Despairing of his tribe's support, and following the death first of his uncle who was his protector, and then of his first wife, Khadija, in 618 A.D., he traveled to the neighboring town of al-Ta'if, seeking support from another tribal group. Disappointed and downcast, he returned to Mecca only to face further hostility.

It was not until a delegation from the city of Yathrib (later renamed Medina) met Muhammad during the pilgrimage season in Mecca that new horizons opened up. The delegates affirmed their belief in his message and confirmed that he was indeed God's messenger. A second and larger delegation arrived in the following year. Its members invited him to travel to Medina and act as a trusted arbitrator between its warring factions. This request gave rise to the idea of *Hijra*, or migration, whereby Muhammad, in 622 A.D., secretly left Mecca under the cover of darkness and traveled with a select group of his companions to a different environment.

Once in Medina, he built a mosque and living quarters and initiated the application of the legal injunctions of Islam. By the mere implementation of those rules, which were revealed in a gradual process, an Islamic state is said to have come into being. This decade is known as the Medinan period (622–632 A.D.).[28]

It was after the emergence of what may be called "political structure" that *jihad* against polytheists, Meccans, and recalcitrant Jewish tribes of Medina was proclaimed to mean fighting the way of God. After Muhammad's victory over the polytheists and the Jews, whereby Mecca itself was conquered, he began to prepare for military campaigns outside the Arabian Peninsula.

Qutb, al-Maududi, and Khomeini, unlike the Prophet Muhammad, confronted a totally different situation. Their immediate aim was not to build a nonexistent state but to overthrow well-established and highly developed state structures. Perhaps the seizure of power by the Bolsheviks in 1917, or the march on Rome organized by Mussolini in 1922, would serve as better models in inspiring twentieth-century radicalists.

To Qutb and al-Maududi *jihad* was a total state of war, designed to disarm one's enemy in order to reinstate the *shari'a*. Both thought that the backwardness of Muslims in the contemporary world resided in the absence of a reliable and organized Islamic movement. An Islamic revolution could not, therefore, be brought about without the existence of a well-disciplined group with its own leadership and agents and a proper moral environment. The history of the French, Russian, and Nazi revolutions, according to al-Maududi, furnished the best evidence of this theory. Thus "German Nazism" could not have succeeded in establishing itself except as a result of the theoretical contributions of Fichte, Goethe, and Nietzsche, coupled with "the ingenious and mighty leadership of Hitler and his comrades."[29]

Qutb contends that Islam does not have to justify itself or present its precepts in a defensive manner. An Islamist has to be bold, strident, and radical in stating his case. His tone and conduct should never be apologetic, hesitant, or conciliatory. Unflinching and infused with pride, he stares death in the face. A believer stands his ground, never runs away, and meets the enemy in open combat. If killed, he is promised martyrdom by God, the highest honor to be gained by a Muslim. A martyr is not washed but buried in his clothes, as he has already been purified. He enters paradise bearing his unmistakable labels and eternal identity. There he enjoys the everlasting pleasures promised by God. Triumphant and towering above his enemies, he paves the way for the advent of "the Kingdom of God" on earth and acts as a magnet that attracts the onlookers, who form the greatest majority of every society.[30]

In order to ensure the world domination and the unquestionable hegemony of Islam, the validity of *jihad* must become perpetual and timeless. Under such circumstances, terms such as "offensive" or "defensive" struggle lose their meaning and become redundant. The necessity of the daily assertion of God's absolute sovereignty demands the existence of a constant state of war. Hence, a clear distinction must be drawn between "the Party of God" and "the Party of Satan," or righteousness and falsehood. Today, as opposed to former times, the danger of mixing with idolatrous individuals, without the prior purpose of admonition, surpasses in its repercussions all other innovations. Consequently, the nature of the task to be undertaken by the vanguard is itself imposed by the universality of religious ignorance.[31]

An Islamic vanguard, Qutb reiterates, has to arm itself with a clear-cut and permanent criterion. This criterion would ensure its doctrine against dilution and render its complete detachment from a corrupt environment a positive achievement. Accordingly, Qutb divides the world into two spheres: the Abode of Islam and the Land of War. The first includes every country in which the legal judgments of Islam are applied. This condition obtains even in countries that happen to be composed of a Christian or Jewish majority. As long as the wielders of political power are Muslims and adhere to the injunctions of their religion, conversion is not required. The second sphere comprises every territory in which Islamic rules are not applied, irrespective of claims made by their rulers or inhabitants.[32]

In the Abode of Islam, property, life, and public order are sacrosanct. Those who violate its laws would be punished in accordance with Islamic justice. The inviolability of an Islamic society is the result of its virtuous and sublime character. It is a society that guarantees full employment and affords financial sufficiency to its disadvantaged members. It also creates incentives to encourage righteous deeds and discourage vice or evil. Abounding with all these amenities, bestowing plentiful benefits on all its citizens, and governed by just instincts, an Islamic state is entitled to consider anyone who violates public order to be a transgressor and to treat him as a criminal deserving the severest punishment.[33]

As for the Land of War, its inhabitants are not worthy of such guarantees and rewards. As long as Islamic law is not applied there and the sovereignty of Islam is not recognized, it becomes for the Muslims an open territory to be conquered. Its inviolability or sanctity, as far as the Muslims are concerned, is null and void, unless a treaty is concluded between it and the Abode of Islam for a brief and prescribed period. In the contemporary world, Qutb continues, this division has become obsolete. Since no Islamic system of government exists anywhere in the world, no treaties are to be concluded or abided by. Consequently, the entire world has become for a true Muslim a Land of War.[34]

Thus, *jihad* is the only option available to the new Islamic vanguard. It is a spiritual, financial, and military endeavor undertaken to assert God's sovereignty. These multifarious aspects form an organic whole and constitute the process of political struggle. However, the highest and most honorable aspect is the military engagement—the violent act in which a believer either triumphs over the enemy or dies and becomes a martyr.[35]

Khomeini was less precise than either al-Maududi or Qutb in defining the characteristics of *jihad* or the validity of armed struggle. He simply contended that political authority in Islam rightfully belonged to the custodians of Qur'anic legal rules, the jurists. All other forms of government, be they democratic or monarchical, were illegitimate. This tenet applied in particular to the kingship of the Shah, an institution that was abhorrent in Islam. He thus called upon the religious leaders to denounce all tyrannical authority (*taghut*).

Such a straightforward message, Khomeini thought, would create its own momentum and mobilize millions and millions. At that stage, and spurred on by their religious leaders, these millions would rush onto the streets, defying, with their faith, bare chests, and clenched fists, the bayonets and guns of the Shah's army. One martyr would follow another. Each would be given a mass funeral—a procession of remembrance—and each would be celebrated for his courage and envied for his success in winning a prominent place in paradise. As martyrs multiplied and funerals proliferated, the Shah, along with the two Satanic powers (the United States and the Soviet Union), would weaken and falter. With the cries of *Allahu Akbar* ("God is Great") resounding through the streets, alleys, and lanes of the land, the enemy would be steadily intimidated. The hour of his surrender would draw closer and closer. The masses' faith in God and revolution would steel them against all attempts to sow dissension in their ranks or force them to compromise. The downtrodden, the oppressed, and the deprived were for Khomeini the invincible army of Islam. To cleanse society of decadence and corruption, as defined by Khomeini, represented the urgent task of a new theocracy organized to exercise power under a self-appointed and absolute jurisconsult.[36]

Qutb, al-Maududi, and Khomeini articulated a new Islamic theory and established the contemporary discourse of a variety of Islamic political organizations. To them, change had to be total, comprehensive, and revolutionary. They saw no possibility of coexistence between Islam and other political or social systems. Gradual improvements and partial amendments of the status quo were considered inimical to the nature of a true Islamic approach. Society as a whole had to be remolded in the image and spirit of Islam.

They all opposed and argued against Western concepts of democracy, socialism, and nationalism. Their line of argumentation excluded even the remotest resemblance between Islam and other systems. To them, apparent similarities in the growth of human institutions were accidental and did not warrant a comparative and fruitful study.

NOTES

1. This paper appeared as a chapter in Abdel Salam Sidahmed and Anoushiravan Ehteshani, eds., *Islamic Fundamentalism* (Boulder, CO: Westview Press, 1996). A shortened version of this chapter was published under the title "Theoretical Paradigms of Islamic Movements," *Political Studies*, 41, No. 1, March 1993, pp. 108–116.
2. See Paul Rabinow, ed., *The Foucault Reader* (Middlesex: Penguin Books, 1984), p. 114. It is interesting to note that despite postmodernist pronouncements on "the death of the author," Foucault had to admit that "founders of discursivity" were "unique in that they are not just the authors of their own works. They have produced something else: the possibilities and the rules for the formation of other texts." Foucault singled out Freud and Marx as such founders.
3. S. Qutb, *Fi zilal al-Qur'an* (Under the Aegis of the Qur'an) (Beirut: Dar al-Shuruq, 1981), p. 280.
4. Ibid., p. 115.
5. S. Qutb, *Jahiliyyat al-quar al-'ishrin* (The Pagan Ignorance of the Twentieth Century) (Cairo: Matba'at Wahbah, 1963), pp. 9–11.
6. S. Qutb, *Fi zilal al-Qur'an*, pp. 510, 3616.
7. S. Qutb, *Milestones* (Beirut: The Holy Koran Publishing House, 1978), pp. 181–186.
8. S. Qutb, *Fi zilal al-Qur'an*, p. 146.
9. Ibid., pp. 266, 349, 556, 3451.
10. Ibid., p. 584.
11. Ibid., pp. 193, 932–933.
12. Ibid., pp. 230, 500, 1743.
13. Ibid., pp. 3563, 2373.
14. Ibid., pp. 112, 3165, 3343, 1754, 3165.
15. S. Qutb, *Al-Islam wa mushkilat al-hadara* (Islam and the Problems of Civilization) (Beirut: Dar al-Shuruq, 1980), pp. 179–180.
16. A. al-Maududi, *The Economic Problem of Man and Its Islamic Solution* (Lahore: Islamic Publications Ltd., 1978), pp. 23–29; S. Qutb, *Fi zilal al-Qur'an*, pp. 331, 1087, 3524. Qutb often quotes the fictitious *Protocols of the Wise Men of Zion* to substantiate his claim regarding Jewish domination in high or international finance. Zionism is seldom mentioned by al-Maududi or Khomeini in the same context.
17. I. Khomeini, *Islam and Revolution*, translated and annotated by Hamid Algar (Berkeley, CA: Mizan Press, 1981), pp. 45, 77; S. Qutb, *Fi zilal al-Qur'an*, pp. 331, 3187, 3524.

18. A. al-Maududi, *The Economic Problem of Man and Its Islamic Solution*, pp. 33–37.
19. Ibid., p. 38.
20. S. Qutb, *Fi zilal al-Qur'an*, pp. 1866, 3514–3515.
21. A. al-Maududi, *Bayan al-da'wa al-qawmiyya wa al-rabita al-islamiyya* (The Nationalist Creed and the Islamic Bond) (Cairo: Dar al-Ansar, 1967), pp. 9–38.
22. S. Qutb, *Fi zilal al-Qur'an*, pp. 1441, 1886–1889.
23. Ibid., pp. 511–512.
24. Khomeini, *Islam and Revolution*, p. 332.
25. A. al-Maududi, *Al-usus al-akhlaquiyya li al-haraka al-islamiyya* (The Moral Foundation of the Islamic Movement) (Cario: Dar al-Ansar, 1952), pp. 6–18.
26. Ibid., pp. 19–52.
27. A. al-Maududi, *Jihad in Islam* (Lahore: Islamic Publications, Ltd., 1978), pp. 17–18.
28. This account draws on traditional Islamic historiography. It is thus not intended to be a critical account having as its premises more recent scholarly studies.
29. A. Al-Maududi, *Minhaj al-inquilab al-islami* (The Method of Islamic Revolution) (Cairo: Dar al-ansar, 1977), p. 19.
30. S. Qutb, *Fi zilal al-Qur'an*, p. 143.
31. Ibid., pp. 1013–1015, 1129–1130, 1946. For further elaboration, see Y. M. Choueiri, *Islamic Fundamentalism* (London: Pinter Publishers, 1992), pp. 125–140.
32. S. Qutb, *Fi zilal al-Qur'an*, pp. 873–874.
33. Ibid., pp. 294, 873–874.
34. Ibid., pp. 873–874.
35. Al-Maududi, *Jihad in Islam*, pp. 16–26; S. Qutb, *Fi Zilal al-Qur'an*, pp. 1429–1469, 1634, 1735.
36. Khomeini, *Islam and Revolution*, passim.

PART THREE

INDIAN POLITICAL THOUGHT

INTRODUCTION

When moving from Islamic civilization to the Indian subcontinent one needs to cross a cultural divide—but a divide which is bridged or rendered passable by a number of historical factors. First of all, due to the prolonged Moghul rule, Islam is also present on the subcontinent. In fact, contemporary India with a total population of about 1.2 billion is home to a larger number of Muslims (about 120 million) than most Muslim countries in the Middle East. Secondly, there is a linguistic bridge. Classical Indian language, called Sanskrit, belongs to the family of Indo-European languages and thus has a distinct affinity with classical Greek. Several idioms in Northern India today are actually derived from Sanskrit. Finally, there is the religious or spiritual factor. In many ways, the ancient Vedic pantheon resembles aspects of the Greek and Roman pantheon—although Vedic deities are distinguished by an unusual spiritual or metaphysical depth. This latter feature also plays a role in the later flourishing of Indian mysticism and mystical poetry—something which is only rarely matched in medieval European culture.

From a present-day perspective, India is often extolled—and not without good reason—as the largest or most populous functioning democracy. In a country of that size, democratic government—with all its shortcomings—is indeed a remarkable accomplishment, something which people around the world can study for benefit. During her long history, India has only experienced short periods of despotic or tyrannical rule; most of the time, political rule—both Hindu and Muslim—has tended to be moderate and benign (though often inefficient). From a contemporary angle, modern India also stands out for another reason: its practice of "muticultural-ism" on a large scale, long before that term became popular in the West. Despite some two dozen major languages and a large panoply of ethnic and religious group-ings, the subcontinent was only rarely the scene of religious warfare or attempts at ethnic cleansing. Only in recent times, largely due to the prodding of demagogues and extremist political leaders, there have been outbursts of interethnic and interre-ligious conflicts. However, the legacy of the great Mahatma Gandhi—leader of the Indian independence movement—stands as an indictment of such derailments.

To some extent, multiculturalism derives from a series of early migrations into the subcontinent and the subsequent amalgamation of the indigenous and the migrant populations. A major group of migrants was an Indo-European tribe that called itself "Aryans" (the Noble Ones). When entering the subcontinent, the Aryans discovered an indigenous culture, which is often called "Harappan" or "Dravidian" culture and which formed the core of a larger Indus Valley civilization (3000–1500 B.C.). As anthropology teaches, that culture was quite complex, displaying urban develop-ment, commercial activities, and an idiographic script. Some of the Harappan deities seem later to have been incorporated into the Hindu pantheon. The relation between Aryans and Dravidians was initially marked by tension; however, over time an amal-gamation or syncretism developed (again like in England).

The migrant people entering India brought with them a rich culture, apparently drawing on a common pool of Indo-European ideas and mythologies. In the religious or spiritual domain, Aryan sages wrote a number of scared texts, the so-called *Vedas* (meaning sacred teachings), which later became the foundation of "Hinduism" or Hindu religion (which is also called *sanātana dharma* or "eternal religion"). Politically, the emerging Hindu culture was fragmented into hundreds of kingdoms or principalities, resembling sometimes Greek city states. In semi-Platonic fashion, the states were divided into four castes or classes (*varnas*): priests and learned sages (*brahmins*, sometimes spelled *brahmans*); warriors and political officers (*kshatriyas*); merchants and farmers (*vaishyas*); and workers and servants (*shudras*). A fifth group outside these castes were the untouchables (*pariahs*). The learned scholars during that time wrote law codes, of which the "Laws of Manu" are the most famous. They also composed treatises (*shastras*, sometimes transcribed as *sastras*) on ethical conduct (*dharmashastras*) and on politics and policy-making (*arthashastras*). The basic point of these books was that politics and the pursuit of political power should always be in harmony with ethical principles. In this respect the scholars simply repeated or reinforced the central Hindu teachings about the four so-called "goals of life" (*purusharthas*): pleasure (*kama*), worldly success (*artha*), ethical duty (*dharma*), and salvation/liberation (*moksha*)—goals that were meant to be in basic harmony and could only be so if duty and salvation retained their guiding role.[1]

The Hindu culture of the Vedic Age presents the picture of a complex organic whole whose different components all uphold or supplement each other. The question remained, however: What lies behind these visible components? What is the inner well-spring that pervades and gives meaning to the organism? This question was addressed by post-Vedic sages in a series of writings called *Upanishads* (meaning: "sit down here beside me"; teacher to student). In these texts the sages reveal the deeper spirit inhabiting the universe, a spirit dwelling in all elements, but not identical with any: the *brahman*. The meaning of this idea was further spelled out in other writings like *Brahmanas* (about rituals) and *Aranyakas* (forest teachings). A major text in this literature, but of somewhat later date, is the "gospel" of Hinduism: the *Bhagavad Gita* ("Song of the Blessed Lord"). The post-Vedic period also witnessed some radical challenges to the Hindu organic order, challenges proceeding from a trans-organic and non-hierarchical worldview. The two most prominent names associated with these challenges are Gautama Buddha (563–480 B.C.) and Mahavira (about 550–475 B.C.), the founder of Jainism. Politically, the period saw the continued flourishing of many Hindu kingdoms and also the emergence of the so-called Mauryan Empire around Pataliputra (modern Patna), an empire in which later on the Buddhist Emperor Ashoka (269–232 B.C.) became the most famous ruler, distinguished by his edicts against violence and ecological destruction. It is also during this period that one of the most well-known political treatises was composed: the *Arthashastra* of Kautilya (who is sometimes identified with Chanakya, a chief minister during the early time of the Mauryan dynasty).

In his essay, "Some Reflections on the Hindu Tradition of Political Thought," Bhikhu Parekh comments on the centrality of the concepts of duty or virtue (*dharma*) and political power (*danda*) in traditional Hindu thought. To sort out the proper relation between these concepts was the chief aim of the great treatises of the time: the *dharmashastras* and *arthashastras* (the latter also called *dandaniti* referring to the science of politics). As Parekh shows, the relation between *dharma* and *danda* corresponded to the respective leadership roles of *brahmins* and *kshatriyas* in the Hindu kingdoms of the time. Parekh also reflects on the meaning and origin of duty or virtue.

As he points out, the social *dharma* reflected the principles of an ordered cosmos (governed by *Rta*). Social *dharma* was differentiated in accordance with castes (*varnas*) and life stages (*ashramas*). The concrete content of *dharma* was spelled out in *shastras*, in traditional customs (*vyavāhara*), precedents, and royal edicts (*rājasasana*). The rise of Buddhism, he notes, had religious as well as political consequences. Politically, Buddhists rejected the Hindu caste system; hence, Buddhist regimes eliminated or reduced the influence of *brahmins* and *kshatriyas* and relied on a broad alliance of groups (mainly *vaishyas*), leaving unspecified the role of Buddhist monks. By way of conclusion, Parekh lists some general features of traditional Hindu political thought: its inegalitarian bias; its pluralist or multicultural character; and its basic conservatism (making it necessary for Buddha and Mahavira to exit from, rather than transform the system).[2]

In the following essay, "Of *Artha* and *Arthashastra*," K. J. Shah discusses in detail the place of *artha* and the *arthashastras* both in the Hindu "goals of life" and in the Hindu system of sciences or fields of learning. In the latter respect, four main types of knowledge were recognized: religious knowledge (*trayi*, relating to the Vedas); philosophy (*darshana* or *anviksiki*); economics (*vartta*); and political science (*arthashastra* or *dandaniti*). The four sciences were thought to be interrelated hierarchically in the same way as the four goals of life (to which they correspond). According to Shah, *artha* (pursuit of success or power) would not be legitimate unless it is in accord with *kama*, *dharma*, and *moksha*. In his reading, Kautilya's *Arthashastra* is basically in agreement with this hierarchical structure (despite some concessions to "realpolitik"): In order to be legitimate, politics and the policies of political regimes have to be in harmony with the precepts of *dharma*. In the words of Kautilya (resonating closely with the teachings of Aristotle): "In the happiness of the subjects lies the happiness of the king and in what is beneficial to the subjects, his own benefit." To achieve this caring or unselfish attitude, Kautilya stressed the importance of royal education along two lines: training in the four sciences and training in practical self-control. Comparing classical Indian with modern Western thought, Shah raises the question of individual rights as a possibly "missing concept" in classical times. As he notes, Indian governments in those times were basically limited by the virtue of rulers and social customs; hence, there was less need for a special protection of individual rights. It is mainly the atrophy of virtue and customary restrictions that dictates in modernity this special protection.

The Vedic Age and the post-Vedic era were followed by a long period witnessing the spreading and deepening of popular Hinduism (about 200 B.C. to 1200 A.D.). Elaborate stories or narratives (*puranas*) were written about all the various deities of the Hindu pantheon. At the same time, there was a growth of mystical or inner-directed faith (*bhakti*) and of religious poetry. On the more rational-intellectual level, the period saw the emergence of a number of major philosophical schools or perspectives (*darshanas*) such as Vedanta (based on the *Vedas* and *Upanishads*); empiricism (*vaishesika*); logic (*nyaya*); and interpretation theory (*mimamsa* and *purva-mimamsa*). Politically, the postclassical age was marked by the flourishing of medium to large-size kingdoms in the North (Gupta kingdom, 320–450 A.D.) and the South (Chola kingdom, 800–1250 A.D.). The political theory informing these regimes continued to be the one outlined in the earlier *dharmashastras* and *arthashastras*.

Starting in the thirteenth century, Muslim rulers began to invade northern India, coming from what later would be called Turkey and Afghanistan. One larger force of invaders succeeded in establishing a Sultanate in Delhi (around 1250–1526 A.D.) patterned along the lines of the earlier regional dynasties. Confined strictly to the North, the Sultanate did not impede the strong survival of Hinduism in South India where some of the most spectacular temples or temple cities were built during this time (e.g., Madurai, Rameshwaram, Konarak, and Khajurao). Muslim rule in Delhi was followed by the more powerful and expansive Moghul Empire (1526–1858 A.D.) discussed earlier. Again, despite the massive Muslim presence in the North, some Hindu kingdoms survived in the South and occasionally led forays against the Muslim rulers. One particularly noteworthy example was the Maratha kingdom in the state of Maharashtra, led by the warrior hero Sivaji. Around 1500 A.D., European colonial and imperialist ambitions began to put pressure on the subcontinent. In 1498 A.D., Vasco da Gama landed in Calicut in the South, and soon afterwards the Portuguese established a foothold in Goa. Similar advances were made by the French and the British. By 1619 A.D., the British East India Company (created shortly before) had carved out trading posts in India. Over the next century and a half, trading centers mushroomed into a vast network of commercial and political influence, with the result that the East India Company developed into a kind of "shadow government" behind the steadily weakening Moghul façade. By 1828 the British Parliament formally began legislating for India, and in 1858, following the Sepoy Mutiny, the Indian subcontinent became part of the British Empire (the "jewel in the crown").

The steady advances of European powers and ultimate take-over of the subcontinent by Britain triggered profound reactions among Indian intellectuals and the Indian population at large. The presence of foreign colonial powers aroused nationalist sentiments and political self-awareness to an extent that the earlier Muslim invasions had not been able to produce. As in the case of the Islamic civilization, the reaction to the European challenge took mainly three forms: rejection or nationalist extremism; assimilation or radical modernism; and compromise or moderate reformism. As long as the Europeans relied mostly on military force, rejection and violent opposition were often the strategy adopted by local Indian rulers. However, once the Europeans relied more heavily on educational and administrative changes, moderate reformism became the preferred option among many Indian elites. In many ways similar to the Muslim *salafiyya*, Hindu reformism—often called "Hindu Renaissance"—sought to adopt the best innovations the West had to offer while combining them with the best Indian traditions and customs.

The leading Hindu reformer during the early nineteenth century was Raja Rammohun Roy (1774–1833), a distinguished scholar from Bengal who knew Indian and Western modern languages in addition to Arabic, Persian, Hebrew, and Greek. In 1828 Roy founded the *Brahmo Samaj* (Brahman Association), which aimed to combine the universalist teachings of the *Upanishads* (the unity of *brahman*) with the progressive rational and scientific ideas of the modern West. He and his associates worked for the strengthening of popular education, the reduction of caste differences and the abolition of *sati* (widow burning). His initiative was continued by Devandranath Tagore (1817–1905) and also the latter's son, the great poet and Nobel laureate Rabindranath Tagore (1861–1941). In his essay "The Socio-Religious and Political Thought of Rammohun Roy," Thomas Pantham comments on Roy's vast erudition and familiarity with sacred and secular literatures of East and West, an erudition which prompted Tagore to call him the "inaugurator of the modern age in India" and C. F. Andrews to celebrate him as the "pioneer of the whole world movement." The accent of Pantham's essay is on Rammohun's effort to instigate religious and social reform in India, without lapsing into either a worship of the modern West or a nostalgic hankering for the past. In essence, his reformism pointed toward a kind of religious "unitarianism" (in conformity with the world spirit announced in the *Upanishads*). Economically, he favored a modified liberal trade policy while, politically, he advocated the introduction in India of a balanced constitutional system patterned loosely on the British model.

Slightly more traditionalist in outlook was another reformist movement, the *Arya Samaj* founded in 1875 by Swami Dayanand Saraswati (1824–1883). Instead of just harking back to the *Upanishads*, this society sought to revive the older teachings of the *Vedas*, while also advocating educational reform, social welfare programs, and the reduction of caste differences. More loosely affiliated with the reform agenda was the neo-*bhakti* movement in India, which concentrated less on scholarship and intellectual training than on concrete devotion and social practice. A leading figure in this movement was Ramakrishna Paramahamsa (1834–1886) who aimed to reconcile popular polytheism with the belief in one God present in all religions. His most famous disciple was Swami Vivekananda (1862–1902), a proponent of the doctrine of "Advaita Vedanta" (non-dualism) or divine immanence in the world (deriving from the great Indian philosopher Shankara). Vivekananda founded many "Ramakrishna missions" devoted to the uplifting of the poor and low-castes and to social welfare programs. His dream was to create "a European society with India's religion" or spirituality.

The Hindu reform movement got caught up in the struggle for independence from Britain, which saddled it with a complicated task: the task of seeking to remove foreign rule while simultaneously not rejecting all European imports. As the struggle went on, reformism was increasingly challenged or contested by radical traditionalists or "rejectionists" who in due course morphed into defenders of Hindu nationalist extremism. One of the founders of this outlook was Raja Radhakanta Deb (1784–1867); he was later followed by V. D. Savarkar (1883–1966), promoter of the ideology of "Hindutva" (India for Hindus), and M. S. Gowalkar, organizer of paramilitary bands. In the political domain, reformers in 1885 founded a political party called Indian National Congress designed to be a broad rallying force and principal agent in the transition from British to Indian self-rule. However, the Congress soon split into a "moderate" and a more "extremist" wing. Among moderate reformist leaders were Dadabhai Naoroji (1825–1917), Mahadev Govind Ranade (1842–1901), and Gopal Krishna Gokhale (1866–1915). Prominent among the more "extremist" politicians were Bal Gangadar Tilak (1856–1920) called the "father of Indian unrest"; the "mystic" patriot Aurobindo Ghose (1872–1950); and the "lion of the Punjab" Lajpat Rai (1865–1928). The situation was further complicated by the creation of the Muslim League in 1906 as a competitor to the National Congress. Alongside moderate reformers and rejectionists there was always a wing of "modernists" composed of secular humanists, liberals, and socialists. Among the latter one may mention Narendranath Bhattacharya (1887–1954), Jayaprakash Narayan (1902–1979), and above all Jawaharlal Nehru (1889–1964), the first prime minister of independent India.

Throughout the turbulent decades of the struggle for independence, a stabilizing loadstar was the work of Mohandas Gandhi (1869–1948), variously described as a reformer or moderate traditionalist. Gandhi drew his inspiration from classical Hindu scriptures, especially the *Bhagavad Gita*, as well as scriptures from other religions; at the same time, he was closely familiar with modern Western thought and modes of life, having studied law in London for three years. His initial political awakening occurred in South Africa where he experienced apartheid policies first hand. In 1894 he founded the Natal Indian Congress Party (a replica of the Congress Party in India). A few years later he started his unique political strategy of nonviolent resistance or *satyagraha* (meaning a force or struggle dedicated to truth). In 1909 he wrote his book *Hind Swaraj* (Indian Homerule), which presented a strong critique of Western political practices and a roadmap for the achievement of Indian independence. On his return to India in 1915, he was greeted by Rabindanath Tagore as "Mahatma" (great-souled person) and began advocating nonviolence (*ahimsa*) and home-grown industries (*khadi, swadeshi*). In 1922 he started a noncooperation campaign and in 1930 he led a large mass of people to the sea in protest of the British salt tax. Like Nelson Mandela later, Gandhi spent several years in jail. In 1940 he launched a *satyagraha* against the war and two years later a "Quit India" campaign. Having struggled throughout his life for harmony between Hindus, Muslims, and other groups, he was devastated when the British in June of 1947 announced the plan to "partition" India, a plan which led to large-scale massacres and which he deplored as "a spiritual tragedy." On January 30, 1948 he was assassinated by a Hindu extremist and follower of the doctrine of "Hindutva."[3]

One of the leading experts on modern and contemporary Indian political thought is Anthony Parel. In his essay titled "Gandhi and the Emergence of the Modern Indian Political Canon," Parel presents Gandhi as a moderate reformer who tried to combine the best features of the Indian tradition with the best features of modernity. As he points out, classical or traditional India subscribed to a set of political ideas—a political "canon"—which lasted for over a millennium. Among these ideas were the attachment to monarchy and to a hierarchical order of society (based on castes), the endorsement of four basic "goals of life" (*purusharthas*) and the cultivation of a number of sciences corresponding to these goals. Western colonialism and the rise of modern culture put pressure on, and nearly extinguished, this canon. It was Gandhi's great accomplishment to foster the rise of a balanced new political outlook. From the past he retained chiefly the notion of diverse goals of life and the cultivation of different forms of knowledge. What he rejected in the classical tradition were the primacy granted to monarchy and the hierarchical structure of the caste system. In lieu of these features, Gandhi introduced four basic new ideas or principles: the idea of civic nationalism, the principle of constitutional government, the respect for human rights, and the practice of a modern, but ethically guided market economy. Summing up all these changes, Parel credits Gandhi with nothing less than the inauguration of a new political canon, a new kind of *arthashastra* combining or reconciling tradition and modernity.

This essay can usefully be compared with another paper authored by Parel titled "Mahatma Gandhi's Critique of Modernity" (not included in this volume).[4] The paper portrays Gandhi as a critic of certain excesses of Western modernity, but not as a radical antimodernist (or "rejectionist")—hence basically again as a reformer. Relying in part on *Hind Swaraj* (Indian Homerule), Parel shows that modern Western civilization for Gandhi was in many respects flawed or tarnished but "not an incurable disease"; it could be corrected through self-reform and self-control (*swaraj*) and the struggle for truth and justice (*satyagraha*). With particular reference to modern democracy, Parel's argument is supported and fleshed out in a paper by Ronald Terchek titled "Gandhi and Democratic Theory" (not included in this volume).[5] As Terchek points out, democracy for Gandhi meant not just a set of procedural rules but a substantive-ethical regime presupposing the capacity for moral self-rule; moreover, it had to be built from the ground up, that is, from the level of villages and village councils (*panchayat*). According to Terchek, Gandhian democracy rests on four philosophical pillars: nonviolence (*ahimsa*) directed against both personal and structural violence; search for truth (*satya*), which requires dialogue and the virtue of tolerance or mutual recognition; individual freedom, but a freedom governed not solely by self-interest but by duty (*dharma*) and responsibility; and equality, meaning equality of citizenship, of labor, and of the ability to satisfy basic needs. With its distinction between selfish interests and basic needs, between base desires and ethical strivings, Gandhian democracy (Terchek notes) harkens back to the classical republican tradition of Cicero, Harrington, Montesquieu (and perhaps Jefferson)—a tradition which can serve as a corrective to the contemporary Western model.

Directly opposed to the tolerant and pluralist outlook of Gandhian reformism stands the tradition of nationalist extremism or Hindu "fundamentalism." In an essay titled "The Ideology of Hindu Nationalism" (not included in this volume), Prabha Dixit outlines the background and central teachings of this tradition.[6] As Dixit points out, a major catalyst prompting the rise of Hindu extremism was the partition of Bengal decreed by the British government in 1905 (in accordance with the policy of "divide and conquer"). As a result, even formerly moderate Hindus were radicalized and began to sponsor "fundamentalist" policies; this was true of Bal Gangadar Tilak, Aurobindo Ghose, and Lajpat Rai (all mentioned before). Some of the Hindu nationalists began to advocate the conversion of Muslims to Hinduism (possibly by force); but, in a more reformist spirit, they also favored the "purification" (*shruddhi*) of low-caste Hindus to create a more unified community. As the struggle for independence intensified, Hindu nationalism expanded and became more solidified—as manifest in the growth of the "All-India Hindu Mahasabha" (great council) during the 1930s. Dixit discusses in some detail the life and activities of extremist Hindu leaders, especially V. D. Savarkar and M. S. Gowalkar. Relatively more moderate, Savarkar's program of "Hindutva" promised some protection to non-Hindu minorities. Somewhat ambivalent about British rule, his teachings failed to gain mass appeal. Anxious to attract popular support, Gowalkar embarked on a more radical policy. In 1947 he founded a "Hindu volunteer corps" (*Rashtriya Swayansevak Sangh* [RSS]) dedicated to the transformation of the secular state of India into a Hindu state (a parallel to "Islamic" republics). He also sponsored socially reactionary policies, such as the maintenance of the caste system (minus untouchability) and the substitution of elite control for democratic procedures.

Among Indian secularists or modernizers it is customary to give pride of place to Jawaharlal Nehru—although as a friend and associate of Gandhi, he was far from being a radical modernist or a despiser of Indian traditions. He was the son of Motilal Nehru, a "moderate" in the Indian National Congress, and throughout his life he followed in his father's footsteps (though with more Western leanings). In his essay "The Political Ideas of Jawaharlal Nehru," (reprinted below), R. C. Pillai discusses Nehru's life story and political commitments. He was almost entirely Western-educated, first at Harrow and later in Cambridge and London (where he received his law degree). During these years, he became imbued with modern Western trends and ideologies, such as secularism, liberalism, nationalism, and socialism. More than anything else he was dedicated to nation-building (paralleling the ongoing nation-building in the Muslim world). He served repeatedly as president of the Indian National Congress and, after independence, became India's first prime minister for several terms (1947–1964). Pillai examines in detail Nehru's various ideological commitments: his secular liberalism with its emphasis on rationality and scientific progress; his socialism that first took the form of a slow-paced "Fabianism" and later of a more robust democratic socialism; and his nationalism involving struggle for *swaraj* and against imperialism. In the economic domain, Nehru promoted a "mixed economy" as an alternative to capitalism and communism and later spearheaded several five-year plans. At the meeting of the Congress in 1931 he defended the privatization of religion and the neutrality of the state vis-à-vis all faiths. Under his guidance, the Indian Constitution of 1950 included a charter of individual rights, including freedom of religion. Internationally, he pursued as prime minister a policy of nonalignment and the goal of peace under the umbrella of an international world federation.

As a strongly modernizing reformer Nehru left his deep imprint on India. Two years after his death, he was followed as prime minister by his daughter Indira Gandhi who, for many years, sought to continue her father's middle-of-the-road and nonalignment policies. However, like in the Muslim world, ideological tensions soon began to assume center-stage and to divide the country into warring camps. Very disturbing and unsettling was the upsurge of Hindu extremism under a new nationalist party (*Bharatya Janata* Party). This upsurge threatened to upset the delicate constitutional balance engineered by Nehru and his fellow nation-builders. Alarmed by the new (right wing) orientation—as well as disillusioned by corruption in the Congress Party—new left-leaning parties emerged with more radical progressive ideas. In the midst of the brewing conflict, Indira Gandhi in 1975 declared a state of emergency and suspended civil liberties—an action that triggered her downfall two years later. She managed to get reelected in 1980, but was assassinated in October 1984, to be followed by her son Rajiv Gandhi who took over as prime minister after Indira Gandhi's death. Although defeated in 1989, Rajiv Gandhi attempted a comeback in 1991, but was in turn assassinated during the election campaign (which the Congress Party actually won). In the meantime India has experienced rapid economic and industrial progress, and has embarked on strong modernizing agendas in many areas. What still needs to be achieved or recovered is the sense of balance and good judgment, which prevailed during the struggle for, and early decades of, independence. More importantly, advances in material well-being are of little lasting avail unless they are accompanied by the cultivation of ethics (*dharma*), nonviolence (*ahimsa*), and self-rule as self-discipline (*swaraj*)—as Gandhi had taught.

NOTES

1. For a detailed discussion of the "goals of life" in relation to Gandhi's practices see Anthony J. Parel, *Gandhi's Philosophy and the Quest for Harmony* (Cambridge, UK: Cambridge University Press, 2006).
2. Regarding the inegalitarian or hierchical character of traditional Indian culture, the leading work to be consulted is Louis Dumont, *Homo Hierarchicus* (Chicago, IL: University of Chicago Press, 1980).
3. As Albert Einstein is reported to have said: Generations to come "will scarcely believe that such a one as this, ever in flesh and blood, walked upon this earth."
4. Anthony Parel, "Mahatma Ganhi's Critique of Modernity," in Parel and Ronald C. Keith, eds., *Comparative Political Philosophy: Studies Under the Upas Tree*, 2nd ed. (Lanham, MD: Lexington Books, 2003), pp. 163–183.
5. Ronald J. Terchek, "Gandhi and Democratic Theory," in Thomas Pantham and Kenneth L. Deutsch, eds., *Political Thought in Modern India* (New Delhi: Sage Publications, 1986), pp. 307–324. A similar argument has been presented by Indian political theorist Thomas Pantham in his essay "Beyond Liberal Democracy: Thinking with Mahatma Gandhi" in the same volume, pp. 325–346. Pantham stresses as central components of Gandhian democracy such ideas as integral self-rule (*purna swaraj*), ethical governance (*ramaraja*), and social order promoting the common good (*sarvodaya*). Additional features are the "trusteeship" notion of property, the notion of participatory democracy (through *satyagraha*), and the role of education in promoting ethical maturation.
6. Prabha Dixit, "The Ideology of Hindu Nationalism," in Pantham and Deutsch, eds., *Political Thought in Modern India*, pp. 122–141.

SOME REFLECTIONS ON THE HINDU
TRADITION OF POLITICAL THOUGHT*

Bhikhu Parekh

In this chapter, I will examine critically some of the distinctive features of the Hindu tradition of political thought. To avoid misunderstanding, it would be useful to begin by clarifying four points. First, as it forms a relatively coherent and analytically convenient subject of investigation, I shall concentrate on the Hindu tradition from its early Vedic beginnings to the arrival of the Muslims in the eight century A.D. and shall ignore its subsequent development altogether.

Second, I shall not summarize the ideas of individual Hindu political thinkers, but only explore the basic framework within which they thought about politics. India was subjected to several foreign invasions and experienced several social and economic changes during the period in question. In response to these, Hindu political thinkers of different periods had to deal with different problems and approach familiar problems from different angles. Despite these developments, however, their basic framework of thought—that is, their basic concepts, concerns, and problems— retained a remarkable continuity. It is in this sense that one can legitimately talk about the Hindu *tradition* of political thought.

Third, I shall use the term "politics" and its derivatives rather widely to refer to the affairs of a territorially organized community held together by allegiance to a common authority. And, finally, I am concerned here with examining not the inarticulate beliefs and assumptions underlying and informing Hindu political institutions and practices, but rather the body of ideas Hindu political thinkers developed in their systematic treatises on politics.

Hindu political thinkers conceptualized political life in terms of two central concepts, namely, *danda* and *dharma*. For them, political life or ruling a territorially organized community ultimately consisted in using *danda* to maintain *dharma*. The term *danda* means discipline, force, restraint, constraint, or punishment. Hindu political writers generally used it to refer to the punitive use of the coercive power of government. *Dharma* is a much more difficult concept. It comes from the Sanskrit root *dhr*, meaning to hold. *Dharma* is that which holds a society together. Since the Hindus thought a society was held together by each individual and group doing his or its specific duties, they used the term to mean duties. Some writers used it broadly to mean all duties, whereas others confined it to religious or religiously prescribed duties.

I

Hindu political thinkers described the systematic study of political life as *niti* or, more commonly *sastra*. *Niti*, which comes from the Sanskrit word meaning "to lead," refers to a study of policies. Thus *dandaniti*, a term sometimes used to describe a systematic study of political life, means a study of the best ways of using the coercive power of government. The term *sastra* means a systematic study of the general principles and detailed organization of a specific form of human activity. Thus *dharmasastra* refers to a systematic treatise on the general principles and detailed content of righteous conduct. Sometimes the term *sastra* [or *shastra*] is given the additional connotation of an authoritative text, and the principles and rules laid down in a treatise are given the status of injunctions. Thus the principles and rules of *dharmasastras* are not merely analytical and elucidatory but also authoritative and binding in nature. This additional connotation, however, is absent in other usages of the term. Thus the principles laid down in Bharat's *Natyasastra* and Kautilya's *Arthasastra* are largely elucidatory and, at best, recommendatory.

As we saw, the Hindu political thinkers regarded *dharma* and *danda* as the two most basic features of political life. Although the two features were accepted by them as complementary, different Hindu writers chose to concentrate on one or the other and explored political life in terms of it, thereby giving rise to two different trends or strands of political thought. The *dharmasastra* writers concentrated on exploring the *dharma* of individuals and social groups, including the government. They discussed the sources of *dharma* as well as what was to be done when these conflicted. And they also provided a detailed prospectus of duties. They were not moral philosophers but law-givers, and generally didactic and prescriptive. Since they did not concentrate on the government and attempted to provide a code of conduct covering the entire human life, they did not write books specifically on politics. Political *dharma* was incidental to their main concern and did not form a distinct and autonomous subject of investigation.

In contrast to *dharmasastra* writers, the authors of *arthasastra* were interested in the organization and mechanics of *danda*, that is, the way the government, the agent of *danda*, could be most effectively organized. They concentrated on the nature and organization of government, the nature and mechanics of power, the way power is acquired, weakened and lost, the sources of threat to government and the best way to deal with them, and so on. Since the *arthasastra* writers were primarily concerned with the government, their works were specifically political. Further, since they concentrated on the government, they appreciated the autonomy of political life and its distinctive problems to a much greater degree than the authors of *dharmasastras*.

It would, however, be a mistake to draw too neat a contrast between the two strands of Hindu political thought. It is true that the authors of *dharmasastras* were rather moralistic, and those of *arthasastras* realistic to the point of sometimes bordering on cynicism. However, the former were not politically naive and freely acknowledged the political need to disregard moral principles and values under certain circumstances, even as the *arthasastra* writers acknowledged and indeed insisted on the observance of *dharma*. Again, it is true that the *dharmasastra* writers occasionally ignored the contingencies and frailties of human affairs; however, they were not nervous about the need to use force. Similarly, although the *arthasastra* writers occasionally tended to treat political power as an end-in-itself, they did not generally lose sight of the moral ends of government. It would also be wrong to suggest, as is sometimes done, that the two approaches represent totally different views of man and society for, as we shall see, their views on these subjects were basically the same.

The two approaches differed primarily in their subject matter, one choosing to explore political life from the standpoint of *dharma*, the other from that of *danda*. This naturally led to differences in emphasis and orientation. Since the *dharmasastras* were concerned to lay down *dharma*, they were legalistic and religious in orientation, whereas the *arthasastras*, concerned with analyzing the structure and functions of government, concentrated on institutions and policies and were secular in orientation. Neither approach was complete by itself, and this was fully appreciated by its followers. The two together constitute the Hindu tradition of political thought. The commentators who equate it with one of them and contend that it is either wholly moralistic or wholly cynical, or either legalistic or institutional, offer a distorted account of it.

II

The Hindu tradition of political thought displays remarkable continuity. It did, of course, undergo important changes in response to new theoretical and practical problems posed by the rise of new religious movements (especially Buddhism), new philosophical movements (especially the *Lokayata*), new castes, guilds and corporations, waves of foreign invasions, settlements of foreigners, and so on. Amidst all these changes, however, its basic theoretical concerns remained more or less constant.

For the Hindu political thinkers the universe is an ordered whole governed by fixed laws. It is characterized by *Rta*, the inviolable order of things. Society replicates the order of the universe and becomes an ordered whole when held together by *dharma*. For the Hindus, society is not a collection of individuals but a community of communities. It consists of castes, each of which is engaged in the performance of certain common functions and is related to the others in a hierarchical manner. Its characteristic functions and place in the social hierarchy define the perimeter of its *dharma*. An individual's *dharma* is derived from the caste of his birth. For the Hindu, an individual's birth into a particular caste is not accidental but a result of his *karma* or actions in his previous life. *Dharma* and *karma* are integrally connected. An individual's *karma* determines his caste, and therefore his *dharma*, and his *dharma* defines his rightful *karma*. In addition to caste, an individual also occupies other social positions. He is a father or a son, a husband, a brother, an uncle or a nephew, a cousin, a neighbor, a subject or a ruler, and so on. As an incumbent of each of these roles, he has a specific *dharma*. The Hindu writers divided man's life into four distinct chronological stages or *āshrams*, and each stage was again characterized by a specific *dharma*.

For the Hindu writers, *dharma* is the basis of personal and social life. It alone holds society together; violation of *dharma* shakes the society to its very foundations and constitutes a mortal threat to its existence. As was to be expected in a society under constant foreign invasion and based on domination by the two highest castes, the Hindu thinkers were most fearful of social disintegration. Accordingly they laid down detailed rules governing almost every aspect of human conduct and insisted that any deviation from them spelt disorder and chaos. Every Hindu was to adhere strictly to the *dharma* of his specific stage in life, his specific social positions and roles, and above all his caste. Doing things that pertain to another caste is *adharma* or immoral. The *Gita* observes that an individual who disregards *svadharma* courts unhappiness and destruction; and it is better to die doing one's *dharma* than to attempt to perform someone else's. According to Hindu law-givers, whoever deviates from his caste duties runs the risk of forfeiting his social status; he may be made an outcaste and deprived of his right to follow certain types of occupations.

According to Hindu political thinkers, each individual does his *dharma* in an ideal society. There is, therefore, no disorder, and hence no need for *danda* or force, and obviously no need for government. For some Hindu thinkers men were once in such a state; for others they have always had refractory impulses; for yet others human history is cyclical in nature and characterized by a regular and inexorable alteration of four distinct epochs representing different degrees of human corruption. In any case, once men become corrupt and incapable of *swaraj* or self-rule, they begin to ignore their *dharma*. This results in *varnasankara* or "confusion of castes," *arajakata* or lawlessness, *matsyanyaya* or the law of the sea (the Hindu equivalent of the Western law of jungle) according to which the big fish eat the small, and the eventual disintegration of the social order. For some Hindu political thinkers, such a situation did once prevail; for others it is only a definite possibility haunting every society. In any case, it must at all cost be remedied or avoided, and hence the institution of government becomes necessary. Although Hindu thinkers were familiar with the republican and other non-monarchical forms of governments, they concentrated on monarchy.

The king's main function was to maintain the established social order. Since a society was believed to remain well-ordered only so long as each individual observed his personal and caste *dharma*, the king's *dharma* consisted in maintaining the rule of *dharma* in society at large. In concrete terms, this meant that he was to facilitate the study of the *Vedas* and philosophy, encourage the development of industry and commerce, maintain proper relations between different castes, ensure the observance of parental, filial, matrimonial and other duties, enforce *dharma* pertaining to different stages of individual life, and so on. The king derived his authority from the fact that he needed it to maintain *dharma*. He was, therefore, to use it only for that purpose and in a manner consistent with it. If he used it for other purposes, or to enforce *adharma*, or in a manner disallowed by *dharma*, he was considered a tyrant. Some Hindu thinkers urged that a tyrant should be disobeyed, and even killed. Some others authorized disobedience only if led by "respectable" men of "status," while others proscribed it altogether.

The king's duty to enforce *dharma* raised the obvious question as to who determined the content of it. The Hindu writers generally pointed to the *Vedas*, the *smritis* and *vyavahāra*. The *Vedas* were not moral treatises, and such moral principles as they contained were highly general. The *smritis* were largely digests of prevailing social practices. And thus *vyavahāra* or custom was the operative source of *dharma*. Each caste had been in existence for a long time and had acquired a specific body of traditions and usages. So long as they were not in conflict with Vedic injunctions, they constituted its *dharma*. Similarly, each family had developed a body of usages over time, and these constituted its members' *kuladharma*. From time to time the Hindu law-givers made a study of the traditions and usages of different social groups and wrote detailed digests.

Over centuries, the social and political structure of India underwent important changes and many different types of social groups began to appear. In the aftermath of successive foreign invasions, fairly large communities of foreign settlers came into existence. Heretical groups began to appear within the fold of Hindu society itself. New religious movements and communities—especially the Buddhists and Jains—appeared. With the development of commerce and trade, corporations and guilds of traders, artisans and craftsmen began to appear. New castes came into existence as a result of inter-marriages or new occupations. Large empires (especially those of the Mauryas and the Guptas) appeared on the scene, and they had to rule over far-flung territories within some of which rather different conceptions of caste *dharma* prevailed.

The Hindu writers dealt with the situation in terms of their traditional concept of *dharma*. Even as they had maintained that each caste had its traditional *dharma*, which it had the authority to enforce, the king intervening only when necessary, the Hindu writers argued that the new social groups must be accepted as autonomous and self-governing communities entitled to have their traditions and customs upheld and to make their own rules. Thus the communities of foreign settlers, corporations, religious communities, heretics, even atheists, villages and districts, guilds and new castes, were recognized as having their own distinctive *dharma*, which they were free to enforce on their members and whose legitimacy was accepted by the king. The Vedic injunctions were not binding on those groups that either consisted of non-Hindus or were essentially economic in nature. The Hindu writers realized that the customs and traditions of various groups might be ambiguous, or harm public interest, or remain silent about certain aspects of social conduct. In such cases the king was to make appropriate laws. In short, the Hindu political thinkers broadened their earlier theory and recognized *vyavahāra* (traditions and customs), *caritam* (conduct of good man), and *rajasasan* (royal edicts and civil laws) as the legitimate bases of *dharma*.

The Hindu political thinkers did not invest the ruler with arbitrary and despotic power as the theorists of Oriental Despotism have maintained. They viewed society as an organic structure articulated in terms of social groups. Each group had its own *dharma*, which was not laid down by the ruler and with which the ruler could not generally interfere. Further many of the groups were quite powerful. The castes were strong social groups, enjoying autonomy and their own distinctive structures of authority. Like the castes, many villages too had a long tradition of self-government. And many guilds and corporations consisted of powerful and wealthy men.

The ruler was therefore an integral part of a highly differentiated and uncentralized social order. He did not stand above the social order. He was one of its several parts, albeit an important part, but still only a part. His authority was hedged in by the relatively inviolable authority of the various autonomous centers of power, and regulated by his own specific *dharma*. Since he was never seen as outside of, let alone above society, the very conceptual framework required by the idea of Oriental Despotism was absent. The king did, of course, sometimes misuse his authority and interfered with the private lives of his subjects. However, his authority was considerably limited by the autonomous institutions, which were not his creations and had independent sources of legitimacy, and the rise of trade and commerce from around the third century B.C. meant that the royal monopoly of land was no longer a formidable source of power. Not so much the government as the religiously sanctioned social structure, helped no doubt by the government, was generally the source of oppression in ancient India.

Having briefly discussed *dharma*, we will now turn to the Hindu examination of *danda*. In their exploration of the structure of government, Hindu political writers were guided by certain common considerations. The king's duty to maintain *dharma* meant that he was to rely on the advice of people well-versed in the *Vedas* and the *Sastras*. The Brahmans, therefore, enjoyed considerable power and prestige. Indeed Hindu polities were for centuries based on and run by a "holy" (or unholy?) alliance of the Ksatriyas and the Brahmans. Not surprisingly, almost the entire Hindu tradition of political thought was based on the unquestioned assumption of a close alliance between the two highest castes. It analyzed political life within the framework of the alliance, and rarely ventured to explore alternative modes of constituting the polity.

In India, political power never really shifted from the Brahmans and the Ksatriyas. The two did, of course, initially struggle for supremacy. However, over time, a *modus vivendi* was reached between them. The Brahmans acknowledged the Ksatriyas' right to rule; in return the Ksatriyas acknowledged the Brahmans' social superiority, gave them a share in the exercise of political authority and made generous donations of land and money. The Ksatriyas had the monopoly of state power, the Brahmans that of learning and teaching. The former were to specialize in *danda*, the latter in *dharma*. By and large, the Brahmans were expected not to interfere with the use of *danda*, and the Ksatriyas with the interpretation of *dharma*. The Ksatriya kings upheld the social order that gave the Brahmans moral and religious authority and material wealth; the Brahmans, in turn, used their monopoly of "intellectual production" to produce ideological systems justifying the established political order, including the king's power and wealth. The corporate spirit in each of the two castes was most developed, as also the spirit of identity of interests between them. By contrast, the other castes were too fragmented and isolated to develop such a spirit. The *Vaisyas* and the *Sudras* could never unite, and the *Vaisyas* were too large and their range of occupations too varied to allow them to develop a sense of corporate identity and collective power.

Some Hindu political thinkers distinguished between authority and power. Authority implied an *adhikar*. *Adhikar*, a difficult and complex Hindu concept, meant a deserved right, a right one deserves to possess as judged by established social norms. A ruler acquired *adhikar* to power when he was judged to possess appropriate intellectual and moral qualifications and was duly crowned by the Brahmans in a ceremony known as *abhiseka*. In this ceremony, the Brahmans anointed and blessed him, symbolically raised him to the status of a Brahman and identified him with the territory and its people, and declared him *satyaraja*, a true or rightful king. For most Hindu political thinkers, however, even an usurper acquired authority if he had appropriate qualifications and ruled his kingdom righteously.

Hindu political thinkers were constantly haunted by the fragility of political authority. It could not be based on *dharma* alone, for people's sense of *dharma* is generally weak and ambitious and powerful men would want to plot against the ruler. Nor could it be based on *danda* alone, for fear cannot sustain a society long. Accordingly, Hindu political thinkers insisted that political authority rested on the twin foundations of *dharma* and *danda* (that is, on the popular recognition of the fact that the king was devoted to the maintenance of *dharma* and would not hesitate to use *danda*). They did not say much about the nature and basis of political authority and legitimacy, and devoted considerable attention to political power.

The Hindu political thinkers suggested various ways in which political power could be acquired and maintained. They insisted that the king should be a man of great intellect and character and advocated his rigorous intellectual and moral training. They insisted also on him having reliable and competent counselors and ministers. Most Hindu writers distinguished between *mantrins* and *amatyas*. The former were men of independent social status, attended public functions with the king and acted as his advisors; the latter were executive officers in charge of day-to-day administration. The Hindu political thinkers insisted that since there was nothing more dear to a man than his customs and usages, the king should not generally interfere with them. They also advocated the importance of efficient administration, constant checks on subordinate officials, programs of welfare provision, and so on.

As for the exercise of *danda* and instilling fear in the subjects, the Hindu political writers relied on several devices of which two deserve some attention, namely espionage and punishment. Nearly all of them stressed the need for an all-pervasive network of spies. According to the *Mahabharata*, every kingdom has "its roots in spies and secret agents". Megasthenes found them so numerous that he referred to them as a special class of Hindu society. They were so pervasive and evoked such terror that they were referred to in a Pallava inscription as *Samcarantakas* (moving agents of death).

Kautilya assigned considerable importance to them and indeed thought that their importance was next only to that of the ministers. He offered a detailed description of the cunning ways in which they were to be planted in society and the techniques they were to deploy. They were to go out in such varied disguises as merchants, mendicants, classmates, prisoners, and beggars, and were free to use all kinds of treachery, sacrilege, cruelty, and immoral devices. According to Hindu thinkers, the spies reported to the king the activities of his officers, family members, foreigners, courtesans, and potential troublemakers; they also spread false information and created divisions among the subjects; and they also spied on the private lives of the citizens and reported on the trends in public opinion and feelings.

The Hindu political thinkers were also preoccupied with the possible conflict between *danda* and *dharma*. They knew that the king may sometimes have to be untruthful, cruel, deceitful and so on, and questioned if and how this was justified. They were all convinced that it was justified, largely on the ground that the preservation of society was the highest political value. The preservation of society meant not just the physical security of the subjects but also the maintenance of the social order and the preservation of *dharma*. In the *Mahabharata*, even Krishna, the Lord Himself, tells a few lies and practices deception on a few occasions. These were all justified on the ground that they were required to uphold *dharma*. As far as relations with foreign rulers were concerned, the Hindu writers generally emphasized the considerations of self-interest and saw little reason for moral restraint.

The Hindu tradition of political thought met its most radical critique at the hands of Buddhism. Buddhism was atheistic in the sense that it did not see the need to postulate the existence of God; it denied the divine origin and the authority of the *Vedas*; it rejected the caste system; it admitted women to the religious order; since it had originated under a republican (or rather semi-oligarchical) system of government, it had pronounced quasidemocratic sympathies; it founded monasteries, organized them along the lines of the republican assemblies, and gave India the first experience of organized religion; and so on. More important, Buddhism attracted the loyalty and support of the economically powerful but socially inferior class of traders, cultivators, artisans, merchants and skilled craftsmen. It also welcomed and assimilated such foreign settlers as the Greeks, Shakas, Kushanas, and Huns whom the caste-based Hindu society had kept out of its fold. Buddhism also attracted the Sudras, who could shed their low social status by joining a caste-free religion and improve their material circumstances by escaping the expensive religious rituals required by the Brahmans. Buddhism thus represented a mass movement consisting of the bulk of the Vaisyas, some Sudras, foreigners, women, and the isolated tribal republics that had still managed to survive.

Buddhism developed a new political theory. It advanced a quasicontractualist theory of the origin of the government. It postulated a peaceful and harmonious state of social existence when men had few desires and were at peace with themselves and with their fellowmen. Over time men began to develop limitless wants and desires, and the institutions of private property and family came into being. Disorder and discord set in, and the institution of the government became necessary. People elected one of the "noblest" among them as a ruler and authorized him to rule over the rest. He was to exercise his authority in cooperation with the assembly of people's representatives, who were not generally elected but were heads of noble families and men of status. The Buddhist writers advocated legal and social equality, but did not extend it to the poor, the propertyless and the Sudras. They accepted the Hindu view that the king's principal duty was to maintain *Dhamma*, but rejected its caste-based definition and content. *Dhamma* for them largely meant the basic social morality as expounded by the Buddha. They stressed the autonomy of corporations, guilds and *sanghas* [religious orders], and advocated religious tolerance.

The Buddhist challenge did not, however, lead to a radical reformulation of the Hindu tradition of political thought. The Buddhist political theory was not sufficiently radical and subversive. It continued to share such basic Hindu beliefs as, life is full of sorrow, desires are bad, a man's *karma* in his previous life determines his destiny in this life, and the ruler must maintain *dharma*. Furthermore, while it challenged the power and authority of the Brahmans, it upheld those of the Ksatriyas. Basically, Buddhism attempted to replace the *Ksatriya-Brahman* alliance with the *Ksatriya-Vaisya* alliance under the former's leadership.

Thus it did not involve a radical break with the traditional form of political domination, only its reconstitution. The Buddhists did, of course, challenge some Hindu beliefs, to which the Hindu writers typically responded by accepting some Buddhist criticisms, ignoring some others and putting up a strong defence against the rest. Hence, in response to Buddhist criticisms such Hindu authors of *dharmasastras* (as *Yajnavalkya*, *Narada*, *Brahaspati*, and *Katyayana*) accepted the autonomy of guilds and corporations, recognized *vyavahāra* as a valid source of law, gave the *Vaisyas* a larger share of power, laid greater stress on the importance of *artha*, paid greater attention to the republican institutions than they had done so far, and so on. At the same time, however, the Hindu thinkers rejected the Buddhist criticism of the caste system and advocated an even more rigid version of it. They also took a leaf out of the Buddhist book and relied on the ruler to take an active part in fighting Buddhism and defending the Hindu social order. Naturally, this led them to glorify the role of the government and to invest the ruler with even greater power and majesty than he had enjoyed so far.

I have outlined in the foregoing some of the basic features of the Hindu tradition of political thought. Obviously, a tradition that has developed over several centuries is too rich and complex to permit an easy summary. Our account of the Hindu tradition is, therefore, bound to involve distortions and omissions. It was intended, however, to provide neither a detailed summary of all its ideas, nor an outline of all the important phases in its development, but only to sketch the broad outlines of the general framework of ideas within which the Hindu writers attempted to understand political life.

III

A careful examination of the Hindu tradition of political thought shows that it is distinguished by several important features. It would be useful to briefly spell out some of the more important ones in order that we can grasp its general character.

First, the Hindu tradition is basically inegalitarian. Although it developed the idea of the moral equality of all men, and indeed of all sentient beings, it never developed the idea of social, legal, and political equality. It made caste the basis not only of society but also of the polity, and integrated it into its very structure. As we saw, only the members of higher castes were entitled to the rights of citizenship or to be appointed as royal advisors; different kinds and degrees of punishment were meted out to men of different castes; and so on. In the name of maintaining *dharma*, the Hindu political thinkers subordinated the polity to the demands of a hierarchical social structure. As a result, they were rendered incapable of grasping the polity as a qualitatively different kind of organization from society, and the government as an agent of social change.

Second, the Hindu tradition of political thought is pluralist in orientation. As we saw, the Hindu political writers from the very beginning recognized the autonomy of social groups. Initially, of course, the castes alone enjoyed the autonomy. However, over time, several different types of social groups were recognized as autonomous and self-governing. This had become such a common feature of Hindu life and thought that it must not be regarded as accidental but a matter of deliberate policy growing out of the considerations of not just political expediency but a deeply held moral principle of respect for others. The policy had obvious advantages. It facilitated social harmony, encouraged diversity, developed habits of self-government, allowed the Hindu religion and moral values to survive in the midst of political upheavals, and so on. The policy, however, also had its drawbacks. It did not allow the institution of the state to grow; it left individuals at the mercy of groups, some of which were oligarchically constituted; it allowed so many different systems of law to flourish that a common legal system could not develop; it heightened the judicial role of the government and did not allow it to acquire a major legislative role; and so on.

Third, the Hindu tradition of political thought is largely uncritical and apologetic of the established social order. Most Hindu political thinkers justified (or rather simply took for granted) the caste system, the caste-based conception of *dharma*, the largely fatalist concept of *karma*, the degradation of the Sudras and the slaves, the extensive moral interference of the state, and so on. There were, no doubt, several exceptions, such as the Buddhist, Jain, and Carvak writers. However, the first two were outside the mainstream Hindu tradition, and the last denied the value of any kind of organized society and were largely apolitical.

While the Hindu tradition of political thought, therefore, lacked variety and provided little more than an elaborate justification of the hierarchical social order, the Hindu philosophical tradition was very different. It threw up a remarkable variety of brilliant and imposing philosophical systems, some of which presented a formidable critique of the dominant Brahmanical tradition. The Hindu philosophers explored such areas as metaphysics, ontology, epistemology, logic, philosophy of language, linguistics, and grammar, and developed several different and fascinating theories, some of which have stood the test of time. Prima facie, it appears paradoxical that a culture with a rich and critical tradition of philosophy should have a relatively poor and uncritical tradition of political thought.

Fourth, since the Hindu tradition of political thought was largely apologetic or hostile to change, it almost entirely ignored the whole area of social conflict. No Hindu thinker examined the nature of sectional interests, the reasons why social groups come into conflict, the way political conflicts arise from clashes of material interests and ideologies, how a group acquires political power and presents its interests as general interests, and so on. The Hindu writers did, of course, appreciate that no social order is or can ever be wholly free of disharmony. However, they traced disharmony to such *personal* desires as greed and ambition, and rarely to the objective conflicts of interest and ideology between social groups. In other words, they overlooked the very essence of political life (namely, latent and open conflicts between organized groups). Since they ignored social conflict, they were unable either to explore its basis or to develop an institutional structure for expressing, articulating, and resolving it. Not surprisingly, they remained haunted by the frailty of political authority and felt compelled to rely on such methods as extensive espionage and harsh punishment.

Fifth, the Hindu tradition of political thought is largely didactic and practical. Many Hindu writers, whether they wrote *dharmasastras* or *arthasastras*, wrote mainly for the attention of the rulers, and their works are largely manuals of ethics or of administration. The authors of *dharmasastras* aimed to lay down authoritative statements of the duties of individuals and social groups; those of *arthasatras* were concerned with discussing the most effective manner of organizing the government and maintaining power. Since their concerns were essentially didactic and practical, neither attempted to interpret, understand and explain political life—that is, to offer a systematic and comprehensive philosophical theory of it. It is, of course, true that no systematic discussion of political life is possible without some theorizing. However, the theorizing in Hindu political texts is largely incidental, patchy, implicit, and lacking in rigor.

This is not to say that the Hindu writers did not engage in philosophical exploration of political life. While the *arthasastras* have little philosophical content, other writings such as the *dharmasastras* and the two epics contain some penetrating and profound philosophical discussions of several political themes. As we saw, the Hindu thinkers conceptualized political life in terms of the two basic concepts of *danda* and *dharma* and addressed themselves to three basic themes (namely, the nature and organization of *danda*, the nature and basis of *dharma*, and the relation between the two). Each theme raises large philosophical questions, to some of which Hindu writes addressed their attention. They did not find anything philosophically problematic about *danda* and have little of philosophical interest to say about it. Most of them concentrated on *dharma* and its relation to *danda*. They have much to say about *dharma*—its nature and basis, how it is grounded in the social nature of man, why man cannot be dissociated from his social group, how *dharma* is a form of *yajna* (or sacrifice), how it integrates man into the universal order, and so on. They also have something to say about the relationship between *danda* and *dharma*; that is, how the two can conflict, how the conflict can be resolved, and if and when violence can be justified.

These and other discussions notwithstanding, it would not be inaccurate to say that the Hindus did not develop a tradition of political philosophy. The discussions referred to above are incidental, fragmentary, and episodic; they are often designed to solve personal problems; they are scattered in various texts; they are not comprehensive and exclude several large questions; they are sometimes not critical and probing enough, as, for example, the discussion of the nature of castes and their *dharma*; they sometimes consist of simple assertions, some of which are penetrating and profound, but these are not backed by arguments; and so on. If we added up the philosophical discussions of various themes scattered in several Hindu texts, we could certainly reconstruct Hindu political *philosophy*. However, we would still be left with the conclusion that the Hindus did not have political *philosophers*.

Why the Hindus did not develop a systematic tradition of political philosophy is a large question that lies beyond the scope of this chapter. The answer to it may perhaps be found in a critical examination of the social structure of classical Athens where the Western tradition of political philosophy first made its appearance. After all, political philosophy, like any other form of inquiry, does not grow in a social vacuum, nor is it produced by creative minds out of their heads. It comes into existence when the wider social structure requires and calls for it, that is, when it becomes a social necessity. We need to ask why and how the social conditions in ancient India made political philosophy neither possible nor necessary.

NOTES

*   This chapter is an excerpt from first publication in Thomas Pantham and Kenneth L. Deutsch, eds., *Political Thought in Modern India* (New Delhi: Sage Publications, 1986). The Hindu political ideas discussed in this paper are outlined in several standard commentaries on the subject, such as those by Beni Prasad, U. Ghoshal, K. P. Jaiswal, R. Mazumdar, J. Spellman, and H. N. Sinha.

Of Artha and the Arthasastra[1]

K. J. Shah

> This science (*arthasastra*) brings into being and preserves spiritual good, material well-being, and enjoyment of pleasures; and destroys spiritual evil, material loss and hatred (ill-will).
>
> *Arthasastra*

Introduction

In this chapter, I want to present a structure of thought, pertaining to the management of the affairs of the state, with reference but not confined to the *Arthasastra*.[2] I do so, however, in my own fashion. Various issues are raised: some internally (e.g., does the *Arthasastra* work out a scheme of *artha* according to *dharma*?) and others externally (e.g., does it escape being authoritarian and an obstacle to the freedom of the individual? If it does, why is there no mention of rights?) It is my hope that this many-sided (though brief) exploration of the structure of thought in the *Arthasastra* will throw some new light on the text and that a study of the text will help us in our enquiry to understand traditional thought.

I would like to add that I have taken the thought of the past seriously, i.e., I have allowed it to speak for itself before judging it to be more or less adequate compared to any contemporary understanding of the same issues. This approach reveals that the thought under examination is not merely a collection of maxims, but has a structure and focus capable of presenting to us at least one way of realizing the values or goals, individual and social, of human life—the *purushartha*.

In brief, our purpose is to present a broad outline of the nature and scope of the thought, and to make a beginning in the dialogue between the past, the present and the future. Pursuantly, I discuss, in the next section, the account of the sciences and their interrelationship as presented in the *Arthasastra*. Next, I consider the institution of law and its relationship to *dharma* and, in the following two sections, the institution of kingship and the various ways in which it was sought to be kept on the path of *dharma*. In the two sections that follow, I discuss first some implications of my argument for the relationship between *dharmasastra* and *arthasastra* and, then, the problem of method in the *Arthasastra*.

The Sciences and their Interrelationship

For properly understanding *artha* as a *purushartha*, as a goal of life, one must begin, perhaps, where Kautilya himself begins: the consideration of the nature of the sciences and their relationship. The sciences are: *anviksiki* (*darshana* or philosophy); *trayi* (the three Vedas); *vartta* (the science of the means of livelihood); and *dandaniti* (*arthasastra* or the science of politics) (AS.I.ii.1).

The sciences are so called because through them we can know what is material and moral well-being. *Dandaniti* and *vartta* give us knowledge of material well-being, and *trayi* and *anviksiki* of moral well-being (AS.I.ii.9). This raises three questions: viz., (a) What is the nature of these sciences? (b) What is the relationship between them? (c) What are the implications of these relationships?

Beginning with the nature of the sciences, it may be recalled that Kautilya clarifies the notion of *anviksiki* by means of examples. Thus, the three philosophical or metaphysical systems, *Samkhya*, *Yoga*, and *Lokayata*, are said to illustrate it, but the goal is not stated in metaphysical terms that are not the same for the different systems. It is rather stated in concrete terms: a rational enquiry into *dharma* and *adharma* (good and evil); *artha* and *anartha* (economic and uneconomic); *naya* and *apanaya* (politic and impolitic); and the relative strength of these three. It confers benefit on the people, keeps the mind steady in adversity and prosperity, and illuminates thought, speech, and action (AS.I.ii.10).

This account of *anviksiki* gives rise to many questions but my purpose here is to make only some general points. These are as follows:

1. One could say that the goal is to bring into focus, to bring a unity to, the thought, speech, and action of the individuals and society. One might, in the usual terminology, say that the goal is self-realization, whatever the theoretical terms in which it may be presented.
2. Insofar as the description of the goal and the theoretical structure to support this are different in different systems, the relationship between the system and its goal cannot be logical in the sense in which this term is usually understood.
3. It is important to note that though the terminology of *purushartha* may have sectarian associations, the issues which are being discussed are not sectarian; in fact, they are universal. This is borne out by the fact that among the systems that can secure unity of thought, speech, and action, *Lokayata*—which does not accept either transcendence as *Samkhya* does, or transcendence and God as Yoga does—is mentioned. Thus Indian pluralism is more plural than it is often supposed to be and includes a materialistic system (*Lokayata*) also.

The next science, *trayi*, is the three *Vedas*, *Rg*, *Sama* and *Yajur*, which give us the knowledge of *dharma* and *adharma*, of the duties of the four *varnas* and the four *ashramas*, and of the duties common to all the *varnas* and the *ashramas* (AS.I.iii.1 and 4). Ordinarily the science of *dharma* will be a *dharmasastra*, like the *Manusmrti*, *Yajnayavalkyasmrti*, etc., but here it is said to be the Vedas. This need not be held out as an objection, because among the sources of *dharma*, *sruti* is the one mentioned first in the *Manusmrti* (II. 6); and the *Vedas* are *sruti*. Therefore, it is not necessary to overemphasize such variations in emphasis.

Vartta is concerned with agriculture, rearing of cattle, and trade. It is a science concerned with the techniques of the various means of livelihood (AS.I.iv.l). Not much is said about this; so much so that it is not clear whether it has a separate status, or is only a distinguishable adjunct to *dandaniti*.

The last of the sciences, *dandaniti*, is concerned with the use of power for the sake of the internal and external security of the state (AS.I.i.iv.3). The more frequently used term for *dandaniti* is *arthasastra*, and it is the means of securing the safety and strength of the three sciences. It enables us to gain what we do not have, to protect what we have, to increase what is protected, and to bestow it on a worthy recipient. Thus, the use of power is not narrow and selfish, as it is very often supposed to be, but manifold.

Coming to the relationship between the sciences, this is linked by Kautilya to the question of the number of sciences, as can be seen from what follows.

The followers of Manu say that the sciences are only *trayi*, *vartta*, and *dandaniti*; and *anviksiki* is only a special aspect of the *trayi*. The followers of Brhaspati say that *vartta* and *dandaniti* are the only sciences; and *trayi* is only a synopsis to one who knows the affairs of the world, that is, *trayi* and *dandaniti*. The followers of Usanasa say that the only science is *dandaniti*; it is the beginning and the end of all the sciences (AS.I.ii 2–8). Does the acceptance of the relationship between the sciences also mean the acceptance of the doctrine about the number of sciences? This is a very important issue as will be seen from the following discussion.

To say that the *trayi* is nothing but a summing up of the principles, which are known already to one who knows the affairs of the world, seems to imply that the exercise of *danda* is brought into focus by the principles of *dharma* and *adharma*—a consideration different from that of mere power, or lack of it, which might determine the exercise of *danda*. This situation can be described in one of two ways: (a) It may be said that there are considerations of power (and lack of power) and of wealth (and lack of wealth) and there are considerations of *dharma* and *adharma*. There are, therefore, two sciences, viz., *dandaniti* concerned with power (and economy) and the *trayi* concerned with *dharma*. (b) Only *dandaniti* based on the considerations of *dharma* and *adharma* is truly *dandaniti*. Therefore, there is only one science of *dandaniti*, of which *dharma* and *adharma*, on the one hand, and power or the lack of it, on the other, are aspects.

In a similar way we can argue about *anviksiki* and *trayi*: (a) It may be said that there are considerations of *dharma* and *adharma*, and there are considerations of unity and lack of unity. There are, therefore, two sciences, viz., *trayi* and *anviksiki*. (b) The *trayi* without the considerations of unity and lack of unity is not truly *trayi*. Therefore, there is only one science, *trayi*, with two aspects, of *dharma* and *adharma* and of unity and lack of unity.

If we take the foregoing account into consideration as a whole, we could say either that there are four sciences, which are interrelated, or that there is one science with four aspects: those of *anviksiki*, *trayi*, *vartta*, and *dandaniti*.

We may now look at some implications of the relationship between the sciences.

1. It is important to note that the question of relationship is independent of the question of the number of sciences. In one case it can be a relationship between different sciences, and in the other, a relationship between different aspects of a science.
2. It is also an interesting point to note that when a science is eliminated, the consideration relevant to that science is not eliminated. For example, when *anviksiki* is eliminated as a separate science, the consideration of *anviksiki*, i.e., that of bringing unity to thought, speech, and action is not eliminated. It is made part of the *trayi* and so on. Similarly, when it is said that *dandaniti* is the only science, the considerations relevant to *vartta*, *trayi*, and *anviksiki* are not eliminated; they are made part of *dandaniti*. As a result, *artha* is not *artha* unless it is sought in the context of these other sciences also.
3. If *artha* and *vartta*, in order to be *artha* and *vartta*, need focusing by *dharma* and *anviksiki*, it is important to remember that the relationship holds the other way also. That is, if *anviksiki* or *dharma* is not to be an empty form, it must have

the content of *artha* and *vartta*. Without this content, or a reference to it, they cease to be what they are.

The foregoing discussion would imply that none of the sciences could be truly itself without reference to considerations of all the other three sciences. Insofar as this is so, any one of the four sciences could not be the only science; or any one of the four sciences could be the only science, but each with a different focus from the other, *artha*, or *vartta*, or *dharma*, or unity of thought, speech, and action. In other words, there is only one science—the science of man, or the science of human goals (*purushartha*) interacting with one another.

4. It is important to note here that the goals of the four sciences are not the same as the traditional four goals of human life. The goals of the sciences are *artha* (political), *vartta* (economic), *dharma* (moral), and *anviksiki* (spiritual). The traditional goals are *artha* (political), *kama* (psychological), *dharma* (moral), and *moksa* (spiritual). The first two goals of science are combined into *artha*, the first traditional human goal. (This is partly at the root of the confusion regarding the meaning of *arthasastra*—a science of economics, or a science of politics, or a science of political economy?) I do not know what to make of this discrepancy. However, the more important consideration is the following.

As we have seen, our discussion of the sciences has taken their goals to be interactional, not hierarchial.[3] Is there a mistake here, or does the hierarchy of the traditional four goals need to be understood differently from what is usual? I think that the latter is the case. We must realize that *artha* will not be a *purushartha* unless it is in accord with *kama*, *dharma*, and *moksa*; *kama* in turn will not be *kama* unless it is in accord with *dharma* and *moksa*; and *dharma* will not be *dharma*, unless it too is in accord with *moksa*. Equally *moksa* will not be *moksa* without the content of *dharma*; *dharma* will not be *dharma* without the content of *kama* and *artha*. The four goals, therefore, constitute one single goal, though in the lives of individuals the elements may get varying emphasis for various reasons.

If this is so, what becomes of the hierarchy of human goals? When it is said that, if one has to choose between *artha* and *dharma*, one must opt for the latter, the choice does not imply that *artha* be completely sacrificed for *dharma*. It generally means the choice of less *artha* than may be available if one were to ignore *dharma*. In the extreme case, where complete sacrifice of *artha* is entailed, it means that if instead of *artha*, *dharma* were to be sacrificed, the former would cease to be human goal; therefore, one's humanity demands such a sacrifice. The foregoing could perhaps be summed up in the following slogans: *artha* alone as a goal is greed, *kama* alone is lust, *dharma* alone is mechanical ritual, and *moksa* alone is escapism.

5. The account of the relationship between the sciences raises a number of questions. What is the relationship between the goals of *anviksiki* and *trayi*? In other words, what is the relationship between religion and morality? How does the study of *anviksiki* help in the attainment of the goal of *anviksiki*? Put differently, the question will be, what does a philosophical system do?

Let us return to the implications of the alternative ways of describing the situation. If we say that there are four sciences, it is suggested that each one of them could be studied on its own, and its principles established without reference to the considerations relevant to the others. This brings out the possibilities of a particular science to the fullest extent, and also suggests which of these can be actualized. Alternatively, if we say that there is only one science with four different aspects, all the considerations are brought to bear on a particular problem; therefore, reference to other aspects will prevent the investigation of the full possibilities of any particular aspect. If one or the other of the foregoing two possibilities is adopted, each would fail to take account of the other and would, therefore, have a certain inadequacy. However, it is possible that each one of the possibilities could be pursued keeping in mind the other.

Insofar as Kautilya accepts that there are four sciences, and yet does not deny a relationship between them, we could say that he would want the other possibility of the relationship between the sciences to be always kept in mind. In this respect, it would appear that the approach of the *Arthasastra* is different from the modern approach. The latter emphasizes the autonomy of the sciences even when it adopts an interdisciplinary approach; per contra Kautilya emphasizes the unity of the sciences: "Therefore, the three sciences have their root in the proper administration of the rule (rod)" (AS.I.v.1). But this could mean that only in an ordered society is it possible to pursue the sciences; it need not mean that *artha* alone is the goal independently of other goals. But Kautilya also says: "*Artha* (material well-being) is the first chief of the three—*dharma, artha* and *kama*, because *dharma* and *kama* are rooted in *artha*" (AS.I.vii. 6,7).

It is true that what we think of as first, we sometimes also think of as the most important; but it need not be so. Without *artha*, there can be no *kama* and *dharma*; but if there is *artha* without *kama* and *dharma*, what is the point of *artha* by itself? Further, *artha* will not be *artha* if it is not in accordance with *dharma*. That Kautilya thinks so is shown by the following: "...that he (the king) should not be without pleasures, but he should enjoy pleasures which ate not against *dharma* and *artha* (consistently with the pursuit of *dharma* and *artha*). Or he should pursue the three equally which are bound up with one another." If any one is pursued in excess, it harms itself and the other two (AS.I.vii.3–5). Also, at the end of the *Arthasastra* (XV. i.72) occurs the statement that I have adopted as the motto for this essay. All this shows that it could not have been the intention of Kautilya to say that *artha* is the most important goal. If what we have said is right, then *arthasastra* lays down a structure to establish political institutions that are in accordance with *dharma*. This does not, however, accord with the reputation of Kautilya and the *Arthasastra*. He is supposed to be an unashamed advocate of power,[4] in both the internal administration and the external relations of the state. Internally he advocates a system of spying where there is no question of morality. Externally he advocates an expansionist policy, which is limited only by one's power and circumstances. The justification is to maintain a society in the performance of *dharma*. The question is to maintain a society in the performance of the *dharma*. The question is whether this can be achieved by the means suggested in the *Arthasastra*. If so, the recommendations of Kautilya do not negate, at least in theory, the understanding that *artha* has to be pursued in accordance with *dharma*. What are the institutions and structures suggested so that the individual and society may achieve such fulfillment? I will consider only law and kingship to try to show how these institutions are structured to attain both *artha* and *dharma*, or *artha* according to *dharma*, or *dharma* consistently with *artha*.

LAW AND DHARMA

An examination of the *Arthasastra* reveals that *dharma* plays a central role in the settling of disputes, in the constitution of the court, and in the rules of evidence.

In the settlement of disputes, according to Kautilya, four factors were regarded as relevant: *Dharma* (code of conduct), *vyavahara* (the actual transaction in a particular case), *caritra* (the history of similar cases, tradition, precedents), *rajasasana* (the order of the king). Truth is the basis of *dharma*, witnesses of *vyavahar*, history of *caritra*, and the decision of the king of the order of king (AS.III.i.39, 40).

In this context, how is *dharma* understood? This word has been translated as "law" by Kangle (1972, see note 1) and as "sacred law" by Shama Sastri (*Kautilya's Arthasastra*. Mysore: Mysore Printing and Publishing House, 1967). I would like to suggest, however, that this concept is best understood in terms of the relationship of *samanya dharma* (*dharma* common to all castes and stages) and *visesa dharma* (dharma specific to various *varnas* and *ashramas*). Taken holistically, *dharma* may be said to be the code of conduct. The sources of this *dharma* are *sruti* (the *Vedas*), *smrti* (the *dharmasastras*), *sadachar* (the conduct of good men), and *atmatusti* (self-satisfaction) (MS.II.6). These sources have been understood to be hierarchically arranged in decreasing importance. However, the relationship is much more complex, and the sources are better described as a matrix of interacting factors (see K.J. Shah "The Concept of Dharma", *Journal of the Indian Academy of Philosophy*, 12(1): 35–45). It follows that it is not correct to translate *dharma* as law, because the code of conduct is not enacted by any one; or as sacred law, because the sources include the conduct of good men and self-satisfaction. This *dharma* is rooted in truth. One might think of it as moral and social consensus.

The terms *vyavahara*, *caritra*, and *rajasasana* do not need explanation, but one may point out how the four factors operated in the implementation of *dharma*. It is a matter of commonsense. In the settlement of a dispute, the appropriate rule or law is provided by *dharma*. No law can exhaustively describe all the possible situations. In order to implement the law, therefore, the facts of the transaction (*vyavahara*) must be known. However, such facts or details may not have occurred for the first time. Therefore, it is necessary to have the precedents (the *caritra*), if the implementation is not to vary from case to case even when the facts are the same. But when the facts of the case do not fit into the existing law or precedents, it is the decision of the king or the state that must decide the issue.

What is the relation between these factors? Kautilya says that "*paschimo purvabadhakah*" (ASS.III.i.39–47). This has been translated as: "the latter factor supersedes, or is superior to the former." But this is not at all clear: how can *vyavahara* supersede *dharma*? One could possibly mean that if the transaction is not according to *dharma*, then the terms of the transaction should prevail. This does not seem intelligible in view of the following two considerations: (a) on the same basis, one would have to say that precedent (*caritra*) should supersede *vyavahara*—the terms of the transaction. But if the terms of the transaction are to be regarded as superior to *dharma*, it is not clear why they should be regarded as inferior to precedent. (b) Later on, it is said that if *vyavahara* or *caritra* contradicts *dharma*, then it is to be rejected. Surely this is not to say that *vyavahara* is superior to *dharma*.

To avoid the problem arising from this last statement, it is said that it must be an interpolation. This view is sought to be supported by pointing out that the word used here for precedent is different (*samstha*) from the one used earlier (*caritra*). But this is not sufficient ground for thinking that we have here an interpolation. In any case, the question is: Is there a need for such an explanation?

There is no such need if we once again go back to the beginning and attempt to understand the kind of relationship that can exist between *dharma* and *vyavahara* and *caritra*. Surely, *dharma* may be implemented only in the context of a particular transaction and the precedents; the latter, in some ways, condition, but do not prevent, such implementation. This is the meaning that the phrase "*pascimo purvabadhakah*" can quite easily bear. If this is so, the later statement that, if the *vyavahara* or *caritra* contradicts *dharma*, then *dharma* must prevail, need not at all conflict with the first account; in fact, it is consistent with the understanding of the *Arthasastra* as a whole. But to this pre-eminence of *dharma* there is one apparent exception. When there is conflict between rational or just decision (*dharmanyaya*) and *dharma*, the former must prevail and not *dharma*. This is only an apparent exception because, in such a context, *dharma* undergoes a change. This possibility is quite in accordance with the four-fold sources or characteristics of *dharma*: *sruti*, *smrti*, *sadachar* and *atmatusti*. We had pointed out that this four-fold characterization shows that *dharma* is not static and that its change can be brought about by persons who are themselves good.

This brings us to the court which was constituted of three members conversant with *dharma* and three officers of the king, providing sufficient knowledge both of *dharma* and administration. The law of evidence gives sufficient scope to the defender as also to the accused, but it is not the same for both. For example, the defender is given time for answering the charges made against him, but not the complainant (ASI.III.i).

From the foregoing account, we can see that *dharma* has a pre-eminent place in the administration of law. But there is one serious difficulty here: is not the king given a dominant position in which he can override *dharma*? It is he who acts in the name of rational law; also it is he who is to establish *dharma* when all sense of duty has disappeared from society (AS.III.i.38). Does this not endanger the role of *dharma*? There can be no doubt that this is a serious possibility and it would have been actualized quite often, and a time may have come when this was generally the case. However, there can be no structure that is foolproof and free from difficulty; what is required is that it should be possible to deal with this difficulty more often than not. And we find that Kautilya has taken precautions to see that this difficulty is prevented as far as possible from getting the upper hand. The manner in which he does this will now be discussed.

THE KING AND HIS TRAINING

At many places in the *Arthasastra* the king is reminded of his duties and of the consequences of his failing to perform them. Thus "In the happiness of the subjects, lies the happiness of the king and in what is beneficial to the subjects, his own benefit. What is dear to himself is not beneficial to the king but what is dear to the subjects is beneficial to him" (AS.I.xix.34).

It is not left to chance, or to his good sense, that the king will do his duty. To inculcate in him a sense of duty, an elaborate two-fold course of training is laid down for the king: first, the training in the sciences we have already mentioned: *anviksiki*, *trayi*, *vartta*, and *dandaniti*; second, the training in the control of the senses. The former is to be received from the respective experts: "he should learn economics from the heads of departments, and the sciences of politics from its theoretical and practical exponents" (AS.I.v.8). The training in the sciences, especially the *anviksiki* and the *trayi*, makes one realize the need for the control over the senses, the need to overcome lust, anger, greed, pride, arrogance, and foolhardiness (AS.I.vi.I). Kautilya emphasizes this point further by mentioning the consequences of indulging in each one of the six vices mentioned, giving two illustrations each (AS.I.vi, 4–12).

But to suggest or to provide a course of training is not necessarily to secure the intended results. It is not at all clear that competence in the sciences will give one control over the senses. Insofar as they are independent of each other, it is possible that the king has both, neither, or only one of the two. There is no problem when the king has both, or when he has neither; but there is a problem when a king has

ther. There will also be a question of preference between one who
competence and one who has competence but is not good. In any
il to get a ruler who will uphold *dharma*; in such a situation the
between different kinds of failings and/or virtues will be there.
ssed a large number of possible situations and tried to come to a
.... However, it is an attempt to make the best of a bad bargain.

Another way in which Kautilya attempts to avoid such a situation is through
advice to the king regarding discipline and competence.

> He who when taught understands spiritual good and practices, the same is one
> possessed of sagacity. He who understands but does not practise them is one
> with intellect requiring to be goaded. He who is ever full of harm and hates
> spiritual and material good is one of evil intellect. If such be the only son, he
> (the king) should endeavour to get a son born of him. Or he should get sons
> begotten on an appointed daughter. An old or a diseased king, however,
> should get a child begotten on his wife.... But he should not install on the
> throne an only son, if undisciplined (AS.I.xvii, 44–51).

Thus, there is no doubt that every attempt was made to see that the king who will
occupy the throne would be just. But when a king turns out to be bad, the people
will have to suffer and they would have no alternative but to wait until he perishes in
one way or another. But they may not wait; in fact, there are other texts, besides the
Arthasastra that advocate that the people should kill the king in such extreme cases.
Kautilya does not directly advocate the killing of the king but he does say that an
undisciplined, evil, and impious king will, by his own negligence and indolence,
produce decline, greed, and disaffection among his subjects who may then kill him.
"Subjects, when impoverished, become greedy; when greedy they become disaffected; when disaffected, they either go over to the enemy or themselves kill the
master. Therefore, he should not allow these cases of decline, greed and disaffection
among the subjects to arise, or, if arisen, should immediately counteract them"
(AS.VII.v.19–28).

This indeed is a way out, but it is an extreme way out, involving considerable
hardship to the people before they take recourse to such an action. But the alternative could be an invitation to unvirtuous kings to do what they wish and to the
people to be long-suffering. This situation arises because the policy of Kautilya suffers from a fundamental defect in that there is no conception of rights—the rights of
the citizens, especially against the state—in it.

RIGHTS: PROBLEM OF THE MISSING CONCEPT

One very striking difference between traditional and modern societies is that in the
latter alone the rights of the individual citizens, even against the state, are recognized. This is one reason for the assertion that traditional society is authoritarian and
modern society, free. What is the real significance of this distinction?

First, let us see what happens to freedom in a traditional society. As already
noticed, the king did not make the law in traditional society, except in special circumstances. Law, therefore, was customary, it was the law of the *dharmasastra*. This
itself was a great check on arbitrariness. Further, *dharmasastra* made it difficult for
the king to cover this arbitrariness under the guise of law. Though there were no

legal processes against such behavior, surely the moral and social processes were present; and even if these processes could be controlled by the authorities, the control must have been much more limited than what it can be today. This was the kind of risk that society took: the risk was not, as is sometimes imagined, the total and continuous absence of freedom; it was the possibility of arbitrariness, now and then, getting the upper hand.

What was the scope of arbitrariness? It could have been an unduly high collection of revenues, or personal harassment of one kind or another, which must have been limited to a few. If it went beyond the limit, it was not impossible to deal with it more or less effectively. If the kingdom was small, it was possible to leave the kingdom; if large, the pressure of arbitrariness would have been limited. Thus, on the whole, the freedom of the people would have been maintained on the one hand by the social and moral sanctions, and on the other hand, by the limited nature and power of government.

However, it might be argued that the recognition of the rights of citizens is definitely an improvement on this, and it gives to the citizen greater scope to realize human goals, individual and social. There can be no doubt that there must have been a time when the institution of rights must have facilitated the attainment of human goals—especially when the ruler had become much stronger in many ways, and the citizen much weaker, such that it had become very difficult to challenge the arbitrariness of the ruler. However, this does not mean that this would be so at all times and places; or that this arrangement would not be open to subversions of one kind or another, as the traditional arrangement was open to subversion. For example, even when there are legal rights, many people will lack the time, energy, and resources to assert these rights and, therefore, the rights will become a tool in the hands of the powerful against the weak.

At a different level, a similar argument can be used against the notion of universal human rights also; for example, freedom of information could become, in fact it is, a tool in the hands of the powerful states against the weak states. Insofar as this is so, the rights of the weak can be ignored with impunity. As greater and still greater efforts are made to avoid such a possibility, law becomes increasingly complicated (including legal assistance at public expense) and even if the situation does not become worse, it continues to be as bad as ever. This sort of development, on the one hand, leads to the acceptance of law as a standard of behavior, and, on the other hand, social norms take a back seat. Thus there comes about a kind of situation that makes things difficult for the straightforward while easy for the crooked. Further, in such a situation, where the ruler does not merely administer law, but also makes it, he can disguise his arbitrariness in the shape of law. These are the degenerations and risks involved in a society where rights are accepted. Not that there are no safeguards against these, but there are situations in which the safeguards are too weak to counter the trends mentioned above.

The foregoing analysis shows that there is no such thing as a foolproof structure that cannot be subverted, or which cannot degenerate; further, it would be difficult, if not impossible, to reject the traditional or the modern approach as fundamentally, inherently inadequate. Nor can we say that each kind of society has not tried to meet the difficulties that are likely to arise. However, situations might arise that might strain the systems to such an extent that they may break down. It is wrong, therefore, to think that traditional society neglected the freedom of the individual whereas modern society gives him his rightful place. Perhaps the best way of choosing between the two structures will be to opt for one where, in the prevailing circumstances, degeneration is not likely to become uncontrollable.

The crux of the matter seems to be that in traditional society duties are at the center, whereas in modern society rights are so located. Thus there is the recognition of value in modern society, which is not there in traditional society; and in modern society the possibilities and opportunities for the individual have increased immeasurably. It would be impossible and also unnecessary in this context to carry this controversy forward to a conclusion, because my purpose is not to choose between traditional and modern society but to institute a meaningful dialogue between the two.[5]

It has often been held that there are universal human rights, inalienable human rights, or natural rights. These terms may have had different uses, but I take them to mean the same thing: human beings, just because they are human beings, have certain rights, such as the right to life, liberty, equality, etc., irrespective of difference in time or place. There may be differences in the account of what specifically are such rights. However, my purpose is not to determine what these rights are, but to understand the notion of universal human rights.

One could approach the problem by considering the implications of the assertion of an individual's decision or resolve to do something. This raises the issue of personal liberty. Now, personal liberty is an element in one's being oneself in the attainment of happiness, in the achievement of the goals of life, viz., *moksa, kama,* or *dharma* (sometimes said to be individually the only goals of life), or *dharma, artha, kama,* and *moksa* taken together as the goal of life. If this conception of personal liberty is granted, then the assertion of an individual right is also part of one's goals of life.

These goals, it is often held, are both the given and the normative ends of human endeavor. But how do we establish that they are the goals of life? *Artha* and *kama* do not, perhaps, pose a serious problem but that is not true of *dharma* and *moksa.* However, we have earlier seen how these goals are said to be related, and only in their interrelationship do they manifest their true nature. We might even say that these goals are the a priori conditions of being a human being. Insofar as *dharma* and *moksa* are also sought along with *artha* and *kama,* these are the goals and these also ought to be the goals.[6]

To return to our question about the assertion of an individual resolve to do something, does it belong to any one of the elements in its true nature? Our problem is not to answer this question but to see that a right, if there is one, will follow from the fact that certain goals are goals that one ought to pursue. Insofar as this is so, the doctrine of rights is essentially a mode of making duty operative.

The distinction between the traditional and modern societies is thus seen to be not fundamental. In other words, it is not such that one recognizes a fundamental value which the other does not. In fact, the difference is that in modern society, the performance of one's duty requires a right as an instrument. A legal safeguard is needed because a social or moral safeguard does not operate.

DHARMASASTRA AND ARTHASASTRA

So far we have examined Kautilya's account of the administration of law and kingship. But *dharmasastra* also lays down rules in both these respects. If *artha* is to be pursued in accordance with *dharma,* what is the point of having both *dharmasastra* and *arthasastra*? This question has not been raised explicitly but it is possible to consider it in more than one way.

One way of considering it would be to compare the sources of the rules in the *Manusmrti* and the *Arthasastra.* According to the former (as already stated above), the sources of *dharma* are *sruti, smrti, sadachar* (conduct of good men), and *atmatusti* (self-satisfaction). Further, and again as we have seen, the sources of law in the *Arthasastra* are *dharma*, *vyavahara*, *caritra*, and *rajasasana*. (It is true these are said to be the four factors that are relevant to the settlement of disputes but by being so relevant they become the source of the *dharma* which is to be implemented.) Moreover, there are rules of conduct and punishment that are there in the one text but not in the other; in some cases the two overlap. The important question to ask would be, what is the significance of the foregoing differences and similarities between the two texts?

I think the reason for the differences/similarities are not always the same, as may be illustrated by considering the rules regarding marriage and verbal and physical injury in the two texts (MS.III.I.44 and VIII, 267–287; AS.III.ii. 1–13; III.xviii. 1–12; and III.xix. 1–36). It will be seen that in some matters, social control is considered adequate—e.g., in the case of advice regarding the kind of girl one should marry. In other cases, it must have been thought that the matter is such as cannot be controlled by law or that law can do precious little in the matter—e.g., the abuse of one's parents. It is some or more of these reasons that would explain why the common code of conduct, which is known as *samanya dharma* and includes such virtues as forgiveness, speaking the truth, etc., are not included in the *Arthasastra*.

Now let us note some of the things that are there in the *Arthasastra* but not in the *Manusmrti*. The most important feature of the rules in the former is that the description and classification of situations, events, offences, etc., are detailed, precise and clear. Thus, in it, different types of marriage are said to be lawful if only the father has approved, or both father and mother have approved, irrespective of the caste of the parties concerned. In the *Manusmrti* a type of marriage is lawful for certain castes but not for others.

As more and more cases arise, there is always a tendency that case-law is built up and so are precedents. This would certainly lead to a more specific and clear definition of situations, events, etc., so that the law is clearly established, there is no ambiguity, and similar situations are dealt with in the same manner. As long as this crystallization does not occur, and there is no machinery to enforce the rules and the punishment, it is possible to lay down unrealistic punishments as in the *Manusmrti* but once there is a machinery of enforcement, it seems punishments also become realistic as they are in the *Arthasastra*.

However, there are areas of conduct in which both our texts give details, which are practical, and relate the consequences to the nature of the action; for example, this is so in the case of rules stating the duties of husbands and wives, or regarding rules of inheritance. The difference between the two texts here is a matter of detail and not one of nature.

At any time, in any society, there are some kinds of conduct that are not left only to informal social control, but are also formally controlled. This is the beginning of the difference between the rules in the *Manusmrti* and the *Arthasastra*. In any society, it is found necessary to leave certain areas of conduct to only social sanctions or moral sanctions. Equally, it is found necessary not to leave certain other areas of conduct to such sanctions only but to formalize the rules as also the institutional structures for their enforcement. However, there can be no definiteness or universality regarding where the line will be drawn between the formal and the informal. It is not, therefore, surprising that the *Manusmrti* contains some rules that are formal and like the rules of the *Arthasastra* in nature. This is how there are not only differences between the two texts but also similarities. With the passage, of time, imperceptibly but inevitably, the generality and informality of the rules must have been replaced by specificity and formality regarding more and more areas. This must have led to the crystallization of the distinction between *dharmasastra* and *arthasastra*. But however much this process goes on, it would not be possible to have only an *arthasastra* without a *dharmasastra* because, as we have already seen, in any society, it is not possible to bring all activities under formal control. However, a change from the informal to the formal code of conduct does not alter the basis of the code of conduct, which remains *dharma*; there is change only in the mode of its operation in certain areas of conduct. To describe this process, as is sometimes done, as a change from the religious approach to the secular approach is a grievous mistake.

NOTES

1. This essay was first published in Anthony J. Parel and Ronald C. Keith, eds., Comparative *Political Philosophy: Studies under the Upas Tree*, 2nd ed., (Lanham, MD: Lexington Press, 2003).
2. The English translation of the text used here is by R.P. Kangle, *The Kautiliya Arthasastra*. (Bombay: University of Bombay, 1972). References to the text are by book, chapter, and verses.
3. Shah's use of the term "hierarchical" is a conventional one (with reference to the simple ranking and needs to be distinguished from Louis Dumont's notion of Hierarchy).
4. For an earlier and unequally worked out challenge to the image of Kautilya, see K. Raghavendra Rao, "Kautilya and the Secular State," *Journal of the Karnatak University*, vol. 2, pp. 1–7.
5. Both these themes—viz., the value placed on individualism in modern society and the methodology of cross-civilizational comparison—are, of course, of central importance in Dumont's work. See Louis Dumont, *From Mandeville to Marx: The Genesis and Triumph of Economic Ideology*. (Chicago, IL: University of Chicago Press, 1977).
6. There is a big jump here in my argument but Sundararajan ("The Purusarthha in the Light of Critical Theory," *Indian Philosophical Quarterly*, Vol. 2, No. 3, pp. 339–350) has argued this point in detail.

THE SOCIORELIGIOUS
AND POLITICAL THOUGHT OF
RAMMOHUN ROY[1]

Thomas Pantham

In 1933, at a meeting held to commemorate the centenary of Raja Rammohun Roy's death, several thinkers (e.g., Rabindranath Tagore, Sarvepalli Radhakrishnan, and Bipin Chandra Pal) spoke of him as the "Father of Modern India." In his address, entitled "Inaugurator of the Modern Age in India," Tagore referred to Rammohun as "a luminous star in the firmament of Indian history."[2] By his numerous tracts, pamphlets, memoranda and books and public activities for religious, social, educational, economic, and political reforms, Raja Rammohun Roy inaugurated the age of enlightenment and liberal-reformist modernization in India.

In doing this, he drew on his wide knowledge of Perso-Arabic, Classical Greek, Vedantic, and modern Western thought. He had learnt as many as ten languages—Persian, Arabic, Sanskrit, English, Urdu, Hindi, Hebrew, Greek, Latin, and French—and was influenced by such contemporary events as the French Revolution and the freedom movements in Naples, Spain, Ireland, and Latin America. Hence, his concerns as a reformer and thinker were not confined to India. This has been acknowledged by, among others, Jeremy Bentham, C. F. Andrews, Brajendranath Seal, and Rabindranath Tagore. Andrews called him the "pioneer of the whole world movement,"[3] while Bentham, before he met Rammohun during the latter's visit to England, addressed him in a letter as an "intensely admired and dearly beloved collaborator in the service of mankind."[4] Tagore has assessed Rammohun's work in the following words:

> There was a day when, all alone, Ram Mohun Roy took his stand on the common claim of humanity and tried to unite India with the rest of the world. His vision was not dimmed by obsolete conventions and customs. His generous heart, and his equally generous mind, prompted him to accept the message of the West without belittling the East. He braved the wrath of his countrymen in his attempts to impart to them a knowledge of the universal rights of man as man. He taught us that truth belongs to all men, that we Indians belong to the whole world. Ram Mohun extended India's consciousness in time and space.[5]

Brajendranath Seal, the Brahmo philosopher, has explained the significance of Rammohun's contribution:

> For a right understanding and estimate of the Raja's thought and utterance, it is necessary to bear in mind the two essentially distinct but indispensable parts

which the Raja played on the historic stage. There was Raja Rammohun Roy, the Cosmopolite, the Rationalist Thinker, the Representative Man with a universal outlook on human civilisation and its historic march.... But there was another and equally characteristic part played by the Raja—the Nationalist Reformer...the Renovator of National Scriptures and Revelations.[6]

LIFE AND TIMES

Rammohun Roy was born on May 22, 1772 in an orthodox Brahman family at Radhanagar in Bengal, which was then beginning to come under the direct administration of the British East India Company. His father, Ramakanta Roy, was a revenue official and dependent land-holder under the Maharani of Burdwan. Soon after the 1793 Permanent Settlement of Land Revenue by the British (more about which we shall see later), he bought several *mahals* and became an independent zamindar (land holder).

Rammohun's early education included the study of Persian and Arabic at Patna, where he read the Koran, the works of the Sufi mystic poets of Persia and the Arabic translations of the works of Plato and Aristotle. After completing his Islamic studies at Patna, he went to Benares, where he studied Sanskrit and read the ancient Hindu scriptures, especially the *Vedas* and the *Upanishads*. Returning to his village at the age of sixteen, he wrote a rational critique of Hindu idol worship. This displeased his father greatly and Rammohun had to leave his home. His wanderings took him, among other places, to Tibet, where he secured a first-hand knowledge of Buddhism, and to Benares, where he undertook further studies of the Sanskrit texts of the Advaita-Vedanta school. From 1803 to 1814, he worked for the East India Company as the personal *diwan* first of Woodforde and then of Digby. The association with these English civil servants, especially Digby, was instrumental in Roy's study of modern Western thought.[7] In 1814, he resigned from his job and moved to Calcutta in order to devote his life to religious, social and political reforms. By that time he had acquired ownership of two *taluks* and four *patni taluks* under the 1793 Permanent Settlement. He also had a money-lending business in North Calcutta. After shifting to Calcutta in 1818, he came into close contact with the British free traders and invested his money in the Agency House of Mackintosh and Company. He also renewed his interactions with the scholars of the Fort William College and the Sadr Diwani Adalat in Calcutta, with whom he had been in contact in the course of his business dealings in Calcutta prior to 1803. Notable among his English friends in Calcutta were James Young, a merchant and follower of Jeremy Bentham, David Hare, the philanthropist, and J. S. Buckingham, the radical editor of *Calcutta Journal*. The writings of Locke, Hume, Bentham, and the Christian unitarians exerted much influence on Rammohun.

We shall return later to Rammohun's Calcutta writings and activities as a liberal-reformist modernizer. To complete this life sketch, it may be noted here that in November 1830, he sailed for England to be present there to counteract the possible nullification of the Act banning *sati* (widow-burning); powerful propaganda had been mounted by the orthodox Brahmans against the banning of *sati* in 1829 by William Bentinck, the British Governor-General of India. Incidentally, it may also be noted that Rammohun was given the title of "Raja" by the titular Mughal Emperor of Delhi, whose grievances the former was to present before the British king. In England, Rammohun was well-received by the king and the directors of the East India Company. Among his important activities in England was the presentation of a memorandum to the Select Committee of the House of Commons on the Revenue and Judicial Systems of India. He fell ill and died at Bristol on December 27, 1833.

RELIGIOUS AND SOCIAL THOUGHT

Rammohun Roy's immediate problem was the religious and social degeneration of his native Bengal. His biographer has given description of the then decadent condition of that society:

> Thick clouds of ignorance and superstition hung over all the land; the native Bengalee public had few books and no newspapers. Idolatry was universal and was often of a most revolting character; polygamy and infanticide were widely prevalent and the lot of Bengalee women was too often a tissue of ceaseless oppressions and miseries while, as the crowning horror, the flames of the *sati* were lighted with almost incredible frequency even in the immediate vicinity of Calcutta.[8]

Several of the degenerate features of Bengal society were singled out scornfully in Rammohun's first published work, *Tuhfat-ul Muwahhiddin* (*A Gift to Deists*), published in 1803–4 at Murshidabad, where he was living at that time. It was written in Persian with a preface in Arabic. In it, he exposed such irrational religious beliefs and corrupt practices of the Hindus as the belief in revelations, prophets, and miracles, the seeking of salvation through "bathing in a river and worshipping a tree or being a monk and purchasing forgiveness of their crime from the high priests" and the "hundreds of useless hardships and privations regarding eating and drinking, purity and impurity, auspiciousness and inauspiciousness."[9]

Rammohun was particularly concerned with sectarian religious dogmas and practices. He noted that in the name of their separate religious orthodoxies, people develop discord among themselves by "giving peculiar attributes to that Being and . . . [by] holding different creeds consisting of the doctrines of religion and precepts of *Haram* (the forbidden) and *Halal* (the legal)."[10] In the introduction to his Bengali translation of the *Sama Upanishada*, he pointed out the need "to correct those exceptionable practices which not only deprive Hindus in general of the common comforts of society but also lead them frequently to self-destruction."[11]

Rammohun identified himself with the victims of religious orthodoxies, which, he wrote in *Tuhfat*, "have become causes of injury and detrimental to social life and sources of trouble and bewilderment to the people, instead of tending to the amelioration of the condition of society."

How is it that the irrational and corrupt religious beliefs and practices which militated against the social comforts and political unity of the people were actually followed by them? Rammohun's answer was that the priestly class, which invented and perpetuated those dogmas and doctrines, derived benefits from them. He wrote:

> Many learned Brahmans are perfectly aware of the absurdity of idolatry, and are well informed of the nature of the purer mode of divine worship. But as in

the rites, ceremonies, and festivals of idolatry, they find the source of their comforts and fortune, they…advance and encourage it to the utmost of their power, by keeping the knowledge of their scriptures concealed from the rest of the people.[12]

From this diagnosis, Rammohun concluded that religious reform is both social reform and political modernization. He conceived of reformist religious associations as instruments of social and political transformation. Accordingly, he founded the Atmiya Sabha in 1815, the Calcutta Unitarian Association in 1821 and the Brahmo Sabha in 1828, which later became the Brahmo Samaj. The original manifesto which he himself wrote for the Brahmo Samaj reads as follows:

No graven image shall be brought in the Samaj. No sermon, discourse, prayer or hymn shall be delivered except such as may have a tendency to promote the contemplation of the Author and Preserver of the Universe, to the furtherance of charity, morality, piety, benevolence, virtue, and the strengthening of the bonds of union between men of all religious persuasions and creeds.[13]

The significance of these religious *sabhas* or *samajs* for social reform is brought out by Charles Heimsath:

Secular reformist crusades, usually for legislative social enactments or caste reform, succeeded in drawing adherents, but alterations in personal and family lives in India required revising religious beliefs and practices. Roy foresaw this connection, as Gandhi did a century later.[14]

Rammohun came to the conclusion that for the emancipation of the people, the monopoly of the orthodox Brahmans over the sacred texts had to be undermined. In other words, their exclusive rights to read and interpret the books of knowledge had to be challenged. "In order to vindicate my own faith and that of our forefathers," he wrote, "I have been endeavouring to convince my countrymen of the true meaning of our sacred books."[15] Accordingly, he set himself the task of interpreting the Vedantic literature and translating them into the vernacular. During the period 1815 to 1823, he published *Translation of an Abridgement of the Vedanta* and translations of several of the *Upanishads* into Bengali, Hindi and English. In this respect, Rammohun was a modern Indian Luther. In fact, the former is reported to have said to the Scottish Presbytarian missionary, Alexander Duff:

As a youth, I acquired some knowledge of the English language. Having read about the rise and progress of Christianity in apostolic times, and its corruption in succeeding ages, and then of the Christian Reformation which shook off these corruptions and restored it to its primitive purity, I began to think that something similar might have taken place in India, and similar results might follow here from a reformation of the popular idolatry.[16]

As a reformation thinker and Enlightenment rationalist, Rammohun applied the criteria of reason and social comfort or utility to the sacred texts. In his *Tuhfat-ul*, he argued that each individual has an innate natural faculty to know the truth and falsity of various religions "without the instrumentality of prophets, religious authority, and traditional revelation." He wrote:

> There is always an innate faculty existing in the nature of mankind that in case
> any person of sound mind, before or after assuming the doctrines of any reli-
> gion, makes an enquiry into the nature of the principles of religious
> doctrines,...without partiality and with a sense of justice, there is a strong
> hope that he will be able to distinguish the truth from untruth and the true
> propositions from the fallacious ones, and also he, becoming free from the
> useless restraints of religion...will pay attention to the good of the society.[17]

Again,

> [T]he fact of God's endowing each individual of mankind with intellectual
> faculties and senses implies that he should not, like other animals, follow the
> examples of his fellow brethren of his race, but should exercise his own intel-
> lectual power with the help of acquired knowledge, to discern good from bad,
> so that his valuable divine gift should not be left useless.[18]

Rammohun adopted three approaches to socio-religious reform: (i) exposing and discrediting those religious dogmas and practices which are irrational and/or contrary to social comfort; (ii) the promotion of modern Western education; and (iii) state action in support of both these programmes.

Rammohun Roy's attitude to modern Western education and socio-religious reform was different from his conservative and radical contemporary Bengali intellectuals. The conservatives, led by Raja Radhakanta Deb (1784–1867), favoured modern Western education. However, they did so not for its scientific spirit or emancipatory ideas but merely for its instrumentality for career advances in the professions and services under the British. Their approach conformed to the Macaulyan scheme of English education. Far from regarding Western education as a means of social transformation, they vigorously defended the social and religious status quo. They fully endorsed the British colonial government's policy of noninterference in the socioreligious orthodoxies of the native peoples. In fact, as Radharaman Chakraborti has pointed out, the "state-society interaction had long been under suspension as a result of recoiling of the Hindu society in the face of the consolidation of Muslim rule in India. For ages the social process not only remained truncated from the mainstream of politics but slowly stagnated into clusters of local orthodoxy."[19] Rammohun Roy pioneered the movement for state intervention for social and religious reforms.

Rammohun's reformism was also opposed by the young radicals led by the Anglo-Indian teacher of the Hindu College, Henry Louis Vivian Derozio (1809–1831). Influenced by Voltaire, Hume, Jeremy Bentham, and Thomas Paine, Derozio became a rationalist free thinker and denounced Hindu religion. He called Rammohun and his group "half-liberals" and opportunists. He wrote:

> What his [Rammohun Roy's] opinions are, neither his friends nor foes can
> determine. It is easier to say what they are not than what they are....
> Rammohun, it is well-known, appeals to the Vedas, the Koran, and the Bible,
> holding them all probably in equal estimation, extracting the good from each
> and rejecting from all whatever he considers apocryphal.... He has always lived

like a Hindoo.... His followers, at least some of them, are not very consistent. Sheltering themselves under the shadow of his name, they indulge to licentiousness in everything forbidden in the shastras, as meat and drink; while at the same time they feed the Brahmans, profess to disbelieve Hinduism, and never neglect to have poojahs at home.[20]

Derozio obviously did not grasp the emancipatory or progressive nature of Rammohun's synthesis of "the Vedas, the Koran, and the Bible".

From his comparative study of religions, Rammohun concluded that there are three basic tenets in all religions: (i) belief in one universal supreme being; (ii) belief in the existence of the soul; and (iii) belief in life after death. Rammohun accepts these beliefs on the basis of reason and/or social utility. Other than these basic tenets, he finds many false and many objectionable dogmas and doctrines in Hinduism as well as in other religions. These, he says, must be rejected, for which he offers the following justification:

> If mankind are brought into existence, and by nature formed to enjoy the comforts of society and the pleasure of an improved mind, they may be justified in opposing any system, religious, domestic or political, which is inimical to the happiness of society, or calculated to debase the human intellect.[21]

His attack was directed, in particular, against polytheism and idolatry. As a result of his studies of Perso-Arabic literature and interactions with the Muslim scholars of the Sadr Diwani Adalat, he was attracted to Islamic monotheism. Monotheism, he maintained, is also the fundamental message of the Vedanta. In his *Tuhfat*, he wrote: "I travelled in the remotest parts of the world, in plains as well as in hilly lands, and I found the inhabitants thereof agreeing generally in believing in the existence of One Being Who is the source of creation and the governor of it."[22]

Rammohun's idea of a single, unitarian God was his corrective to the polytheism of orthodox Hinduism and to Christian trinitarianism. He believed that monotheism supported one universal moral order for humanity, while polytheism justified sectarian moralities. The significance of this aspect of Rammohun's work was recognized by Bentham when he wrote "Rammohun Roy has cast off thirty-five millions of gods and had learnt from us to embrace reason in the all important fields of religion."[23] Rammohun's conception of the fundamental unity of all religions has been endorsed by several subsequent thinkers of India (e.g., Vivekananda, Tagore, Gandhi, and Radhakrishnan). What these thinkers advanced, it must, however, be noted here in passing, was not Benthamite or utilitarian internationalism but spiritual-universalist cosmopolitanism. Rammohun Roy was himself called a "religious Benthamite."

The ground of Rammohun's opposition to polytheism and idolatry was their underlying anthropomorphic conception of the one supreme being. Moreover, idol worshippers and ritualists make idols and rituals the center of their devotion and worship, and neglect the purification of their mind or the self. Those who rely on rituals and ceremonies do so in the expectation of this-worldly or other-wordly rewards. They are not done from a sense of duty or in a spirit of detachment and as such are a bad means to spiritual or moral ends. For the ritualists and ceremonialists, what matters are such mundane considerations as the appearance of one's ritual robes or the lavishness of the feast that one hosts.[24] Rituals or ceremonies, he says, do not yield morality which according to him comes from spirituality. He says that just as the religious or spiritual degeneration of Hinduism generated and sustained bad moral norms, so also the morality codes of the Christians were corrupted by orthodoxies. He, therefore, turned his attention to raising the moral level of orthodox trinitarian Christianity. He expressed his views on Christianity in his 1820 publication, *The Precepts of Jesus, A Guide to Peace and Happiness.* The controversy it generated among some Christian missionaries led Rammohun to write three tracts, each entitled *An Appeal to the Christian Public in Defence of the Precepts of Jesus.*

Rammohun rejected the divinity of Christ but admitted that his moral teachings, best summed up in his Sermon on the Mount, are a "guide to peace and happiness" and "best calculated to lead mankind to universal love and harmony." Christ's central teachings, Rammohun noted, are love of God and of one's fellowmen. Rejecting the Christian doctrine of the trinitarian God, Rammohun said that by his prayer, "Our Father," Jesus indicated that he and God were not ontologically one. The original, pure unitarian Christianity, Rammohun maintained, became corrupt with the intermixture of polytheistic and idolatrous ideas and practices introduced by the Greek and Roman converts. Orthodox Christianity, he noted, had its "idols, crucifixes, saints, miracles, pecuniary absolutions from sin, trinity, transubstantiation, relics, holy water, and other idolatrous machinery."[25]

In 1821, Rammohun supported the founding of the Calcutta Unitarian Committee, of which he and his eldest son became members. He also set up a Unitarian Press in Calcutta. Although he believed that Indians would benefit from the moral teaching of unitarian Christianity, he did not become a Christian convert. Once believing that he had become a Christian, the Bishop of Calcutta congratulated him for "embracing the purer faith". To this, Rammohun's reply was: "My Lord, you are under a mistake—I have not laid down one superstition to take up another."[26] He believed that the original Vedantic message of the unity of God was superior to the anthropomorphic conception of God contained in the Judeo-Christian Bible. He held that while Christianity justifies the death of Christ, God's son, for the atonement of man's sin against God, the Vedanta teaches that the "only means of attaining victory over sin is sincere repentence and solemn meditation."[27] To Rammohun, it seemed "heathenish and absurd" that for the crime of a person another person had to be killed. He said that each sinner must make restitution for his sins and it is to be done through self-purification and repentence, and not through sacrifices and rituals.

Arguing that Rammohun used "Unitarianism in an Indian way," David Kopf writes:

> [His] comparativist approach coupled with a modernist outlook placed the Hindu reformation movement on an Orientalist foundation by which indigenous traditions could be defended at the same time they were modified according to progressive values in contemporary Western societies. Though the foundation was a precarious one, it saved the Hindu reformation repeatedly from the snare of militant nationalism.[28]

Rammohun is well known for his pioneering thought and action on the emancipation of women and especially on the abolition of *sati* or widow-burning. He, to use the words of David Kopf, found Bengali Hindu women "uneducated and illiterate, deprived of property rights, married before puberty, imprisoned in *purdah*, and murdered at widowhood by a barbaric custom of immolation known as *sati*."[29] Unless women were freed from such inhuman forms of oppression, Rammohun felt,

Hindu society could not progress. He characterized *sati* as "the violation of every humane and social feeling" and as symptomatic of "the moral debasement of a race." Just as he opposed the orthodox Christian doctrine of Atonement, so he rejected the theory that the wife can, or has to, atone for the sins of her husband. He also cited the sacred texts to show that they permitted the wife to continue her life after her husband's death. Largely as a result of Rammohun's campaign, *sati* was banned by Lord Bentinck in 1829. Rammohun also advocated widow remarriage, female education, and the right of women to property.

Rammohun's attitude toward the caste system was somewhat ambivalent. While he practiced some of the overt caste rules (e.g., the wearing of the sacred thread), he noted that God makes no distinction of caste and that "our division into castes . . . has been the source of want of unity among us."[30]

Rammohun was a pioneer of modern Western education which, he believed, would enlighten the Indians against the superstitions and injustices of religious orthodoxies. The mere study of ancient, Sanskrit texts, he said, would only "keep the country in darkness." In his famous letter on education to Lord Amherst, he wrote:

> If it had been intended to keep the British nation in ignorance of real knowledge, the Baconian philosophy would not have been allowed to displace the system of the school-men which was the best calculated to perpetuate ignorance. In the same manner the Sanskrit system of education would be the best calculated to keep this country in darkness if such had been the policy of the British legislature. But as the improvement of the native population is the object of the Government, it will consequently promote a more liberal and enlightened system of instruction, embracing Mathematics, Natural Philosophy, Chemistry, Anatomy, with other useful sciences.[31]

In 1816, Rammohun founded an English school and some years later he lent support to the founding of the Hindu College. In 1825, he started the Vedant College, in which the study of Western knowledge was combined with that of Indian learning.

ECONOMIC AND POLITICAL THOUGHT

In Rammohun Roy's economic and political thought, there are some ambivalences between liberal-capitalist and feudal-aristocratic values as well as between colonial and postcolonial orientations. These ambivalences in his thought had to do with the fact that he was a zamindar with investments in free-trade business in an emerging colonial political economy. As Rajat Ray has noted, Rammohun was a participant in a three-fold process of modernization:

> the consolidation of the position of the traditional high caste rural gentry on the land, the transformation of medieval literati into a modern intelligentsia, and the transition from Company monopoly to free trade imperialism (this was ultimately to lead to the failure of Indian capitalist enterprise after its brief development in partnership with the European free-traders).[32]

The sociohistorical changes that Rammohun was responding to did not permit any neat and simple theoretical and philosophical treatment or paradigmatic encapsulation.

In the face of the unprecedented sociohistorical changes that were unfolding before him, he, in his writings, advocated the cause of what he felt were the liberating and growth-promoting forces and opposed what seemed to him to be the oppressive and growth-inhibiting features of the emerging political economy.

Initially, as he himself has acknowledged, he had a "great aversion" to British rule, but subsequently he became its admirer and responsible critic. He wrote:

> When about the age of sixteen...I proceeded on my travels, and passed through different countries, chiefly within, but some beyond, the bounds of Hindoostan, with a feeling of great aversion to the establishment of the British power in India. When I had reached the age of twenty...I first saw and began to associate with Europeans, and soon after made myself tolerably acquainted with their laws and form of government. Finding them generally more intelligent, more steady...I gave up my prejudice against them, and became inclined in their favour, feeling persuaded that their rule, though a foreign yoke, would lead more speedily and surely to the amelioration of the native inhabitants.[33]

Broadly speaking, there were two main reasons for Rammohun's favorable attitude toward British rule in India. First, he was persuaded that British rule, unlike the despotic and tyrannical rule of the Mughals or the Rajputs, provided security and other civil liberties to the Indian people. Second, and relatedly, he felt that the introduction of capitalist norms and principles by the British were contributing to India's economic development.

Rammohun's economic ideas were shaped by, and supportive of, two of the most important institutional measures through which the Indian economy was linked with the British colonial system, namely, the Permanent Settlement of 1793 and the Agency Houses of *private* British trade with India.

The Permanent Settlement introduced the system of private landed property in India as part of a new system of land revenue. Prior to the Settlement, about a third of the cultivable land in Bengal, Bihar, and Orissa lay waste. The British felt that by giving permanent land tenures in return for a system of fixed revenue, private individuals could be induced to extend and improve cultivation. It was hoped that "the magic touch of property would set a certain productive principle in operation," from which would result a general increase in revenue.[34] The new class of secure landlords, it was also believed, would serve as property-defending supporters of the British empire, in addition to constituting a consumers' market for British manufactures.

The Permanent Settlement did contribute to the increase in the area under cultivation and to making the new middle class of landlords loyal supporters of the British Empire. But these results were obtained at the expense of production principles and to the detriment of the actual cultivators, namely, the ryots and peasants. These were exploited by the zamindars, who "became more and more pure rentiers and performed no economic functions toward the improvement of agriculture."[35] The Permanent Settlement and subsequent enactments gave the zamindars exploitative powers over the ryots and the peasants. Thus Regulation VII of 1799 empowered the zamindars to dispossess the ryots of all their personal property and even to arrest them for arrears of rent. Similarly, the Patni Taluk Regulation of 1819 legalized a system of subinfeudation, which was severely hurtful to the actual tillers of the land. In short, the Permanent Settlement led to the setting up of a semifeudal system of land-ownership, which subserved imperial interests through the mediation of the semi-feudal, semi-capitalist zamindars.

As we saw earlier, Rammohun derived his income from the zamindari and money-lending business. He also made investments in a free-trade business house. Defending property rights, he wrote: "Every man is entitled by law and reason to enjoy the fruits of his honest labour and good management."[36] In his submissions on the revenue system of India before the Select Committee of the House of Commons in 1831, he maintained that the Settlement was advantageous to both the British rulers and the Indian landlords, "though not perhaps in equal proportion." He proposed some reduction in the extent of revenue demand on zamindars. His greater concern and compassion, however, were expressed for the peasants, whose miserable plight he lamented. "[S]uch," he wrote, "is the melancholy condition of the agricultural laborers, that it always gives me the greatest pain to allude to it." He bemoaned the fact that as the cultivators were left with no surplus for accumulation, they were unable to improve the production system. He exhorted the "enlightened Government" of Britain to follow standards of justice. He pleaded against the enhancement of rents and for the security of the tenants. The resulting loss in revenue, he said, could be made up by taxing luxury goods and effecting economy measures in the revenue administration.[37]

Rammohun Roy's ideas for reforming the Permanent Settlement were denounced by the spokesmen of the conservative association, the Dharma Sabha. To them Rammohun seemed to be too harsh on the zamindars. But the *Bengal Hurkaru* found Rammohun's views too supportive of the zamindars and of British colonial administration. To the *Hurkaru*, the Rammohun of the 1831 was a "mere Zamindar"![38] To me, this seems to be an unfair criticism since Rammohun Roy pointed out the injustices of the revenue system and demanded their rectification.

During Rammohun Roy's life, there was a long, drawn-out conflict between those favoring the British East India Company's monopoly rights to trade with India and the British private free-traders. This conflict ended with the victory of the latter over the former. The opening of the East India trade to private enterprise was begun by the Charter Act of 1813 and culminated by the Act of 1833. In this long conflict, Rammohun sided with the free traders and endorsed their ideology of utilitarian liberalism. He participated in the Calcutta Town Hall meeting of free traders in December 1829, which petitioned Parliament "to throw open the China and India trade, and to remove the restrictions against the settlement of Europeans in India."[39]

In his political thinking, as we noted earlier, he admired the British system of constitutional government for the civil liberties it gave to the people. He wanted to extend the benefits of that system of government to the Indian people. He wrote: "I am impressed with the conviction that the greater our intercourse with European gentlemen, the greater will be our improvement in literary, social and political affairs."[40] He sympathized with the freedom struggles of the Greeks and the Neapolitans. The French Revolution gladdened him. He rejoiced at the passage of the Reform Bill of 1832 by the English Parliament and the successful revolt by the Spanish colonies in South America. Yet he welcomed British rule over India! Commenting on his philosophy, B. Majumdar writes:

> He was the first Indian who imbibed the spirit of the English constitution and demanded civil liberty with all its implications. Fully aware as he was of the limitations of the Indians of his age he never thought of demanding political liberty for them. He was conscious of the ignorance and superstitions that enveloped the minds of his countrymen, who betrayed a deplorable lack of

public spirit in their conduct. So he could not think them capable of exercising self-government. The great problem which confronted the well-wishers of India in the first half of the nineteenth century was not autonomy for India but the bare recognition of the principles of justice and security of life and property.[41]

Rammohun Roy attributed India's decline in the immediate pre-British period to the "tyranny and oppression" of the Rajput rulers and the despotism of the Muslim rulers. In contrast, British rule appeared to him as providing to the Indians a God-sent opportunity of securing civil liberties. In his Appeal to the King-in-Council against the 1823 Press Regulation, he noted that "under their former Muhammadan Rulers, the natives of this country enjoyed every political privilege in common with Mussalmans, being eligible to the highest offices in the state." But, he added, "their property was often plundered, their religion insulted, and their blood wantonly shed," till "Divine Providence at last, in its abundant mercy, stirred up the English nation to break the yoke of those tyrants and to receive the oppressed Natives of Bengal under its protection."[42] Rammohun Roy believed that the British rulers, who enjoyed civil and political liberties in their country, could "also interest themselves in promoting liberty and social happiness, as well as free inquiry into literary and religious subjects, among those nations to which their influence extends."[43]

Rammohun Roy believed that in his time, Indians could derive the advantages of the liberal spirit of British public or political life if the laws for India were made by the British Parliament rather than by an Indian Legislative Council located on Indian soil. If such a legislative council was set up, he feared that it would be controlled by the British Governor-General of India and his Council. That would be in contravention of the principle of separation of powers, of which Rammohun was an ardent supporter. "In every civilized country," he wrote, "rules and codes are found proceeding from one authority, and their execution left to another. Experience shows that unchecked power often leads the best men wrong and produces general mischief."[44] He maintained that if legislation for India was left to the British Parliament, it would benefit from the liberal public opinion in England. He was aware of the difficulties involved in making liberal legislation for a distant land. He, therefore, proposed three measures to ensure that the British Parliament makes good laws for the Indian people: (i) a free press; (ii) commissions of inquiry; and (iii) ascertaining the views of "gentlemen of intelligence and respectability."[45] Only these classes seemed to him to be able to exert any influence on the government in those times.

Both through his writings and through his activities, Rammohun Roy supported the movement for a free press in India. When press censorship was relaxed by Lord Hastings in 1819, Rammohun founded three journals: *The Brahmanical Magazine* (1821); the Bengali weekly, *Samvad Kaumudi* (1821); and the Persian weekly, *Mirat-ul-Akbar* (1822). John Adams, who succeeded Lord Hastings as Governor-General, reimposed press censorship in March 1823. Against this censorship, a petition was made to the Supreme Court by Rammohun Roy, Dwarkanath Tagore, and several others. When the petition was rejected by the court, Rammohun submitted an appeal to the King-in-Council which too was rejected. The British colonial case against a free press in India was that India's was a colonial administration and not a representative constitutional government and that there was no effective public opinion in India. Rammohun argued that a free press will help to generate such a public opinion. He also maintained that precisely because India was a colony, it stood in greater need of a free press if a revolutionary overthrow of the rulers was to be avoided. In his famous appeal to the King-in-Council, he wrote:

> [M]en in power hostile to the Liberty of the Press, which is a disagreeable check upon their conduct, when unable to discover any real evil arising from its existence, have attempted to make the world imagine that it might, in some possible contingency, afford the means of combination against the Government, but not to mention that extraordinary emergencies would warrant measures which in ordinary times are totally unjustifiable.... Your Majesty is well aware that a Free Press has never yet caused a revolution in any part of the world, because, while men can easily represent their grievances arising from the conduct of the local authorities to the supreme Government, and thus get them redressed, the grounds of discontent that excite revolution are removed; whereas, where no freedom of the press existed, and grievances consequently remained unrepresented and unredressed, innumerable revolutions have taken place in all parts of the globe, or if prevented by the armed force of the Government, the people continued ready for insurrection.[46]

RAMMOHUN ROY AND HIS CRITICS

We have already seen in the earlier part of the chapter that in his life time, Rammohun Roy was criticized by Radhakanta Deb, Henry Derozio, and the *Bengal Hurkaru*. Let us turn now to some very recent critical appreciations of Rammohun's contribution.

To some of his interpreters, it has been disappointing that even though he favored the freedom struggles in other countries, he welcomed the British imperialist domination of India as an act of divine providence. According to Asok Sen, Rammohun Roy's ideals of modernity and his determination to lead his land away from medieval decay had some basic weaknesses as they were "largely locked up in a sense of identity with the forces of empire".[47] Rammohun and the other members of the new middle class were thus participants in making India a colonial political economy under Britain. Sen finds "most untenable" Rammohun's views "about the benefits of expanding British trade, about the identity of his country's interests with the liberal stances of the British industrial revolution, or even about the prospects of his reformed, Permanent Settlement."[48] Sen concludes his excellent study by noting that these basic weaknesses in Rammohun Roy's thought were the tragic inevitabilities of his circumstances in history which he had no opportunity to choose.

Similarly, Sumit Sarkar points out that the process of modernization pioneered by Rammohun Roy was a transition from precapitalist society in the direction "not of full-blooded bourgeois modernity, but of a weak and distorted caricature of the same which was all that colonial subjection permitted."[49] "The ideology and role of Rammohun Roy's group," writes Rajat Ray, "marked it out quite clearly as a *comprador* group" in the development of subimperialist capitalism in India.[50] They failed to see that colonization undermined the process of industrial accumulation in India and that through unproductive operations, the new middle classes were exploiting the productive labor of the peasants. Despite these shortcomings of his thought, Rammohun Roy is praised by Rajat Ray for "the striking modernity of his philosophical premises and social vision, the concrete achievements of his fruitful career in Calcutta that led to the emergence of a modem urban culture containing the seeds of future Indian nationalism."[51]

Asok Sen, Sumit Sarkar, and Rajat Ray are indeed correct in pointing out that Rammohun Roy did not grasp or anticipate the evils of the imperialist penetration of India. In his writings, there were no expressions of patriotic or nationalist sentiments. Such sentiments would have been highly premature in his historical circumstances. His preoccupations were different. He regarded British rule as *fait accompli* and sought to "reform" it to the advantage of the subject peoples, who, he said, should enjoy the same civil liberties which the colonizing peoples enjoyed at home. This was indeed a very courageous and progressive stance. He regarded the capitalist-industrial economy, which was then being introduced into India, as superior to the old feudal economy. The contradictions which the capitalist system has acquired over the years were hardly visible in Rammohun Roy's historical context. He thought that compared to the old feudal economy, capitalism and its ideology of liberalism were truly progressive and emancipatory changes.[52] It was tragic that the capitalist-industrial economy and the liberal ideology were introduced in India in a distorted manner under imperialist auspices.

Rammohun Roy was concerned to mitigate that tragedy. While he welcomed British rule, he entertained a vision, howsoever faint it was, of a postimperialist world order. This vision is ignored, it seems to me, by Asok Sen and Sumit Sarkar. Also while highlighting the economic aspects of both colonialized Bengal and Rammohun Roy's thought, they seem to underestimate his important contribution to the formation of a transnational culture. It is perhaps from an inadequate appreciation of the role of such a culture that Barun De writes that "Rammohun's political and economic ideas merit veneration only by those who worship the history of India's liberalism."[53]

TOWARD A SYNTHESIS OF CULTURES

Rammohun Roy's appreciation of "England's work in India" was centered on his grasp of the scope it held for the extension of the liberal revolution to the Indian society. His support of British rule was not due solely or mainly to the economic or career benefits it brought to him and to the other members of his new middle class. No doubt he shared in, and appreciated, those benefits. Yet, his main hope from British rule, which he accepted as a *fait accompli*, was that it would be instrumental in extending liberalism's civil and political liberties to the Indian society. This is clearly indicated in some of the earlier citations as well as in the following passage:

> Many of those . . . who engage prosperously in commerce, and of those who are secured in the peaceful possession of their estates by the Permanent Settlement, and such as have sufficient intelligence to foresee the probability of future improvement which presents itself under the British rulers, are not only reconciled to it, but really view it as a blessing to the country. But I have no hesitation in stating, with reference to the general feeling of the more intelligent part of the Native community, that the only course of the policy which can ensure their attachment to any form of government would be that of making them eligible to gradual promotion, according to their respective abilities and merits, to situations of trust and responsibility in the states.[54]

In the extension of the liberal revolution to the Indian society, Rammohun saw an opportunity for reforming and reordering the imperialist world system. While he did not deny or resist the political and economic integration of India into the British imperialist system, he strove to reform that system. Both the colonized and coloniz-ing societies, he said, must be reformed in their religions, cultures, politics, and economy. The norms or values of such reforms, he said, were not the monopoly of either the colonizing, modern West or the colonized, traditional Eastern countries such as India. For the reform of the then emerging world system, he felt, a new humanist culture had to be synthesized. Accordingly, he worked toward a synthesis of the world-affirming rationalist-deistic strands of Islamic thought, the liberal and scientific attitudes of modern Western thought and the spiritual and communitarian values of Advaita Vedanta.

Rammohun Roy believed that the system of sovereign states is not permanent but historically contingent on developments in such areas as property-systems, linguis-tics, and religion. This he indicated in his *Tuhfat-ul Muwahhiddin* in the following words:

Although it cannot be denied that the social instinct in man demands that every individual of this species should have permanent regulations for the (different) stages of life and for living together, but social laws depend on an understanding of each other's meaning (or ideas) and on certain rules which separate the property of one from that of another, and provide for the removal of the pain which one gives to another. Making these the basis, the inhabit-ants of all the countries, distant islands and lofty mountains have according to their progress and intellectuality, formed words indicative of the meaning and origin of faiths on which at present stand the governments of the world.[55]

It was Rammohun Roy's declared objective to help remove some of the bases of the barriers imposed by the "present governments" against the fulfilment of the species-wide "social instinct in man." He saw orthodox religions as one important type of such barriers. Hence he wrote: "May God render religion destructive of differences and dislike between man and man, and conducive to the peace and union of mankind."[56] Rammohun Roy also maintained that national sovereignty had to be transcended in solving the problems of the people. In a letter to the French Foreign Minister, he made the following proposal for a Congress of Nations:

But on general grounds, I beg to observe that it appears to me the ends of constitutional government might be better attained by submitting every mat-ter of political difference between two countries to a Congress composed of an equal number from the Parliament of each; the decision of the majority to be acquiesced in by both nations and the chairman to be chosen by each nation alternately, for one year, and the place of the meeting to be one year within the limits of one country and the next within those of the other; such as Dover and Calais for England and France.

By such a Congress all matters of difference, whether political or commercial, affecting the natives of any two civilized countries with constitutional govern-ment might be settled amicably and justly to the satisfaction of both and pro-found peace and friendly feelings might be preserved between them from generation to generation.[57]

Rammohun Roy's focus, however, was not on any organizational blueprint for a restructured world order. His preoccupation rather was with synthesizing a transnational, humanist culture. He appreciated the liberal, scientific, world-affirming attitude of modern Western thought. But he critiqued its foundation in the conflictual cosmology of the Judeo-Christian tradition of thought, which justifies the violence done unto one being or person in atonement for the sins of another. He appreciated the spiritual (inner self and self-purification) and communitarian values of Advaita Vedanta. But he disapproved of its world-denying and self-denying assumptions. By such a critique of cultures and religions, he undermined the cultural arrogance of orthodox Brahmans, Christian missionaries, and Macaulayan educationists. Thus, he, as noted by Brajendranath Seal, paved the way for "a synthesis between Eastern and Western social values and postulates against the common background of universal humanity." In other words, he pointed the way "to the solution of the larger problem of international culture and civilization in human history, and became a precursor...a prophet of the coming Humanity."[58] Hailing Rammohun Roy as the herald of a world society, Rabindranath Tagore writes:

Rammohun was the only person in his time...to realise completely the significance of the modern age. He knew that the ideal of human civilization does not lie in isolation of independence, but in the brotherhood of inter-dependence of individuals as well as nations. His attempt was to establish our peoples on the full consciousness of their own cultural personality, to make them comprehend the reality of all that was unique...in their civilizations in the spirit of sympathetic cooperation.[59]

NOTES

1. This essay was first published in Thomas Pantham and Kenneth L. Deutsch, eds., *Political Thought in Modern India* (New Delhi: Sage Publications, 1986).
2. Rabindranath Tagore, "Inaugurator of the Modern Age in India," in *The Father of Modern India, Commemoration Volume of the Rammohun Roy Centenary Celebrations*, 1933, edited by Satish Chandra Chakravarti (Calcutta: Sadharan Brahmo Samaj, 1935).
3. C.F. Andrews at the Rammohun Roy Centenary Celebrations at Cuttack, Orissa, in 1933, as cited in D.R. Bali, *Modern Indian Thought* (New Delhi: Sterling, 1980), p. 7.
4. J. Bowring, ed., *The Works of Jeremy Bentham* (Edinburgh: W.Tait, 1843), Vol. 10, p. 589.
5. Rabindranath Tagore in *Bharatpathik Rammohun Roy*, as cited in V.S. Naravane, *Modern Indian Thought* (Bombay: Asia, 1964), p. 23.
6. Translation of several principal books, passages, and texts of the Vedas, and of some controversial works on Brahmanical theology by Raja Rammohun Roy with an Introductory Memoir, *Memorial Education* (Calcutta: Society for the Resuscitation of Indian Literature, 1903), pp. lxxi-lxxii; as cited in A.K. Majumdar, "Religion of Rammohun Roy" in V.C. Joshi, ed., *Rammohun Roy and the Process of Modernization in India* (Delhi: Vikas, 1975), pp. 69–70.
7. While Digby was in England on leave in 1817, he published from London Rammohun Roy's translations of the *Kena Upanishad* and *Abridgment of the Vedanta*.
8. Sophia Dobson Collet, *The Life and Letters of Raja Rammohun Roy*, edited by Dilip Biswas and Prabhat Gangopadhyay (Calcutta: Sadharan Brahmo Samaj, 1962), pp. 60–61.

9. As cited by Sumit Sarkar in V.C. Joshi, ed., op. cit., p. 50.

10. See D. H. Bishop, ed., *Thinkers of the Indian Renaissance* (New Delhi: Wiley Eastern, 1982), p. 7.

11. As cited in Radharaman Chakraborti, "Rammohun Roy: His Vision of Social Change," in A.K. Mukhopadhyay, ed., *The Bengali Intellectual Tradition* (Calcutta: K.P. Bagchi, 1979), p. 23.

12. *The English Works of Rammohun Roy* (Calcutta: Sadharan Brahmo Samaj, 1947), Vol. 2, p. 44.

13. As cited in V.S. Naravane, op. cit., p. 26.

14. Charles H. Heimsath, "Rammohun Roy and Social Reform," in V.C. Joshi, ed., op. cit., p. 154.

15. *The English Works of Rammohun Roy*, p. 90.

16. S.D. Collet, *op. cit.,* p. 280. There were, however, the following differences between Rammohun Roy and his Bengal society, on the one hand, and Reformation Europe and Luther, on the other. The incipient nationalism of Reformation Europe against the claims of the Papacy was absent in the colonized society of Bengal. Moreover, while Luther wrote his German Bible in the common language of the peasants, Rommohun Roy used the Sanskrit-based Bengali of the emergent urban *bhadralok*.

17. Kissory Chand Mitter, *Rammohun Roy and Tuhfat-ul Muwahhiddin* (Calcutta: K.P. Bagchi, 1975), p. 7.

18. As cited in D.H. Bishop, op. cit., p. 11.

19. Radharaman Chakraborti, op. cit., p. 20.

20. As cited in A.F. Salahuddin Ahmed, "Rammohun Roy and His Contemporaries," in V.C. Joshi, ed., op. cit., p. 100.

21. See Bimanbehari Majumdar, *History of Indian Social and Political Ideas* (Calcutta: Bookland Pvt. Ltd., 1967), p. 27.

22. D.H. Bishop, op. cit., p. 7. In 1833, in a critique of Rammohun Roy's interpretation of the Upanishads, K.M. Banerjee wrote that the Upanishads teach monism and not monotheism. See K.M. Banerji, *Review of the Mudock Upanishad by Ram Mohan Roy* (Calcutta: Enquirer Press, 1833), pp. 9–10. According to V.P. Varma, however, the Upanishads "tend to blur the distinction between a personal supreme god and the impersonal absolute." V.P. Varma, *Modern Indian Political Thought* (Agra: Lakshmi Narain Agarwal, 3rd ed., 1967), p. 19. It may also be noted in this context that in the Vedanta literature, there is also a blurring of the distinction between ontology and ethics.

23. J. Bowring, ed., op. cit., p. 571. According to Rajat Ray, before Rammohun Roy was influenced by British utilitarianism, he was influenced by "the secularist, rationalist and deistic trend in the Perso-Arabic literature of seventeenth and eighteenth century India." See Rajat Ray in V.C. Joshi ed., op. cit., pp. 7–8.

24. In Rammohun's anti-ritualist views, he was influenced by Islam and Buddhism.

25. As cited by David Kopf in V.C. Joshi, ed., op. cit., p. 27.

26. As cited by A.F. Salahuddin Ahmed in V.C. Joshi, ed., op. cit., p. 94.

27. See note 24 above.

28. David Kopf, "Rammohun Roy and the Bengal Renaissance: An Historiographical Essay," in V.C. Joshi, ed., op. cit., p. 28.

29. Ibid., p. 37.

30. D.H. Bishop, op. cit., p. 21.

31. *The English Works of Rammohun Roy*, Vol. 4, p. 108.

32. Rajat K. Ray, "Introduction" to V.C. Joshi, ed., op. cit., p. 11.
33. *Rammohun Rachanabali* (Calcutta: Haraf Prakashani, 1973), p. 449, as cited in Tapan Chattopadhyay, "Rammohun Roy: An Analysis in Historical Perspective," *Calcutta Journal of Political Studies*, Vol. 2, No. 1, Winter 1981, p. 108.
34. See Asok Sen, "The Bengal Economy and Rammohun Roy," in V.C. Joshi, ed., op. cit., p. 113.
35. Ibid., p. 115.
36. See B. Majumdar, op. cit., p. 43.
37. See V.C. Joshi, op. cit., pp. 101–102 and 118.
38. See Asok Sen in V.C. Joshi, op. cit., pp. 119–121.
39. S.D. Collet, op. cit., p. 270.
40. *The English Works of Raja Rammohun Roy*, p. 917.
41. B. Majumdar, op. cit., pp. 431 and 449.
42. S.D. Collet, op. cit., pp. 431 and 449.
43. As cited in B. Majumdar, op. cit., p. 36.
44. Ibid., p. 37.
45. Ibid., p. 34.
46. As cited in V.P. Varma, op. cit., p. 22.
47. Asok Sen in V.C. Joshi, op. cit., p.111.
48. Ibid., p. 128.
49. Sumit Sarkar, "Rammohun Roy and the Break with the Past," in V.C. Jodi, ed., op. cit., p. 63.
50. Rajat Ray in V.C. Joshi, op. cit., p. 17.
51. Ibid., p. 20.
52. It is interesting to note that some two decades after Rammohun Roy's death, Karl Marx wrote that British imperialism played a regenerative role in India. For an interesting comparison of Rammohun Roy and Karl Marx's views on this, see Subrata Mukherjee, "Political Ideas of Rammohun Roy," *Democratic World* (New Delhi), 9 September 1984, pp. 10–11. See also T. Chattopadhyay, op. cit.
53. Barun De, "A Biographical Perspective on the Political and Economic Ideas of Rammohun Roy," in V.C. Joshi, ed., op. cit., p. 147.
54. As cited in B. Majumdar, op. cit., p. 26.
55. *The English Works of Raja Rammohun Roy*, p. 947.
56. As cited in B. Majumdar, op. cit., p. 49.
57. As cited in D.H. Bishop, op. cit., pp. 23–24.
58. B. Seal, *Rammohun, The Universal Man* (Calcutta: Sadharan Brahmo Samaj, 1933), p. 1.
59. As in note 1 above.

Gandhi and the Emergence of the Modern Indian Political Canon[1]

Anthony J. Parel

As is evident from Kautilya's *Arthasastra*,[2] classical India had a political canon of its own. Because of this, there was an original, recognizably Indian mode of political thought. By the beginning of the nineteenth century, however, with the introduction of the modern Western political thought by the colonial state, it was faced with the threat of extinction. Modern Indian political thinkers, whether of the liberal or the Marxist persuasion, adopted a Western framework of thought in their effort to understand and modernize India. They thought and acted as if the Indian political canon had never existed. What they succeeded in producing, however, was political thought in India, not genuine Indian political thought. There were of course several exceptions to this—M. K. Gandhi being the most important. Genuine modern Indian political thought is possible only if the framework of thought and analysis is Indian and modern at the same time. Gandhi produced such a framework. He updated the ancient Indian canon by deleting what was obsolete in it, preserving what was valid and viable, and adding to it what was new and modern. By doing all this, he was able to liberate the Indian mind from intellectual dependency and give Indian political thought a new direction. This essay is a critical examination of his achievements in this regard. It begins with a brief account of the ancient canon, which provides the necessary background for the present discussion.

The Ancient Indian Political Canon

By about the end of the fourth century BC, four ideas had attained canonical status in Indian political thought. First, a plurality of sciences (*vidyas*)—among them the science of politics (*danda niti*)—were recognized as being indispensable for human flourishing. Second, monarchy was accepted as the normal form of government. Third, a hierarchical order of society, based on the four *varnas* (in the current terminology, "castes") was endorsed as the right form of human society. And fourth, the overall aim of political science was to create the cultural conditions necessary for the pursuit of the four great ends of life, the *purusharthas*—ethical goodness (*dharma*), wealth and power (*artha*), pleasure (*kama*), and spiritual transcendence (*moksha*).

These ideas received their formal recognition in Kautilya's *Arthasastra*. Subsequent writers such as Kamandaki in the fifth century AD, Somadeva in the tenth century AD, and the author of *Sukraniti* in the fourteenth century AD, all followed the canon more or less faithfully.[3] The great epics of India, the *Mahabharata* and the

Ramayana, were careful to pay due attention to the canon. So were the works in the dharmasastra tradition, such as Manu's *Dharmasastra.* The same was true even of the *Kamasutra,* a work on sexual pleasure. Major writers in secular Sanskrit literature, such as Kalidasa (fifth century AD), were all mindful of the canonical status of these ideas. Given their importance and longevity,[4] it is necessary to examine them in some detail. For reasons of space, however, I shall limit the enquiry mostly to the *Arthasastra.*

The *Arthasastra* opens the discussion of the science of politics with a wider discussion of the necessity of the three other sciences known in its day. Such a holistic approach to political science is noteworthy in itself. The sciences mentioned, in the order presented, were philosophy (*anviksiki*), the Vedas, economics, and of course political science. The implication was that political science, though necessary, was not sufficient to bring about all the conditions necessary for human flourishing. The latter required the contributions of the other sciences mentioned, and it was necessary that political science from the very start was mindful of this.

How many sciences were necessary for full human flourishing was itself a matter of debate. That these issues were debated tells us something about the level of intellectual vitality and sophistication of the times. Kautilya mentions three schools opposed to his position. It is not clear whether they were contemporary schools or schools belonging to the past. His lack of detailed analysis of their claims suggests the latter. In any case, the school of Manavah maintained that only three sciences were needed, since philosophy could be considered as an offshoot of the science of the Vedas. The school of Brahaspati on the other hand held that only two sciences— politics and economics—were needed, since the other two sciences were "a cloak for those conversant with the ways of the world."(1.2.5). According to the school of Usanas, there was need for only one science—the science of politics. "For, with it are bound up undertakings connected with all the sciences." (1.2.7).

It is against this background that Kautilya advances his own position: " 'Four indeed is the number of sciences,' says Kautilya. Since with their help one can learn what is spiritual good [*dharma*] and material well-being [*artha*], therefore the sciences are so called." (1.2.8–9).

Philosophy was placed first on the list of sciences. By philosophy was meant the discipline that investigates "by means of reasoning" (1.2.11) the internal structure of all the sciences. The philosophy's business is to question the basic assumptions of the sciences. To make reasonable basic assumptions was the prerogative of the sciences themselves. The role of philosophy, by contrast, was to investigate whether the claims made were rationally consistent and intelligible. Thus philosophy examined "the relative strength and weakness" of the three sciences, what was spiritual good and spiritual evil according to the teachings of the Vedas, what was material profit and material loss in economics, and what constituted good policy and bad policy in political science (1.2.11). That is to say, without the techniques of philosophy no coherent understanding of any of theses sciences was possible. As such, philosophy was a precondition for a thorough and systematic understanding of any branch of knowledge.

It is not surprising that Kautilya is effusive in his praise of philosophy. It "confers benefit on the people, keeps the mind steady in adversity and prosperity and brings about proficiency in thought, speech and action." (1.2.11). Philosophy is "the lamp of all sciences," a lamp that dispels the darkness of ignorance and inconsistency (1.2.12). He mentions by name the Samkhya, the Yoga, and the Lokayata schools of philosophy known in his day. The first two dealt with the issue of spiritual liberation while the third dealt with the issue of materialism—allowing the inference that philosophy was neutral and "secular" as far as the basic assumptions of the various systems of knowledge were concerned. Its distinctive role was to make the sciences argumentative in their procedure.

As modern scholars have noted, philosophy according to the ancient Indian canon does not mean what it means today in modern West.[5] Modern Western philosophy (or at least certain branches of it) is liable to be hostile to spiritual philosophy generally—a liability that Indian philosophy, ancient and modern, does not carry. Philosophy according to the ancient Indian canon remains neutral between materialism and spiritualism. This becomes very clear when we turn to the role it plays in the science of the Vedas, second on Kautilya's list.

The science of the Vedas deals with "revealed truths," i.e., truths whose ultimate justification rests directly on the "seeing" of the seers and only indirectly on reason. Such truths are concerned with the ultimate meaning of existence, the nature of the immaterial *atman* or *purusha* or self and its relationship to the supreme Self. The science of the Vedas is an integral part of the human sciences. The Vedas also concern themselves with the ultimate basis of ethical values, worship, religious sacrifices, rituals, and chants used in worship and the like. The study of theses aspects of the Vedas depended on a host of subsidiary sciences, such as grammar, phonetics, prosody, and astronomy.

The crucial issue in the science of the Vedas from the perspective of the present discussion is its epistemology. The knowledge of revealed truths is said to be derived from the internal spiritual "experience" (*anubhava*) of the "seers." Such knowledge is not derived in the first instance from reason or empirical sources. As far as revealed truths are concerned, "seeing" has priority over reasoning. It may be said that in the beginning was "seeing." Only after "seeing" do thinking, reasoning, speaking, writing, and acting come.

Even so, philosophy has a role to play in the development of the science of the Vedas. It delves into the data provided by the seers and helps produce systems of philosophy called "*darshana*" (literally, "what is seen"). The basic assumptions of the well-known six systems of Indian "philosophy"—Samkhya, Yoga, Nyaya, Visesika, Mimamsa, and Vedanta—rest ultimately on the authority of the Vedas. But that is not the whole of it. These systems of spiritual "philosophy" can develop only when they become argumentative. This can happen only if philosophy as a neutral discipline intervenes. That is to say, the very development of the spiritual "philosophies" depends on *anviksiki*, to use the original name for philosophy.

Two things are noteworthy here. The first is that according to the old canon the science of revealed truths does have a place among the human sciences. That the premier text of Indian political philosophy should say this makes the saying very striking. In comparative terms, it is as if Machiavelli were to say that theology is an integral part of the human sciences. However that might be, the revealed truths of the Vedas were open to investigation by human reason. What originates in "seeing," is subjected to rational investigation. Only such investigation can establish their status as science (*vidya*). Indeed, it is from such investigation that the six systems of spiritual "philosophy", already mentioned, arose.

The second noteworthy feature of the ancient canon is the relationship of the science of the Vedas to philosophy. There is no suggestion in the *Arthasastra* of any incompatibility, much less of active hostility, between the two. Distinction does not imply or require opposition. The presumed harmony between the two is an important aspect of the ancient canon of Indian political thought. That political science, which is concerned with power interests, should recognize the validity of the science of the Vedas is something that would have a lasting impact on the entire history of Indian political philosophy.

The science of economics (*vartta*) is third on Kautilya's list. It maintains its relative independence among the other sciences. He does not go into a detailed analysis of this science, being content with mentioning that agriculture, cattle breeding, and trade are the chief sources of wealth production. Most importantly, however, he points out that success in both domestic policy and foreign policy depends on the treasury and the strength of the economy (1.4.1–2).

Turning now to political science itself, the *Arthasastra* makes five points that are highly relevant to the present discussion. The first is that political science is the science of maintaining and protecting a wealthy and powerful political community or a territory inhabited by people. "The source of livelihood of men is wealth, in other words, the earth inhabited by people. The science which is the means of the attainment and protection of that earth is the Science of Politics [*arthasastra*]." (15.1.1–2). Secondly, political science is necessary for protecting humans from "the law of the fishes" (*matsya nyaya*), according to which the strong swallows the weak (1.4.13–15). The natural tendency of humans is to dominate one another unilaterally. The political order is a remedy against this tendency. The remedy consists of just punishment or the exercise of the Rod. From the symbol of the Rod, political science derives its other name, *danda niti*, the science of the just application of *danda* or punishment. The political order, to this extent, is a coercive order, but coercion applied only in the interest of justice. Punishments, states *Arthasastra*, should be neither severe nor lax but "just." (1.4.7–10).

Thirdly, monarchy is the accepted form of government. In his domestic policy, the monarch is obliged to enforce the hierarchical social order based on *varna* or "caste". In his foreign policy, however, he is free to promote the power interests of the state. It is in the nature of states to seek to expand, conquer and subjugate. It was the ambition of every king to become one day a king of kings or a conqueror. The symbol of conquest was the wheel (*chakra*), from which was derived the title of the conqueror, *chakravarti*—the wielder of the wheel. Once set in motion, the wheel moves in all directions—north, south, east, and west, until it conquers everything before it or stopped by another wheel similarly in motion. Hence the second title of the conqueror, *digvijayi* or the conqueror of the four quarters. The state system as envisaged in the old canon was an imperial war-system.

The science of politics, then, is also the science of acquisition and expansion. It has "for its purpose the acquisition of things not possessed, the preservation of things possessed, the augmentation of things preserved and the bestowal of things augmented on a worthy recipient. On it is dependent the orderly maintenance of worldly life."(I. 4. 3–4).

Fourthly, political science has an indispensable positive cultural role to play in society. Without political science establishing conditions of order and stability, the other sciences would not be able to flourish. "The means of ensuring the pursuit of philosophy, the three Vedas and economics is the Rod, wielded by the king." (1.4.3). Again, "the three sciences have their root in the just administration of the Rod." (1.5.1).

Finally and most importantly, political science is the indispensable means of creating the cultural conditions necessary for the pursuit of the great ends of human existence, the *purusharthas* (1. 4.11). It is as if humans cannot attain their destiny, both material and spiritual, without the support of political science. *Arthasastra* considers this point so important that it takes the unusual step of repeating it several times. To begin with, the king himself should set an example to his subjects by demonstrating how the *purusharthas* may be successfully pursued. "He should enjoy sensual pleasures without contravening his spiritual good and material well-being; he should not deprive himself of pleasures. He should devote himself equally to the three goals of life which are bound up with one another. For, any one of the three, viz., spiritual good, material well-being and sensual pleasures, if excessively indulged in, does harm to itself as well as to the other two." (1.7.3–5). As far as political science is concerned, however, *artha* has relative primacy, because "spiritual good and sensual pleasures depend on material well-being." (1.7.7). Again, the pursuit of these goals being so important, the education of the prince should include training in the pursuit of the *purusharthas* (1.17.33). The same point is made in 15.1.64: "He [the royal preceptor] should instruct him [the prince] in what conduces to spiritual and material good, not in what is spiritually and materially harmful."

It comes as no surprise that *Arthasastra* should end with a strong plea on behalf of the *purusharthas*. The connection between political science and the *purusharthas* could not have been better defended. It is as if political science has no higher end than the defense of the theory of the *purusharthas*. It is as if Kautilya wrote his work to establish this truth. One need only to read the penultimate sentence of the entire work to grasp this: "This science brings into being and preserves *dharma*, *artha*, and *kama*, and destroys spiritual evil, material loss and hatred." (15.1.72).

THE PLACE OF ARTHA AMONG THE FOUR PURUSHARTHAS

Given the importance that the old canon had attached to the theory of the *purusharthas*, it is useful to give, at this stage of our argument, a brief account of it and of the position that *artha* occupies in it. The term *purushartha* is made up of two Sanskrit terms: *purusha*, meaning "immaterial spirit," and *artha*, meaning (in this instance) "for the sake of." It therefore carries the literal meaning of "that which is done for the sake of the immaterial spirit." In Indian philosophical anthropology, humans are understood to be composites of nature (*prakriti*) and spirit (*purusha*). The former provides the material/physiological/psychological substratum of human personality, and the latter its spiritual "foundation." Accordingly, human activities are seen, ultimately, as those that are pursed for the sake of the *purusha*. It is this reference to the *purusha* that gives ultimate meaning to *all* human activities, material, psychological, ethical, aesthetic as well as spiritual. Not that the body and its interests do not have their own relatively autonomous purposes, but that in ethical and philosophical terms those purposes acquire their full human significance only in so far as they retain a reference, however remote, to the interests of the *purusha*. Any human activity that deliberately excludes this reference is considered *pro tanto* not beneficial to human well-being.[6]

The position occupied by *artha* among the *purusharthas* had been different in the different intellectual traditions. In the *arthasastra* tradition, as we saw above, it had a very crucial role to play in the system of the *purusharthas*: it operated interactively with the other three, and there was no suggestion of any incompatibility between it and *moksha* (1.3.14). Later works in the *arthasastra* tradition, such as the fifth century *Kamandaki Nitisara* did the same.[7] However, in the *moksha-sastra* traditions, viz., in the six systems of Indian philosophy, *artha* had a very low status, and was treated as though it was incompatible with the serious pursuit of *moksha*. The pursuit of *moksha* according to these systems was supposed to require a gradual withdrawal from the real world of politics and economics. As a result, *artha* became marginalized to the point of being treated as a negative value. The consequences were disastrous. As P. V. Kane remarks, intellectuals from the eleventh century onward took no interest in the sciences of politics and economics, being totally committed to "mental gymnastics about logic, Vedanta, Poetics and similar subjects."[8] Interest in *artha* became so low that, as Sheldon Pollock points out, "even commentarial literature" on the subject was stunted, and "the discourse on polity" was absorbed within the *dharmasastra* tradition.[9] The neglect of *artha* continued into the nineteenth century. The thinker who did more than others to rescue and modernize it was Mahatma Gandhi.

STABILITY AND CHANGE

No political culture can long survive without its canon. And no political canon can long continue without timely change. There is a subtle but real connection between canon, stability, and change. A political canon reflects stability, but to be relevant, it should also be willing to change. However, because of the preponderance of the *moksha* tradition in Indian culture of the medieval period, the old political canon was unable to develop further. This remained the case even after the fourteenth century, when a radically new political canon—the *sharia*—was introduced in Indian territories under Muslim rule.

This is not the place to raise the question of why the Indian political canon and the *sharia* did not enter into a creative engagement with one another. However, the fact that no such engagement took place needs to be noted. Not that Indian political thinkers of the Middle Ages were unaware of the *sharia*, but that they chose to do nothing more than just take note of it. *Sukraniti*, for example, mentioned the "theory of the Yavanas" (medieval Indian name for Muslims), and included it in its list of thirty-two sciences.[10] "Yavana philosophy is that which recognizes God as the invisible creator of this universe, and recognizes virtue and vice without reference to *Sruti* [the Vedas] and *Smriti* [Tradition], and which believes that *Sruti* contains a separate religious system."[11] The Yavanas, noted *Sukraniti*, did not follow the caste system. They "have all the four castes mixed together. They recognize authority other than the Vedas and live in the north and west. Their *Sastras* have been framed for their welfare by their own masters."[12]

Totally different, however, was the reception accorded to the Western canon, introduced by the colonial state in the nineteenth century. It produced an unprecedented intellectual ferment in India that made Indians look critically at their social and political institutions. The role that the ascetic tradition played in Indian culture came under critical scrutiny. The same happened to the caste system and monarchy itself. Western ideas such as individual liberty, equality, the right to self-determination, nationalism, rule of law, and the religious neutrality of the state, etc., were warmly welcomed.

However, there was one striking aspect to this welcome. It was as if the welcome party was unaware of the existence of India's ancient political canon. Both Indian liberals and Indian Marxists seemed to suffer from cultural and intellectual amnesia. In the case of the latter, the forgetfulness was perhaps deliberate. They forsook Gandhi and took after Mao, Gramsci, Lukacs, and others, believing that Marxism was the new universal canon superseding all the others, whether Indian, Chinese, or Islamic.

There is no question that modern Indian political thinkers, including Indian Marxists, wrote about Indian political issues—theory of history, colonialism, nationalism, self-determination, socialism, class war, individual liberty, equality and a host of other things. But their writings produced what may be termed "political thought in India." They did not produce "Indian political thought," if by Indian political thought is meant a body of thought produced with the help of and within an Indian framework of thought and analysis. The framework of thought and analysis that these writers employed was not specifically Indian; it was normally either liberal or Marxist. Take for example A. Appadorai's classic two-volume *Documents on Political Thought in Modern India*.[13] As their very title indicates, these volumes are about *political thought in India*, not about "Indian political thought." The writers in question were of course writing about India; but only few of them were conscious of the need to use an Indian framework of analysis. There is some truth in Sri Aurobindo's criticism that "the last generation merely attempted to imitate and reproduce with a servile fidelity the ideals and forms of the West."[14]

However that might be, India once had a political canon of its own. If it was to have a new canon, the old one had to be updated. Now updating an old canon is no easy task. The charisma of the writer or writers has to respond to the needs of the times. India was fortunate to have had a number of great writers who contributed important elements towards the updating of a modern Indian political canon. Among them were Rabindranath Tagore, B. G. Tilak, Sri Aurobindo, S. Radhakrishnan, Jawaharlal Nehru, Maulana Azad, and B. R. Ambedkar. However, the thinker who pulled all the elements together and inaugurated the modern Indian political canon was M. K. Gandhi.

SEVERAL IDEAS DELETED

There is no doubt that Gandhi wanted to be an innovator of the old Indian political canon. He could become one only if he were prepared to delete what was obsolete, add what was new, and preserve what was essential. This exactly was his strategy. "My *swaraj* is to keep intact the genius of our civilization," he had written. "I want to write many new things but they must be all written on the Indian slate. I would gladly borrow from the West when I can return the amount with decent interest."[15] At the same time he did not want to drown himself, as he put it, "in the waters of our ancestors' well." Preserving everything from the past would indeed be suicidal. The innovator's task was to increase the patrimony of the past and make it productive. "I believe that it is our duty to augment the legacy of our ancestors and to change it into current coin and make it acceptable to the present age."[16] His efforts to update the old political canon are best seen in the light of these sentiments. I shall sketch below the process of deletions and additions that was involved.

Deleted from the old canon were ideas relating to the monarchy and the caste system. The "law of fishes," the old justification for the political order, was dropped in favor of the idea of *swaraj* or self-rule. Likewise the idea that political power was something that had to expand, conquer and subdue was replaced by the idea of political power as the legitimate means of coercion solely for purposes of internal order and external security.

Disposing of the monarchy was relatively painless. It did not require civil war, revolution or regicide. By mid-twentieth century, the rajahs and maharajahs were pensioned off and their territories integrated into republican India. Gandhi's political theory in general and his theory of nonviolence in particular contributed greatly to India's transition from monarchy to republic.

Dealing with the caste system was an altogether different matter. Although by 1890s Gandhi had become convinced of the illegitimacy of the system, he was painfully aware of the fact that the system had its sanction the Vedas (*Rg Veda*, 90: 11–12) and the *Bhagavad Gita* (4: 13; 18: 41–48). Because of this, he had to tread cautiously. He first took the position that "caste" in its original form as *varna* was egalitarian and that its corruption into *jati* (the assignation of caste by birth) was "a hideous travesty of the original." Instead of the original four divisions, there was now a multitude of castes—clear evidence "that the law of *varna* [had] become a dead letter."[17] By 1935 he took a firm stand against the caste system: "Caste Has to Go," was the title of an essay that he published in that year.[18] Campaign against the practices of "untouchability" soon became one of the most important projects of the new canon.

However, the scriptural justification of the caste system raised its own difficulties, which forced him to examine the rules of interpretation of the scriptures. The issue became critical as B. R. Ambedkar, the leader of the so-called "Untouchables" (and the future draftsman of the new Indian Constitution) threatened to abandon Hinduism altogether, arguing that nothing less than the rejection of the scriptures themselves was needed.

Gandhi sought to find a way of both getting rid of the caste system and safe-guarding the integrity of the scriptures. A correct interpretation of the scriptures, he argued, would show that the caste system had only a historical, not permanent, validity. This followed from the criteria of the interpretation of the scriptures that he employed. The criteria he chose were conscience, reason, learning, holiness of life, and the inner experience of the truths to be interpreted. "The scriptures properly so called can only be concerned with eternal verities and must appeal to any conscience, i. e., any heart whose eyes of understanding are opened. Nothing can be accepted as the word of God which cannot be tested by reason or is capable of being spiritually experienced... Learning there must be but religion does not live by it. It lives in the experiences of its saints and seers, in their lives and sayings. When all the most learned commentators of the scriptures are utterly forgotten, the accumulated experience of the sages and saints will abide and be an inspiration for ages to come."[19]

One "eternal verity" that the Hindu scriptures taught was that humans were capable of self-determination, self-development and spiritual liberation. All other facts about humans had to be interpreted in the light this truth. The interpretation of the scriptures by saints and seers were more reliable than were those by mere scholars: for the former had spiritual experience of the truth they were interpreting, while the latter lacked it altogether. Gandhi's point was that the Hindu scriptures, rightly interpreted, could favor the evolution of an egalitarian society. Seen in this light, the caste system as it had evolved in India had only historical, not permanent, validity. The scriptures, reinterpreted, would call for the end of caste system. As historical awareness changes, so would the attitude towards caste. A combination of historical knowledge, spiritual experience and sound reasoning led him to delete the caste system from the old Indian political canon.

As for the "law of fishes," he replaced it with the idea of self-rule or *swaraj:* all humans were free and capable of self-determination, self development, and self-transcendence. According to the new canon, the justification for a democratic political order arises from this principle.

Deleted also was the notion that state power was something that of necessity required expansion and conquest. According to old theory, power was antinomian, a law unto itself, recognizing no other law. States tended to invoke national interest (*prajana swartha*)[20] as their supreme law of conduct. Gandhi's theory of nonvio-lence, which is not a pacifist theory but a theory of the legitimate use of coercive force, challenged the antinomian character of state power. The "law of fishes" did not constitute a moral law. It merely referred to a mode of behavior, a "faculty of acting," as Samuel Pufendorf, in the seventeenth century was to point out.[21] Gandhi, going further, argued that the law of humanity required that states in their mutual relations could use power only for internal order and external security, and never for external expansion and imperial domination. What the world needed today was not "absolutely independent states warring one against another but a federation of friendly interdependent states."[22] His demand for the end of modern colonialism, which was an integral part of his theories of *swaraj* and non-violence (*ahimsa*), was simultaneously a demand for a change in the old *Arthasastra* conception of state power.

FOUR IDEAS ADDED

Updating the old canon required the addition of new ideas that came mostly from the West. They included ideas of civic nationalism, the limited constitutional state, fundamental human rights and modern political economy.

Nationalism for Gandhi was a theory of political community. The "nation" was to take the place of "caste." Though a Western ideology, it had its cultural antecedents in Indian history. Already the *Arthasastra* had spoken of India as a sphere of imperial expansion (a *chakravartin* sphere) stretching from the Himalayas in the north to seas to the south and a thousand *yojanas* across (9.1.18). In *Hind Swaraj* he vigorously defended the view that Indians constituted a nation, arguing that all Indians—Hindus, Muslims, Buddhists, Jainas, Christians, Sikhs, Zoroastrians, Jews, and others—had a shared sense of history and culture.[23]

The old canon was no longer adequate to deal with the modern reality of a multireligious and multilingual India. The viability of modern India depended on the availability of a modern theory of political community that could weld the country's multiplicities into a working unity. Gandhi believed that civic nationalism was that theory. Its defense became part of the new canon.

Nationalism, however, was not a monolith ideology, as Gandhi was soon to learn. There was a nationalism based on religion that the separatist Muslims wanted; there was a nationalism based on *hindutva* (Hinduness) that a minority of Hindus wanted; and there was civic nationalism that the vast majority of Indians under the banner of the Indian National Congress wanted. The political history of modern India was a struggle for supremacy by these three forms of nationalism—M. A. Jinnah (1875–1948) taking the leadership of religious nationalism, V. D. Savarkar (1882–1966) taking that of ethnic or *hindutva* nationalism, and Gandhi taking that of civic nationalism.

What distinguished civic nationalism from the other two was its universalistic core. According to Gandhi, a civic nation is a people who, in addition to inhabiting a specific territory and sharing a common history, share a sense of justice, rights, and duties. The civic nation attaches the greatest importance to the individual as a self-determining and self-developing being and as a bearer of certain inalienable rights. Of the three forms of nationalism, only the civic nation recognizes and respects these rights. This recognition and this respect constitute its inner core. The civic national identity alone could transcend all prepolitical identities, whether based on religion or language or caste or ethnicity. Civic nationalism recognizes and respects these identities too but within a broader context of a pan-national identity. Briefly, civic nationalism is a component part of the new Indian political canon.

Hind Swaraj (1909) is the primary text of Gandhi's civic nationalism. However, in 1946, on the eve of national independence, he hit upon the wonderful metaphor of "oceanic circle" for India as a civic nation. Contrasted with the oceanic circle (the new India) was the pyramid—the metaphor for the old, hierarchical India. The term "oceanic" signified inclusiveness and the term "circle," signified the formal distinction of the oceanic circle from other nations. The center from which the oceanic circle is drawn is the individual. From the center as many concentric circles as the individual wishes may be drawn, so long as they do not break the outer circumference of the oceanic circle. That is to say, Indians may belong to as many small inner circles as they wish: there would be room for all in the oceanic circle. Whichever circles they belong to, the individuals are not a collection of isolated atoms but are held together by a "free and voluntary play of mutual forces." "Life will not be a pyramid with the apex sustained by the bottom. But it will be an oceanic circle whose centre will be the individual always ready to perish for the village, the latter ready to perish for the circle of villages, till at last the whole becomes one life composed of individuals, never aggressive in their arrogance but ever humble, sharing the majesty of the oceanic circle of which they are integral units. Therefore the outermost circumference will not wield power to crush the inner circle but will give strength to all within and derive its own strength from it."[24] The oceanic circle has a special place in the new canon.

Turning now to Gandhi's notion of the state, the state that would be compatible with the oceanic circle is a "parliamentary *swaraj* according to the wishes of the Indian people"—a mixture of the Indian idea of self-rule and the Western idea of representative government.[25] The phrase "according to the wishes of the people of India" emphasizes the notion of government based on consent. The state according to the new canon would be neither the old *Arthasastra* type nor the new Hobbesean/Machiavellian type: it would be a constitutionally limited democracy.

The Gandhian state has four additional characteristics. First, it would be secular: *artha* (the category to which the state belongs) is a secular, not religious, category. Besides, religion had nothing to do with the structure of India as an oceanic circle.[26] Secondly, state sovereignty is not absolute but relative to the needs of peace between states. What "the better mind of the world" desires is "universal interdependence" rather than absolute independence.[27] Thirdly, as explained in his short treatise, *Constructive Programme: Its Meaning and Place* (1941), the state would work in tandem with the organs of civil society, viz. nongovernmental organizations.[28] Finally, it would operate according to the general principles of Gandhian nonviolence. Those principles recognize the right of the state to self-defense even by military means, if necessary. As he stated at the constitutional conference of 1931 held in London (the only such conference he ever attended), a state that did not have the control over its defense could not be a responsible state. The ability to defend itself is of "the essence" of a state's existence.[29] At the same time, the Gandhian state also has the obligation to develop civilian means of self-defense and to engage in progressive disarmament. What the new canon is trying to achieve was a reasonable balance between moderate political realism and the imperative of world peace.

Turning now to fundamental human rights—the third addition that he made to the modern Indian canon—they are quintessentially part of modernity. They had their historical origin in Western thought. Yet when transferred to Indian conditions, he managed to give them a recognizably Indian face—that of *satyagraha*. As he famously defined it, *satyagraha* was "a method of securing rights by personal suffering: it is the reverse of resistance by arms."[30] The Gandhian method of civil disobedience is different from the Western method, even from that made famous by Henry David Thoreau in mid-nineteenth century.[31] The Western method was open to the use of violence in defense of human rights even in internal politics. Gandhi's method, by contrast, made "personal suffering" a means of their defense. As Joan Bondurant has pointed out, of all the elements that constitute *satyagraha*, self-suffering is "the least acceptable to a Western mind."[32] Historically, the Western mind had accepted violence—such as the violence involved in street riots or in political revolutions, such as the French Revolution—as a means of asserting human rights. Gandhi's method marks an advance on the Western method. *Accepting* "self-suffering" does not mean *seeking* it in a pathological manner. It simply means accepting peacefully "the consequences of disobedience." This, he pointed out "was what Daniel did when he disobeyed the laws of the Medes and the Persians."[33] What makes civil disobedience "civil"—not violent—is precisely the peaceful acceptance of the penalty attached to civil disobedience.

Apart from transforming the Western mode of civil disobedience into *satyagraha*, Gandhi made an additional contribution to Indian political thought: he formally introduced fundamental human rights into the political discourse of modern India. This he did in 1931 by means of the famous resolution on "Fundamental Rights and Economic Changes." Jointly drafted by him and Jawaharlal Nehru, he personally presented the resolution at the annual meeting of the Indian National Congress—which assured its easy acceptance. As Granville Austin has pointed out, this resolution is the "spiritual antecedent" of the Directive Principles of the new Indian Constitution.[34]

As for Gandhi's fourth addition to the modern Indian canon, it strictly speaking is not an addition but a reintroduction. For, as we saw above, economics had a canonical status in the *arthasastra* tradition. What he did was to give modern economics its due place in the new canon. His initial access to modern economic thought was mostly through the economic writings of John Ruskin—*The Political Economy of Art* (1857), reissued in 1880 under the title *'A Joy For Ever': And Its Place in the Market*, and *Unto This Last* (1860)—and of a host of other friendly critics of nineteenth century industrial capitalism.[35] The Gandhian economic corpus—writings on *khadi* (cloth manufactured by cottage industry), rural economic development, option for the poor, appropriate technology, the relationship of economic development to moral development, and the like—is very substantial indeed. The scale of Indian poverty so affected him that in 1921 he took the dramatic step of changing his bourgeois attire to the much despised loincloth of the poor villager. The gesture was meant not to glorify but to critique poverty. The economic emancipation of the poor was as important to him as was the political emancipation of the nation itself. Political emancipation without economic emancipation would be nothing more than a cruel joke played on the poor. *Swaraj* (self-rule) had to come in all its four forms—political, moral, spiritual, *and* economic.

The single most important influence on his economic thought was John Ruskin. His *Unto This Last* produced, as he tells us, "an instantaneous and practical transformation" in his life.[36] He wanted Indians to understand Ruskin's basic orientation and to this end, in 1908, he published a paraphrase of that book in his weekly newspaper, *Indian Opinion*. Later it was published as a booklet under the title *Sarvodaya* ("the well-being of all"), a name that he gave to his economic philosophy as well.[37]

Ruskin's overall aim was to fight the antihuman elements that had crept into nineteenth century British capitalism and to bring a reformed capitalism into the mainstream of Western civilization. This is not the place to go into a detailed analysis of Ruskin, but the main points that Gandhi took from him may be briefly noted. The good of the individual is contained in the good of all. Labor is an equalizing activity and, even in the industrial age, the labor of the artist, the craftsman and the peasant has great economic as well as civilizing value. Given humans are body-soul composites, soul-force is as much a motivating force in economic activities as is enlightened self-interest. Granted that economics is the science of wealth, it is a mistake to see wealth only as possessions of exchangeable value. The wealth of a nation consists above all in its people who enjoy health, freedoms, and moral dispositions that enable them to use their wealth fittingly. It is necessary therefore to shift the focus from wealth as possessions to wealth as people. The aim of a sound political economy should be to meet the material needs, not just of the greatest number, but of every member of society. A reformed capitalism can accomplish all this only when it integrates principles of ethics and virtue into its economic practice.

Applying these ideas to India, Gandhi became convinced that the elimination of mass poverty was a primary task of political independence. In general terms, this called for investment in areas that would foster development from below. It required production by the masses rather than mass production. The right to private property was to be respected, but within the bounds of social responsibility. What was surplus to your reasonable needs were to be treated as if you were its trustee. Modern industrial capitalism had two defects that needed urgent remedy. The first was the damage it was doing to nature, the urban areas and the countryside, and the second was its inability either to satiate the greed of the rich or to alleviate the misery of the poor. The first required "appropriate technology," and the second required economics with a social conscience that could humanize the forces of the market.

Gandhi is not Gandhi unless he is able to write on the Indian slate. Regarding modern economics, he managed to find enough room on that slate to write something Indian. Quite ingenuously, he found support for the views mentioned above in the Upanishads, the *Bhagavad Gita*, and the *Yoga Sutra*. He interpreted the first verse of the *Ishopanishad* as teaching a lesson of great economic significance: God alone is the sovereign of the material world. Humans may enjoy them as its trustees, renouncing any claim to absolute ownership. In doing so, they should avoid coveting what belongs to fellow human beings. The *Gita* according to him taught a lesson in work ethic: no one was entitled to his food unless he or she had worked for it. Two virtues listed in Yoga philosophy—*astea* (prohibition against theft) and *aparigraha* (moderation in possessive desires)—with due modification, were converted into economic virtues necessary for healthy, modern economic activities.

Two Ideas Retained

Gandhi retained two pivotal ideas from the old canon—with some modification, of course. The first concerned the need for a plurality of sciences for the good life, and the second, the need for a plurality of life-goals or the *purusharthas*.

The old canon had held that there was no necessary incompatibility between revealed truths and truths based on reason. With this in the background, Gandhi had no difficulty in accepting modern science and its methods. In all his activities—as lawyer, political activist, social reformer, religious thinker—he was scrupulous to apply the methods of modern science. One example out of many would suffice—the advice that he gave to the workers engaged in the cottage industry of *khadi* (home-spun cotton cloth). This was not a highly educated group—most of them barely literate. Yet he was urging them to learn modern scientific methods. The passage, despite its length, is worth citing:

> A person who is scientifically inclined does not take the truth of anything for granted; he tries to prove it himself. In this way he develops his own intellect and also obtains knowledge of the potentialities of things. Why does an apple fall off the tree, why does it not fly up? It is said that this question arose in Newton's mind and he discovered the law of gravitation. Is the earth flat like a plate? Is it stationary? Such questions arose in Galileo's mind and he discovered that the earth is spherical like an orange and revolved on its axis. Such discoveries have produced great results.
>
> A *khadi* worker should adopt a similar scientific attitude. Newton or Galileo did not ponder over the problem of...[mass poverty]. They followed an intellectual quest. The *khadi* worker has however to find a solution to the problem of feeding the hungry masses. That is why their attitude should be all the more scientific.
>
> ....Many of my activities are undertaken in good faith or intuitively. But they are not conducted on the basis of inspiration alone; I have tried to place my convictions on a sound scientific foundation while propagating them. I have made and am still making all possible experiments based on reason and I encourage my co-workers to do so...[A complex problem] does involve a lot of statistics as also knowledge of economics, psychology, particularly of the Indian mind, and also of ethics. A mere statistical solution will not do, nor will a mere economic solution, because we cannot ignore our most fundamental and vital principles. We do not want to spread *khadi* through coercion. We want to do our work by changing people's sense of values and habits. Hence our researches should proceed from all angles.[38]

Gandhi's problem, then, was not with modern science and its methods,[39] but with the ideology of science, the ideology that asserted that there was incompatibility between scientific truths and the spiritual truths based on revelation. He was deeply concerned about the impact that this ideology had had, and was still having, on modern Western civilization. It was promoting, he felt, a culture of unbelief in the name of positivistic reason. "This civilization is irreligion, and it has taken such a hold on the people in Europe that those who are in it appear to be half mad," he had written in 1909.[40] His explanation for this phenomenon was that Western civilization was no longer able to maintain the right balance between the material aims and the spiritual aims of human life. In his language it was interested only in the pursuit of wealth, power and pleasure (*artha* and *kama*), and not at all in that of *dharma* and *moksha*. This was a dangerous course to take: "This civilization is such that one has only to be patient and it will be self-destroyed."[41]

He was anxious to protect modern Indian civilization from the onslaught of modern materialism. He believed that India was still "sound at the foundation." "What we have tested and found true on the anvil of experience, we dare not change."[42] The "foundation" and "the anvil of experience" he is referring to, are of course the "experience" (*anubhava*) by the seers of the divine. It is from the experiences of the seers, the sages and the prophets that humanity comes to know what the ultimate meaning of life is. The new canon that he was trying to introduce sought to reconcile aspects of modernity with spirituality, science with religion, rational knowledge with spiritual experience. If Gandhi had anything to say about it, there would indeed be an Indian version of modernity.

An assumption present in Gandhi's philosophy is that "seeing" or "experiencing" has epistemological validity. His theory of compatibility between revealed truths, modern science, and the truths of political science, rests on this assumption. That he claimed such compatibility is evident from his life and writings. His *Autobiography*, for example, spoke of his desire "to see" the universal and all-pervading Spirit of Truth face to face. It was this desire for "seeing," he said, that had brought him to the field of politics, the field best suited in modern times to the pursuit of the highest vision of Truth.[43]

Thanks to Gandhi, the assumption of the harmony between the science of revealed truths and natural sciences became a distinguishing feature of the new Indian political canon. Indian theologies belong to the broad field of the human sciences. In his view, the Western notion that science alone is sufficient for human well being is something that emerged from a particular direction that modern Western thought had taken. Such a notion does not apply elsewhere. The modern Indian political canon stands squarely against the claim that modern science (and philosophies that are subservient to it) is the only knowledge sufficient for human well-being. This is monism in the disguise of science. He rejects it in favor of a plurality of sciences. There would be two epistemologies producing two types of knowledge—knowledge based on "experience" and knowledge based on positive reason.

Turning now to the theory of the *purusharthas*, the second element that he retained from the old canon, Gandhi soon discovered that the concept of *purushartha* was in need of redefinition. Over the centuries, it had acquired a somewhat misogynist connotation—not in high culture, but in popular culture. Since the term "*purusha*" meant "a man" as one of its meanings, *purushartha* in popular culture came to be associated with manliness, with its perceived misogyny. This corruption of meaning greatly bothered him and he wanted to remedy it. He sought advice from his female friends. The outcome was that he was able to provide a gender-neutral meaning to the concept. "The word *purusha* should be interpreted in its etymological sense," he wrote, "and not merely to mean a man. That which dwells in the *pura*, the body, is *purusha*. If we interpret the word *purushartha* in this sense, it can be used equally for men and women."[44] He went further: *purushartha* signified a specifically spiritual power common to men and women, a power that enabled them to unify all human activities into a working harmony—activities directed toward the values of wealth, power, pleasure, aesthetics, moral integrity, and spiritual transcendence. This power distinguishes humans from the rest of material universe. "All human beings, and animals too, struggle. The only difference is that we believe that behind our struggle there is an intelligent purpose."[45] Only activities of the *purushartha* type can rise to the level of genuine human activities. "Only effort aimed at the welfare of the *atman* can be described as *purushartha*. . . . All else is futile expenditure of energy."[46]

Gandhi continued with his exploration of the meaning of *purushartha*. Not only could it unify the diverse strivings of humans, it could also help humans in their struggle against fate, destiny and *karma*. "In one sphere, fate is all powerful, and in another *purushartha*."[47] "Fate is the fruition of *karma*. Fate may be good or it may be bad. Human effort [*purushartha*] consists in overcoming the adverse fate or reducing its impact. There is continuous struggle between fate and human effort [*purushartha*]. Who can say which of the two really wins? Let us, therefore, continue effort [*purushartha*] and leave the result to God."[48] Again, "Between destiny [*bhagya*] and human endeavor [*purushartha*] there is incessant struggle. Let us continue to endeavor [*purushartha*] and leave the result to God. Let us not leave everything to destiny [*bhagya*], nor be vain about our endeavor [*purushartha*]. Destiny will take its own course. We should only see where we can intervene or where it is our duty to do so, whatever the result."[49]

Reflections such as these show how profoundly the concept of *purshartha* had penetrated Gandhi's mind. In the final analysis, *purshartha* for him is the ability "to overcome whatever weaknesses we see in ourselves."[50] What modern Indians needed most was the recovery of their faith in the humanism of the *purusharthas*.[51]

The four canonical *purusharthas* are now seen as four different modes of being human and exercising this inner power.[52] The high calling of modern Indian political science is to help humans acquire this inner power, not as its efficient cause, but as the cause that creates the material conditions necessary for its acquisition.

THE NEW CANON

Deletions and additions prepared the way for the emergence of a new set of modern ideas that have canonical status today—*swaraj*, *satyagraha*, *sarvodaya*, *swadeshi*, *ahimsa*, nationalism, constitutionalism, selfless public service (*anasakti yoga*), and the like. The concept of *purushartha* has been rethought and the relationship of the four *purusharthas* inter se redefined in interactive rather than oppositional terms. The need for a plurality of different sciences for human well being has been reaffirmed. Gandhi in other words has given India a modern *arthasastra*—a recognizably Indian way of thinking politically. Its other features may now be summarized.

All human beings are capable of *swaraj*, self-determination, self-development, and spiritual liberation. Indians in the past had belonged to a monarchy-based and caste-oriented political community; today they belong to the oceanic circle.

Political science is a secular science, whose proximate ends are internal order, material prosperity and external security. Its specific means is legitimate coercion according to the terms set by the constitution, statutes, principles of human rights and universal *dharma*.[53] The state, being part of the sphere of *artha*, is a secular institution. Its coercive power is limited to maintaining internal order and external security; it does not extend to achieving domination over other states. The state is a member of a community of independent and interdependent states. The new *arthasastra* puts an end to the old *chakravartin* concept of the imperial state. In doing so, it has changed the very notion of political power from one that seeks to expand limitlessly to one that limits itself to the requirements of internal order, world peace, interdependence, and universal *dharma*. The state that the new *arthasastra* envisages is a "parliamentary *swaraj*." It recognizes the fundamental rights of the citizens and their freedom to make non-violent protests through the practice of *satyagraha*. It also recognizes the need for the organizations of civil society with which it coordinates its own activities.

The economic system that is compatible with the new *arthasastra* is *sarvodaya*, a reformed form of capitalism that recognizes the principle of private property within the limits of social responsibility. Corresponding to the obligation to work is the right to the fruits of one's work. The creation of wealth, a requisite of *purushartha*, has a positive human value, and poverty is a sign of human degradation, being the outcome of the mismanagement of the nation's labor. What is surplus to one's reasonable needs should be held in trust for society. The centralization of economic power in the hands of the state does "greatest harm to mankind by destroying individuality which lies at the root of all progress . . . the violence of private ownership is less injurious than the violence of the state."[54] The mode of wealth production should be consistent with the use of appropriate technology, the needs of natural environment and the requirements of long-term sustainability. Though India needs industrialization, the kind of industrialization that it embarks upon should be consistent with principles of universal justice. It should learn from the past mistakes of industrialized societies.[55]

There is also a new conception of *dharma* as ethics that corresponds to the new *arthasastra*—the ethic of nonviolence. Two caveats save this ethic from becoming utopian. The first is the need to adapt it to the four different "fields" (communities) of nonviolence[56]—the family, the state, the religious community, and the world community of states. Nonviolence works differently in these fields. What works in one may not work in the others. It therefore needs constant adaptation to the requirements of the given field. The second caveat concerns the "vast majority principle." The ethic of non-violence would work only when the vast majority in a given field had the habit of practicing it. Thus, "a state can be administered on a non-violent basis only if the vast majority of the people are non-violent."[57] The vast majority can become nonviolent only if conditions of justice and political stability prevail. The responsibility for bringing these conditions about depends as much on the state as on the political culture of ordinary citizens. There is a subtle link, then, between the public behavior of the state and the private behavior of its citizens. If the citizens want the state to behave nonviolently, they themselves should behave nonviolently toward one another. That is the implication of Gandhian nonviolence. And if there is a circle of non-violently administered states, and only then, can the relations between such states become nonviolent.

There is also a new conception of *moksha*, corresponding to the new *arthasastra*. Gandhi modernized the mode of pursuing *moksha*, making it less ascetical and more compatible with action in the political and economic fields. The minimum necessary condition for its pursuit is commitment to Truth (in the Gandhian sense), supported by a reflective, spiritual lifestyle. The pursuit of *moksha* should not interfere with the secular character of the state.

Gandhi's unique contribution to the new Indian canon has been to bring the pursuit of *moksha*, a spiritual activity, into a dynamic relationship with the pursuit of *artha*, a secular activity. As A. L. Basham, the great interpreter of Indian civilization in the twentieth century has remarked, "The theoretical purpose of the whole social and political structure of classical India was to promote *moksha*—to help as many individuals as possible to achieve it." The Indian seer, unlike the Chinese sage or the Hebrew prophet, "thought not in terms of the salvation of the whole people," but of individual human beings. The "fundamental individualism," involved in this, Basham thinks, is "perhaps the reason why India, unlike most other colonial countries, has taken enthusiastically to parliamentary democracy . . ." Those who pursue *moksha* in the Gandhian mode exemplify the fundamental harmony between all human strivings. Few perhaps actually attain this harmony, "but the secret of the good life is to travel hopefully towards it."[58] Such is the distinctive feature of the new Indian political canon.

There is, however, a lacuna in Gandhi's political thought. There is no creative dialogue in it with Marxism, which is in contrast to his fruitful dialogue with liberalism. Perhaps this is due to Marx's own all knowing dogmatism. He made an either/ or offer that Gandhi had to decline. Indian Marxists, in their turn, have not helped matters: they were and are bent on changing India on Marx's terms; they simply refuse to change Marxism on India's terms. This explains why Indian Marxism remains outside the modern Indian canon—why it belongs to the category of "political thought in India," rather than to "modern Indian political thought" strictly speaking.

As for the view of the modern Indian canon that basic human goals are compatible with one another, it stands in contrast to the Western liberal canon that they are incommensurable. Difference between the two canons is unavoidable. The best one can do here is to study the difference comparatively.

Gandhi's evaluation of India's colonial experience has been exemplary, for it did not produce any cultural schizophrenia in him. His sense of identity was so authentic that he could integrate Western ideas without undergoing postcolonial angst that afflicts so many today. The remedy against such angst lies in adopting the canon that he has inaugurated. Here his metaphor of the "slate" is helpful. He had no problem writing many new things so long the slate on which he was writing was Indian. So is his other metaphor of "capital and interest." If he borrowed the idea of human rights from the West, which he did, he paid back the capital with interest—in the form of *satyagraha*. If the new Indian political canon has borrowed certain ideas from the West, as it has, it is now in a position to pay something back to the West.

NOTES

1. An earlier version of this essay appeared in *The Review of Politics*, vol. 70 (2008), pp. 40–63.

2. The date of the *Arthasastra* is disputed among scholars. According to Romila Thapar, parts of it go back to the fourth century BC, and the present form of the text goes back to about third century AD (*Early India: From the Origins to AD 1300* [London: Allen Lane, 2002] pp. 184–85). The standard English translation of this work, which is used in this article, is R. P. Kangle, *The Kautiliya Arthasastra*, Parts 1, 2 and 3 (Delhi: Banarsidass, 1997).

3. See *Nitisara or The Elements of Polity by Kamandaki*, edited by Raja Dr. Rajendralala Mitra, revised with English translation by Dr. Sisir Kumar Mitra (Calcutta: The Asiatic Society, 1982); *Niti Vakyamritam of Somadeva Suri*, edited by Ramachandra Malaviya, with extensive Hindi Commentary (Varanasi: Vidyabhavana Samskrta Grantamala, 1972); and B. K. Sarkar, *The Sukraniti* (New York: AMS Press, 1974).

4. For over a millennium these canonical ideas made their appearance in works in the *arthasastra* tradition. I make distinction between *Arthasastra* the book and the *arthasastra* tradition that grew out of it. See U. N. Ghoshal, *A History of Indian Political Ideas* (Bombay: Oxford University Press, 1959), pp. 83, 112, 121, 247, 348, 375, 428, 476–477, 496–497.

5. For a recent discussion of the meaning of *anviksiki*, see Wilhelm Halbfass, *India and Europe* (Albany, NY: State University of New York Press), 1988, pp. 263–286.

6. For more on this see A. J. Parel, *Gandhi's Philosophy and the Quest for Harmony* (Cambridge: Cambridge University Press, 2006), pp. 5–6.

7. The *Nitisara* of Kamandaki, II, v. 17, pp. 41–42, adds *moksha* by name to the list of the *purusharthas*. It proudly states that it is an abridgement of "the mighty ocean" of the *Arthasastra*, ibid., p. 3; and calls Kautilya "our guru", ibid., p. 37.

8. See P. V. Kane, *History of Dharmasastra*, vol. V, part 2, 2nd ed. (Poona: The Bhandarkar Institute, 1977), p. 1623.

9. Sheldon Pollock, *The Ends of Man at the End of Premodernity* (Amsterdam: Royal Netherlands Academy of Arts and Sciences, 2005), pp. 63–64.

10. See *Sukraniti*, chapter. IV, section 111, p. 153.

11. Ibid., p. 156.

12. Ibid., p. 164.

13. A. Appadorai, ed., *Documents on Political Thought in Modern India*, vol. 1 (Bombay: Oxford University Press, 1973), and vol. 2 (Bombay: Oxford University Press, 1976).

14. A. Appadorai, *Indian Political Thinking from Naoroji to Nehru* (Madras: Oxford University Press, 1971), p. 151. The opening lines of this book verify my point here: "The object of this book is to survey the history of *political thought in India* from 1857 to 1964..." p. xi. Italics added.

15. M. K. Gandhi, *Young India*, 26-6-1924, p. 210.

16. M. K. Gandhi, *The Collected Works of Mahatma Gandhi*, 100 vols. (New Delhi: Publications Division, Ministry of Information and Broadcasting, Government of India, 1958–1994) (hereafter *CW*), 51: 259.

17. *CW*, 59: 64, 66.

18. *CW*, 62: 121–22.

19. *CW*, 63: 153.

20. M. K. Gandhi, *Hind Swaraj and Other Writings*, ed., Anthony J. Parel (hereafter *HS*) (Cambridge: Cambridge University Press, 1997), p. 87.

21. See J. D. M. Derrett, "Social and Political Thought and Institutions," in *A Cultural History of India*, ed. A. L. Basham, (Delhi: Oxford University Press, 1998), pp. 124–140. As Derrett at p. 140 points out, the famous "law of fishes" migrated to the West and found a place in Talmudic literature, "whence, via Spinoza," it found a place in Western political thought. Pufendorf criticized Spinoza for speaking of it in terms of a moral law. Fishes, he pointed out, do not have a "right" but only "a faculty of acting," which by itself did not indicate a right. See S. Pufendorf, *De Jure Naturae et Gentium* (1688), vol. II, tr. C. H. and W. A. Oldfather (Oxford: Clarendon Press, 1934), bk. 2, ch. 2, p. 159.

22. *CW*, 25: 481–482.

23. *HS*, pp. 51–57.

24. *CW*, 85: 33.

25. *CW*, 19: 278.

26. *HS*, pp. 52–57.

27. *CW*, 25: 481.

28. For the complete text see *CW*, 75: 146–166.

29. *CW*, 48: 304.

30. *HS*, p. 90.

31. *Satyagraha* was invented in 1906, a year before Gandhi read Thoreau, which was in 1907. See *CW*, 61: 401.

32. Joan V. Bondurant, *Conquest of Violence: The Gandhian Philosophy of Conflict*, revised edition (Berkeley: University of California Press, 1967), p. 29.

33. *CW*, 16: 51.

34. G. Austin, *The Indian Constitution: Cornerstone of a Nation* (Delhi: Oxford University Press, 1966), pp. 56–57.

35. Of the twenty books listed in Appendix I of *Hind Swaraj*, twelve were on economics. They were, besides the books of Ruskin mentioned, three by Leo

Tolstoy, one each by G. Blount, Robert Sherard, Edward Carpenter, Henry Thoreau, Thomas Taylor, D. Naoroji, and R. C. Dutt.

36. *CW*, 39: 239.
37. See M. K. Gandhi, *Ruskin: Unto This Last, A Paraphrase*, translated from the Gujarati by Valji Desai (Ahmedabad: Navajivan, 1989).
38. *CW*, 74: 278–279.
39. This is a point well made by Lloyd Rudolph and Susanne Rudolph in *Postmodern Gandhi and Other Essays* (Chicago: University of Chicago Press, 2006), pp. 232–239.
40. *HS*, p. 37.
41. Ibid.
42. Ibid., p. 66.
43. *CW*, 39: 401.
44. *CW*, 44: 80. The dweller in the body is the *purusha*.
45. *CW*, 32: 350.
46. Ibid., p. 351.
47. *CW*, 32: 360.
48. *CW*, 79: 258.
49. *CW*, 79: 433.
50. *CW*, 38: 64.
51. Among modern Indian writings on the theory of *purusharthas*, the following are especially relevant to the present discussion: K. J. Shah, "Of *Artha* and the *Arthasastra*," in A. J. Parel and R. C. Keith, (eds.), *Comparative Political Philosophy*, 2nd ed. (Lanham: MD, Lexington Books, 2003), pp. 141–162; "*Purushartha* and Gandhi," in Ramashray Roy (ed.), *Gandhi and the Present Global Crisis* (Shimla: Indian Institute of Advanced Study, 1996), pp. 155–161; and R. Sundara Rajan, "The *Purusharthas* in the Light of Critical Theory," *Indian Philosophical Quarterly* VII (1979–80), pp. 339–350; and "Approaches to the theory of the *purusharthas*: Husserl, Heidegger and Ricoeur," *Journal of Indian Council of Philosophical Research*, vol. 6 (1988–9), pp. 129–147.
52. The various steps that Gandhi took to realign the four *purusharthas* are discussed in A. J. Parel, *Gandhi's Philosophy and the Quest for Harmony*, pp. 14–21.
53. These principles were non-violence (*ahimsa*), truthfulness (*satya*), uprightness, freedom from malice, compassion and forbearance. This list goes as far back as *Arthasastra* 1. 3.13.
54. M. K. Gandhi, *Sarvodaya*, ed., B. Kumarappa (Ahmedabad: Navajivan, 1984), p. 74. However, if "unavoidable," "a minimum of state-ownership" may be accepted. Ibid.
55. Gandhi had specifically warned modern India of the dangers of copying the nineteenth century model of industrialization: "We can never industrialize India, unless of course, we reduce our population from 350 millions to 35 millions [Gandhi was writing in 1934, when India, Pakistan and Bangladesh were one political entity] or hit upon markets wider than our own and dependent on us...We cannot industrialize ourselves, unless we make up our minds to enslave humanity." *CW*, 58: 400.
56. *CW*, 72: 248–50; 271–272; 281–282.
57. *CW*, 71: 407.
58. A. L. Basham, ed., *A Cultural History of India*, pp. 498–499.

THE POLITICAL THOUGHT OF
JAWAHARLAL NEHRU[1]

R. C. Pillai

Jawaharlal Nehru is widely acclaimed as one of the architects of modern India. His remarkable personality was an unusual combination of an intellectual and a practical political leader. The role that he played in the long struggle for national freedom, and later as the greatest political leader of free India, has had a profound effect on Indian political thinking. He belonged to that group of Western-educated Indian elites who drew their inspiration mainly from the intellectual currents of the nineteenth and twentieth centuries. If in the early part of his career he had absorbed many of the ideas and impulses of modern democratic thought, in his later years "he acquired a deeper appreciation of Indian history and philosophy, and enriched the basis for subsequent thought and action."[2]

Nehru had a long span of public life stretching for more than forty-five years. After his education at Harrow and Cambridge, he returned to India in 1912 when the national political scene was at a low profile. He was not inspired by the politics of the moderate group although his father, Motilal Nehru, was a vocal supporter of it. Be believed rather strongly that individual and national self-respect required a more aggressive attitude to foreign rule. By nature he was an intense nationalist and an open rebel against authoritarianism. As he disliked the politics of prayer and petitions, he was naturally inclined to accept the programme of the extremist group, headed by B.G. Tilak, who was then the embodiment of militant nationalism in India. But though the aggressive nationalism of Tilak appealed to Nehru emotionally, it contained deep religious motivations that he totally disliked. His demand for a more fighting attitude towards foreign domination was a purely psychological urge and he continued to express it even after Gandhi's emergence on the political scene.

LIBERAL NATIONALISM

Nehru was aware that nationalism, particularly as it existed in the colonial world, was both a composite and a living force and could make the strongest appeal to the spirit of man. He also knew of its many-sided contributions to the development of modern civilization. It had all along been a driving force for freedom and independence. It gave a certain degree of unity, vigor, and vitality to many people all over the world.

But he was also conscious of the fact that Indian nationalism, though mainly rooted in the universal virtues of "pacifism, liberalism and rationalism," was not free from limitations. According to him, Indian nationalism did lack certain vital elements although it was free from violence and hatred. He wanted Indian nationalism to be limited, liberalized, and balanced as he thought it would be harmful if it ever made the people conscious of their own superiority or aggressive expansionism. Nehru's intense nationalism, coupled with his urge for effective political action, made him a constructive critic of the Indian National Congress. What he demanded was the introduction of a secular, rational, and scientific, international outlook as the essential ingredients of Indian nationalism. In other words, he was the most vocal critic of the religious metaphysical and revivalist outlook, which, according to him, was greatly harmful to the cause of national liberation as well as to the growth of nationhood.

ANTI-IMPERIALISM

Nehru was a crusader against imperialism. His anti-imperialist attitude found its first open expression at the Brussels Congress held in February 1927. There he stressed the common element in the struggles against imperialism in different parts of the world. His close contact with European revolutionaries and movements created in him a new awareness of the forces, which were shaping the destiny of humankind. His association with the "League Against Imperialism"[3] and his short visit to the Soviet Union later in November 1927 brought about a radical change in his political perception. The Indian nationalist movement, according to him, was part of the worldwide movement and its serious impact would naturally be felt in most other countries. He, therefore, made it a point to appeal to all progressive forces all over the world to lend their support to the Indian struggle.

Nehru's anti-imperialism was largely the product of his own understanding of the historical evolution of the laws of social change. His partial acceptance of the Marxist interpretation of history gave him an insight into the facts of social evolution. Though he made no deeper analysis, he believed that the dominant class—the class which controlled the means of production—was the ruling class and that class conflicts in an exploitative and oppressed society could not be avoided. As an intellectual, he diagnosed the social maladies and understood their socio-economic consequences. But on the practical side of his politics he remained extremely cautious.

Nehru was clear in his mind that so long as imperialism was not rooted out, mankind would continue to suffer both exploitation and oppression. Therefore, he asserted that "the nationalist movement had to be uncompromisingly anti-capitalist, anti-feudal, anti-bourgeois,...and of course anti-imperialist," and its sole objective should be the establishment of a democratic socialist republic in a free and independent India.[4] Nehru was fairly in agreement with Lenin's ideas on imperialism and the Soviet Union's firm anti-imperialist position. "So I turned inevitably with goodwill towards communism," wrote Nehru in his autobiography, "for whatever its faults, it was at least not hypocritical and not imperialistic."[5] Here his political outlook seemed to be that of a "self-conscious radical" and throughout his life his sympathy lay broadly with the socialist countries.

UNCOMPROMISING STAND TOWARD
COMPLETE INDEPENDENCE

Nehru's new radicalism reaffirmed his enthusiasm for more purposeful political action. His whole effort during the twenties was to redefine the concept of *swaraj* in terms of complete independence. The content of *swaraj* as demanded by the nationalists remained largely vague and insufficient and so he had made up his mind to move in a different direction. As a first step, he tried to persuade the Congress for an open commitment to the goal of complete independence. With a deep sense of courage and determination, Nehru moved a resolution on complete independence at the Madras Session of the Congress held in 1927 and it was formally adopted there.

Though the resolution on independence was formally adopted by the Congress, Nehru had a genuine fear whether the Congress would follow it in both letter and spirit. The doubt arose because of the Congress' refusal to incorporate it in the constitution. Nehru, therefore, took immediate steps to form two new organizations— The Republican League and the Independence for India League. The former was mainly intended to work for the establishment of complete national independence while the latter was to carry on a vigorous campaign for the same cause.

At the Calcutta Session of the Congress held in 1928, Nehru noticed that some attempts were being made to obscure the issue of independence. He immediately stepped in and accepted the presidency just "to prevent, as far as I could, the swing back to moderation and to hold on to the independence objective."[6] In a sharply worded rejoinder to all those who were still harping on Dominion Status, Nehru said, "If India has a message to give to the world, it is clear that she can do so more effectively as an independent country than as a member of the British group."[7] Despite the pulls and protests from many of his colleagues, he was able to hold on to the independence objective and, in a sense, he had the satisfaction that the pressure that he built in the Congress in favor of complete independence had a positive effect.

SOCIALIST IDEAS

The beginning of Nehru's interest in socialist ideas can be traced to his Cambridge days when the Fabianism of Bernard Shaw and the Webbs attracted him. But that was, as he confessed, purely an academic interest. He was also influenced by the ideas of Bertrand Russell and John Maynard Keynes, in the sense that he used to regularly attend their lectures although his own university curriculum contained only science and not economics.[8] The vague ideas of socialism which he had nurtured during his student days were subsequently revived and sharpened in the light of the sweeping political, social, and economic changes taking place throughout the world.

Nehru was not a pioneer in the field of socialism in India; compared to others, he was certainly not in the forefront of the socialist movement. Some kind of a vague socialist thinking was already a part of the political process right from the early twenties. Marxian theory was increasingly influencing many individuals and this tendency was further strengthened by the developments in the Soviet Union, the workers' trade union movement and a majority of the youth leagues and socialist leanings. However, it was entirely at the insistence of Nehru that the Congress committed itself very vaguely to the principle of socialism in 1929. In 1931, the Congress under his influence took a more definite step in that direction by adopting an economic programme at the Karachi Session. As he had occupied a high position in the Congress, he had the advantage of making his influence felt much more than others. He was also looked upon by the youth and the weaker sections of the masses as a symbol of their hopes and aspirations. Moreover, as the Congress began to enlist the active support of the masses for its political programme of national liberation, the organization felt more and more compelled to take up economic issues for consideration. As a matter of fact, Nehru continuously kept up his pressure on the organization in favor of socialism and, consequently, a number of vague socialist resolutions were adopted by the Congress from time to time.

Socialism was not a mere economic doctrine for Nehru. "It is a vital creed which I hold with all my head and heart," he stated in 1936.[9] His early radicalism convinced him that there was no other way of ending the appalling mass poverty and sufferings in India except through socialism. He was, therefore, determined not only to work for that cause but was keenly interested in making the Congress an effective instrument of social and economic change. Nehru declared:

> I work for Indian independence because the nationalist in me cannot tolerate alien domination; I work for it even more because for me, it is the inevitable step to social and economic change. I should like the Congress to become a socialist organization and to join hands with other forces in the world who are working for the new civilization.[10]

More than most of his colleagues, Nehru had a clear understanding of the character of the National Congress and the movement it was piloting then. The Congress, during the preindependence period, was a great movement; but that movement was neither a proletarian nor a peasant movement. It was purely a bourgeois movement whose objective was not of changing the social structure but of winning political freedom. However, there were quite a few in it who could think far beyond their surroundings. They stood for drastic socioeconomic transformation and were quite enthusiastic about it. This group was asserting itself within the Congress with the sole aim of persuading others to accept socialism and Nehru was undoubtedly the spokesman of that group. In all his speeches and writings during this period, Nehru repeatedly stressed the need for *swaraj* and socialism as the joint objectives of the movement and he firmly believed that India could not have one without the other. It was also his conviction that political freedom could no longer be separated from economic freedom since world events were forcing the issue to the forefront.

Nehru's vigorous campaign for socialism continued for long, even after independence, and the Congress, under his undisputed leadership, adopted official resolutions to that effect. But his concept of socialism remained largely undefined throughout. He had no rigid adherence to any brand of socialism as such. He was solely guided by the practical considerations of Indian society and its concrete situation as it appeared before him. His approach to the fundamental problem of social transformation was, therefore, extremely cautious. He was aware that the Congress, constituted as it was, could hardly accept any revolutionary programme of social action. Had the issue been forced on it, the Congress, being a loose organization, would have probably split. Even in the years of power, Nehru paid no serious attention to reorganizing the Congress into a cadre-based party with a deep sense of commitment to socialism. Inside the organization he was not unwilling to cooperate, even with those who did not accept his socialist ideas. He had no intention either of forming a new party or group in order to carry out his socialist objective.

However, in the pursuit of his "vague-socialist ideal" Nehru had to face certain serious problems. The question of providing social justice without sacrificing individual freedom was certainly uppermost in his mind. It was, therefore, in the choice of method and general approach that Nehru revealed his pragmatism more apparently than anything else. Unlike the communists, Nehru chose the method of persuasion or peaceful democratic pressures as against the "methods of destruction and extermination."[11] He was critical of both the communists and the socialists who, according to him, were largely influenced by the literature on European socialism. In India, Nehru argued, nationalism and rural economy constituted the core of the problem and, as such, it could not be dealt with in terms of the industrial proletariat. European socialism had never dealt with such conditions. Nehru was, therefore, convinced that if socialism was to be established in India, it would have to grow out of Indian conditions.

Nehru did not subscribe to the Marxian theory of class-war and the dictatorship of the proletariat. His admiration for the finer aspects of Marxism (as evident both in his works as well as in his numerous speeches) was never uncritical or unqualified. He totally disliked the "communist policy of ruthless suppression" of political dissent and the "wholesale regimentation." Moreover, he was completely opposed to the methods of violence and hatred. He honestly believed that it was possible to liquidate poverty and ensure a minimum standard of life for all without any violent overthrow of the existing order. Even if conflicts did exist between classes, the best way of resolving that conflict, according to him, was to put an end to it by peaceful methods.[12]

It was Nehru's political conviction that India would have to march gradually in the direction of socialism, but that march, he asserted, would be on different lines, different from a violent overthrow of the existing social order. "Nothing is so foolish," he argued, "as to imagine that exactly the same process takes place in different countries with varying backgrounds."[13] India, therefore, will have to find her own way to socialism, which would avoid unnecessary sacrifice and the possibility of chaos.

Nehru's political ideas were conditioned by some of the liberal democratic traditions of the nineteenth century. The brand of socialism that he advocated could be achieved only through the democratic process. He strongly believed that democracy and socialism were not contradictory but complementary to one other. His concept of social democracy did not amount to any serious infringement of individual freedom and civil liberty. "I do not see why under socialism there should not be a great deal of freedom for the individual, indeed far greater freedom than the present system gives...."[14] His tremendous respect for human freedom and individual rights, on the one hand, and his total opposition to authoritarianism and regimentation, on the other, and above all his practical considerations arising out of his desire to carry the bulk of the people with the system, possibly prevented him from accepting an ideologically rigid position.

"Nehru was a practical idealist."[15] He did not want to rely on idealistic principles while dealing with the massive problems of an amorphous plural society with a clear semifeudal background. The problem with Nehru was that the intellectual in him prompted him to be a critic of both communism and capitalism. He was aware of the inherent limitations of both and he wanted to avoid them in the developmental model that he initiated. His lip service to some of the fundamental tenets of Marxism was a mere intellectual exercise. But Nehru the political man, faced with the appalling socioeconomic conditions of a semifeudal society, with all his awareness of the actual character of the Indian National Congress, found favor with liberal democracy. Also looking at the mass poverty, illiteracy, and social backwardness in the country, Nehru could not think of anything other than a socialist solution to that gigantic problem. But revolutionary socialism was neither feasible nor inevitable because the human values of a free society had to be preserved. His concept of socialism could be achieved only through a full democratic process, through the consent of a majority.

The task before Nehru was, therefore, to continuously educate the people in the spirit of democratic socialism in order to win them over to that cause. This was obviously a pragmatic approach based on political expediency and compromise and not on any ideological conviction. Choosing the method of persuasion rather than that of coercion, he said: "I do not want India to be drilled and forced into a certain position, because the costs of such drilling are too great; it is not worthwhile; it is not desirable from my point of view...."[16] In any case, the freedom and dignity of the individual was well preserved in Nehru's model which, if analyzed objectively, was nothing but welfare capitalism.

ON PLANNING AND DEVELOPMENT

Another significant aspect of Nehru's model of economic development was the creation of a consciousness of economic planning. Since the early 1940s, it became quite apparent that his bitter antagonism to capitalism was being modified. By that time, in several countries of the West, "capitalism had been civilized, tamed and toned down, and many of its old evils extricated by the insistent demand of the masses...."[17] These countries were working vigorously to provide a better life for the masses. Nehru who was aware of these developments, however, continued to stress the importance of socialism for tackling contemporary economic and social problems. But, finally, he threw himself in favor of a mixed economy as the most suitable and most practicable for India. It would be an economy, he asserted, in which socialist principles and ideals would prevail generally, along with a fair share of capitalism. Thus the concept of a welfare state, on the basis of a mixed economy, in place of a completely socialized economy, became Nehru's political creed and model of economic development.

Much before the advent of freedom, Nehru realized the need for planning for the modernization and development of society. Insistence on planning for socio-economic reconstruction thus became a cardinal feature of his thought. He was also deeply impressed by the Soviet economic development through planning which, according to him, caught the imagination of the world. In 1938, when the Congress decided to set up a National Planning Committee with Nehru as its chairman, he boldly accepted the challenging task. He took up the work in all earnestness and the statement of objectives made by him as Chairman of the Planning Committee became a significant document on economic planning in India.

To Nehru, planning was an inevitable process of a socialist economy in a democratic structure. But he had no intention of frightening away any section of the people by stressing the socialist aspect. He, therefore, chose to remain vague and imprecise while formulating the aim of planning. His concept of planning was not based on any dogmatic or doctrinaire considerations. He was guided more by the desire for quick results than by any ideological adherence. His only interest was to put the people on the road of steady economic and social progress. "I do not care what ism it is that helps me to set them on that road, if one thing fails, we will try another."[18] It was this uncommitted and flexible attitude that led him to believe that a mixed economy was the most suitable for India.

Nehru's concept of a mixed economy envisaged the simultaneous participation of the public and private sectors in developmental activities. Key sectors of the economy were to be wholly under state control while the private sector would operate in other spheres. However, the private sector must be subject to state control so as to make it function within the objective of the national plan. While commenting on the role of the private sector, Nehru observed: "The control over the private sector will relate not only to its dividends and profits but will extend to all the strategic points in the economy of the country."[19] He envisaged gradually more and more state control over the private sector in order to make the mixed economy sufficiently capable of adapting itself to changing conditions.

Nehru's arguments in favor of a mixed economy might sound logical in the peculiar Indian conditions. According to him, the choice before the country lay essentially between the socialist and capitalist systems. But he was not prepared to exercise the choice in view of the limitations inherent in both. Nehru argued:

Western economics, though helpful, have little bearing on our present-day problems. So also have Marxist economics which are, in many ways, out of date even though they throw considerable light on economic progress. We have thus to do our own thinking, profiting by the example of others, but essentially trying to find a path for ourselves suited to our own conditions.[20]

Thus it was clear that Nehru did not want to imitate any economic model of other countries. India must evolve a system which suited her own requirements and genius. The ideal of a mixed economy was thus considered to be the best. Stressing this point rather heavily, Nehru declared:

...(economic) change will have to be in the direction of a democratically planned collectivism....A democratic-collectivism need not mean an abolition of private property, but it will mean the public ownership of the basic and major industries.... In India especially it will be necessary to have, in addition to the big industries, cooperatively controlled small and village industries. Such a system of democratic collectivism will need careful and continuous planning and adaptation to the changing needs of the people.[21]

Nehru was quite sincere and earnest in his efforts to develop an Indian model of planning and development. However, the fact of the situation is that his efforts could not produce the desired results. Despite his best intentions, a certain minimum standard of living was still a far cry for a sizable section of the masses. The alarming growth of private capital and the colossal waste of the national resources resulting from misplaced national priorities in planning have all contributed to the ever-widening gap between the rich and the poor.

LIBERAL DEMOCRATIC IDEAS

Jawaharlal Nehru was the greatest champion of liberal democracy in India. Throughout his life, he stressed the importance of democracy and passionately desired that free India went along the full democratic process. His sensitive mind had absorbed much of the dominant concepts of modern democratic thought. In fact, the intellectual and social influence of the West appeared to have largely molded his liberal democratic ideas. This he confessed when he wrote: "My roots are still perhaps partly in the nineteenth century and I have been too much influenced by the humanist liberal traditions to get out of it completely."[22]

Nehru's concept of democracy had certain specific implications. In the early years of the struggle for independence, democracy meant the ideal of self-rule or responsible government. During the later years, his socialist ideas altered his views on democracy, stressing more and more its economic aspect. In an ultimate analysis, democracy implied a mental approach applied to political and economic problems. Broadly, democracy emphasized equality of opportunity for all in the political and economic field and freedom for the individual to grow and develop to the best of his personality. It also involved a high degree of tolerance and a certain inquisitive search for the truth. Democracy was thus the dynamic concept for Nehru.

Nehru had tremendous respect for the freedom of man. He firmly believed that the creative and adventurous spirit of man could grow only in an atmosphere of rights and freedom. To promote and preserve the human values, both society and the individual must enjoy freedom. Explaining the reasons for accepting the democratic process in India, Nehru observed:

> It is not enough for us merely to produce the material goods of the world. We do want a high standard of living, but not at the cost of man's creative spirit, his creative energy, his spirit of adventure, not at the cost of all fine things of life which have ennobled man throughout the ages. Democracy is not merely a question of elections.[23]

His concept of individual freedom necessarily implied freedom of speech and expression, of association and many other fields of creative activities. The general health of a society, he believed, was largely determined by the freedom of its people.

In Nehru's democratic thought, there was an integrated conception of political, economic, and social freedom, which could not be separated from one another. Realizing that the danger to democracy lay essentially in the economic structure of society, Nehru pointed out that democracy could grow and flourish only in an equal society. A serious weakness of Western democracy, according to him, was that political power there became the monopoly of the dominant class. The democratic machinery was often exploited to perpetuate class privileges and interests. It also failed to solve the burning problem of inequality. "The spirit of the age is in favour of equality though practice denies it almost everywhere," said Nehru, explaining the democratic principle of equality in the Indian context.[24]

One of the reasons for Nehru's fascination with democracy (as against authoritarianism) was that the former was based on rationalism while the latter relied on dogmatism. Free discussion and an inquisitive search for the truth, which found no place in authoritarianism, constituted the essence of democratic theory. Nehru had a tremendous faith in the spirit of man. The dismal failures of mankind never depressed him. Being a liberal by taste and temperament, he believed in the potentiality of human reason and man's ability for survival. However, he was very clear about his social objective of establishing an economic democracy, which, in his terminology, was to be a socialistic pattern of society. Such a society was to be based on cooperative effort providing equal opportunity for all.[25] It is, however, significant to note that when Nehru defined democracy in terms of individual freedom, popular government, or social self-discipline, he was speaking of the realities of the actual life. When he defined democracy in terms of economic and social equality, he was speaking of an ideal, a distant goal to be achieved in due course.

Nehru frequently referred to the Gandhian doctrine of ends and means; he obviously seemed to be under its impact when he stressed the importance of social self-discipline. It was his strong belief that social and political objectives must be sought only by nonviolent methods. If democracy was to ensure individual liberty, Nehru held then that liberty was to be considered in the larger context of social responsibility.

SCIENCE FOR MODERNIZATION

Gifted with a fascinating scientific temper, Nehru recognized from the beginning the supreme importance of science and technology for the modernization of Indian society. One of the most striking characteristics of Western civilization, according to Nehru, was its rational and scientific temper. By virtue of these, the Western mind was able to free itself from the shackles of medievalism, from "unreason, magic and superstition." Rationalism and scientism seem to have had a profound impact on Nehru's

POLITICAL THOUGHT OF JAWAHARLAL NEHRU   175

thinking. His persistent demand for them was based on his conviction that India must break with much of her past and not allow the past to dominate the present. In other words, India must get out of her traditional ways of thought and action.

During the long course of human history, Nehru observed, science revolutionized the conditions of human life more than anything else. Humanity secured considerable relief from the burden of miseries by the application of science and the scientific approach. The conquest of the physical world by the human mind was so remarkable that nature was no longer regarded as something apart or distinct from humans.[26] But science must have a social objective apart from being an individual's search for truth and knowledge. Its objective should be to ward off the ills and evils of the community. In a country like India, "science must think in terms of the suffering millions."[27] "It was science alone," Nehru asserted, "that could solve these problems of hunger and poverty, of insanitation and illiteracy, of superstition and deadening custom and tradition, of vast resources running to waste, of a rich country inhabited by starving people."[28]

Nehru insisted that a scientific approach be accepted as a way of life, as a guiding principle, as a process of thinking. This was absolutely essential, according to him, to build the foundation of modern India. The scientific temper was exceedingly manifest in Nehru when he said, "We have to build India on a scientific foundation to develop her industries, to change that feudal character of her land system, and bring her agriculture in line with modern methods to develop the social services which she lacks so utterly today."[29] He strongly believed that national progress could be achieved neither by a repetition of the past nor by its denial. New patterns must be developed and integrated with the old. This was all the more necessary for India because, instead of relying on the present, India had heavily depended upon the past. She must get out of her obsession "with the supernatural and metaphysical speculations." Religious, ceremonial, and mystical emotionalism not only crippled the mental discipline in India but also stood in the way of understanding ourselves and the world at large.[30] People in India will have to come to grips with the present, Nehru said, because there was only a one-way traffic in time and progress.

SECULARISM AS A SOCIAL IDEAL

It was mainly due to Jawaharlal Nehru's efforts that India emerged as a secular state in the mid-twentieth century. Much before independence, he played a heroic role in the development of a secular basis for Indian polity. For him, secularism was essentially a social ideal to be promoted in the interest of national unity and progress. He used every single opportunity to impress upon the people the danger of mixing religion and politics. Communalism, he believed, could not only weaken the very fabric of a society but also threaten its very existence.

Nehru's secularism found expression officially for the first time in the resolution drafted by him on "Fundamental Rights and Duties" which was adopted by the Karachi Congress in 1931. Clause (1)(ix) of the resolution read: "The State shall observe neutrality in regard to all religions."[31] The secular state did not in any sense imply that religion ceased to be significant in the life of the individual. It only meant the separation of the state from religion—a cardinal principle of modern democratic practice. Nehru was vehemently opposed to the idea of a theocratic state which, in his view, was both medieval and antidemocratic in character and had no place in the mind of a modern individual.

Nehru favored a strong secular base for the state primarily for the maintenance of social stability and religious harmony among diverse groups. It was his firm conviction that a secular state alone could better serve a community divided by diverse religious creeds and faiths. With the state pledged to a secular way of life, the Constitution of India guaranteed the right to freedom of religion as a fundamental right. Nehru was specially interested in the enumeration of the "Directive Principles of State Policy," which suggested the creation of a uniform civil code for all in India. In order to maintain national unity and thereby to ensure orderly progress, a secular approach was considered to be an imperative need. Nehru's achievement in this direction was most praiseworthy and was acclaimed by even his critics.

WORLD OUTLOOK

Long before independence, Nehru realized that national isolation was neither desirable nor possible in a world that was fast changing and becoming more of a unit. He had a deep sense of history. What he did observe in history was the strong urge in humans to come together, to cooperate and work out their problems in common. It was from that cooperation, Nehru felt, that humans were able to progress from barbarism to civilization. In that ever-growing spirit of cooperation, nations too were becoming interdependent and none could go against that historical tendency. India, therefore, Nehru argued, "must be prepared to discard her narrow nationalism in favor of world cooperation and real internationalism."[32]

Nehru had all along possessed a rare ability to analyze the international situation by placing the national problem in the wider world context. It was he who persuaded the Congress to realize that the Indian struggle for freedom was part of a global struggle and that its strategy and tactics should be such as would fit into the context of world developments. "If we claim independence today," Nehru said, "it is with no desire for isolation; on the contrary, we are perfectly willing to surrender part of that independence in common with other countries to real international order."[33]

Time and again Nehru insisted that the states should maintain a reasonable balance between nationalism and internationalism. Every state should strive for an adjustment of its national interests with those of the other states in order to promote international harmony and cooperation. He probably visualized the emergence of a world federation in which India was to become an active member after independence. But it must be, according to Nehru, a world republic and not an empire for exploitation.[34]

When the Constitution of India was framed, Nehru was keenly interested in incorporating in it some basic guidelines for the country's foreign policy. This was provided in Part IV dealing with the Directive Principles of State Policy (in the enumeration and drafting of which he was specially interested). Apart from many other things, the Directive Principles enjoined that the country's foreign policy shall be directed with a view to promoting international peace and security. The state should strive for maintaining just and honorable relations between nations, by fostering respect for international law and treaty obligations, and by encouraging the settlement of international disputes by arbitration. In fact, the policy of nonalignment initiated by Nehru after independence was mainly aimed at the attainment of the same objective. It is a great tribute to him that "he insisted that India should be nonaligned in the insane struggle for power which has preoccupied the United States and the Soviet Union at the expense of the welfare of mankind."[35]

Nehru had a deep sense of cosmopolitanism. He believed that his policy of democratic collectivism would ultimately lead to political and economic internationalism and India would inevitably play a leading role in international affairs. His optimism sounded well during his lifetime, although his hopes were belied by the events that followed.

SCIENTIFIC HUMANISM

Nehru had a deep sense of respect for India's heritage. He was visibly moved by its past glory and present predicament. He passionately desired that the Indian people liberate themselves from the shackles of the past. At the same time, he urged them to recondition their mind, equipping themselves with the problems of the present and a perspective on the future. This, according to him, was possible only when the people tried to imbibe the highest ideals of the present age—humanism and scientific sprit. Despite an apparent conflict between the two, there was "a growing synthesis between humanism and scientific spirit, resulting in a kind of scientific humanism."[36] What Nehru wrote in his *Discovery of India* probably revealed much of his mind. Here he stated: "The modern mind, that is to say the better type of the modern mind, is practical and pragmatic, ethical and social, altruistic and humanitarian. It is governed by a practical idealism for social betterment.... Humanity is its god and social service its religion."[37]

Nehru was a multifaceted personality. As a political leader, he did create in the Indian mind an awareness of the movements and the significance of events in the outside world. As an intellectual, he could think far ahead of his surroundings, and his ideas did influence the progressive forces in and outside the country. As a humanist, he championed the cause of humanity and devoted himself to the ideas of social progress. More than most of his contemporaries, Nehru had a clear vision of modern India emerging as an integral part of a free world community. He aspired to build a political order based upon the universal values of freedom and social justice.

NOTES

1. This essay was first published in Thomas Pantham and Kenneth L. Deutsch, eds., *Political Thought in Modern India* (New Delhi: Sage Publications, 1986).
2. Michael Brecher, *Nehru—A Political Biography* (London: Oxford University Press, 1959); p. 181.
3. In February 1927, Nehru was elected one of the five honorary presidents and a member of the Executive Committee.
4. B.N. Pande, *Nehru* (London: Macmillan, 1977), pp. 122–123.
5. Jawaharlal Nehru, *An Autobiography* (London: The Bodley Head, 1955, reprinted), p. 163.
6. Ibid., p. 168.
7. Jawaharlal Nehru, "Statement on the Independence Resolution," The Tribune, January 27, 1928, in S. Gopal, ed., *Selected Works of Jawaharlal Nehru*, vol. 3 (New Delhi: Orient Longman, 1972), pp. 22–23.
8. Frank Moraes, *Jawaharlal Nehru—A Biography* (New York: Macmillan Co., 1956), p. 42.
9. Jawaharlal Nehru, "Presidential Address to the National Congress in 1936," in *India and the World* (London: George Allen and Unwin Ltd., 1936), p. 83.
10. Ibid., pp. 83–84.
11. Jawaharlal Nehru, *The Basic Approach*, a note published in A.I.C.C. *Economic Review* (New Delhi: All-India Congress Committee, August 15, 1958).

12. *Jawaharlal Nehru's Speeches*, vol. 3 (Delhi: Publications Division, Govt. of India, 1958), pp. 136–137.

13. Jawaharlal Nehru, *Where Are We?* (Allahabad and London: Kitabistan, 1939), p. 60.

14. Ibid., p. 59.

15. Willard Range, *Jawaharlal Nehru's World View—A Theory of International Relations* (Athens: University of Georgia Press, 1961), p. 16.

16. Jawaharlal Nehru, *India and the World* (London: George Allen and Unwin Ltd.), p. 259.

17. Willard Range, op. cit., p. 71.

18. Jawaharlal Nehru, *Independence and After*, p. 191, quoted in D.E. Smith, *Nehru and Democracy: The Political Thought of an Asian Democrat* (Calcutta: Orient Longman, 1958), p. 121.

19. *Jawaharlal Nehru's Speeches* (1949–53) (Delhi: Publications Division, Govt. of India, 1957), p. 97.

20. Jawaharlal Nehru, "The Basic Approach," in *Nehru's Speeches*, (Sept. 1957 to April 1963), vol. 4 (Delhi: Publications Division, Govt. of India, 1964), p. 123.

21. Jawaharlal Nehru, *The Discovery of India* (Calcutta: Signet Press, 1946), pp. 635–636.

22. Jawaharlal Nehru, *An Autobiography*, p. 591.

23. Jawaharlal Nehru, "Away from Acquisitive Society," in *Nehru's Speeches* (March 1953 to August 1957), vol. 3 (Delhi: Publications Division, Govt. of India, 1958), p. 53.

24. Jawaharlal Nehru, *The Discovery of India*, p. 634.

25. Jawaharlal Nehru's Broadcast, December 13, 1952, *Building New India* (New Delhi: A.I.C.C., 1958), p. 53.

26. *Jawaharlal Nehru's Speeches* (Sept. 1957 to April 1963), p. 114.

27. Jawaharlal Nehru, "Presidential Address at the 34th Indian Science Congress" (Delhi, January 3, 1947), in S. Gopal, ed., *Selected Works of Jawaharlal Nehru*, vol. 1 (Second Series), (New Delhi: Nehru Memorial Fund, Teen Murti House, 1984), p. 372.

28. J.S. Bright, ed., *Before and After Independence (A Collection of Important Speeches)*, Vols. 1 & 2 (1922–1950), (New Delhi: Indian Printing Works, red.), p. 292.

29. Ibid., p. 293.

30. Jawaharlal Nehru, *The Discovery of India*, p. 633.

31. Jawaharlal Nehru, *The Unity of India* (London: Lindsay-Drummond, 1948, third impression), p. 406.

32. Jawaharlal Nehru, "Whither India," in *Recent Essays and Writings* (Allahabad: Kitabistan, 1934), pp. 23–24.

33. Jawaharlal Nehru, *An Autobiography*, p. 419.

34. Willard Range, *Jawaharlal Nehru's World View—A Theory of International Relations*, p. 54.

35. Bertrand Russell, "The Legacy of Nehru," *Illustrated Weekly of India* (Bombay, May 27, 1984), p. 44.

36. Jawaharlal Nehru, *The Discovery of India*, p. 681.

37. Ibid., p. 680.

PART FOUR

EAST ASIAN POLITICAL THOUGHT

INTRODUCTION

In moving from India to East Asia we encounter again a great cultural divide—or several cultural divides. And the voyage is not easy. We are leaving the Indo-European family of languages and the confines of the three Abrahamic religions. We are entering a civilization (or civilizations) with very different mythologies, intellectual traditions, and ways of life. We encounter a highly literate culture (or cultures) whose script is not based on alphabets but on pictorial images or pictograms. By contrast to Abrahamic and also Indian religions, East Asian religiosity is not, or not heavily, focused on God or deities, but rather on the order of the cosmos or universe. One of the most central concepts of East Asian religiosity is *tao* or "the way," which is not a deity or a philosophical principle but a way of being in accord with the cosmic order. Perhaps the strongest contrast with Western and Indian "God-talk" can be found in Buddhism with its emphasis on no-God and no-self (*anatman*)—which is not a simple endorsement of secularism or atheism but a denial of the ability to domesticate or control the divine.

Despite these differences and contrasts, however, there is again a bridge facilitating our journey. For, in moving from India to East Asia we follow, in a way, the path that Buddhism traveled since the time of Gautama Buddha, also called Buddha Shakyamuni (563–483 B.C.). As pointed out in the preceding part, Buddhism arose initially as a challenge to the Indian pantheon and the prevailing caste system. In opposition to the existing system, Buddhism introduced a greater degree of social egalitarianism and also a network of monasteries whose monks were, in a fashion, detached from the traditional social order. The central teaching of Gautama Buddha was not about God or Gods but about the basic condition of human life, distilled in the "four noble truths" (*arya-satya*): the truths that life is suffering or disjointedness (*dukha*); that the source of suffering is selfish desire or craving (*trishna, tanha*); that to overcome suffering selfish clinging has to cease (*nirodha*); and that there is a path or a "way" leading to the cessation of suffering, the so-called "eightfold path" (*ashtangika marga*) involving a complete turning around of the human being leading to liberation (*satori, nirvana*).

From its origins in India, Buddhism developed in several directions, not all of which can be pursued here. The initial outreach was toward the South and Southeast of India (Sri Lanka, Thailand, and Burma). Buddhism at this point took an austere form, relying on individual self-control; because of this austerity it is called the "small vehicle" (*Hinayana*). In subsequent centuries Buddhism traveled eastward over Tibet to the Far East. Less rigid in outlook, Buddhism now became a "great (or large) vehicle" (*Mahayana*) aiming at the liberation of all peoples and beings. Instead of relying purely on self-control, the *Mahayana* version envisaged the beneficial intervention of Buddha-like helpers (called "*bodhisattvas*") moved by compassion (*karuna*) for all suffering beings. The most celebrated among these helpers is the "*bodhisattva* of unlimited mercy" (*Avalokiteshwara*). The Dalai Lama, the head of Tibetan Buddhism, is said to be an incarnation of this *bodhisattva*.[1] A prominent subdivision of the *Mahayana* school is the "Middle Way" (*Madhyamika*) branch, which, among other things, developed the philosophical implications of "emptiness" (*sunyata*), meaning both the egoless character of the human individual and the contingency or nonfixity of the world.

It was in its *Mahayana* form that Buddhism entered China in the middle of the Han dynasty (202 B.C. to 221 A.D.). Due to diligent efforts to translate Buddha's *Sutras* (sermons) and other *Mahayana* texts, Buddhist teachings rapidly spread through the land. A few centuries later, prominent Indian Buddhists visited China to clarify the message, among them, Kumarajiva (344–413 A.D.), Paramartha (499–569 A.D.), and Bodhidharma (sixth century). Buddhist monasteries and schools sprang up and numerous Chinese pilgrims went to India to study the original sources. The rapid rise of Buddhism, however, triggered native resentment and several times led to severe persecutions (the first between 450 and 550 A.D., the second around 850 A.D.). In many ways, these latter events sealed the political fate of Buddhism in China (and the Far East in general). Although, following the persecutions, Buddhists were able to regain their place in society, they remained politically on the sidelines. The sociologist Max Weber has claimed that Buddhism is an "anti-political status religion" aiming at personal salvation, which is surely an overstatement (remembering Emperor Ashoka and other Buddhist rulers). What is true, however, is that Buddhism assumed a distance from social hierarchies and imperial dynasties (especially those not ruled by *dharma*). For more than a millennium, this distance favored an attitude of noninvolvement or critical aloofness.[2] Things changed, however, in late modernity, partly under the impact of colonialism and native tyrannical regimes. At this point, we witness the upsurge of a politically "engaged Buddhism" or "Buddhist resistance movement" (as will be shown below).

When moving into China, Buddhism did not enter a cultural no-man's land, but rather a country with rich cultural and spiritual traditions. The two main indigenous traditions were Confucianism and Daoism. Actually, the reception of Buddhism in China was facilitated because of a certain affinity between Buddhist and Daoist beliefs (with some Daoists viewing Buddhists as siblings from the "barbarian" West). There is also a political affinity between the two beliefs in the sense that, like Buddhism, Daoism over the centuries has shied away from direct political involvement, preferring the role of critical gadfly.[3] Politically and socially, the most prominent tradition in China has always been Confucianism originated by Confucius (Kungfu-tzu, 551–479 B.C.) during the Chou dynasty. Confucius basically set himself the task of rescuing the ethical and political ideals of earlier times from oblivion. His teachings, like those of Aristotle, are based on a series of personal and public virtues. Foremost among these virtues are: humaneness or benevolence (*ren*); natural propriety or decorum (*li*); ethical fittingness (*yi*); loyalty (*chung*); filial piety (*hsiao*); power of moral example (*te*); and civility or peacefulness (*wen*). A person embodying these virtues is called a good or noble person (*chün-tzu*), similar to the "*phronimos*" in ancient Greece. His teachings are collected in a number of writings, the most important being the *Analects* (*Lun-yü*). Confucius held public offices, especially as supervisor of royal lands, but suffered from political intrigues. He attracted a large member of students and followers, among them Mencius (Meng-tzu, 372–289 B.C.) and Hsün Tzu (313–238 B.C.).

Approached from a Western vantage point, Confucianism is hard to pinpoint or classify, because it escapes customary categories. Philosophically considered, it is not properly speaking a form of "idealism," if that term means the assumption of ideal essences. Nor is it a form of empirical "realism," if that term means the acceptance of the world "as it is" without ethical transformation. Its outlook resembles in some ways that of American "pragmatism" because of a shared emphasis on practical conduct, ethical striving, and education. However, whereas pragmatism has often been narrowly future-oriented and dismissive of the past, Confucius endorsed traditional ancestor-worship and always sought inspiration from "ancient" ways of life. In his teachings, Confucius avoided talking about God or speculating about the "after-life," arguing that we should first know more about this life before we contemplate after-life. In a way, his thinking was this-worldly or "secular" but not in the sense of modern secularism or atheism. Pointing to its peculiar "immanent" religiosity, one expert speaks of Confucius's treatment of "the secular as sacred."[4] As a corollary, one can describe Confucianism as a "humanism," but without anthropocentrism or selfish individualism. Socially and politically, Confucius was opposed to autocracy and despotism, but without dismissing legitimate authority. His personal conduct in his relation with others displayed a strong democratic temper—without prompting an ideological commitment to democracy.[5]

In this essay "The Value of the Human in Classical Confucian Thought," Tu Weiming emphasizes the central role of the metaphor of the "Way" (*tao*). As he states: "The Confucian Way suggests an unceasing process of self-transformation as a communal act." Hence, pursuit of the Way for Confucius is neither a narrowly individualistic nor a collectivist enterprise; although it centers on finding one's way in this world, it does not neglect the "Way of Heaven" (testifying to an immanent religiosity). Examining the *Analects*, Tu Weiming comments on the importance of education or learning (*hsüeh*) not just for the purpose of accumulating knowledge or information but as a process of "training the self to be responsive to the world and culture at large." He also points to the close correlation between the cultivation of humaneness (*ren*) and the observation of propriety or ritual (*li*), with the two closely complementing each other. The Confucian emphasis on learning was continued by Mencius who stressed not only the "mind" but also the "heart" and who upheld the possibility of human self-perfection if pursued in accordance with virtue and the Way of Heaven. The same outlook prevails in a text known as "The Mean" (*Chung-yung*), which likewise celebrates a worldly religiosity. In Tu Weiming's words, in that text, "the relationship between Heaven and man is not that of creator and creature but one of mutual fidelity; and the only way for man to know Heaven is to penetrate deeply into his own ground of being." Contrary to allegations of bland conformism, Confucianism for the author makes rooms for individual "internality"—which, however, is far removed from Lockean or Hobbesian self-interest or Kierkegaardian loneliness.

In the political domain, the main competitor to Confucianism in China was the school of "Legalism" or political "realism" (arising around 300 B.C.) stressing the need for harsh control to combat corruption. Confucians and Legalists often clashed; the Qin dynasty (221–206 B.C.) witnessed the brutal persecution of Confucians by the forces of "law and order." In a way, the conflict between the two schools resembles the tension between "*dharma*" and "*danda*" in ancient India, between those relying mainly on the cultivation of virtue and those privileging political power. In his essay "Law and Society in Confucian Thought," Ronald Keith discusses the struggle between Legalists and Confucians through the centuries. As he notes, the motto of the former was: "the virtuous are few and the worthless are many"— meaning that government can only be maintained by power. To be sure, Confucians also recognized the role of law (*fa*)—but as something subordinate or ancillary to benevolence (*ren*) and propriety (*li*). Mencius also accepted law (especially punitive law) as a supplement to self-cultivation. Over the centuries, the two schools moved closer to each other; one speaks in this context of the "Confucianization of law" or the legalization of *ren/li*. As Keith points out, Legalism of a sort was restored to prominence around 1978 by the Chinese Communist regime—but at that time Legalism denoted something like a general "rule of law" or "dignity of law" in opposition to arbitrary political rule. Basically, the idea of a "lawful society" (*fazhi shehui*) was extolled as an antidote not to Confucianism (which by then had been sidelined) but to the "personality cult" of Maoism.

To be sure, on an intellectual or philosophical level, Legalism was not really on a par with Confucianism, seeing that it lacked the latter's rich panoply of texts and learned treatises. Intellectually, the real competitors of Confucianism in China were always Buddhism and Daoism; in fact, the three are widely recognized as the "Three Teachings" in China. As indicated before, Confucianism always enjoyed a political preeminence among them. In the early Sung dynasty (960–1279 A.D.), a civil service examination system (introduced earlier) was formally established, with Confucian texts serving as the central topic of examinations. Henceforth, public officials in China were required to be closely familiar with Confucian texts and teachings. As it happens, the same period also witnessed a growing interaction of the "Three Teachings," with the result that Confucianism developed a more metaphysical outlook able to compete with Buddhist and Daoist ideas (though without replicating the Buddhist focus on meditation nor the Daoist concern with physical and psychic cultivation). On the whole, one can characterize the Sung dynasty as an early time of intellectual and political "reformism" (preceding by several centuries similar movements in the Islamic world and India). The most prominent development at the time was the rise of "neo-Confucianism" led by a number of outstanding Confucian scholars who reformulated the Confucian "canon" by establishing the centrality of "Four Books" (*Analects*, Mencius, "Great Teaching," and *Chung-yung*). The most prominent of these innovators was Chu Hsi (Zhu Xi, 1130–1200 A.D.) who offered a profound new analysis of key Confucian terms.

The following centuries saw the growing interest of European powers in China (as exemplified by the travels of Marco Polo and Matteo Ricci). The real upsurge of European colonialism, however, occurred during the final Ch'ing or Manchu dynasty (1644–1911 A.D.).[6] At this time, European powers made concerted efforts to establish footholds in China. As in the case of India, it was first of all European mercantile interests that were eager to tap the vast Chinese markets. One of the most lucrative economic interests was the trade in Opium, which the British companies sought to inflict on Chinese people despite its corrupting effects. When the Ch'ing dynasty sought to curb this pernicious trade, the British government reacted with military force, triggering the so-called Opium War (1839–1842), at the end of which China was compelled to cede Hong Kong for 100 years to Britain. Soon other European powers joined in, exploiting the weakness of the Chinese government; the result was a series of "concessions" or "unequal treaties" granting semigovernmental functions in various regions to European powers. After the Ch'ing regime was further weakened and humiliated by being soundly defeated by the Japanese (in the Sino-Japanese War of 1894–95), the United States in 1899 forced an "Open Door Policy" on China, leaving domestic industry and manufacture unprotected from foreign exploitation. It was at this point that hordes of Chinese people literally took things into their own hands and, in the so-called "Boxer Rebellion" (1900), marshaled their "righteous fists" against colonial guns, only to be brutally repressed.

Here it is useful to remember the discussions in Parts Two and Three. As in the case of India and the Islamic civilization, the reaction to Western colonial assaults took mainly three forms: outright rejectionism or radical traditionalism; radical modernism or assimilation; and moderate reformism. The attitude of the Chinese in the Opium War and the Boxer Rebellion was clearly one of rejectionism. But soon cooler heads prevailed. At the onset of the twentieth century, the Chinese regime embarked on various legal and administrative reforms. By 1905, the traditional civil service examinations were abolished; a few years later, a movement for constitutional reform was launched which ultimately led to the downfall of the Imperial regime and the establishment of the Republic (in 1911). Somewhat earlier, similar developments happened also in Japan—which culturally was always somewhat influenced by China. Confucianism had entered Japan in its early history—although its influence there was circumscribed from the beginning by Shintoism (Emperor worship). Buddhism traveled to Japan in the middle of the sixth century A.D. and for a time even became the official state religion. During the Nara period (eighth century), there were already some six schools of Buddhism in the country. Subsequent centuries saw the rise of the popular or devotional "Pure Land" branch of Buddhism and the more austere "Zen" school (Chinese: Chan). By the middle of the sixteenth century Dutch and Portuguese traders and missionaries began to arrive. The real upsurge of European colonialism, however, occurred during the Tokugawa Shogunate (1603–1867), when Western powers were eager to penetrate Japanese markets. In 1854 the American Commodore Perry, through an act of gun boat diplomacy, forced Japan to open its ports to Western business. It was at this point that Japan was compelled seriously to confront the Western challenge. The initial reaction was a form of modified rejectionism: the so-called Meiji Restoration (1868) carried out under the motto "revere the Emperor, expel the barbarians." However, soon the spirit of moderate reformism prevailed: the Meiji Constitution (1869 revised in 1890) established a constitutional monarchy with the Emperor as head.

In an essay titled "East Asia's Modern Transformation" (not included in this volume), Theodore de Bary reflects on the different responses of China and Japan to Western modernity and colonialism.[7] As he points out, China's response was slower and delayed, whereas Japan hurried more rapidly from moderate reform to assimilation. "Within fifteen years of Perry's arrival," he writes, "the Japanese moved from an initial defensive stance, not unlike that of the Chinese, to a dynamic, outward-looking policy that would bring Japan quickly into the West's modern world." To illustrate this point in the case of Japan, de Bary discusses two examples: the samurai Yoshida Shōin (1830–1859) and the Emperor Meiji himself (who reigned 1868–1911). Trained in both neo-Confucian and samurai traditions, Shōin sought to combine the East's "moral and spiritual values" with Western science and technology, but he did so with an intense nationalist fervor hard to reconcile with reformism. Emperor Meiji, by contrast, managed a steady balancing feat: to accomplish a constitutional "revolution" in the name of tradition and renovation. In the long run, however, renovation came to tip the balance against tradition. Turning to China under the Ch'ing dynasty, de Bary highlights the role of the so-called "self-strengtheners" and especially the reform program of K'ang Yu-wei during the "Hundred Days of Reform" in 1898—a program deeply tainted with a nostalgic Confucian traditionalism. Confucian nostalgia, however, could not permanently salvage the Ch'ing regime. The latter was swept aside by the constitutional upheaval of 1911, which—though initially reform-oriented—set China on the path of radical innovation. Through many detours this path would eventually lead to the rise and final triumph of an ideological movement which—basically Western in origin—sought to revolutionize an Asian peasant society: Mao Tse-tung's communism.

As we know, the period from 1911 to the establishment of the Chinese People's Republic (in 1949) was a period of arduous nation-building overshadowed by domestic ideological rivalries and foreign interventions. The beginning of the first Republic witnessed the emergence of a strong modernist and nationalist movement, called the

"May 4th" (1919) movement, wedded to the twin goals of modern science plus democracy. Sun Yat-Sen who served as President for several years (1921–1925), became the leader of a major party (Kuomintang) dedicated to the transformation of China into a modern nation-state (but without extensive social and economic changes).[8] Roughly at the same time, however, Mao Tse-tung together with some others launched the Marxist Communist Party, a development that drove many earlier reformers into the arms of right-wing nationalist leaders. Compounded by Japanese invasion, factional strife and civil war continued throughout World War II and until 1949 (when the Kuomintang retreated to Taiwan.) The policies of mainland China ever since 1949 have been basically modernist and antitraditionalist in character; high points of radical modernism were the "Great Leap Forward" (1958–1960) and the "Cultural Revolution" (1965–1976) aimed at the destruction of all traditional vestiges. In more recent times, however, a softening of these policies has taken place. Economically, China has made limited concessions to Western neoliberal market principles. Intellectually, there is a pronounced revival of older cultural and religious traditions, most importantly Confucianism, Buddhism, and Daoism. Although it is too early to predict the outcome of this readjustment, it seems that mainland China is embarking on a path of moderate adaptation, not too far removed from the reformers of the Ch'ing period.

In their essay "The Contemporary Relevance of Confucianism," Daniel Bell and Hahm Chaibong discuss the contributions the Confucian legacy can make both to the future development of China and to the emergence of a global civilization integrating Eastern and Western traditions. The essay serves as Introduction to an edited volume titled *Confucianism for the Modern World*.[9] As the editors point out, Confucianism in China during the last 100 years has been under siege, being frequently harassed and vilified by modernists (whether liberal or communist). In recent times, however, new currents of thought have emerged seeking to vindicate Confucian teachings in many domains. The main emphasis of the essay is on the possible symbiosis of Confucianism and democracy, and on the readjustments needed on both sides. Additional attention is given to Confucian perspectives on law as well as on economics, especially capitalism. The basic preference of the editors is for a sensible reformism, which would give both the past and the present and future their proper due. As they write: "The contributors to this volume are somewhat disenchanted with Western-style liberal democracy," and especially "its inability to articulate and institutionalize the kind of communal life that can ensure human flourishing." At the same time, the contributors "do not argue for the wholesale restoration of premodern Confucianism" (that is, for a radical traditionalism). As Bell and Hahm note, some kind of reformism has actually been endemic to Confucianism through the centuries. The whole effort then, they add, is "reviving Confucianism for the modern world by bringing about a creative synthesis between the two, an endeavor that would have been entirely familiar to Confucian intellectuals in the past" (a statement that would be congenial both to Gandhians and to Muslim supporters of *salafiyya*).

In a similar manner, of course, one can also ask about the contemporary "relevance" of Buddhism and Daoism. As in the case of Confucianism, some kind of reformism has certainly been present in Buddhism in past centuries—as is evident in the continuous readjustment of schools of thought and the close interrelation between the "Three Teachings" throughout the rise of neo-Confucianism. Nevertheless, the preponderant political stance of Buddhism during the Imperial period was one of quiescent withdrawal or else subdued criticism. It was only in the twentieth century—under the impact of colonialism and the turbulence of Asian nation-building—that Buddhism (or certain Buddhist schools) emerged from this withdrawal and entered the political arena as agent(s) of nonviolent political change. To make this new stance possible, a basic teaching of traditional Buddhism had to be revised or reformulated: the stress on individual awakening/liberation had to be expanded to encompass liberation from social oppression, injustice, and misery. In an essay titled "The Shapes and Sources of Engaged Buddhism" (not included in this volume), Christopher Queen offers an overview of the historical background and religious teachings of politically "engaged" Buddhist movements.[10] As he indicates, the new outlook does not radically depart from the past; what is involved is rather a move from narrow individual self-reform to broader social and political reformism. A major aspect of this reformism is the emphasis on "skillful means" (*upaya*): that is, on education, public dialogue and nonviolent action. As Queen adds importantly, the goal of engaged Buddhism is not to seize political control of the "state," but rather to exert ethical influence in civil society (in classical Indian terminology: to bring *dharma* to bear as a restraint on *danda*).

Forms of engaged Buddhism are present in East Asia as well as in South and Southeast Asia today. Prominent leaders of this kind of neo-Buddhism have been or are: A. T. Ariyaratne in Sri Lanka (born 1932); Buddhadasa Bhikkhu (1906–1993) and Sulak Sivaraksa (born 1953) in Thailand; Thich Nhat Hanh (born 1926) in Vietnam; and the Dalai Lama (born 1935) in Tibet. In his essay "Buddhist Principles in the Tibetan Liberation Movement" (reprinted below), José Cabezón focuses on the historical development of Lamaism in Tibet and on the life and teachings of the present (14th) Dalai Lama. As Cabezón notes, despite his personal suffering and the suffering of his people—he was exiled from China in 1959 and now lives in Dharamsala, India—the Dalai Lama has always pursued toward China a moderate policy of peaceful negotiation (becoming to a Buddhist). In conformity with central tenets of engaged Buddhism, the philosophy of the Dalai Lama stresses a two-pronged path of change: social transformation joined with, and predicated on personal transformation. In line with traditional teachings, he upholds the equal Buddha nature of all humans (*tathagatagarbha*) and the basic interdependence of all beings (*pratitya-samutpada*). In intersocial relations, the Dalai Lama has always upheld the value of compassion (*karuna*) and nonviolence (*ahimsa*), adding that the maxim to "love one's enemy" does not necessarily imply quiescence but rather demands peaceful resistance to oppression and injustice. (In all these respects, the affinity between the Dalai Lama and the Mahatma Gandhi is evident.)

As the mentioned essays demonstrate, the contemporary relevance of both Confucianism and Buddhism is in large measure predicated on their ability to steer a middle (or reformist) path between tradition and innovation, between a nostalgic clinging to the past and an overly zealous embrace of Western modernity. Indications are that this path is being pursued with at least some success in Asia (and elsewhere). Of course, opposition to this path is still formidable in many quarters: The linkage of modernization and globalization fuels on the one hand an intense modernism (amounting to "Westoxification"), a mood that is countered on the other side by an equally fervid radical traditionalism cum nationalism. The advantage of the middle path is not only its reconciliation of past and future, but also its relative openness toward alternative traditions struggling along parallel paths, that is, its inclination toward tolerance and mutual recognition among cultures.

In East Asia, the relationship between the "Three Teachings" offers an instructive example of the benefits of multicultural dialogue and interpenetration. This kind of interrelationship has to be expanded today to the global, cross-civilizational level, to the encounter between East and West. In the concluding essay, "East Asia and the West: Catching Up with Each Other," Theodore de Bary ponders the possibility as well as the difficulties of such an expanded learning process. As he writes: "No real dialogue can take place between East Asia and the West unless both parties are equally and deeply involved; but for all the West's desire to understand East Asians, so far its effort has not been equal to theirs." In our contemporary world overshadowed by "terror wars" and "ethnic cleansings," the prospects for deeper cross-cultural learning are dim, but the moral task is nonetheless imperative. In de Bary's words again:

> What we need is not new worlds to conquer, star wars, and all that, but a new parochialism of the earth or planet. This should start, as the Confucians did, with self-reflection and self-restraint. Conscious of the interrelatedness of all things, and of one's own place in an interdependent world, their view should develop a sense of equal responsibility for oneself and others and of reciprocal support for a life-sustaining environment.

This passage could serve as a guiding motto for the emerging enterprise of comparative political theory in our time.

NOTES

1. For the main differences between the *Hinayana* (or *Theravada*) School and the *Mahayana* School see Huston Smith, *The World's Religions: Our Great Wisdom Traditions* (New York: Harper Collins, 1991), pp. 125–126. In China, *Avalokiteshwara* is venerated in female form as Kwan Yin.
2. In the words of Wm. Theodore de Bary: "It is fair to say that in contrast to the concern of Hinduism with caste and class, and of Confucianism with kinship and community, Buddhism was from its beginning a homeless wisdom, a mendicant and missionary religion.... Buddhism had little to say specifically about the organization and conduct of family life or the state. Empty-handed in these respects, it remained free to adapt to native tastes." See *East Asian Civilizations: A Dialogue in Five Stages* (Cambridge, MA: Harvard University Press, 1988), pp. 24–25. For some political expressions of Chinese Buddism see Hui Yuan, "A Monk Does Not Bow Down before a King," in de Bary et al., *Sources of Chinese Tradition* (New York: Columbia University Press, 1960), vol. 1, pp. 280–286; and "The Humane King as Protector of Buddhism," in the same *Sources*, p. 477.
3. On Daoism compare Huston Smith, *The World's Religions*, pp. 197–220.
4. See Herbert Fingarette, *Confucius—The Secular as Sacred* (New York: Harper & Row, 1972).
5. In the words of Huston Smith: "There was nothing other-worldly about him. He loved to be with people, to dine out, to join in the chorus of a good song, and to drink, though not in excess. His disciples reported that 'When at leisure the Master's manner was informal and cheerful. He was affable, yet firm; dignified yet pleasant.' His democratic attitudes have...been remarked upon." See *The World's Religions*, p. 157. By comparison, Mencius had a more clearly "idealist" outlook, as he assumed a "good essence" in human beings. Going beyond Confucius, and anticipating John Locke, he granted to people the right to rebel against tyrants or corrupt rulers.

6. Curiously, the beginning of the Ch'ing dynasty witnessed the late flowering of traditional Chinese political philosophy, especially in the work of Huang Tsung-his (Huang Zongxi, 1610–1695). On that work see de Bary et al., eds., *Sources of Chinese Tradition*, vol. 1, pp. 530–542.

7. William Theodore de Bary, "East Asia's Modern Transformation," in his *East Asian Civilizations: A Dialogue in Five Stages*, pp. 67–104.

8. Regarding the "May Fourth" movement and Dr. Sun Yat-sen (1866–1925) compare Shu-hsien Liu, "Contemporary Neo-Confucianism: Its Background, Varieties, Emergence, and Significance," *Dao: A Journal of Comparative Philosophy*, vol. 2 (2003), pp. 213–233. Liu mentions among modernizing intellectuals at the time chiefly Hu Shi (1891–1962), a scholar strongly influenced by Deweyan pragmatism. The essay also distinguishes between several generations of recent neo-Confucians, paying special attention to Xu Fuguan (1903–1982), Tang Junyi (1909–1978), and Mou Zongsan (1909–1995). Compare also Hao Chang, *Chinese Intellectuals in Crisis: Search for Order and Meaning, 1890–1911* (Berkeley, CA: University of California Press, 1987); and Tse-tsung Chow, *The May Fourth Movement: Intellectual Revolution in Modern China* (Cambridge, MA: Harvard University Press, 1960).

9. Daniel A. Bell and Hahm Chaibong, eds., *Confucianism for the Modern World* (Cambridge, UK: Cambridge University Press, 2003).

10. Christopher Queen, "The Shapes and Sources of Engaged Buddhism," in Queen and Sallie B. King, eds., *Engaged Buddhism: Buddhist Liberation Movements in Asia* (Albany, NY: State University of New York Press, 1996), pp. 1–44.

THE VALUE OF THE HUMAN IN CLASSICAL CONFUCIAN THOUGHT[1]

Tu Weiming

The root metaphor in the Confucian classic, the *Analects*, is the Way (*tao*).[2] The Confucian Way suggests an unceasing process of self-transformation as a communal act. It is specified as a human way, a way of life. The Way of Heaven also features prominently in Confucian literature and an understanding of the meaning of death is essential for a comprehensive appreciation of the Confucian perception of humanity. But it seems that the ontic weight in the Confucian spiritual orientation falls on the lived experience of ordinary human existence.

The *Analects* places a great deal of emphasis on commonly shared human concerns. It characterizes the method of humanity as an analogical reflection on that which is near at hand as its point of departure. One's own existence, body and mind, provides the primary context wherein the Way is pursued concretely. Without this basic grounding, the Way can never be found and one's humanity can never be realized. The Way does not in itself give full expression to humanity; it is through human effort that the Way is manifest.

Analogy, in this sense, far from being an imperfect form of deductive reasoning, signifies a mode of inquiry significantly different from linear logic but no less rigorous and compelling. To think analogically is to develop self-understanding by a continuous process of appropriating insights into the human situation as a whole and one's particular "location" in it. This involves systematic reflection and constant learning.

As an integral part of a comprehensive quest for self-knowledge, Tseng Tzu, a disciple of Confucius, is recorded to have engaged in daily self-examination on three points: "Whether, in transacting business for others, I may have been not faithful; whether, in inter-course with friends, I may have been not truthful; whether I may have not mastered and practiced the instructions of my teacher."[3] This attempt to inform one's moral self-development by constantly probing one's inner self is neither a narcissistic search for private truth nor an individualistic claim for isolated experience. Rather, it is a form of self-cultivation, which is simultaneously also a communal act of harmonizing human relationships.

By implication, the centrality of learning (*hsüeh*) in the *Analects* must also be interpreted as a process of training the self to be responsive to the world and culture at large. Thus, one studies poetry (*shih*) in order to acquire "language" (*yen*) as a necessary means of communication in the civilized world, and *ritual* (*li*) in order to internalize the "form of life" characteristic of one's own community. Accordingly, learning is a way to be human and not simply a program of making oneself empirically knowledgeable. The whole process seeks to enrich the self, to enhance its strength and to refine its wisdom so that one can be considerate to others and honest with oneself.

Needless to say, learning in the Confucian perspective is basically moral self-cultivation. It is a gradual process of building up one's character by making oneself receptive to the symbolic resources of one's own culture and responsive to the shar-able values of one's own society. Thus, Confucius observes, "In order to establish oneself, one should try to establish others; in order to enlarge oneself, one should try to enlarge others."[4] This sense of mutuality is predicated on the belief that learning to be human is by no means a lonely struggle to assert one's private ego. On the contrary, human beings come into meaningful existence through symbolic interchange and reciprocal relationship, which affirms a commonly experienced truth.

Inherent in this belief is a deep-rooted concern for the human as a communicable and sharable value. It is inconceivable that one's humanity could be realized in isola-tion or expressed by a private language. Of course, periods of self-imposed morato-rium, such as the observance of the mourning ritual, are a highly respected aspect of life in virtually all schools of Confucian thought. But even there, the primary focus is on social solidarity through an elaborate reenactment of commonly experienced roles and scenes. Indeed, the memory of the dead intensifies the care for the living.

The central concern of knowledge in this connection is to cultivate the human way and the way of life. Understandably, teaching and learning by example is considered the authentic and perhaps also the most effective method of education. One learns to be benevolent, truthful, courageous, and firm not by following a set of abstract moral rules but by a continuous encounter with the multiplicity of existential situations exemplified in the life of the teachers. The teacher, who must also be a dedicated stu-dent, responds to specified questions about self, society, politics, history, and culture not merely as an informed elder but also as an experiencing and loving fellow wisdom-seeker on the way.

This is probably the main reason that the value of ritual assumes such a central significance in the *Analects*. Like language, ritual is a form of communication and self-expression. Without a growing awareness of the ritual language, one cannot become a fully participating member of one's own society. Maturation entails a cre-ative appropriation of the prescribed values shared by the community at large. Ritual as a nonverbal mode of human interaction is particularly emphasized in Confucian literature because it involves a commitment not only synchronically to a form of life but also diachronically to a living tradition.

However, despite the apparent indication that the ontic weight of the *Analects* tends toward human sociality, it is misleading to characterize the Confucian percep-tion of learning as sociological. For one thing, Confucius himself maintains that real learning is for the sake of the self (*wei-chi*) rather than for the sake of others (*wei-jen*).[5] Indeed, the learning of the profound person is a learning to gain personal knowledge, which implies a way of life that can never be completely objectified as a blueprint for behavior. Exemplary teaching so conceived necessitates a sense of dis-covery. After all, the dialogical encounter as an incessantly confirming and renewing process of self-understanding always involves creativity. The way of the profound person is therefore as much a process of internal self-transformation as a demon-strable communal act. The internality and immediacy of the way to be human is such a recognized value in the *Analects* that Confucius unequivocally asserts, "Is humanity (*jen*) indeed far away? If I wish to be human, and lo! humanity is at hand."[6]

It is also in this sense that ritual is thought to come afterwards because it has to be built upon humanity.[7] And without humanity, ritual practice easily degenerates into formalism. Confucius' response to Yen Hui's inquiry into the meaning of humanity is most instructive. Instead of characterizing humanity as loving and caring as he does in other contexts, Confucius explains to his best disciple that humanity consists in self-mastery and returning to ritual.[8] In the light of this seminal idea, it is vitally important to note that if ritualization is the Confucian way to be human, it is inseparable from a more fundamental Confucian concern for self-mastery.

A significant development of the Confucian concern for self-mastery is found in Mencius' philosophical anthropology. By conceptualizing learning as nothing other than the quest for the lost heart, Mencius underscores the centrality of heart in his thought.[9] To him, the way of learning to be human is primarily a purification and nourishment of the heart. But since the Chinese word *hsin* in *Mencius* connotes conative as well as cognitive and affective meanings, the cultivation of the heart involves not only harmonizing one's feelings but also refining one's consciousness and establishing one's will. Actually the Mencian heart, far from being merely a physiological or a psychological idea, is an ontological basis for moral self-cultivation. Mencius claims that it is because of the heart, which is also set forth as the "great body" (*ta-t'i*), that morality is not drilled into us from outside, but inherent in our nature.[10]

It is in this connection, I think, that Mencius insists upon a fundamental distinction between inability (*pu-neng*) and unwillingness (*pu-wei*).[11] While Mencius fully acknowledges differences in temperament, talent, intelligence, and environmental influences among human beings, he refuses to grant that the ability of learning to be human as a quest for moral self-development is not readily available to each member of the human community. The willing faculty itself, namely the inner decision of the heart, is not only the ultimate reason but also the actual strength for self-realization. Indeed, Mencius' moral philosophy further articulates the Confucian belief in the power of the human will: "Although the commander of the three armies can be snatched away, the will of even a commoner cannot be snatched away."[12] As I have noted elsewhere, Mencius' unflagging faith in human perfectibility through self-effort is a direct result of his commitment to the view that no matter how disturbed and destroyed the human heart has become, its inner strength for rejuvenation can never be subdued.[13] Actually this deceptively simple appeal to what may be called the indestructibility of the true self is closely related to a theory of human nature, which emphasizes the commonality and universality of the value of the human.

By focusing his attention on "what is common in all our hearts," Mencius wishes to show that moral goodness is not merely a potential inherent in human nature but a universally experienced reality. Surely Mencius is critically aware of "all too human" atrocities against nature, mankind, and the self. After all his age is historically designated as the period of the "Warring States," known for its numerous cases of internecine struggles among those of the same surname and of the same family. The allegory of the Niu Mountain, denuded of trees by woodcutters and even of buds and sprouts by browsing cattle and goats, clearly indicates that Mencius knows well the deprivation of the human condition. However, notwithstanding his realistic appraisal of the actual state of humanity, he propounds the thesis that "the sage and I are the same in kind."[14] Implicit in this assertion is the message that our existential situation, no matter how degenerate it has become, does not deny us the same reality that enables ordinary human beings to become sages.

This fiduciary commitment to the inner resources of the self is based upon an observation that common human feelings such as commiseration, shame, deference, and a sense of right and wrong, relative and feeble as they are at times, are the concrete foundations of moral self-cultivation.[15] The very fact that we, as ordinary human beings, can experience alarm and concern when we suddenly see a child about to fall into a well sufficiently demonstrates that we are endowed with an ability to sympathize with others. To be sure, our sympathy is sometimes latent, and occasionally it is no more than a "spark" buried in the dust of selfish worries. Yet, the nature and function of the heart is such that it can regain its vitality as soon as it is preserved and nourished. Although one can lose one's heart, it is inconceivable that one cannot find it upon willing. Needless to say, the act of willing itself is also an activity of the heart. The apparent circularity of thinking is subtle but not vicious. Mencius is absolutely serious in claiming that if anyone with moral feelings "knows how to give them the fullest extension and development, the result will be like fire beginning to burn or a spring beginning to shoot forth."[16] This is actually the way by which an ordinary human being can eventually become a sage, symbolizing humanity in its all-embracing fullness. The primary concern of learning in Mencius is thus the quest for self-knowledge. To seek the lost heart is a spiritual discipline whereby primordial feelings, such as commiseration, shame, deference, and a sense of right and wrong are transformed into moral qualities, such as humanity, righteousness, propriety, and wisdom.

However, it is misleading to conclude that in Mencius' thought knowledge has lost its objective validity and self-knowledge is no more than the self-awareness of an isolated self in transformation. For one thing, the prominence of "internality" (*nei*) as Mencius would have it is neither a concern for privacy nor an attachment to individuality. Rather, it intends to show that personal knowledge is an authentic way to genuine communication as well as to deep self-understanding. This is in accord with the Confucian instruction that learning for the sake of the self is the best way to manifest common humanity: the ability to take one's own feelings as a guide is the course of human-relatedness.[17]

Undeniably, strong human feelings are often associated with instinctual demands, such as appetite for food or sex. Although Mencius strongly recommends that the cultivation of the heart depends on making our desires few,[18] he never advocates asceticism. On the contrary, he not only recognizes but proposes that basic physiological and psychological needs be properly fulfilled. Actually he insists that it is the duty of the political leader to feed and enrich the people as a prior condition for educating them. Without an adequate livelihood, Mencius maintains, it is senseless to impose moral standards upon the people.[19] Yet it is vitally important to point out that the gratification of animal desires is no more than the minimum requirement of being human. If one is preoccupied with food and sex at the expense of one's "great body," one can hardly appreciate the value of the human in its full expression. This is like the short-sighted man who is fixated on nourishing his finger to the exclusion of rest of the body.[20] In response to the question, "Since we are all human beings, why is it that some follow their great body and others follow their small body?" Mencius states, "When our senses of sight and hearing are used without thought and are thereby obscured by material things, the material things act on the material senses and lead them away."[21]

By implication, it is "thinking" (*ssu*) that can free us from the limitation of the small body. Lest we should mistake this view for a kind of intellectualism, thinking in the Mencian context involves not only the heart and the mind but also the body. It signifies a holistic and integrated way of learning. Thus, Mencius observes that "if we first establish the great body in us, then the small body cannot overcome it. It is simply this that makes a person great."[22] It is also in this sense that Mencius maintains that only the sages can fully realize their "bodily designs" or their "human forms."[23] In other words, the development of the true self, as differentiated from the expansion of the privatized ego, is a process that opens oneself up to an ever broadening and deepening horizon of values shared by the enlarging community of likeminded moral persons. This is a concrete path leading toward a universalizable experience of personal identity and communication. Against this background, it seems fitting that Mencius concludes that if we can fully develop our hearts, we can completely realize our human nature; and if we completely realize our human nature, we will know Heaven.[24]

This seems on the surface no more than a naive faith in the ability of the heart to fully develop itself and in so doing not only to realize humanity in general but also to know the ultimate reality, Heaven. However, a fundamental assumption in classical Confucian thought underlies this seemingly unbridled romantic assertion of the unity of the human way and the Way of Heaven. The prescriptive reason is given in a short but highly suggestive text, *Chung yung*, commonly known as the *Doctrine of the Mean*. In my study on *Chung-yung*, which I translate as "centrality and commonality," I have made the following observation:

> Professing the unity of man and Heaven, *Chung-yung* neither denies nor slights a transcendent reality. Actually, since human nature is imparted from and confirmed by Heaven, it is inconceivable in *Chung-yung's* view that man can be alienated from Heaven in any essential way. As an integral part of Heaven's creative process, man is not only endowed with the "centrality" (the most refined quality) of the universe but is charged with the mission of bringing the cosmic transformation to its fruition. Therefore the Way is nothing other than the actualization of true human nature. In a strict sense, the relationship between Heaven and man is not that of creator and creature but one of mutual fidelity; and the only way for man to know Heaven is to penetrate deeply into his own ground of being. Consequently, an inquiry into philosophy or religion must begin with a reflection on the problem of man here and now.[25]

This rudimentary formulation of *Chung-yung's* philosophical anthropology may give the impression that the Mencian line in the Confucian tradition, of which *Chung-yung* is a part, seems to advocate the thesis that "man is the measure of all things." But as I have further observed:

> One can [certainly] argue that learning and teaching in *Chung-yung* are basically concerned with the problem of how to become a person, and that doctrines such as the unity of man and Heaven and the harmony of man and nature are manifestations of this humanistic concern. Spiritualism and naturalism as such do not play a key role in *Chung-yung*. But we would be ill-advised to interpret *Chung-yung's* humanism as a form of anthropocentrism, ignoring its spiritualist and naturalist dimensions.[26]

Actually it is not difficult to see that in the perspective of *Chung-yung*, the realization of the deepest meaning of humanity entails a process transcending the anthropological realm. The logic is readily comprehensible: since human nature is

imparted from Heaven, it shares a reality that underlies the myriad things. To actual-
ize this underlying reality, therefore, is not to transcend humanity but to work
through it. This is predicated on the belief that ontologically human nature is
endowed with the "original ability" and the "original wisdom" to realize the ultimate meaning of Heaven in ordinary human existence. But the task of actualizing
the ontological truth of humanity in concrete, everyday experience requires a continuous process of self-cultivation, which is reminiscent of Tseng Tzu's description of
the way and burden of the profound person: "For humanity (*jen*) is the burden he
has taken upon himself; and must we not grant that it is a heavy one to bear? Only
with death does his journey end; then must we not grant that he has far to go?"[27]

It is in this sense that the person who realizes his own nature to the full necessarily becomes a paradigm of authentic humanity. "What is being realized, then,
signifies not only his personal humanness but humanity as such and as a whole. And
since humanity is an integral part of the 'myriad things,' a complete realization of
humanity must lead to the realization of things as well."[28] Against this background,
the sincere, true, and real persons are thought, through their quests for self-
knowledge, to have transformed the universe as well. The following statement from
the *Chung-yung* can thus be taken as an articulation of the Confucian faith in human
perfectibility.

> Only those who are absolutely *sincere* can fully develop their nature. If they
> can fully develop their nature, they can fully develop the nature of others. If
> they can fully develop the nature of others, they can then fully develop the
> nature of things. If they can fully develop the nature of things, they can then
> assist in the transforming and nourishing process of Heaven and Earth. If they
> can assist in the transforming and nourishing process of Heaven and Earth,
> they can thus form a trinity with Heaven and Earth.[29]

Indeed, "The profound person, through a long and unceasing process of delving
into his own ground of existence, discovers his true subjectivity not as an isolated
selfhood but as a true source of creative transformation."[30]

The apparent conflict between the search for inner spirituality and the commitment to social responsibility is no longer relevant. Even the tension between self and
society, one of the most salient characteristics of "religious" experience, also assumes
a rather different shade of meaning. "Internality" in the Mencian tradition of
Confucian thought denotes an experienced human value, a personal knowledge of
the good. It is inconceivable that the ripening of one's inner moral sense of humanity
and righteousness does not lead to a growing concern for social well-being. Indeed,
the real threat to the maturation of the self is selfishness. A privatization of the self
is, in Mencius' terminology, the frustration of the great body by the small one. The
cultivation of the heart, then, is to make it receptive to the universal power of the self
to communicate with other structures of being.

The humanist vision, which first appeared in the *Analects*, then developed in the
Book of Mencius, and eventually attained a remarkable fruition in *Chung-yung*, is a
holistic approach to the perennial human concern for self-understanding and self-
realization. Confucian humanism is therefore fundamentally different from anthropocentrism because it professes the unity of man and Heaven rather than the
imposition of the human will on nature. In fact the anthropocentric assumption that
man is put on earth to pursue knowledge and, as knowledge expands, so does man's
dominion over earth is quite different from the Confucian perception of the pursuit

of knowledge as an integral part of one's self-cultivation. To be sure, the belief that knowledge implies power is not totally absent in the Confucian tradition. Hsün Tzu, for example, strongly advocates the position that since culture is man-made, the human transformation of nature is not only necessary but also highly desirable. Yet, what Hsün Tzu proposes is hardly a form of aggressive scientism. Indeed, he is so painfully aware of the principle of scarcity that his general attitude towards natural resources is not manipulative but conservationist.[31]

The human transformation of nature, therefore, means as much an integrative effort to learn to live harmoniously in one's natural environment as a modest attempt to use the environment to sustain basic livelihood. The idea of exploiting nature is rejected because it is incompatible with the Confucian concern for moral self-development. Once our attention is focused upon the external, so the argument goes, our internal resources will be dissipated. In Mencius' words, the interaction between material things and material senses can form a vicious circle. As the things act upon the senses, the senses will demand more things for gratification. This will lead to an uncontrollable expansion of the "small body," a kind of inflated ego. As a result, the true self (the human heart), will be lost. This seems to support the modern socio-logical observation that the glorification of the technocratic power may produce a protean creature whose flexibility is disproportional to his miserably limited inner freedom. In other words, his adaptability is merely symptomatic of the brute fact that, having been shaped into many unnatural forms by man-made environments, he is no longer capable of experiencing his own selfhood.

However, it is helpful to note that the Confucian quest for a vision of the whole from a humanist point of view is by no means incongruous with the scientific spirit of acquiring empirical knowledge, although it is certainly in conflict with the dog-matic positivistic assertion that only verifiable knowledge is philosophically sound. Actually empirical knowledge is such a cherished value in the Confucian tradition that its way of learning to be human entails a comprehensive program of education, which includes, among other subjects, the natural world of grass, trees, birds, and animals. Also, it should be mentioned that the Confucian "six arts," prerequisites for the educated person, involve arithmetic, as well as ritual, music, archery, charioteer-ing, and calligraphy.[32] Furthermore, it is not difficult to see that the Five Classics are rich sources for the study of astronomy, geography, government, history, poetry, and art. Understandably the *Great Learning*, a highly compact essay on Confucian edu-cation, begins its instruction with the precept of "investigating things."[33] To be sure, the extension of knowledge in the Confucian sense is always conceived as an integral part of a holistic way of humanization. But the value of knowledge is abso-lutely irreducible in Confucian humanism; it is inconceivable that one can become fully human without going through a conscious process of learning to do so.

Implicit in this spiritual orientation is a concerted effort to maintain a delicate balance between freedom as an inner moral direction and knowledge as a self-disclosure to the cosmos as a whole. It rejects both an introspective affirmation of the self as an isolable and complacent ego and an unrestrained attachment to the external world for the sake of a limitless expansion of one's manipulative power. The myth of the Faustian drive or of the unbound Prometheus, symbolizing the human passion to know, to change, and to conquer, is alien to the Confucian concept of man not because it dramatizes self-transcendence but because it glorifies a complete destruction of the primordial order. When Mencius observes that the great man does not lose his childlike heart, he is perhaps also making a general statement about knowledge and its relationship to human nature.[34] To him, the value of knowledge lies in its contribution to the wisdom of self-fulfillment, of communality, and of union with Heaven. In other words, knowledge helps us to realize our original nature. If knowledge is pursued for its own sake to the extent that it becomes completely beyond human self-understanding, it will turn out to be a serious threat to our inner freedom.

On the other hand, the appropriation of knowledge in the Confucian tradition never intends to be a possession, as a way of controlling nature. Rather, it implies a movement of opening up the self to nature. To live a full life, then, requires the willingness and the courage to transform the limited and limiting structure of the ego into an ever deepening and broadening self. It is in this sense that true subjectivity is not only compatible with but also essential for the development of an experienced universality. The real challenge to self-realization is not the external world but self-ignorance and egoism. The Confucian Way, suggesting an unceasing process of self-transformation as a communal act,[35] is therefore an attempt to show that knowledge, properly understood as a humanist value, can ultimately free us from the constrictions of the privatized ego.

This approach to the problem of the self naturally leads us to a comparative observation: the Confucian tradition either omits or rejects a large category of Western ideas, which is thought to have been the necessary outgrowth of a more refined philosophical understanding of humanity. The category includes ideas of self-interest, private property, spiritual loneliness, and psychological egoism as positive contributions to the formulation of respectively political, economic, religious, and ethical individualism. Indeed, it can be further pointed out that a conflicting, if not contradictory, category of ideas assumes great prominence in Confucian thought: for example, duty-consciousness, public service, mutuality between man and Heaven, and a sense of community. Of course, we need to examine the different stages of Chinese history to determine the genetic reasons found in economic conditions, political organizations, social structures, and other relevant constraints for the seeming asymmetry, mainly from the Western viewpoint, between ideas of individualism and their social practices.

Does this imply that the Confucian perception of the dignity of man is separable from the individual's autonomy, privacy, and self-development? Surely, equality in Confucianism is defined in terms of man's inner worth, his inherent ability to attain moral excellence. Since the ontological basis as well as the actual strength of self-realization is considered to be anchored within the structure of human nature and mind, respect for the dignity of man, as a corollary, is believed to be egalitarian in a universal sense. However, it does not necessarily follow that since respect is equally due to all per-sons in virtue of their being persons, there is no way of criticizing autonomy as self-centeredness, privacy as self-isolation, and self-development as an expression of egoism.

It is difficult to argue that a man's dignity can be preserved if he does not decide and choose in a self-determined way. Yet, to say that his dignity depends on the fact that his actions are solely determined by his conscious "self" is not without serious ambiguity. Specifically when and how a person acts autonomously is often problematic. More intriguing is the ethicoreligious question: What kind of person can really experience a sense of inner freedom and thus claim to be autonomous? Similarly, to define privacy as freedom from interferences and obstacles is predicated on the belief that, in Isaiah Berlin's words, "a frontier must be drawn between the area of private life and that of public authority." Unfortunately the notion of "frontier" is morally debatable and can be easily abused in the political sphere. Even in the case of self-development, although the practice of egoism does not seem to us as dangerous as the inculcation of ideologically controlled collectivistic ideas in the unsuspecting mind, it is nevertheless a perversion of human growth.

Historically, the emergence of individualism as a motivating force in Western society may have been intertwined with highly particularized political, economic, ethical, and religious traditions. It seems reasonable that one can endorse an insight into the self as a basis for equality and liberty without accepting Locke's idea of private property, Adam Smith's and Hobbes' idea of private interest, John Stuart Mill's idea of privacy, Kierkegaard's idea of loneliness, or the early Sartre's idea of freedom. While I am sympathetic to Steven Lukes' conclusion that "the only way to realize the values of individualism is through a humane form of socialism,"[36] I suspect that the task may have to begin with an inquiry into the value of the human with all its far-reaching philosophical implications.

NOTES

1. This is the fourth chapter in Tu Wei-ming, *Confucian Thought: Selfhood as Creative Transformation* (Albany, NY: State University of New York Press, 1985).

2. For a general discussion on this root metaphor, see Herbert Fingarette, *Confucius—The Secular as Sacred* (New York: Harper & Row, 1972), pp. 18–36. I have also written on the subject in reference to Confucius' spiritual self-identification; see my essay on "The Confucian Perception of Adulthood," *Daedalus: Journal of the American Academy of Arts and Sciences*, vol. 105:2 (Spring 1976), 109-123. This essay is included in *Adulthood*, ed. Erik H. Erikson (New York: W. W. Norton & Company, 1978), pp. 113–127. I wish to note that Paul Ricoeur's "multi-disciplinary studies of the creation of meaning in language" have been most inspiring to me in my research on this particular aspect of Confucian thought; see his *The Rule of Metaphor*, trans. by Robert Czerny (Toronto: University of Toronto Press, 1977).

3. *Analects*, 1:4.

4. Ibid., 6:28.

5. The statement in the *Analects* reads: "The scholars of antiquity studied for the sake of the self; nowadays scholars study for the sake of others" (14:25). Arthur Waley correctly interprets this to mean that "[i]n old days men studied for the sake of self-improvement; nowadays men study in order to impress other people." See *The Analects of Confucius*, trans. by Arthur Waley (London: George Allen & Unwin, 1938), p. 187.

6. *Analects*, 7:29.

7. The statement in the *Analects* reads: "Tzu-hsia asked, saying, what is the meaning of 'Oh the sweet smile dimpling,/The lovely eyes so black and white!/Plain silk that you would take for colored stuff.' The Master said, The painting comes after the plain groundwork. Tzu-hsia said, Then ritual comes afterwards? The Master said, Shang [Tzu-hsia] it is who bears me up. At last I have someone with whom I can discuss the Songs!" (3:8). For this translation see Waley, pp. 95–96. It should be noted that "the Songs" here refers to the *Book of Poetry*, which symbolizes the natural expression of basic human feelings.

8. *Analects*, 12:1. For a consideration of the philosophical significance of this passage in Confucian thought, see my paper "The Creative Tension between Jen and Li," *Philosophy East and West*, vol. 12:1–2 (January–April 1968), 29–39.

9. *Mencius*, 6B:11.

10. For a discussion of Mencius' moral philosophy, see my paper "On the Mencian Perception of Moral Self-Development," *The Monist*, vol. 61:1 (January 1978), 72–81. Also see *Mencius*, 6A:15.

11. *Mencius*, 1A:7.

12. *Analects*, 9:25.

13. "On the Mencian Perception of Moral Self-Development," p. 76.

14. *Mencius*, 6A:7.

15. The term "fiduciary commitment" is here used in Michael Polanyi's sense; see his *Personal Knowledge: Towards a Post-Critical Philosophy* (New York: Harper & Row, 1962), pp. 30–31. See *Mencius*, 6A:6.

16. *Mencius*, 2A:6.

17. *Analects*, 6:28.

18. *Mencius*, 7B:35.

19. Ibid., 1A:7.20; 3A:3.

20. Ibid., 6A:14.

21. Ibid., 6A:15.

22. Ibid., 6A:15.

23. Ibid., 7A:38.

24. Ibid., 7A:1.

25. Tu Wei-ming, *Centrality and Commonality: An Essay on Chung-Yung* (Honolulu: The University Press of Hawaii, 1976), p. 9.

26. Ibid., p. 10.

27. *Analects*, 8:7.

28. Tu Wei-ming, *Centrality and Commonality*, p. 118.

29. *The Doctrine of the Mean*, chapter 22. For this translation, see Wing-tsit Chan, trans., *A Source Book in Chinese Philosophy* (Princeton: Princeton University Press, 1973), pp. 107–108.

30. Tu Wei-ming, *Centrality and Commonality*, p. 140.

31. For a brief account of Hsün Tzu's political and social thought, see Fung Yu-lan. *A History of Chinese Philosophy*, trans. Derk Bodde (Princeton: Princeton University, 1952), vol. I, pp. 294–302.

32. This refers to the famous "six arts" in Confucian education; see the "Ta-ssu-tu" section of the "Ti-kuan" chapter in the *Chou-li*.

33. The precept of *ko-wu* ("investigation of things") was one of the most important foci of intellectual debate in Neo-Confucian thought. It is the first of the "eight steps" of education in the *Great Learning*. See Wing-tsit Chan, *A Source Book*, pp. 84–94.

34. *Mencius*, 4B:12.

35. For a more comprehensive treatment of this point, see my paper on "Ultimate Self-Transformation as a Communal Act: Comments on Modes of Self-Cultivation in Traditional China," *Journal of Chinese Philosophy* (1979), 237–246.

36. Steven Lukes, *Individualism* (New York: Harper & Row, 1973), p. 157.

LAW AND SOCIETY IN CONFUCIAN THOUGHT[1]

Ronald C. Keith

CONFUCIUS AND CHINESE POLITICAL THOUGHT

Within the grand, syncretic Confucian tradition, successive generations of scholar literati engaged in the textual exegesis of Confucius' *Analects, Lunyu*. Down through dynastic history, each generation had to come to terms with the central theoretical issue of the relation of law and state to society. Chinese political theory and practice continuously sought to resolve the tension between the bureaucratic resort to law as a matter of reward and punishment and the commitment of the scholar literati to "teaching by moral example." Bureaucratic legalism strengthened the state's autonomy from society even while political theory regarded the state as the external reflection of the anterior moral ordering of human relationships within society. This debate has had profound implications for the development of modern Chinese political culture, and over the last several years Chinese Marxist-Leninist theorists have self-consciously examined these implications in terms of "feudalism" which has survived the rigors of revolution.

The debate started with Confucius, who happened upon the stage of Chinese history at a critical juncture of social and institutional crisis. He lived in an era of anomie and military conflict. There was then only the myth of the sage kings and the declining prestige of the Zhou dynasty's nominal imperium to sustain men of principle against the spiraling military conflict between feudal states. Confucius did not live to see the germination of the seeds which he planted, but his ideal became the single most powerful unifying force in the subsequent development of the Chinese empire.

His own antecedents were decidedly modest as was his political career. According to the *Shi Ji* (i.e., *Book of History*, which Confucius is said to have edited himself), he was born in 551 B.C. to an impoverished noble family in the state of Lu (part of contemporary Shandong province). His father died when he was three, and he was brought up by his mother. Confucius did not have sufficient noble status to acquire high position. The tradition which suggests he was a high judicial official in Lu is controversial.[2] As a young man he was employed as an accountant and as a field superintendent.[3]

In 497 B.C. he left the service of Lu to become an itinerant teacher. For 13 years he wandered between the various feudal courts offering sagely though at times unwelcome and blunt advice to princes. The *Analects*, which were posthumously compiled by his disciples, provide a rambling anecdotal account of such advice to the bellicose feudal lords.

Within his own temporal and social context, Confucius was a living paradox. His political conservatism had revolutionary implications. Confucius sought sanction for the prevailing moral ordering of society in the golden age of the western Zhou dynasty when apocryphal sage kings ruled. Access to political office in his own time was still largely, although not exclusively, a matter of heredity. The "nobles", *shi*, who acted as state ministers, in contrast to the sons of rulers, acquired their state positions on the basis of ability as well as birth. The *shi* included scribes, warriors and stewards who were the scions of great aristocratic houses.[4]

Confucius, although he was himself a scribal member of the *shi* class, ignored hereditary credentials to choose his own disciples on the basis of their moral worth. The sage kings likewise were thought to have appointed their ministers and successors. In his self-professed modest role as a transmitter of the past, Confucius had an earnest Tory wish to reinstate a traditional moral order, but his advice persisted down through the centuries to challenge the hereditary claims of military aristocracy.

This great historical social dilemma was explicit in Confucius' usage of the term, *junzi*. Past connotations of *junzi* meaning "son of the sovereign" were progressively dropped in favor of *junzi* as a morally superior gentleman.[5] All too often the avaricious, pugnacious feudal lords of his day were more likely to fall into the opposite category of *xiao ren*, or "small man," that is, man of base, materialistic instincts. Confucius' fearless admonitions to feudal lords to aspire to the moral and intellectual level of the *junzi* who seeks "the root of knowledge" may well help explain his own difficulties in acquiring high office; however, his emphasis on moral qualification in government service eventually became the dominant ideal in Chinese imperial history.

Confucius did not live to witness the final repudiation of the Zhou imperial legacy and the full blown development of a feudal system of warfare in the era known as the Warring States Period, 463–222 B.C., but his ideas were carried forward in the context of great debates over the nature of the state and its relation to an understanding of human nature.

Sharply veering toward a pessimistic view of human nature, Legalist rivals frontally challenged Confucius' disciples and their notion of government by virtue. Arguing that the future appearance of sage kings was extremely unlikely, they opposed government by law to government by moral example. Law had previously been reserved for querulous, malodorous foreigners, and commoners whereas the principle of *li* has applied in the application of ritual to the social relationships of the upper classes. Rather than treating the state as the moral extension of society, the Legalists sought to create an autonomous state, which would mold society for its own purposes of "wealth and power." Law as an instrument of the state was designed to contain the evil nature of man through the systematic and efficacious application of punishment and reward. Legalism, however, achieved its own nemesis in its identification with the sheer brutality of the first imperial dynasty, the Qin dynasty, 221–206 B.C. Thereafter, Legalism as a state philosophy was simply politically unacceptable.

Successive generations of Confucian scholars denounced the Legalists for their disparagement of virtue as the basis of government, and for their superficial focus on quantification and measurement. However, even though Legalism had discredited itself, some of its bureaucratic methods of rulership were later surreptitiously incorporated into the Confucian tradition by the Confucian *junzi* themselves. Confucian officials had to resort to law even though its very existence called into question the practicality of government by moral example.

Within the Western democratic context, a certain dignity accrued to the notion of law that may have originated with the influence of some of the more optimistic assumptions of the European natural law tradition. The latter as an exercise in human reason transcended the merely prudential requirements of man's ascent from the perilous state of nature. St. Thomas Aquinas, for example, viewed lowly human law, even with all its imperfections, as the ordinance of reason for the common good. Even so, comparative political thought has not stressed enough on the significance of the status of law as an element of modern political development. Perhaps this is because it is almost axiomatic that a healthy respect for law as the reflection of widely held moral principles in society is a mark of a sophisticated political culture.

Since 1978 and until very recently in China, there has been a strong emphasis on the "dignity of law" as an essential element within "socialist spiritual civilization" (*shehuizhuyi jingshen wenming*), and this chapter will examine the interstices of classical and modern Chinese political thought in relation to the dignity accorded to law in Chinese society.

THE PLACE OF LAW IN THE CONFUCIAN TRADITION

The "Confucian tradition" was a grand eclectic tradition culled from the different interpretative schools of Confucianism as well as from rival schools of Maoism, Daoism, and Buddhism. This tradition encompassed a great debate on the role of law in society, but within Confucian theory, law posed a political dilemma with respect to the legitimacy of "government by virtue."

Confucianism within the "Confucian tradition" was interested in the cosmic immanence of virtue, and the Confucian imperial official was in theory primarily concerned with the moral demonstration of such virtue in society through the compelling example of his own conduct. The latter theoretically rendered the application of law largely unnecessary as the exercise of government focused on teaching by moral example (*shenjiao*). The latter would flow faster than imperial writ. Even so, in the context of his governmental responsibilities, the Confucian as a moral but technically unaccomplished personality was called upon to make legal judgements and to participate in the making of law.

The Confucian official was, thereupon, locked in a resulting contradiction insofar as the use of law drew attention to the failure of his own moral example—a point which had been drawn out in the original arguments of Legalism. Even so, in the Confucian tradition, there is at least some hint of a theoretical linkage between law in human society and the laws of nature. The *Book of Changes* says, for example, that law is derived from "…an understanding of ways of nature and from a study of the activities of men. It is modeled after the constant law of nature, and it is useful to guide the people."[6] However, according to Joseph Needham, who laments the Daoist failure to move towards the systematic identification of the "laws of nature," China did not have an equivalent differentiation between the twin ideas of a natural law tradition and a body of the laws of nature regarding the physical properties of the universe.[7] Like many others, Needham did recognize a rudimentary element of "natural law" in the Chinese intellectual focus on *li*, implying the ritual manifestation of what is right in society, and he concludes: "…*li* was much more important for society than natural law was in Europe."[8]

The secular dimensions of the Confucian tradition may have been overstressed in Western comparative analysis. The highly respected research of Derk Bodde and Clarence Morris, for example, opines: "The contrast of the Chinese attitude to the belief in a divine origin of the law is indeed striking, for in China no one at any time has ever hinted that any kind of written law…could have a divine origin."[9] This general point, however, is qualified with reference to the phenomenological tendencies within the Confucian tradition requiring the application of the full force of the law against any crime which disrupted the sense of order within the cosmos.

Both "*fa*," law, and "*li*," the ritual extension of the inner moral sense of "benevolence" or "humaneness" (*ren*) into social relationships, were theoretically entangled with "filial piety," which focused on the perpetuation of the family through ancestor worship. *Li* was a central aspect of Confucian theory linking man, earth, and heaven as is evident in Confucius' instruction to "first cultivate the self, then regulate the family, then order the state and there will be peace under heaven" (*xiu shen, qi jia, zhi guo, hoping tianxia*).[10] The Legalists disparaged *li* as a specious Confucian justification for privilege and corruption. Alternatively, they offered *fa* as the ordering principle of society, which was to be imposed directly by the state, thus reversing the relation between society and state.[11]

Confucius transmitted the wisdom of the ancients, but he was not a lawgiver. His concern was the living out of moral principles in social life. He did not explicitly advise rulers on what to put in the law; he did advise rulers as to how they might avoid disharmonious litigation among the populace. A priori to government is "knowing the root" (*zhi ben*). Moral self-cultivation by the "superior man" would lead to the regulation of familiar relationships on the basis of *li* as the external social extension of internal benevolence, i.e., *ren*. The wider extension of such relationships became a priori to the ordering of the state. In the *Great Learning*, Confucius compared governing with teaching and he provided a brief internal gloss on the meaning of what subsequently became a famous instruction in order to rightly govern the state, "it is necessary first to regulate the family by saying it is not possible for one to teach others, while he cannot teach his own family."[12] In chapter 4, Confucius highlighted the following question: "In hearing litigations, I am like any other body. What is necessary to cause the people to have no litigations?"[13] Confucius' point was simple enough—if there are no "depraved thoughts" there would be no need of litigation and legal pettifoggers or "litigation sticks", *song gun*. . . .

Confucius taught in the *Analects*: "He who exercises government by means of his virtue [*yi de*] may be compared to the north polar star, which keeps its place and the stars turn towards it." In the same passage Confucius noted: "If the people be led by laws, and uniformity sought to be given them by punishments, they will try to avoid the punishments, but have no sense of shame [*wu chih*]."[14] Confucius disparaged any exclusive preoccupation with uniform standards, and he conceptualized the progression in stages of human moral development from the age of fifteen when the mind turns to learning to the age of seventy, when a "superior man" could "follow what [his] heart desired, without transgressing what was right."[15]

The theoretical debate within early Confucianism posed a major problem for the scholar official working within the Confucian imperial tradition as codified law became a practical necessity. Even Mencius, with reference to the necessity of "benevolent government" (*ren zheng*) conceded: "Virtue [*de*] alone is not sufficient for government; laws cannot carry themselves into practice."[16] Like Confucius, Mencius abhorred the unseemly emphasis on punishment, but he argued that men of "virtue" would, nevertheless, have to make the penal laws clear to the people.

Legalist theory granted the state autonomy from society, and the law was viewed as a precise instrument providing for political stability in society through a clearly defined system of rewards and punishments. Law did not originate with principles derived from the "regulation" of the family and the teachings of "superior men," for as the preeminent exponent of Legalism, Han Feizi, noted: "By common observation, the virtuous are few and the worthless are many." The populace would have trouble understanding the niceties of virtue but could intuitively relate to the necessity of law as a matter of deterrence; hence Han argued that "...the prohibition of evil is a universal standard."[17]

Legalism disputed the continuous existence of "benevolence" in society as the durable basis for government. The Confucian reliance on past moral examples of sage kings was disparaged as was the Confucian preoccupation with feelings of morality, which would allegedly serve to generate confusion in the law and political and social instability within the populace. The issue was not "the avoidance of punishment." Where the Confucians feared contentiousness among the people as the result of written law, the Legalists feared the lack of clarity in law which was necessary in terms of the political stability of the state.

Under this regime law rather than the official becomes the inspirational source of instruction.

THE DIGNITY OF LAW IN CONTEMPORARY CHINA

From the late 1970s through to the present the Chinese Communist Party strongly emphasized "lawful society" (*fazhi shehui*) or the "dignity of law" (*faludi zunyan*) for two related reasons. In the first place, there has recently been a great desire for political stability in reaction to the political devastation of the party during the Cultural Revolution. The party leaders themselves had experienced the arbitrary judgment of competing armed mass organizations that had dispersed rough justice in kangaroo courts and engaged in the "three negations," or the institutional dismantling of the courts, procuratorates, and public security organs. They had a personal stake in establishing institutional checks against the violence of "one-man rule" or "rule by the individual" (*renzhi*). The origins of the latter were theoretically traced to "feudalism" (*fengjianzhuyi*), which had persisted into the present stage of socialism.

The repeated official condemnation of some party members for thinking that they were exempt from the law's authority has some parallel in the Legalist accusation against the Confucians who allegedly excluded themselves from the application of the law. The widespread illegal violence against party leaders during the Cultural Revolution has been attributed in part to the failure to consolidate the legal and democratic system since 1949. Writing in the Central Committee's journal, Li Buyun and Wang Hanging drew the following conclusion:

> The main reason for the imperfect democratic and legal system was that the law did not have lofty dignity.... Our Constitution and laws were unable to stop the leaders from erroneously launching and developing the "Great Cultural Revolution...." Therefore, in order to prevent a repeat of the historical tragedy like the "Great Cultural Revolution"...we must make our party and government leaders...act in strict accordance with the Constitution and laws and we must never allow anyone privilege overriding the law....[18]

Secondly, with the change in the party line de-emphasizing class struggle and underlining the "four modernizations," political stability has become a self-conscious priority which is linked to the success or failure of economic reform, hence the party slogan "grasping construction and reform with one hand and grasping the legal system with the other" featured a positive correlation between the development of the legal system and the interrelated goals of political stability and national economic construction.[19]

While Mao Zedong's theory of contradictions has been retained as a vehicle for understanding social and institutional reality, his focus on the merits of disequilibrium as the motor of human progress has been utterly rejected. Law in the early 1980s became the "regularization of policy" in that it is more deliberately thought out, and it has the advantage of "standardization." This view was underwritten in Deng Xiaoping's objection to the "two-line struggle" of the Cultural Revolution as the basis for interpreting leadership and policy disputes. This polemical struggle was an aspect of "the rule of man" rather than the "rule of law."

In reacting to the need for economic reform and political stability, Deng Xiaoping lamented: "Our country has no tradition of observing and enforcing laws."[20] Why? Since the late 1970s, the party has traced the problem to a persisting feudalism in China's modern society.

"FEUDALISM" AND CHINA'S LEGAL TRADITION

Current events certainly suggest that the Chinese have yet to resolve the tension between "*quanli*," the power which legally derives from formal official position, and "*shili*", the power derived from political prestige and related patronage. However, since the late 1970s a new party consciousness has developed on this question as it relates to "feudalism", defined in terms of the patriarchal absolutism associated with "one-man rule". The Chinese concept of feudalism has to be rigorously distinguished from its European counterpart. In the great span of Chinese history, the term has only a superficial relevance to European notions of "enfeoffment," military obligation and property ownership. In fact its connotation of "one-man rule" as it reflects imperial absolutism would seem to have little to do with the fragmentation of political authority implied in the European phenomenon.

Important to the Weberian discussion of feudalism is the legal definition of the rights of lords and vassals in relation to the prevailing normative conception of honor and loyalty. In contrast, Chinese theory has spent little time on the question of enfeoffment. The focus is shifted to the connotations of absolute patriarchal authority implied in the emperor's role as "Son of Heaven". The Confucian feudal tradition only admitted of one singular source of "truth".

Deng Xiaoping used Mao's theory of contradictions and particularly his conception of "seeking the truth from the facts" to debunk the "whateverist" position in the party that emulated feudalism in its fervent conviction that Mao was absolutely and forever correct. In an important resolution, the party's Central Committee formally described "feudal ideology" as including "patriarchal clannishness, autocratic ways, the tendency to seek privileges and to form factions for selfish purpose...."[21] The issue of feudalism was the key to the trial proceedings of the "gang of four." One judge, Fei Xiaodong, depicted the proceedings themselves, as a vivid lesson in the "rule of law" which countered the tendency during the Cultural Revolution to favor "rule by the individual."[22]

In some respects, the contemporary focus on feudalism is reminiscent of the liberal view of the Confucian tradition prevalent in the 1920s. Legalism had, according to Liang Qichao, addressed the failure of the latter, and it had even anticipated the "modern theory of sociology" in its description of three stages of Chinese social development from the "tribal stage" in which authority rests in the Confucian obsession with familial ties through a complex second stage marked by a division of labor favoring the incipient autonomy of the state from society to a final stage wherein the laws became "fixed" thus providing impersonal standards for all time.[23] In the end, however, Liang could not abide Legalism, for, while it claimed that all were equal before the law, it gave the ruler an unqualified legislative authority. Legalism's interest in the autonomous state did not in the end serve Liang's interest in liberal democracy.

CONCLUSION

The contemporary party focus on feudalism relates to the outstanding problems of twentieth century political leadership as much as it relates to the lack of a legal tradition. While Deng may appear to share the Legalist concern for "fixed standards" so as to achieve the political stability necessary for modernization, he has used "Mao Zedong thought" as the vehicle with which to assert "seeking the truth from the facts" against "personality cult" or "one-man rule." By the "scientific" standards of Mao's own thought, Mao's leadership has been fairly accurately assessed although the party's political-sociological explanation, as it is premised in "feudalism," is a cause for some theoretical confusion.

The frank admission of continuing "partriarchal ways" in the context of modern China may turn out to be very important. Deng raised the issue, only to follow in Mao Zedong's footsteps. In assuming supreme power as "helmsman" (*duoshuo*) he did not personally follow through in his own commitment to the "rule of law". Deng's attribution of the lack of laws and law-abidingness in society to the lack of "tradition" is somehow uninformative. It may distract from the underlying practical issues of political power and leadership in a Marxist-Leninist state and may also distract from an effective theoretical understanding of the complexity and contemporary influence of "tradition."

Within senior political circles, the discussion of Legalism has been conspicuous by its absence. The Chinese leadership in the mid-1980s was in a great rush to create law, and there is the possibility that in the absence of a solid social consensus too much of the responsibility for coping with the infrastructural problems of the newly emerging political regime was placed on the inadequate shoulders of the legal system. The party, even if it was inclined to do so, cannot will into existence a new social consensus underwriting the "lofty dignity of the law."

The Confucian tradition does not offer a direct equivalence to the natural law tradition in Europe in terms of the development of law as an extension of moral principles in society. Chinese political theory needs to move beyond the narrow interpretation of Confucianism as "feudalism" to treat the totality of the "Confucian tradition." Within the Confucian tradition, the scholar official feared too much law would discredit both the social requirements of *li* and the political imperium, and there was no systematic justification for the incorporation of human reason into law. However, Legalism within the same tradition sought to place law on a pedestal for reasons which had little to do with the cultivation of moral standards of behavior within society. In the latter case, the law could have an "educative" moral effect in terms of the purposes of the state, but these purposes were at bottom genuinely authoritarian and inconsistent even with Mao's mass line and the on-going theoretical attempts to define "socialist democracy."

Ironically, it was Deng Xiaoping who identified law and democracy as necessary to the accomplishment of modernization, but even given the ideological commitment to "seeking the truth from the facts" a comprehensive theory has yet to be evolved whereby the "rule of law" and "socialist democracy" can be entwined in the party process of "political restructuring" without seriously challenging the contemporary Marxist-Leninist structures of political leadership and the genuine development of "socialism with Chinese characteristics."

NOTES

1. This is a chapter in Anthony J. Parel and Ronald C. Keith, eds., *Comparative Political Philosophy: Studies Under the Upas Tree*, 2nd ed. (Lanham, MD: Lexington Books, 2003).
2. H.G. Creel challenged official Chinese history on this point. See his *Confucius: The Man and the Myth* (London: Routledge, 1951); and also Vitaly Rubin, *Individual and State in Ancient China* (New York: Columbia University Press, 1976), pp. 6–7.
3. On Confucius' rank and occupational experience see Cho-yun Hsu, *Ancient China in Transition* (Stanford: Stanford University Press, 1965), p. 35.
4. For sociological analysis of the *shi* see Benjamin Schwartz, *The World of Thought in Ancient China* (Cambridge, MA: Harvard University Press, 1985), pp. 58–59; and Hsu, *Ancient China in Transition*, ibid., p. 34.
5. For the changing connotations of *junzi* see Rubin, *Individual and State in Ancient China*, op. cit., pp. 20–21; and H.G. Creel, *Chinese Thought from Confucius to Mao Tse-tung* (Chicago: University of Chicago Press, 1975), p. 27.
6. Liang Ch'i-chao, *History of Chinese Political Thought* (New York: AMS Press, Inc., 1930, 1960), p. 113.
7. Joseph Needham, *The Shorter Science and Civilization in China: 1* (London: Cambridge Press, 1978), p. 305.
8. Ibid., p. 304.
9. Derk Bodde and Clarence Morris, *Law in Imperial China* (Philadelphia: University of Pennsylvania Press, 1978), p. 305.
10. See "*Daxue*" (Great Learning) in *Sishu* (The Four Books) (Macao: Juwendangshu, 1962), p. 7.
11. Originally, "fa" related generally to "standards", but under Legalism's influence it increasingly related to penal law and punishment. Roger Ames provides an extensive commentary on the connotations of "fa" in his *The Art of Rulership* (Honolulu: University of Hawaii Press, 1983), p. 109.
12. Confucius, "*Daxue*", op. cit., p. 23.
13. Ibid., p. 15.
14. Confucius, "*Lunyu*" (The Analects), in *Sishu*, 1962, op. cit., p. 13.
15. Ibid., p. 15.
16. *Mencius*, "*Mengzi*" (Mencius) in *Sishu*, 1962, op. cit., p. 260.
17. Burton Watson, trans., *Han Fei Tzu* (New York: Columbia University Press, 1964), p. 105.

18. Li Buyan, Wang Hanqing, "Adhere to the Principle that All Men are Equal Before the Law, Safeguard the Authority and Dignity of the Law", *Hongqi*, No. 12, 16 June 1986, JPRS-CRF-86-015, August 7, 1986, p. 45.

19. See, for example, Yang Yichen, "Report on the Work of the Supreme People's Procuratorate," *Renmin ribao*, 18 April 1988, in FBIS-CHI-88-017, p. 70.

20. Deng Xiaoping, "Reform the Political Structure and Strengthen the People's Sense of Legality", *Fundamental Issues in Present-Day China* (Beijing: Foreign Languages Press, 1987), p. 146.

21. For the 12th CCPCC Resolution of 28 September 1986 see *Beijing Review*, No. 40, October 6, 1986, Documents, p. v.

22. See the preface to Fei Xiaodong, *A Great Trial in Chinese History* (Beijing: New World Press, 1981), p. 7. In 1985 the party leadership officially endorsed the "rule of law" concept. See Ronald C. Keith, "Chinese Politics and the New Theory of the "Rule of Law", *China Quarterly*, No. 125, March 1991, pp. 109-118.

23. Liang, *History of Chinese Political Thought*, p. 125.

THE CONTEMPORARY RELEVANCE OF CONFUCIANISM: INTRODUCTION[1]

Daniel A. Bell and Hahm Chaibong

Confucians have long been preoccupied with social and political change. According to the standard account, Master Kong (Latinized name: Confucius; c. 551–479 B.C.) left his native state of Lu, hoping to find a ruler more receptive to his ideas about good government. Unfortunately, Confucius did not have any luck, and he was forced to settle for a life of teaching. Several generations later, a student in the academic lineage of Confucius's grandson named Master Meng (Latinized name: Mencius: c. 390–305 B.C.) committed himself to spreading Confucius's social and political ideas. Like the old master, Mencius moved from state to state, looking for opportunities to put his political ideals into practice. Mencius had slightly more success—he served briefly as Minister of the State of Qi—but he became disenchanted with political life and reluctantly settled for a teaching career.

Several hundred years later, however, the social and political ideas of Confucius and Mencius—as recorded in *The Analects of Confucius* and *The Works of Mencius*—proved to be literally world transforming. Following a short-lived experience with Legalism, the newly founded Chinese state of Han adopted Confucianism as its official ideology. For the next 2000 years, the country's best minds sought to interpret and modify Confucianism to make it more relevant in particular situations with novel features. By the late nineteenth century, the whole East Asian region was thoroughly "Confucianized." That is, Confucian values and practices informed the daily lives of people in China, Korea, Japan, and Vietnam, and whole systems of government were justified with reference to Confucian ideals.

Since the advent of modernity in the latter half of the nineteenth century, however, Confucianism has fared less well. Max Weber, one of the earliest scholars to devote serious attention to the relationship between Confucianism and modernity, singled out Confucianism among the major "world religions" as the least conducive to capitalist development. East Asians, for their part, began to condemn this venerable tradition as they deepened their encounter with the West. Nationalists and militarists held Confucianism responsible for their country's inability to withstand the onslaught of Western imperialism. From the other side of the political spectrum, the communists did their best to extirpate every root and branch of Confucianism that they regarded as a feudal and reactionary world view hindering progress. Indeed, for the vast majority of East Asians, modernity had come to mean overcoming Confucianism.

As such, in the postcolonial era, few, if any, East Asians openly declared allegiance to Confucian ideals. For most of the Cold War period, East Asians had to choose between two alternative roads to modernity—Marxism and capitalism—and the Confucian tradition had almost completely disappeared from public discourse. That modernity itself was the ultimate goal was rarely in doubt. In fact, one of the most remarkable aspects of Confucianism's encounter with modernity is that unlike in the case of Islam, Hinduism, and Buddhism, there has never been an organized Confucian resistance to modernization. Confucianism seems to be one "religion" where one would be hard put to find any "fundamentalist" adherents at all.

Perhaps this lack of fundamentalist resistance to modernity underpins the remarkable ability of many of the countries that belong to the "Confucian sphere of influence" to industrialize and, in some cases, democratize. While the contradictions inherent in the communist bloc were becoming more apparent, while other Third World countries were trapped in seemingly inextricable patterns of underdevelopment, and while even the advanced industrialized countries were mired in the vicious cycle of stagflation, the countries of East Asia continued to flourish through the 1960s, 1970s, and 1980s. In fact, the success of the countries in this region became so conspicuous as to require some explanation. The need for a new theoretical framework became all the more acute primarily because the social scientists, both liberal and Marxist, failed to predict or explain the economic success of these "Confucian" states while the Weberian thesis regarding the alleged incompatibility between Confucianism and capitalism rapidly lost credibility.

Since the early 1980s, there has been much discussion regarding the role of Confucianism in the modernization of East Asia, particularly in the economic sphere. Initially, those who found Confucianism to hold the secret to the region's economic success were mostly Western scholars. It was "outside observers" who began attributing the success of East Asia to Confucianism (MacFarquhar, Hofheinz and Calder, Vogel, among others). The irony was that few living in the Confucian world thought that their political and economic success was due to Confucianism. What success they enjoyed, they typically attributed to their success in having overcome Confucianism.

The first among the East Asians to openly and enthusiastically espouse the idea that Confucianism had much to do with the rapid industrialization of the region were politicians. Most notoriously, Singapore's senior statesman Lee Kuan Yew has invoked Confucian values— under the guise of "Asian values"—with the apparent aim of justifying constraints on the democratic process. Authoritarian governments in the region have similarly appealed to Confucian values meant to contrast with Western-style democracy. Even the Chinese Communist Party "rectified" its previous anti-Confucian stance—party leaders have been trying to tap Confucian teachings to help curb rampant corruption and to counter the widespread social malaise that threatens to undermine the Communist Party.[2] These political leaders affirmed the linkage between Confucianism and modernity not only to explain their economic success but also to argue that the political and economic system that they had erected was in many ways superior to that of the West.

Against this trend, anti-Confucian liberal intellectuals and social critics argued that Confucianism is a dead tradition that has been (justifiably) relegated to the dustbin of history. Others recognized that Confucian values continue to exert moral and political influence in East Asia, with the proviso that these values are not desirable in the modern world and thus Confucianism should be opposed whenever it rears its ugly head. Confucianism, it was argued, is incompatible with the social and political manifestations of modernity—democracy, capitalism, and the rule of law. The Confucian emphasis on differentiated and hierarchical relationships as manifested in the Five Cardinal Virtues (*wulun*) leads inevitably to elitism and authoritarianism. The Confucian dictum that one should pursue justice, not profit, conflicts with the commercial ethos that undergirds capitalism and the ethics of self-interest that drives it. The Confucian emphasis on moral cultivation and reliance on a morally cultivated elite to bring just order to society exposes it to the danger of subjective and hence arbitrary rule and clashes with the modern reliance on institutions and procedures that secure the rule of law.

The debate soon came to be mired in polemics. The argument over the alleged superiority of one set of values over another might have revealed some interesting psychology at work among the participants, but it did little to shed light on the linkages between Confucianism and modernity. In fact, given the state of the debate surrounding Confucianism and modernity, it is not surprising that once East Asia was hit by a financial crisis in 1997, those who had been arguing against the Asian values thesis simply began to dismiss the whole issue. Just as the advocates of Asian values tried to reverse Weber's thesis on Confucianism, so now the critics of Asian values tried to treat the whole argument concerning Confucianism as having been completely misbegotten. When they did acknowledge Confucianism's influence on economic development, they now did so only in order to "prove" that it has produced "crony capitalism" characterized by corruption and inefficiency.

In the meantime, another group of East Asian intellectuals and their Western sympathizers has sought to articulate a vision of Confucianism that avoids either of these extremes by highlighting the humanistic and liberal elements in the Confucian world view while recognizing its flaws. Here the assumption has been that Confucianism has indeed underpinned economic and political development in modernizing East Asian societies and the aim has been to understand how Confucianism actually works in economic organization, political ideology, and social behavior.[3] While this enterprise has primarily been descriptive and explanatory, it has also been animated by a normative vision. This group of "Confucian humanists," as Tu Weiming puts it, defends Confucianism on the grounds that it expresses values of universal significance for those concerned with leading moral lives. In the contemporary world, this tradition has the added advantage of buttressing valued forms of communal life against the disintegrating and atomizing forces of economic globalization. As shown by "actually existing" East Asian societies, the Confucian cultural heritage can also underpin relatively egalitarian forms of economic development.

This appealing vision, however, often seems to lack specific proposals for social and political change. That is, the debate over Confucianism continues to be based on values and norms as contained in classical texts and historical past. Little work has been done to investigate linkages between Confucian ideals and concrete practices/institutions, be they political, economic, social, or legal, in the existing "Confucian" societies. It is time for the debate to move beyond the theoretical and speculative stage to more practical and institutional considerations. If Confucianism is to remain viable, it will not be sufficient to "apologize" for the supposedly authoritarian tendencies of its theories and tenets. Rather, proponents of Confucianism need to engage in more affirmative and constructive thinking where the institutional manifestations of Confucianism for modern democratic societies are actively sought and articulated. This means sorting out and clearly articulating those aspects of Confucianism that are feasible and defensible in the modern world. Thus, those trying to negotiate the relationship between Confucianism and modernity need to tackle the following questions: Which particular Confucian values should be promoted in contemporary East Asian societies? How should they be promoted? What are the political and institutional implications of "Confucian humanism"? How do the practical implications of modern Confucianism differ from the values and workings of liberal capitalist societies? Can these differences be justified from a moral point of view? . . . .

CONFUCIAN PERSPECTIVES ON DEMOCRACY

Modern-day governments, it is commonly argued, must be constituted "by the people." Whatever the practical arguments for and against democracy, this form of government has emerged as an ineliminable symbol of equal political recognition in modern societies. Even autocratic leaders such as Lee Kuan Yew recognize that democracy is the best form of government and that all modern countries must eventually adopt this political ideal. The history and culture of the East Asian region, however, may seem to hinder this development. Prior to the twentieth century, not a single political regime in this region was democratic. That is, ordinary people did not have a say in choosing their country's most powerful political decision makers by means of competitive elections, and the majority of "citizens" did not have any other mechanisms for participating in the political process. As the first two contributions show, however, this does not mean that political rulers were "authoritarian" despots who could operate without any checks on their power.

Hahm Chaihark, who teaches Korean studies at Yonsei University, argues that the Confucian concept of ritual propriety (*li*) functioned as a public political norm that effectively restrained and disciplined political rulers in premodern East Asia. The Confucian rulers' political legitimacy depended on correctly regulating their conduct according to *li*, and this meant that rulers had to pay the utmost attention to detailed specification and correct observance of ritual propriety. More importantly, the rulers were surrounded by Confucian scholar-officials who were themselves disciplined by *li* and believed that their mission was to discipline the highest political leader of the country according to ritual propriety.

In modern East Asia, many of the idioms and vocabularies for making sense of politics and rendering value judgments are derived from the Confucian tradition. Given that constitutional norms are more likely to be effective if they are grounded in a society's political culture, Hahm argues that these norms must resonate with the idea of *li* in the East Asian context. Thus, the ruler's power could be effectively checked by modern-day Confucians who are socialized into "the role of disciplinarians of political leaders." Confucian political education can be promoted in families, schools, and other settings with the aim of teaching people the importance of effective and regularized restraints on their government.

It would also be in the ruler's interest to be disciplined by *li*, since this could help to secure legitimacy for the government. Here too, we can learn from past practices. In Korea, Chosŏn dynasty rulers were properly disciplined by various mechanisms and by being educated in the art of governance. For example, the king was obliged to listen to policy lectures by Confucian scholars and he was not allowed to hold audience with his ministers unless he was accompanied by two court historians, one of whom recorded all the verbal transactions while the other recorded all physical movements. Hahm argues that "we should retrieve the notion that a ruler can and should be disciplined by being lectured to all the time, and put under constant surveillance." The need for disciplining political rulers has certainly not diminished in the modern world, and such Confucian disciplinary mechanisms could arguably be adapted to fit modern governmental structures. This may not make the ruler into a paragon of virtue, but it should at least help to prevent obvious corruption—not to mention other indiscretions in presidential offices.

Jongryn Mo, who teaches international political economy in the Graduate School of International Studies at Yonsei University, draws on the example of the Censorate in Korea to argue that there were effective institutional restraints on the ruler's power in Confucian political regimes. In the Chosŏn dynasty, the Censorate consisted of three organs that were designed to prevent abuses in the exercise of political and administrative authority. Mo shows that the censors were not only judicial and auditing agents, "but also voices of dissent and opposition, playing the roles of mass media and opposition parties in modern democracies." Moreover, he argues that the Censorate was well designed for effective horizontal accountability, meaning that Confucian scholar-officials were able to hold agencies of equal power accountable. In effect, the Censorate was a branch of government in a system of checks and balances.

Mo argues for the need to reintroduce elements of the Censorate—such as the practice of appointing censors whose job is to write critical reports on the ruler's conduct—in contemporary East Asian political systems, especially that of Korea. For one thing, this institution is compatible with Confucian political culture and may resonate with the habits and values of East Asian people. With respect to the contemporary Korean context, the Censorate could also help to increase the quality of governance, given that major political actors and some top political organizations have not completely shed their authoritarian ways.

Wang Juntao's essay challenges the perception that political dissidents in China favor uprooting their own tradition in favor of wholesale Westernization.[4] Wang, a doctoral candidate in political science at Columbia University, argues that many of the key figures in the various democracy movements in contemporary Chinese history drew inspiration from Confucian values. From the late nineteenth century onward, leading Chinese intellectuals have struggled to promote "minimal" democracy (i.e., free and fair competitive elections to select political leaders) in their country. It turns out that nearly all the important figures in the history of Chinese democracy movements—Kang Youwei, Zhang Jian, Sun Yatsen, Liang Qichao, Zhang Junmai, Wang Xizhe, and Chen Ziming—tried to revive Confucianism in order to support democratization. Several had received a traditional Confucian education and they argued that democratic institutions such as parliamentary systems, elections, and equal rights are natural extensions of Confucianism. For example, Sun Yatsen, the founding father of the Republic of China, said:

> Our three-*min* principles [nationalism, citizen rights, and the welfare of human beings] originate from Mencius and are based on Cheng Yichuan [a Song dynasty Confucian]. Mencius is really the ancestor of our democratic ideas....The three-*min* principles are a completion of the development of those three thousand years of Chinese ideas about how to govern and maintain a peaceful world.

Others admitted the existence of some weaknesses in Confucianism that blocked China's march toward democracy but added that Confucianism can be reinterpreted to make it consistent with democracy. This project was successfully carried out in the case of Catholicism—Wang reminds us of Samuel Huntington's argument that Catholicism was transformed from an important obstacle to democratization into one of the major ideological factors underpinning the "third wave" of democratization in the world—and Confucianism may hold similar potential.

The political importance of Wang's argument is that democracy may be easier to implement in the Chinese context if it can be shown that it need not conflict with traditional political culture. As Wang puts it, "If Confucianism is consistent with democracy, the traditional culture may be used as a means of promoting democratization in East Asia. At the very least, the political transition will be smoother and easier, with lower costs, since there will be less cultural resistance."

Chang Yun-Shik's essay shows that Confucian values do not merely have the *potential* to support democracy. In the Korean context, Confucianism *in fact* helped to bring about a transition to a democratic form of government. Chang, Professor Emeritus of Sociology at the University of British Columbia, focuses on the ethic of mutual help. This communal ethic has long been embedded in rural farming communities, but it was reinforced and modified by the importation of Confucian values from China. Koreans incorporated the idea of the community compact articulated by the great twelfth-century Neo-Confucian Zhu Xi. Eventually, the community compact—self-regulating local communities under the leadership of an educated moral elite—became the norm in rural farming communities.

Over the last century, social bonds of mutual obligation and trust spread from rural to urban settings. In contemporary Korea, kinship ties continue to play an important role by linking clan members residing in the city to those remaining in the same surname village (*tongjok maŭl*). Moreover, cities provided people with new opportunities to meet and interact, and the ethic of mutual help came to underpin personal relationships beyond the confines of neighborhood and kinship organizations—in schools, workplaces, training centers, churches, and prisons.

Chang argues that this ethic initially proved to be inimical to democracy. Democratic constitutional forms imposed by Western occupying forces were molded by traditional person-oriented norms, with each president fortifying his position by staffing governmental offices from the personal circles of close kin members, friends, and acquaintances who pledged personal loyalty to him. This led to "administrative despotism," corruption, the decline of party politics, and other ills associated with authoritarian government.

However, this same ethic of mutual help also informed the workings of opposition social forces in Korea. Pro-democracy students and dissident church leaders led the struggle for democracy, and the student-church nexus was molded by the ethic of mutual help. For example, groups of students from the same high school or hometown or church formed "study circles" that served as the basic organizational unit for demonstrations. These close ties ensured unity of purpose and mutual support in difficult times. Other groups joined forces to launch their own democratic campaigns, and the increasing number of civic groups committed to the public interest eventually helped to consolidate democracy in Korea.

Democracy, however, is neither stable nor necessarily desirable if it is limited to the minimal idea of free and fair competitive elections. Chang suggests that "personalist democrats" can also help to support more participatory forms of democratic politics. In contrast to "individualist democrats,"

> personalist democrats are not likely to ignore each other or make their political decisions on their own. They will encourage consultation with or advice seeking from others in making decisions on political matters, and they will share information and lend moral support. Does the individual know his interest best? The personalist democrat is likely to think that the group decision is better, wiser, and safer than individual decision making....With emphasis on

mutuality, not on individual autonomy per se, personalist democracy might be able to avoid the widespread tendency among many citizens in individualist democracies to exclude themselves from political processes.

The next contribution develops this vision of a "Confucian democracy" that avoids the excesses of liberal individualism. David Hall and Roger Ames argue that democratic practices should not threaten the preservation and appropriate exercise of Confucian sensibilities when they are imported into East Asian countries. In the contemporary world, it is difficult to detach democratic models from elements of "Westernization"—such as legal formalism that mitigates the role of rituals in the socializing process and an insistence upon individual rights to the detriment of social responsibilities—that worry "communitarian Confucians." To meet this challenge, Hall, formerly of the University of Texas, and Ames, who teaches at the University of Hawaii, appeal to John Dewey's understanding of democracy as a "communicating community." This concept was designed precisely to address these concerns and thus holds the greatest promise for achieving a Confucian democracy in which central Confucian values are still largely intact.

In an ideal Confucian society, human relationships are largely noninstrumental and communication appeals to a shared repository of discourse. As Hall and Ames point out, this ideal still informs conversations among educated Chinese: "Such conversations tend to be highly allusive, involving citations of classical texts and the employments of apothegms and proverbs common to the tradition." This form of communication has the effect of promoting affective bonding and reinforcing attachment to commonly acknowledged cultural models. Moreover, local groups in rural China have been "slowly and quietly enchanting the routine habits of the day" during the course of their struggles for social and political change. But how can affective bonds of this sort be maintained against the seemingly inevitable trend toward the "disenchantment of the modern world"? More ambitiously, how can these bonds be generalized to the national level, particularly now that an extreme form of "winner take-all" capitalism seems to be taking shape in China? The coauthors suggest that John Dewey's educational theory may have something to offer. Dewey particularly emphasized the educative processes meant to realize and sustain "communicating democracy." The aim of education, according to Dewey, is the creation of a community of affect where everyday communication helps to maintain and promote noninstrumental relationships of the sort Confucians value. If Dewey's theory of education is institutionalized in mainland China, this may help to promote an "enchanted world" where desirable traditional values are exhibited on a day-to-day level. In this context, the importation of democracy need not threaten Confucian sensibilities.

Geir Helgesen, Senior Researcher at the Nordic Institute of Asian Studies (Copenhagen), develops a similar argument for the Korean context. He points to the negative social and political effects of globalization and argues for moral education that strengthens affective ties and resonates with Confucian values. According to Helgesen, survey research reveals that globalization contributes to "existential insecurity" among people that can have grave political consequences. If individuals feel helpless and alienated from the political process, they will retreat to the passive realm of consumption. The "centers of meaning production" will shift from the local community and national culture to the standards set by profit-seeking multinationals, resulting in what Helgesen terms "individualistic uniformity." Individual "citizens" will lose their sense of attachment to the political community, participation in national affairs will decline, and "democracy" can only be realized on a formal, institutional level. Without strong affective bonds underpinning relatively participatory forms of democracy, individual "citizens" will lack the motivation to sacrifice for the common good and they will fail to show solidarity with needy members of the political community. This will increase the likelihood of social breakdown and exacerbate economic inequality.

In Korea, the Kim Dae Jung administration promoted restructuring the economy according to the requirements of the International Monetary Fund (IMF). Helgesen argues, however, that it may not have been doing enough to strengthen the affective bonds that underpin "communalistic, solidarity-oriented" democracy. These bonds have been influenced by Confucian social morality for more than half a millennium, and authorities should draw on Confucian resources to combat existential insecurity and strengthen cultural rootedness. More concretely, this means promoting particular Confucian values in Korean schools. Empirical research shows that there is widespread support for such values as ancestor worship, and Helgesen describes his call for a moral education policy as "less of a 'social engineering' project and more of an effort to build on the strengths of continuity and self-confidence." However, this policy should modernize aspects of Confucianism, for example, by challenging gender inequality though without "copying the emancipation struggle of women in the Western world."

The last two essays may contribute to the impression that Confucianism is fundamentally antagonistic to the requirements of global capitalism. The best that Confucianism can do, it seems, is build walls that protect communitarian cultures from the "atomizing" forces of globalization. But is it possible that Confucianism can also help to shape modern market economies in desirable ways? The contributors in the next section examine the Confucian potential for abetting economic development and promoting social justice in market-based economies.

CONFUCIAN PERSPECTIVES ON CAPITALISM

Just as it seems impossible to imagine successful nondemocratic societies in the modern world, so capitalism—an economic system that is dominated by owners of capital who hire wage laborers and produce for profit—seems to be an essential feature of all developed societies. As Karl Marx himself recognized, economic and technological development proceeds more quickly than ever before under capitalism, because capitalists compete with one another to make a profit, and hence they have a special incentive to develop new, ever more efficient means to produce goods. Contrary to Marx's expectations, however, capitalist societies in the West have managed to mitigate some of the negative consequences of capitalist development by redistributing (some) wealth from the capitalist classes to the rest. To what extent does Confucianism provide resources for those thinking about the requirements of modern-day capitalist societies?

Gilbert Rozman, Musgrave Professor of Sociology at Princeton University, argues that Confucianism can provide the ideological underpinning for further dynamism in East Asia. One of the effects of economic globalization is that the state is losing the capacity to control economic activity within its borders. Given the increased tendency toward multiple levels of economic power—both below and above the state—Rozman argues that Confucianism may be particularly appropriate for justifying the transition from state-controlled economies in East Asia.

On the one hand, Confucianism can provide the intellectual and moral resources for promoting an agenda of economic decentralization. By looking back at the history of East Asian countries, Rozman makes the case that Confucian ideals justified limitations on central power and encouraged family and social solidarity to balance controls from above. This translated into reliance on market mechanisms, dynamic local economies, and complex urban networks. Of course, Confucian decentralization has often faced political obstacles, but it has helped to counter the centralizing messages put forward by militarists in Japan and (more recently) by communists in China.

On the other hand, Confucianism can serve as an integrating force for East Asian regionalism. Following the formation of regional trading blocs in Europe and North America, East Asians have been exploring the possibility of their own regional trading bloc that would bring economic payoffs. Rozman suggests that regionalism based on Confucian values and local networks can be enhanced without artificial state manipulation. He points to the formation of hierarchies of cities across borders such as the Hong Kong-Taiwan-Guangdong-Fujian natural economic territory. As intraregional trade of this sort accelerates, people will form their own economic and cultural ties. Through agreeing on a shared agenda of "open, decentralized, Confucian regionalism," East Asian states "could breathe new life into the way each of them develops and create a vision of how the past brings them together as they expand cooperation for the future."

Rozman does, however, cast some doubt on the Confucian agenda. He warns of continued obstruction from those in East Asia who claim to be defenders of traditional values such as community harmony, state benevolence, and family solidarity while protecting narrow vested interests. He also sees a need to embrace more fully meritocracy and openness to globalization as a prerequisite to reviving Confucian themes as a forward-looking foundation.

The next essay—by Lew Seok-Choon, Professor of Sociology at Yonsei University, and two of his graduate students, Chang Mi-Hye and Kim Tae-Eun—points to the economic benefits of Confucian-style affective networks (social ties bound by what Chang terms the "ethic of mutual help") in an overall capitalist context. Focusing on the case of Korea, the coauthors show that individuals are actively involved in the "social investment" of building up affective networks. These networks—rooted in school ties, marriage, work, hometown, and region—have been blamed for corruption, nepotism, tax evasion, and other economically harmful phenomena denounced by critics of "crony capitalism." That, however, is not the whole story.

For one thing, it is a mistake to regard these networks as "premodern" practices that will disappear as the economy develops. Contrary to the predictions of "modernization theorists," the coauthors show that these networks are alive and well in Korea and cannot easily be removed by legal or institutional reform. Moreover, affective networks can be functional for further economic development. The social trust embedded in these networks lowers the costs of supervision and provides for economic efficiency: "When a person is recruited by a company through recommendation or connection, he/she tends to work harder not to disappoint those who recommended him/her and to secure his/her position within the network of personal relations provided by that connection." These networks can also reduce transaction costs, as the strong trust eliminates the need for detailed contracts and modes of enforcement. What makes the Korean affective networks particularly functional is that they are not exclusive or closed to outsiders. An individual can belong to several affective networks simultaneously and boundaries between groups are flexible and extendable depending on circumstances. In this globalizing world of fast-paced, relatively unpredictable change, such open networks can facilitate rapid adjustment and economic restructuring in times of crisis.

Of course, economic development per se may not be desirable if it leads to radical inequalities and social upheavals. As noted above, however, the "East Asian model of economic development" managed to combine rapid economic development with relatively egalitarian distributions of income (relative to many Western countries). In East Asia, the most developed economies are also the most egalitarian.[5]

Throughout Chinese history, Confucians opposed heavy-handed government control and warned of the negative effects of state intervention in the economy. This did not translate, however, into endorsement of an unfettered private property rights regime. As Daniel Bell, a political theorist at Tsinghua University in Beijing, argues, Confucius and Mencius defended constraints on the free market in the name of more fundamental values. These constraints have influenced the workings of East Asian economies and continue to play a role today.

Firstly, the state has an obligation to secure the conditions for people's basic material welfare, an obligation that has priority over competing political goods. The government realizes this aim, according to Mencius, by means of the "well-field system" that allows farmers to make productive use of land while ensuring that enough food is supplied to the nonfarming classes. Chinese rulers adapted the principles of this system to their own circumstances, and Bell suggests that even Deng Xiaoping's rural land reform program may have been influenced by Mencius's ideas.

Secondly, Confucians argued that ownership rights should be vested in the family, not the individual, so as to facilitate the realization of "family values" such as filial piety, the care of elderly parents. Family joint ownership was institutionalized in traditional legal systems—for example, junior members of families could not be accused of stealing, but only of appropriating (for their own use) family property. While modern East Asian countries have incorporated "individualistic" conceptions of property rights to a certain extent, Bell argues that they still tend to emphasize, in both law and public morality, the duty to regard property as an asset of the whole family, including elderly parents.

Joseph Chan, a political theorist at the University of Hong Kong, delineates the basic Confucian principles of social welfare and draws implications for contemporary societies. Taking Mencius's influential view on social welfare as the basis for discussion, Chan argues that Confucians endorse the idea of a multilayered system of welfare assistance in which the family, social networks, and government all have a specific role to play. Welfare responsibility lies first with the family—Confucians are quite explicit that obligations to the family are the most basic. The principle of family caring should then be extended outward. The local community serves as the second tier of help, mutual care being provided through the well-field system and other networks of communal relationships. The government plays the role of last resort, providing direct help to people who cannot help themselves and lack adult family members to turn to.

Chan shows that these principles were put into practice in premodern China. Confucian principles may also help to explain the fact that contemporary East Asian states rely mainly on nonstate agencies—community, firm, and family—to finance and provide welfare services, with significantly less direct state financing of services than other developed states.[6] To further close the gap between the ideal and reality, Chan proposes a voluntary donation scheme that would allow individuals to choose between various charity groups and aid packages. This scheme would be similar to the United Way, except that the central agency would be a government-run institution that expresses, in a symbolic way, public support for voluntary help and mutual caring. Though this proposal might further reduce the need for direct state financing of welfare, it is not meant to completely eliminate the state's welfare responsibilities.

In short, the ongoing, living Confucian tradition helps to explain the distinctive characteristics of East Asian economic systems and welfare states. This tradition may also help those thinking about an economic reform that strikes the right balance between productive economic activity and meeting the needs of the "worst-off" in an overall capitalist framework. All this, however, would seem to assume the presence of a reliable and transparent legal system to enforce Confucian-style contracts, property rights, and welfare entitlements. Not even the most idealistic Confucian argues that the ethic of mutual help could suffice to regulate conflicts in the modern world. Does this mean the Confucian perspective on law—including its notorious aversion to litigation—is completely out-of-date? Put positively, can Confucianism offer any insights for those thinking about legal reform in modern-day societies? The next section turns to this topic.

CONFUCIAN PERSPECTIVES ON LAW

The third main social plank of modern-day societies is the rule of law. Individuals in contemporary societies must be able to rely on a relatively stable, predictable, and transparent legal system that upholds the ideal of equality before the law and promises restitution in cases of injustice. Of course there is often a gap between the ideal and the practice, but any successful contemporary society must at least aspire to this ideal and devote resources to its practical implementation. On the face of it, it may appear that Confucianism is fundamentally incompatible with contemporary notions of the rule of law.[7]

In traditional China, mediation rather than litigation was the preferred means of dispute resolution. According to Albert Chen, professor of law at the University of Hong Kong, the theory and practice of mediation have largely been shaped by Confucian philosophy. Confucians value social harmony, and litigation was considered to be a negative social phenomenon because it exacerbates ruptures and poisons social relationships beyond the point of repair. Litigation was also viewed with disdain because the pursuit of material self-interest that underlies civil litigation was perceived to be inconsistent with the Confucian valuation of moral self-cultivation over selfish interests. Thus:

> in case of potential conflicts with others, the correct attitude would be that of self-scrutiny (to examine oneself to see what wrong one has done and what moral failings one should be responsible for), self-criticism, politely yielding (*rang*) or giving concessions to others, complaisance and compromise, rather than to assert one's interests, claim one's "rights," and press one's case by taking the other party to court.

In practice, the dominant Confucian philosophy translated into reliance on officials to mediate disputes and search for solutions agreeable to and voluntarily accepted by the disputants. By relying on persuasion and education (as opposed to binding judgments on the parties), the ultimate aim was "the reconciliation of the disputants to each other and hence the restoration of the personal harmony and social solidarity that have been temporarily breached by the conflict."

From a modern liberal standpoint, however, the Confucian theory and practice of mediation is deeply flawed. Due to differences in power, wealth, knowledge, and influence, mediated "compromises" often produce unjust outcomes that disadvantage the weaker parties. In contrast to modern litigation, there are no procedural or institutional safeguards to ensure that the mediator is not biased against the socially inferior or weaker party. What looks like social harmony is often obtained at the expense of justice, and the party who has been genuinely wronged gets less than his or her due. Thus, liberals argue that litigation followed by adjudication by the court according to the law is a better vehicle for the realization of justice.

Despite these criticisms, Chen argues that suitably transformed mediation can still have a useful role to play in modern societies. This is recognized in the Anglo-American world, where a movement to introduce means of "alternative dispute settlement" is gaining influence. Various arrangements (e.g., appointing mediators from diverse class backgrounds) can help to minimize the problem of power imbalance, and it may be possible to reach truly consensual settlements that facilitate reconciliation and accommodation. In China, traditional thinking and practice regarding mediation can be revised in light of the modern liberal understanding of the rule of law. For example, it should be ensured that mediation is noncoercive and does not diminish the parties' rights to litigate the matter in court. Mediation may be particularly suitable in cases involving human associations that depend on spontaneous and informal collaboration and where parties have an incentive to maintain collaboration in the future. In such cases, it may not be unreasonable to require mandatory mediation before litigation can be entertained. Chen notes that mediation continues to play an important role in dispute settlement in China (compared to Western countries), and these normative concerns can help to provide guidelines for reform.

Lusina Ho, who teaches law at the University of Hong Kong, considers how Confucian values have been or could be given effect through concrete legal institutions comparable to those in established Western legal systems. Focusing on legislative debates over the law of succession in predominantly Chinese communities, Ho shows that these laws resulted from the influence of Confucian values on the minds of legislators. This is particularly obvious in the case of intestate succession, which involves applying rules devised by the state to distribute a deceased's properties when he or she fails to leave a will. In such cases, the state cannot be neutral—it must appeal to some value system to decide how to distribute the deceased's assets. In mainland China, the state explicitly invokes "traditional Chinese values" to justify maintenance of the elderly, the young, and the needy, with the parents of the deceased being heirs of the first priority. Ho notes, however, that exactly the same rule can be found in the Russian Civil Code, which shows that this rule is not *uniquely* Confucian. But this should not be viewed as a problem; rather, it shows that such laws can also be justified on non-Confucian grounds and thus could potentially be "exported" to non-Chinese communities that do not necessarily subscribe to Confucianism.

In the last part of her paper, Ho draws on the laws and practices surveyed to develop a model of a law of succession with a Confucian foundation that can be accommodated in a Western legal framework. In accordance with the Confucian principle that citizens should be encouraged to practice benevolence, which involves a graduated love depending on the nature of the relationship, the order of the rights of inheritance should correspond to the Confucian hierarchy of relationships. These substantive Confucian norms can be embedded within the technical framework of the laws of common law jurisdictions that balance the conflict between clarity and flexibility. Ho argues that this model can help remedy the defects of poorly thought out succession laws in predominantly Chinese communities such as Hong Kong, where haphazard mixtures of Confucian values and common law frameworks can (unintentionally) lead to anti-Confucian consequences.

Note, however, that Ho does not defend the traditional patriarchal succession laws—prior to the 1931 Civil Code of China, women were not given equal rights of inheritance. In the same vein, Chen takes it for granted that "creatively transformed" mediation will not be biased against women—more than that, he suggests that there is a special affinity between Confucian values and "feminist values," such as compromise, empathy, and sensitivity to context. More generally, none of the contributors discussed above seek to defend traditional patriarchal social and political arrangements in East Asia; it is simply assumed, it seems, that Confucianism for the modern world need not take on "patriarchal characteristics." But is this assumption warranted? The domination of men over women seems to be one of the defining characteristics of Confucian theory and practice—one might even say that patriarchy is the "Achilles heel" of Confucianism. Does it make sense to discuss "nonpatriarchal" Confucianism? Can Confucianism take on board feminist insights without altering its major values? To what extent can legal systems shaped by Confucian values accommodate the interests of women?

Chan Sin Yee, who teaches philosophy at the University of Vermont, discusses the Confucian conception of gender and draws implications for contemporary legal systems. Focusing specifically on the *yin-yang* distinction, Chan argues that *complementariness*, rather than subordination, should be emphasized in women's gender roles. The *yin-yang* distinction is an integral part of neo-Confucianism, and it was taken to imply a hierarchical relationship between the "female" *yin* (associated with dark, cold, night, passivity, softness, weakness, and the moon) and the "male" *yang* (associated with light, warmth, day, activity, hardness, strength, and the sun). However, Chan argues that *yin* and *yang* were not correlated with the genders of male and female when these ideas first emerged in early Confucian texts. Moreover, the *yin* and *yang* were said to be complementary forces in early Confucianism, and *yin* was not meant to be denigrated in comparison to *yang*: "For example: 'Music comes from *yang*, rituals come from *yin*, when *yin* and *yang* harmonize, myriad things are fulfilled' (*Li Ji* 11:5). Since rituals (*li*) are of utmost importance in Confucianism, to conceive of *yin* as their source is indeed to accord *yin* a very respectable status." It was only in Han dynasty Confucianism—not coincidentally, perhaps, the first dynasty to lift Confucianism into official state ideology—that the alignment between *yin-yang* and male-female became codified. Their hierarchical relationship was stressed at the expense of complementariness, and the oppression of women became much more severe than under early Confucianism.

According to Chan, there are no clear philosophical grounds for treating the *yin-yang* distinction as a hierarchical polarity, and whatever practical advantages men enjoyed in Confucian China cannot be justified with reference to this distinction. Still, she recognizes that the *yin-yang* distinction can imply gender essentialism and this may have some implications for gender issues in contemporary society. At most, however, *yin-yang* gender essentialism might justify "ritual" respect accorded to males. This "ritual" respect is similar to the "ritual" honor accorded to the elderly, and it need not affect the distribution of important opportunities and resources. There may also be positive Confucian grounds for the inclusion of women in powerful positions: "the [Confucian] sage-ruler is supposed to act like the parents and assume the roles of both the father and mother to the people. Consequently, in Confucianism, women cannot be excluded from politics on the ground that they lack full human potential as they were in the West." In fact, the practical implications of the *yin-yang* distinction (properly understood) significantly overlap with those of contemporary liberal feminism—"both support the idea of shared parenting, the elimination of many kinds of traditional sexual segregation in the workplace, and equal opportunity of political leadership and political participation." Chan shows, however, that both "schools" will reach these conclusions via different values and justifications. Moreover, there may still be particular areas where the *yin-yang* based conception of gender can lead to legal and political conclusions that worry liberal feminists—for example, *yin-yang* Confucians may be less tolerant of single-parent families that fail to allow interactions and complementariness of the two genders in the family setting and may support divorce laws that discourage the breakup of families and tax laws that reward married couples. One way to address the problem of Confucian intolerance of deviations from gender norms, Chan suggests, is to detach the *yin-yang* based conception of gender from core Confucian ideas, as in pre-Han Confucianism.

Hahm Chaibong, a political theorist at Yonsei University, turns to the more specific issue of Confucian-inspired marriage laws in Korea. On July 16, 1997, the Constitutional Court of Korea struck down the law that maintained the centuries old prohibition of marriages between men and women who have the same surnames and ancestral seats. Confucians were in an uproar whereas liberals celebrated the court's decision, and Hahm argues that these divergent reactions are rooted in deeper philosophical differences.

For the liberal, the family is not valuable in and of itself. It is the means to greater goods that are realized outside the family, such as creativity in work and success in politics. Thus, relegating "women or anyone to the family is seen as a mode of repression, as taking away that person's right to individual freedom and self-expression." Any law that reinforces ties to the family at the expense of opportunities in the public realm should therefore be struck down.

Confucianism, on the other hand, values the family as an end in itself, as an essential part of the good life. It fosters the sense of intimacy and caring that most "civil societies" tend to lack. It is the site where people learn the ties of affection that are subsequently spread to other segments of society. Thus, Confucians argue that the state should do what it can to support the institution of the family.

In Korea, the prohibition on marriages between men and women who have the same surnames is widely regarded as a crucial bulwark of Confucian familism. This prohibition owes its origins to Sung dynasty Confucianism. The Sung neo-Confucians sought a means of guaranteeing their social status even in the event of a failure to pass the examination, and they resolved this dilemma by reconstructing the family system along the ancient *zong* system, that is, the principle of descent through male heirs. The reconstruction of the family was also justified on the philosophical grounds that the family was the main realm in which the Confucian ideals of *li* could be taught and practiced.

These neo-Confucian ideas were rigorously implemented in Chosŏn Korea, a fascinating example of the way in which philosophies developed in one place actually find their fullest and most "orthodox" expression in another. Through a massive state-led effort in translating, interpreting, and disseminating neo-Confucian philosophy and institutions, Korea was transformed into an exemplary Confucian society. The prohibition of marriage between men and women who have the same surname and ancestral seat was one of the means of enforcement of the Neo-Confucian family system, because pre-Chosŏn marriage customs often confounded the hierarchy of a family organized along patrilineal descent. The different clans have kept strict genealogical records of all their descendants, and today these records, some going back over five hundred years, still top the best-seller lists in Korea.

However, Hahm suggests that the marriage prohibition may be less defensible today, given the population explosion that coincided with rapid modernization: "Today there are 3,760,000 Kimhae Kims, 2,740,000 Milyang Parks, and 2,370,000 Chŏnju Lees, the three largest clans in Korea. The chance of meeting and falling in love with someone from one's own clan is much greater in modern-day South Korea, highly urbanized and with a population of forty-five million." In this context, the marriage prohibition becomes counterproductive since many young people, denied the chance to marry the person they love, are turning away from the institutions of marriage and family. Thus, Hahm suggests that Confucians should endorse the Constitutional Court's decision while searching for new institutional means for preserving the family. This would also pave the way for further nonpatriarchal interpretations of Confucianism.[8]

DOES CONFUCIANISM REALLY MATTER?

This book ends with an epilogue by William Theodore de Bary, Provost Emeritus of Columbia University. Professor de Bary—one of the pedagogical pioneers of core curricula in the humanities—stresses that Confucianism is relevant not only in East Asian societies. A multicultural education in the twenty-first century will have to combine an understanding of local and world cultures. He argues that Confucianism should be given a definite (though not uniquely privileged) place within multicultural educational curricula. At a minimum, this would include study of the *Analects*—generations of readers have been attracted by the person of Confucius revealed in its pages. The appeal of Confucius as a person—how he triumphed over political failure and achieved a measure of self-fulfillment (and humility) in difficult circumstances—might help one achieve a sense of personal ease and contentment, whatever the social and political relevance of Confucianism.[9]

Put differently, the contributors to this volume are somewhat disenchanted with Western-style liberal modernity. Most important of all is its inability to articulate and institutionalize the kind of communal life that can ensure human flourishing. Confucianism can help to remedy this flaw, thus altering the character of the modern world as currently defined. At the same time, we do not argue for the wholesale restoration of premodern Confucianism. Obviously the main social and political features of modernity—democracy, capitalism, and the rule of law—are here to stay. The effort to secure human freedom had a historical inevitability and normative force that is hard to deny. Moreover, democracy, capitalism, and the rule of law are still values that need to be defended above and beyond all others in many parts of the world, including parts of East Asia. There is a sense in which the development of democratic rights and the affirmation of the positive role of the market are not only the requirements of globalization, but quite necessary for securing the good life. The rule of law continues to be the minimum standard necessary for any human flourishing.

What then is the sense in which we are questioning these essential features of modernity? Is it not the case that Confucian East Asia needs more of these rather than less? Indeed, East Asians have been actively working to over-throw Confucianism for the better part of the past century. Clearly, many in East Asia continue to argue for more "modernity," not less. Those who still do not enjoy the luxury of democracy cry out for even the most basic human rights and procedural justice. For countries mired in corruption and inefficiency, the introduction of free market principles and private property laws are urgent matters that go beyond considerations of tradition and culture. In countries where women are still relegated to second class citizen status, if not subjected to outright abuse and blatant discrimination, the call for the restoration of "family values" and talk of Confucianism can seem to be nothing less than reactionary.

However, the contributors to this volume have decided to look beyond, to look to the next stage with a willingness to err on the side of Confucianism, so to speak. Our view is that there is little danger that any argument in favor of Confucianism would bring about a reaction to turn the clock back to the Confucian past, however defined. This perhaps arises from the fact that most of the contributors, with important exceptions, hail from countries where basic human rights are secure and the rule of law and democracy have begun to take root. This, coupled with the fact that East Asia continues to exhibit a remarkable ability to generate economic growth and political stability, has provided the authors with the luxury of speculating about improving modernity with Confucian norms and institutions, an idea that might be viewed with skepticism, if not outright suspicion, under different circumstances. Of course, the burden is on us to define what that good life is, in what ways modernity does not measure up, and how Confucianism can contribute to the rearticulation and reformulation of modernity in ways that would measure up to our standards of the "good life."

NOTES

1. This is an Introduction to Daniel A. Bell and Hahm Chaibong, eds., *Confucianism for the Modern World* (Cambridge, UK: Cambridge University Press, 2003).
2. See Tony Lau, "Jiang's Appeal to Virtue Harks Back to Confucius," *South China Morning Post*, February 20, 2001. Some mainland Chinese intellectuals have also "returned" to Confucianism for inspiration: see, e.g., Guoji Ruxue Lianhehui, ed., *Ruxue Xiandai Tansuo* [Search for Contemporary Confucianism] (Beijing: Beijing Tushuguan Chubanshe, 2002), and Tang Kailin and Cao Gang, *Chongshi Chuantong: Rujia Sixiang de Xiandai Jiazhi Pinggu* [Reinterpreting Tradition: Contemporary Evaluation of Confucian Thought] (Shanghai: East China Normal University Publishing House, 2000).
3. See, e.g., Tu Wei-ming, ed., *Confucian Traditions in East Asian Modernity* (Cambridge, MA: Harvard University Press, 1996).
4. Wang Juntao's personal history is sufficient to cast doubt on this claim. He is a long-time democratic activist who was labeled (by the Chinese government) one of the two "black hands behind the scenes" of the May/June 1989 Tiananmen democracy movement. Arrested after the June 4, 1989, massacre, Wang spent five years in jail before being released to the United States on medical parole.
5. See Peter Passell, "Asia's Path to More Equality and More Money for All," *New York Times*, August 25, 1996, E5.
6. See Gordon White and Roger Goodman, "Welfare Orientalism and the Search for an East Asian Welfare Model," in Roger Goodman, Gordon White, and Huck-ju Kwon, eds., *The East Asian Welfare Model: Welfare Orientalism and the State* (London: Routledge, 1998), pp. 13–14. But see White and Goodman's account of the more immediate social and political explanations for the "East Asian welfare model" (ibid., pp. 14–20).

7. This topic relates to the question of the compatibility between Confucianism and modern ideas of human rights. Recent works have explored this question in detail—see especially Joseph Chan, "A Confucian Perspective on Human Rights for Contemporary China," in Joanne R. Bauer and Daniel A. Bell, eds., *The East Asian Challenge for Human Rights* (New York: Cambridge University Press, 1999), and the articles collected in William Theodore de Bary and Tu Wei-ming, eds., *Confucianism and Human Rights* (New York: Columbia University Press, 1998.

8. One of the editors of this book had an interesting experience with Korean-style feminism. He asked a Korean graduate student at Yonsei University who expressed feminist ideals to explain what exactly she would want to challenge in the social and political practices in Korea. The student replied that she was particularly irked that she did not have the "right" to perform rituals of ancestor worship (typically, only males have the "right") and that as an eldest daughter she did not have the "right" to continue the family lineage. In other words, she wanted an equal opportunity to participate in Confucian rituals.

9. For de Bary's own reflections on the negative and unresolved problems of the Confucian tradition, see his *The Trouble with Confucianism* (Cambridge, MA: Harvard University Press, 1991).

Buddhist Principles in the Tibetan Liberation Movement[1]

José Ignacio Cabezón

He who uses mankind badly, uses himself badly.

—Sextus the Pythagorean[2]

Tibet: An Overview

Tibet is a Buddhist country of 6 million inhabitants, occupying an area about the size of Western Europe, in the very heart of Asia. With China to the east and India to the west, it managed to serve as a buffer between these two great civilizations, interacting with both but maintaining its own cultural identity. Tibet had its own unique language, its own currency and postal system, and an independent government that integrated the religious and secular spheres (*chos srid gnyis 'brel*) under the leadership of the Dalai Lama. It developed distinctive traditions of painting, metalwork, and the performing arts and preserved a unique form of Mahayana Buddhism that was monastic, scholastic, and tantric in character.

In 1949 the Chinese invaded Tibet, an event that led to their slowly establishing considerable, and eventually complete, domination over the country. For ten years the Tibetan government, posing little threat to Chinese colonial interests, was allowed to retain nominal power. Various attempts were made by the Dalai Lama and his representatives during this time to regain political control of their homeland. On May 23, 1951, under duress and threats of a full-scale invasion by the People's Liberation Army, a group of Tibetan delegates sent by the Dalai Lama as representatives of the Tibetan government, signed the Seventeen-Point Agreement that, while ceding control of Tibet's external affairs to China, guaranteed the country's *internal* autonomy.[3] Receiving little support from the outside world, the Dalai Lama's government felt they had no choice but to accept the agreement already signed by the Tibetan delegates, despite the fact that the delegates had been prohibited from ever conferring with the central Tibetan government during the negotiation process. Because it promised some semblance of internal autonomy, the Tibetan government hoped that the agreement would allow them to keep Tibetan society, and especially their unique religious heritage, intact.

These hopes were unfounded however, and relations between the Tibetan government and the Chinese continued to deteriorate. Finally, in 1959, after a series of events in which the Dalai Lama's safety was threatened, the people of Lhasa rose up against the Chinese. No match for the overwhelming might of Chinese forces, this culminated in the final military overthrow of one Tibetan government, and the

Dalai Lama's flight to India. Together with almost 100,000 Tibetan refugees, the Dalai Lama continues to live in exile in India to this day.

Tremendous damage was done to the Tibetan culture, people, and land during and following the final Chinese takeover of the country in 1959: multitudes of Tibetans were executed, imprisoned, or forced to enter "re-education camps," monks and nuns were forced to enter lay life against their will, and a great deal of the country's cultural, religious, and artistic heritage was pillaged and sold. This was nothing compared to the losses that would be sustained later during the Cultural Revolution, however. By some estimates, all told, more than 1 million Tibetans have lost their lives at the hands of the Chinese, either directly through torture and execution or indirectly through mismanagement of Tibet's agricultural resources, that is, through policies that led to two 5-year periods of widespread famine and starvation in Tibet. In addition, more than 6,000 monasteries, temples, and historic structures have been destroyed.[4] As regards the natural environment, there has been systematic clearcutting of Tibetan forests, especially in eastern Tibet, and a great deal of Tibet's unique wildlife (the gazelle, wild ass, bar-headed geese, and brahmany duck) has been threatened, in some cases almost to the point of extinction.[5] Although the situation has improved somewhat since the end of the Cultural Revolution, Tibetans still lack the most basic human rights, such as freedom of speech and the right to peaceful protest. Just days before my own arrival in Lhasa, Tibet's capital, in the summer of 1991, for example, five Tibetans were arrested and imprisoned, and one killed, simply for engaging in peaceful protest outside Lhasa's Central Cathedral (*Jo khang*). Based on his interviews with former prisoners, John Avedon wrote that prison life in Tibet is

> ...characterized by unremittant labor, regular interrogation sessions in which the prisoner is beaten, ineffective medical care, borderline rations of black tea and barley, and an ongoing death toll resulting from the harsh conditions. Prisoners sleep on the floor, are chained at night and only have bedding if the family members donate it.[6]

The systematic torture of prisoners has been documented in greater detail in a 1988 report by the Boston-based organization, Physicians for Human Rights, titled *The Suppression of a People: Accounts of Torture and Imprisonment in Tibet*.

To this day, the Chinese continue to practice a policy of covert cultural genocide—the systematic destruction of Tibetan cultural identity—that includes the massive population transfer of Han Chinese into Tibet (a policy whose end it is to make Tibetans a minority in their own homeland).[7] This, coupled with the repression of religious freedoms and the systematic destruction of traditional Tibetan learning, poses grave threats to the continued existence of Tibetan culture.

THE DALAI LAMA

The Dalai Lamas have been the spiritual and temporal leaders of the Tibetan people since the seventeenth century, when the fifth Dalai Lama consolidated political power and unified the country under his rule. Since that time the Dalai Lama has been considered by his followers to be the physical manifestation (*sprul pa*) of Avalokitesvara, the "Buddha of compassion" and the mythical progenitor of the Tibetan people. Successive Dalai Lamas are considered the reincarnations of previous ones, and upon the death of a Dalai Lama a regent assumes power and takes on the responsibility of finding the new incarnation. The present Dalai Lama, Ngag dbang blo bzang bsTan 'dzin rgya mtsho (Ngawang lozang tenzing gyatso), is the fourteenth such incarnation (*sku phreng*).

The fourteenth Dalai Lama was born to humble peasant parents in 'A mdo (Amdo), one of the eastern provinces of Tibet, on July 6, 1935. He was recognized as the reincarnation of the thirteenth Dalai Lama and was enthroned in Lhasa on February 22, 1940. The regent continued to rule and the young Dalai Lama began his studies, which focused primarily on the religious texts of the monastic curriculum of the great monasteries (*gden sa*). Within a few years, however, a series of events, not the least of which was the Chinese invasion, brought great political instability to the country, and on November 17, 1950, the fourteenth Dalai Lama assumed full temporal power as head of state and government. Although he was responsible for the political affairs of the country from this time forward (at least to the extent possible, given the Chinese threat), he continued his religious studies, and in the year 1959, after sitting for public examinations during the annual Great Prayer Festival (*sMon lam chen mo*), he was awarded the highest academic degree, that of *dge bshes lha ram pa* (geshe lharampa).

Within a matter of weeks, as we have seen, the Dalai Lama was forced to leave his homeland and to seek political asylum in India. For the past thirty years, based in the village of Dharamsala in the Himalayan foothills of north India, he has been the major force behind the Tibetan people's efforts at preserving their cultural identity in exile—setting up schools, monasteries, handicraft centers, and even an academy for the performing arts. He has been instrumental in the drafting of a Tibetan constitution, in reorganizing the Tibetan government in exile along representative and democratic lines, and in making major reforms in the monasteries. And, of course, he has been the indefatigable spokesman for Tibetan independence throughout the world.

The Dalai Lama has consistently eschewed violence as a means for achieving Tibetan independence, and on more than one occasion he has been instrumental in actually preventing violent retaliation against the Chinese, both in Tibet and abroad. Instead, he has sought repeatedly to engage in negotiations with the Chinese, and has put forward several proposals that could serve as the basis for such negotiations. The most famous of these is the Five Point Peace Plan that calls for:

1. Transformation of the whole of Tibet into a zone of peace
2. Abandonment of China's population transfer policy that threatens the very existence of the Tibetans as a people
3. Respect for the Tibetan people's fundamental human rights and democratic freedoms
4. Restoration and protection of Tibet's natural environment and the abandonment of China's use of Tibet for the production of nuclear weapons and dumping of nuclear wastes
5. Commencement of earnest negotiations on the future of Tibet and of relations between the Tibetan and Chinese peoples.[8]

On June 15, 1988, he made even greater public concessions to the Chinese in an address before the European Parliament at Strasbourg.[9] But these and other proposals have fallen on deaf ears, and there has been no positive response by the Chinese to the Dalai Lama's repeated call for dialogue.

In 1989 the Dalai Lama was awarded the Nobel Peace Prize in recognition of his unswerving commitment to the peaceful and nonviolent struggle for Tibetan independence. In his Nobel acceptance speech, the Dalai Lama especially stressed the necessity of making of Tibet a zone of *ahimsa* or nonviolence through the demilitarization of the Tibetan plateau; of protecting its natural environment by ending the testing and stockpiling of nuclear weapons and by turning Tibet into "the world's largest natural park or biosphere"; and of maintaining it as a buffer zone between the two most populous states in the world, China and India.[10] Today, under the aegis of the International Campaign for Tibet, hundreds of chapters of the "Friends of Tibet" in every corner of the globe have joined the Dalai Lama in making the plight of the Tibetan people known throughout the world.

With this by way of background, I now move on to the main subject of this chapter, the social philosophy of the Dalai Lama. What are the principles guiding the Tibetan liberation movement? To what extent are they uniquely Buddhist, and to what extent universal? What are the doctrinal and scriptural foundations for these principles? How does a Buddhist social philosophy of liberation contrast with liberation theologies in Latin America?

SOME PRINCIPLES IN THE TIBETAN LIBERATION MOVEMENT AND THEIR BUDDHIST HERITAGE

What began as a response to a specific sociopolitical problem, the Tibetan response to the Chinese occupation of their homeland, has in recent years emerged as a systematic set of universal principles based on Buddhist teachings. Such a movement today might best be described as a Buddhist philosophy of social transformation. The tendency of the Tibetan liberation movement, and others like it, to become more universalized with time is discussed in more detail later. For now it must only be remembered that the universal principles characteristic of the movement today have their roots in a unique historical crisis: the Tibetans' loss of their homeland and their subsequent oppression at the hands of the Chinese. In what follows I shall be discussing some of the main points of the Dalai Lama's more developed and universal philosophy of social transformation, but I hope that in so doing the particular historical origins of these principles will not be lost. The Dalai Lama speaks of love for the enemy, and *for him* this means especially love for the Chinese. When he speaks of truth having the power to overcome evil, for him this means that, despite their small numbers and poor resources, the power of truth shall eventually prevail and Tibetans shall one day regain their independence.

INNER TRANSFORMATION, MATERIAL DEVELOPMENT, AND THE RHETORIC OF PEACE

It is one of the Dalai Lama's unique characteristics as a human being that he likes to tinker with things. In recent years this has led to a very profound interest in the physical and natural sciences, and in psychology. This has also brought him to meet on several occasions with scientists, medical doctors, and psychologists, and has led to his repeated praise of the scientific and technological advances of the West.

This interaction with Western scientists has undoubtedly also influenced his belief that science and technology are not the inherent causes of human alienation. If there exists human misery in technologically advanced societies, it is the fault of human beings, not of science. Hence, in the industrialized West, it is not scientific advancement that has brought alienation, but the fact that that level of material development has been achieved at the expense of inner spiritual development.[11] It is in this context that he frequently compares the Tibetan situation with that of the industrial West:

> Despite an often-stated desire to go beyond this materialistic emphasis, scientific and technological advancement seem to be the greatest pride of the Western world. This point of view stands in direct opposition to that of my own country, Tibet. We were technologically backward, but spiritually very rich.[12]

And it is inner, spiritual development that is perceived to be the true source of peace. Hence, "things depend more on the mind than on matter. Matter is important, we must have it, we must use it properly, but this century must combine a good brain—intelligence—with a good heart."[13]

Science and technology, therefore, are not the enemy. Instead, the true enemy lies within. "Many problems are created by our own mental defects; we suffer due to an internal lack."[14] This means that the most fundamental social problems that we face today are human-made and that their solution involves personal transformation. This is not, of course, to denigrate social action as an external practice, but it is to put it in its place. Without some commitment to personal spiritual transformation, to the betterment of one's mind, talk of peace is only so much rhetoric. "Everybody loves to talk about calm and peace, whether in a family, a national or an international context, but without inner peace, how can we make real peace?"[15] Therefore, true, lasting peace is something that requires inner peace as a prerequisite. "The only alternative is to achieve world peace through peace of mind."[16]

Is the inner transformation required to achieve a socially stable and peaceful world sectarian in character? Is it necessarily Buddhist? The answer seems to be that it is not, that what is needed is a sense of brotherhood and sisterhood, compassion, and the genuine realization of the oneness of all humankind,[17] which are principles espoused by all of the world's religions. Nonetheless, there is a sense in which the Buddhist heritage of Tibet is seen as making a particularly important contribution in this regard:

> Traditionally, Tibetans are a peace-loving and non-violent people. Since Buddhism was introduced to Tibet over one thousand years ago, Tibetans have practiced non-violence with respect to all forms of life.[18]

THE INTERDEPENDENCE OF CONTEMPORARY SOCIETY

The fact that the Dalai Lama begins what is arguably his most important political proposal, "The Five Point Peace Plan," invoking the principle of interdependence, is indicative of its importance to his philosophy of social transformation:

> The world is increasingly interdependent, so that lasting peace—national, regional and global—can only be achieved if we think in terms of broader interest rather than parochial need....As the world grows smaller, we need each other more than in the past.[19]

Interdependence in this sense of the term is a modern phenomenon and is due, among other things, to improved communications. As a result of this, problems—social, economic, and political—can no longer be solved in isolation:

> In ancient times problems were mostly local and therefore tackled at the local level. But now the situation is transformed and we have become very closely connected on the international level. One nation's problems can no longer be solved by itself completely.[20]

The principle of interdependence has its origins in classical Buddhist philosophy.[21] Especially as it is developed by Nagarjuna and his followers, it comes to be the positive analogue of emptiness, the final nature of all phenomena. This is undoubtedly the initial source for the Dalai Lama, but in applying it within the context of his philosophy of social transformation the concept takes on a new life. It takes on a historical tone, becoming a way of distinguishing modernity from "ancient times," and a dynamic, pragmatic principle for solving a variety of practical problems.

DISCRIMINATION AND THE RECOGNITION OF EQUALITY

One of the most important principles in the Dalai Lama's social philosophy is that of the equality of all human beings. Philosophically, this has several loci in Buddhist doctrine. It is, of course, a corollary to the theory of Buddha-nature (*tathagatagarbha*)—the fact that all beings are equal in their potential for perfection. It is also implicit within the discussion of the nature of mind, for according to classical Tibetan Buddhist psychology every individual's mind is of the nature of clarity and cognition, and at the most subtle level all beings, even Buddhas, are equal in having as the substratum for all thought an extremely subtle mental state that, although usually hidden beneath grosser mental functions, does manifest itself in the case of ordinary beings at the time of death. It is this same subtlemost mind, present in every living being, that transforms into the enlightened state at the culmination of the process of mental purification. These two doctrines, the theory of Buddha-nature and speculation concerning nature of the mind, give a metaphysical basis to the principle of the equality of all beings. Perhaps the most important *ethical* source for this idea comes from the *Bodhicaryavatara* of the Indian sage Santideva (8th century), a constant classical locus for much of the Dalai Lama's thought. A particular source of inspiration has been the eighth chapter, on meditation, where the specific form of *bodhicitta* meditation known as "the exchange of self with other" (*bdag gzhan nyams brjed*) is taught. It is in this context, and specifically as an antecedent to the actual exchange of self and other, that the equality of self and others is expounded. We are all equal in that we desire happiness and loathe suffering. As Santideva says:

> Hence, I should dispel the misery of others
> Because it is suffering, just like my own,
> And I should benefit others
> Because they are sentient, just like my body.
> When both myself and others
> Are similar in that we wish to be happy
> How are they different from me?
> Why do I strive for *my* happiness alone?
>
> And when both myself and others
> Are similar in that we do not wish to suffer,

> How are they different from me?
> Why do I protect myself alone?[22]

This equality of self and other has been taken as a theme, and expanded upon, in most of the Dalai Lama's writings. As with the principle of interdependence, it is the practical consequences of this idea that are stressed. Hence

> We are the same human flesh. I want happiness; you also want happiness. From that mutual recognition we can build respect and mutual trust for each other. From that can come cooperation and harmony, and from that we can stop many problems.[23]

In many instances the principle of human equality is used to emphasize the superficiality of cultural differences and the unity of our basic humanity:

> During my travels abroad I have noticed many things which seem to differentiate West from East, and particularly from Tibet. It is easy enough to understand these superficial differences in terms of the varying cultural, historical and geographical backgrounds which shape each particular way of life and pattern of behavior, but I feel that the far more relevant point to be stressed is the unity of these varying cultures and peoples. That unity is basically the human quest for happiness....[24]

It is interesting that this principle of human equality is also, in this system, the philosophical basis for human rights. Our wanting happiness and our desire to avoid suffering is philosophically fundamental in that it is self-evident and requires "no further justification."[25] Moreover,

> Based on that feeling we have the right to obtain happiness and the right to get rid of suffering. Further, just as I myself have this feeling and this right, so others equally have the same feeling and the same right.[26]

Just as equality can serve as the foundation for peace and for respecting human rights, discrimination (in a broad sense that includes not just prejudice but also the act of simply emphasizing differences) is considered the cause of strife and turmoil. Hence, sociocultural, ideological, religious, ethnic, and economic differences are considered both superficial and artificial.[27] At worst, emphasizing such differences can be the cause of discord:

> Philosophical teachings are not the end, not the aim, not what you serve. The aim is to help and benefit others, and philosophical teachings to support those ideas are valuable. If we go into the differences in philosophy and argue with and criticize each other, it is useless.[28] (Dalai Lama, 1984:47)

And in the secular realm:

> Also, in the world of politics such small discriminations create uncontrollable problems...sometimes from race, sometimes from ideology. The same is true

for my own country, Tibet, due to certain attitudes of our great neighbor, the People's Republic of China, that appeared during the Cultural Revolution. In this manner human ways of thinking create problems in addition to the basic ones that we must face.[29]

Hence, ideology, religion, and culture are the constructs of human beings. As such they should serve us and bring us happiness. If instead they become sources of suffering, then we are creating unnecessary grief for ourselves, grief that, unlike natural catastrophes, is within our control.[30] Pragmatically, this suffering can be eliminated by stressing human equality rather than human differences.[31]

LOVE OF ONE'S ENEMY AND THE PRACTICE OF NONVIOLENCE

In his monumental essay, *Civilization and its Discontents*, Freud states that if there is a "commandment" that he finds "even more incomprehensible and arouses still stronger opposition" in him than the commandment that one should love one's neighbor as oneself, it is the commandment, "Love thine enemies," and in the footnote he cites Heine's line that "One must, it is true, forgive one's enemies—but not before they have been hanged."[32] Freud's opposition notwithstanding, love of the enemy has been a pivotal way of expressing the principle of universal love (love for all humans or all beings) in many of the world's religions. It is of course an especially important ethical principle for those peoples who find themselves unjustly persecuted: the Hebrews at different periods in their history, the early Christians under Roman rule, and of course the Tibetans under Chinese domination.

Enemies, like human differences, are an undeniable fact of life. In the Dalai Lama's writings the existence of enemies is not denied, nor does he deny the fact that it is sometimes necessary to react aggressively to a situation:

> For example, if you are genuinely a humble and honest person and act that way, some people may take advantage of you. So in such a situation, it may be necessary to react. But we should react without bad feelings. Deep down, tolerance, compassion and patience must still be present....[33]

External circumstances may demand different types of outward responses—some peaceful, some not. But regardless of the variety of possible external manifestations, one thing that must remain invariant is the internal positive motivation. Even when aggressive behavior is called for externally, the only proper internal motivation remains love and compassion. Indeed, it is love of the enemy that is perceived as being the true test of love:

> Love which is limited to near and dear ones is invariably alloyed with ignorance and attachment. The love being advocated here is the kind one can have even for another who has done one harm.[34]

In the Dalai Lama's analysis, based especially on the sixth chapter of the *Bodhicaryavatara* ("Patience"), gratitude becomes the correct response to the enemy:

> Only when someone criticizes and exposes our faults are we able to discover our problems and confront them. Thus is our enemy our greatest friend. He provides

us with the needed test of inner strength, tolerance and respect for others. Instead of feeling anger toward this person one should respect him and be grateful.[35]

Hence, enemies are to be valued in that they provide us with the opportunity to practice patience.

This attitude toward the enemy is not a mere theoretical principle. In his recent autobiography, *Freedom in Exile*, the Dalai Lama applies this to the case of the Chinese.[36] There he deplores the violence perpetrated against the Chinese by Tibetans in recent years, and although also criticizing the Chinese human rights abuses against Tibetans, he emphasizes that these are the actions of a few and that in many cases the Chinese populace has itself been deprived of fundamental human rights, just as Tibetans have.[37]

A corollary to the Dalai Lama's views on universal love are his views on the ultimate inefficacy of anger and violence as means to resolving problems. Anger-motivated violence is at most a short-term answer to a problem:

Anger, jealousy, impatience and hatred are the real troublemakers; with them problems cannot be solved. Though one may have temporary success, ultimately one's hatred or anger will create further difficulties. With anger all actions are swift. When we face problems with compassion, sincerely and with good motivation, it may take longer, but ultimately the solution is better, for there is far less chance of creating a new problem.[38]

The doctrinal basis of this idea of nonviolence is to be found especially in the *Vinaya* literature of Buddhism, the corpus of monastic discipline that focuses on the avoidance of harm to others. For the Dalai Lama, a prime exemplar of this principle is to be found in Mahatma Gandhi. In his autobiography, the Dalai Lama describes his visit to Rajghat, Gandhi's cremation site, in the following words:

It was a calm and beautiful spot and I felt very grateful to be there, the guest of a people who, like mine, had endured foreign domination; grateful also to be in the country that had adopted *Ahimsa*, the Mahatma's doctrine of non-violence. As I stood praying, I experienced simultaneously great sadness at not being able to meet Gandhi in person and great joy at the magnificent example of his life. To me he was—and is—the consummate politician, a man who put his belief in altruism above any personal considerations. I was convinced too that his devotion to the cause of non-violence was the only way to conduct politics.[39]

UNIVERSAL RESPONSIBILITY AND COMPASSION

Perhaps the most important principles in the Dalai Lama's philosophy of social transformation are those of universal responsibility and compassion. Whereas love is traditionally defined as the wish to bestow happiness on others, compassion is considered the wish to rid others of their suffering. These, together with a third principle called "the superior thought" (*lhag bsam*), taking upon oneself the burden or responsibility of liberating others,[40] are the three prior causes to the generation of *bodhicitta*, the "mind directed to enlightenment," which is the bodhisattva's wish to attain enlightenment for the sake of all sentient beings. It is in the context of the discussion of the doctrine of *bodhicitta* that we find the most extensive discussions of compassion in Tibetan

Buddhism. This, then, is the doctrinal locus for the Dalai Lama's discussions of this subject. The reason why the concept of *bodhicitta* is not introduced as a universal principle within this philosophy of social transformation is clear. The notion of *bodhicitta* is one with clear Buddhist overtones. However, the Dalai Lama has consistently stressed the fact that the principles he is espousing are universal ones that should have applicability even in the secular sphere and "in this life."[41] For the Dalai Lama, making the message universal has meant in part divesting it of religious ideology, that is, making it as religiously neutral, and therefore as widely acceptable, as possible.

> Developing a kind heart does not involve any of the sentimental religiosity normally associated with it. It is not just for people who believe in religion; it is for everyone, irrespective of race, religion and political affiliation.[42]

This would of course exclude from the Dalai Lama's philosophy of social transformation notions with an overtly sectarian religious basis, such as *bodhicitta*, a notion that requires an understanding and acceptance of the specifically Buddhist conception of human perfection.

As we have mentioned, much of the Dalai Lama's discussion of the more general concepts of love, compassion, and universal responsibility are extracted from the discussion of *bodhicitta* and given a pragmatic, worldly flavor. It is a compassionate attitude, and especially *bodhicitta*, which is considered to be the perfect motivation (*kun slong*) for action in Mahayana Buddhism. In the Dalai Lama's thought the notion of proper motivation also plays an extremely important role. Ethically, it is the chief factor that determines whether an action is virtuous or not. When an action is motivated by compassion it becomes virtuous. To use a metaphor from the *Bodhicaryavatara*, like an elixir that can transform ordinary metal into gold, compassion has the capacity to transform worldly action into liberative action. Hence, even politics can become virtuous when properly motivated:

> Sometimes we look down on politics, criticizing it as dirty. However, if you look at it properly, politics in itself is not wrong. It is an instrument to serve human society. With good motivation—sincerity and honesty—politics becomes an instrument in the service of society. But when motivated by selfishness, with hatred, anger, or jealousy, it becomes dirty.[43]

THE POWER OF TRUTH

There is an ancient pan-Indian tradition that ascribes power to truth. Truth has the power to protect the one who speaks it and to set injustice right. In the *Ramayana*, Sita proves her fidelity to her husband, Rama, thereby defending herself against the unjust charge of adultery by stating her position and throwing herself into a fire. Her emerging unscathed serves as proof of the truth of her position. The notion is also present in the Buddhist tradition,[44] and it finds an interesting expression in the context of the Tibetan liberation movement.

In 1960, the Dalai Lama wrote a short work called "Prayer Words Supplicating Truth, to Request the Compassion of the Three Supreme Jewels" (*mChog gsum thugs rje i skul ba'i bden gsol smon tshig*). It is a work that invokes the power of the truth of the Buddha's doctrine to bring about the desired goal of universal happiness and Tibetan liberation. Now although it is primarily the truth of the Buddha's words that is invoked, there is also a sense in which the Dalai Lama's own words of prayer are considered words of truth. Hence, in the very first verse the Dalai Lama invokes the Buddhas of the past, present, and future and asks them to "please hear my anguished words of truth (*bden pa'i smre ngag*)."[45]

Truth, then, both as the reality of a given situation, that is, as the resolution sought by those who find themselves the object of oppression in a given situation, and as the words that express it, has the power to overcome evil, the oppression itself. The truth quite literally has the power to set free the oppressed. Hence,

> I believe that human determination and willpower are quite sufficient to challenge outside pressure and aggression. No matter how strong the evil force is, the flame of truth will not diminish. This is my belief.

Truth, in much of the Dalai Lama's writings, is frequently associated with the will of the people and pitted against the power and propaganda of government. Hence, when he states in his recent autobiography that "no matter what governments do, the human spirit will always prevail," he means in part that truth has a power mightier than institutional power and force. Applied to the Tibetan case this means that Tibetans under Chinese rule should never lose hope, for, in spite of their few numbers and relative military backwardness, the truth is with them, and it has a power greater than material might.

IS SOCIAL TRANSFORMATION IDEALISTIC?

It is not uncommon for proponents of social transformation, even those who do not proclaim utopian goals, to be accused of having idealistic visions. That this has in part been the response to the Dalai Lama's social philosophy is witnessed by the fact that he has found the need to defend himself against this charge. There is even at times in his writings the acknowledgment that his views on nonviolence may in fact *be* idealistic, at least for those who find themselves under the yoke of oppression.

> Yet, in truth, I realize that for most people such words are unrealistic. It is too much to ask. It is not right for me to expect Tibetans, who live their daily lives under such terrible hardships, to be able to love the Chinese. So, whilst I will never condone it, I accept that some violence is inevitable.[46]

For the most part, however, the Dalai Lama attempts to justify his social philosophy as plausible and practical. He concludes a recent talk, "Compassion in Global Politics," with the following words:

> ...no doubt you feel I am talking of an impractical dream. However, we human beings have a developed brain and limitless potential. Since even wild animals can gradually be trained with patience, the human mind can also gradually be trained, step by step. If you test these practices with patience, you can come to know this through your own experience.[47]

Therefore, the defense against the impracticality of such a vision comes in the form of reflection on human nature. If human beings were limited in their ability to change, so too would be society. Since they are not, since it is possible to change through training, the transformation of society is possible.

The idea of the limitless capacities of sentient beings has as one of its doctrinal sources the doctrine of Buddha-nature, which, as we have mentioned earlier, is the claim that all beings with minds have the capacity to achieve perfection. More to the point as regards the doctrinal basis for the limitless capacity of sentient beings, perhaps, is Dharmakirti's defense of the possibility of buddhahood in the "*Pramanasiddhi*" chapter of his *Pramanavarttika*. Be that as it may, in the present context, the claim is more modest and, although not philosophically neutral, inasmuch as it contains metaphysical presuppositions about the limitless possibilities available to human beings, it is at least doctrinally neutral in that it makes no specific reference as to the nature of that limitless state.

At the same time, the Dalai Lama acknowledges that the individual human transformation that is the basis for the transformation of society is difficult at best.[48] It is not something that can be achieved overnight. In fact, even though such a transformation is theoretically possible, there is no guarantee that it will actually take place:

> [A] troubled atmosphere is our current reality. It is very bad, but it is reality. People may feel that the opposite of this, the internal transformation about which I have been speaking is merely idealistic and not related to our situation here on earth....Although to bring about inner change is difficult, it is absolutely worthwhile to try. This is my firm belief. What is important is that we try our best. Whether we succeed or not is a different question. Even if we could not achieve what we seek within this life, it is all right; at least we will have made the attempt to form a better human society on the basis of love—true love—and less selfishness.[49]

BUDDHISM AND LIBERATION THEOLOGY

The Buddhist social philosophy that is emerging from the Tibetan liberation movement is one of a class of religiously based philosophies of social action in the world today. Although each of these movements address distinct, and even unique, problems and issues, it is illuminating to see how the Dalai Lama's philosophy contrasts with another such movement, Liberation Theology. Comparing the two, it seems to me, gives us greater insight into both.

It is one of the central features of Latin American Liberation Theology[50] that it views itself not simply as an addendum or complement to theology as it is currently done but as a critique of the entire theological enterprise. Hence, liberation theologians urge a shift from the traditional concern with the speculative and ahistorical to concern with giving "priority to historical critical thinking as such"[51] and from concern with orthodoxy as "right thinking" and "right speaking" to orthopraxis as "right doing."[52] Hence, for the liberation theologian the starting point of a religiously based philosophy of social action is not theory but practice. It is not ahistorical speculation, but action from within the ranks of the poor that leads to "the whole process of questioning the present social order...leading eventually to the abolition of the current oppressive culture."[53]

There is also a sense in which we might say that the Tibetan social philosophy of liberation is grounded in history, for surely it is a direct result of a historical crisis, the Chinese occupation of Tibet. But although it is born as a concrete response to oppression, it has, not unlike some strands of Liberation Theology itself, taken on a life of its own. It has become universalized, and the principles that it espouses are seen by its followers to have universal applicability. Hence, the message of the Buddhist social philosophy of liberation still developing among the Tibetans is no longer solely aimed at understanding and resolving the particular historical crisis in which the Tibetans find themselves but is instead aimed at a wider, even global, audience.[54]

This tendency for religiously based social philosophies to become universalized, to go beyond their particular historical crises to expound a more general message to humanity, is evident in the African-American freedom movement as well. In his most recent book, *Hope and History*, my colleague Vincent Harding writes:

> When we search deeply enough into the struggles for truth, justice and hope of any human community, moving with disciplined compassion and vision, we emerge from the exploration with lessons that were meant for us all. In other words, when approaching the movement from this perspective, what we realize is that the story of the African-American struggle for freedom, democracy and transformation is a great continuing human classic whose liberating lessons are available to all seekers and discoverers....[55]

In other words, the lessons of the African-American freedom movement too are universal.

In both the Tibetan and the Latin American case, it may be the oppressed that are the inspiration behind the emerging philosophies of liberation, but in both cases, it is an intellectual elite that is the source of this new thinking. It is interesting, however, that the Buddhist social philosophy developing among the Tibetans is evolving not as a bottom-up phenomenon in which ecclesial structures and doctrines become the object of critique but as a top-down one in which the source of the new thinking is the religious hierarchy itself. This is in part due to the fact that the critique is not economic in nature. Whether or not the chief critique in the Latin America case is an economic one, it is certainly the case that such a discussion, and especially a discussion of the Church's role in legitimizing the economic exploitation of the poor, is high on the list of important topics for most Latin American liberation theologians. Such concerns are not absent in the Tibetan case, and indeed the Dalai Lama has himself, on a number of occasions, admitted that internal religious corruption was partly responsible for the eventual demise of the Tibetan government. This being said, it is clear that the most pressing problem, from the Tibetans' own perspective, is not internal corruption but the foreign domination of the Tibetan people by the Chinese. This is understandable. For a country under foreign domination, an economic critique of indigenous, precolonial, political, and ecclesiastical polity can only be considered a secondary task and one that might very well siphon energy away from the primary one of bringing an end to foreign domination. This explains in part why the Tibetan critique has been primarily directed externally by the hierarchy rather than internally toward the hierarchy.

What this has meant as well is that the Buddhist social philosophy emerging out of the Tibetan liberation movement is not envisioned as a radical rethinking of traditional Buddhist philosophy. Although suggesting a new reading of Buddhist texts, a new hermeneutical lens, it does not do so at the expense of the traditional understanding of Buddhist scripture. Instead, the tone in the Tibetan case is internally conciliatory rather than confrontative; it views itself more as a complement to traditional Buddhist philosophical speculation rather than as an undermining of it, and it stresses continuity with the tradition rather than rupture. The idea is not that orthopraxis must supplant orthodoxy but that it must supplement it. Traditional philosophical speculation and scriptural interpretation are not seen as obstacles to social action, as in the case with various liberation theologians.[56] Rather, as we have seen, they are perceived as providing the theoretical and spiritual *basis* for action. In the Tibetan case it is not that the traditional goals of Buddhism (e.g., *nirvana*, the universal emancipation of all beings, and so on) are discarded in favor of action in the world. Instead the two goals, worldly and supramundane, are seen as reinforcing each other, for virtuous action on behalf of the oppressed creates merit and aids in the task of mental purification, while the more traditional spiritual exercises, especially the practice of compassion and wisdom, are seen as providing the basis that ensures the moral goodness of an action and its efficacy.[57]

Among many Latin American liberation theologians there appears to be a rejection (or what might be the same, a radical redefinition) of tradition, especially of contemplative tradition and classical spiritual practice, in favor of immersing oneself into "the very midst of political activity, recognizing all its elements of conflict."[58] In the words of Vidales:

> Right from the start we must realize that human history, the one and only history that exists, is not only the circumstantial locale of salvation but also salvation itself—as yet unfinished but moving toward its final fulfillment.[59]

Such a rejection of traditional doctrine and spiritual practice in favor of worldly involvement is alien to the form of Buddhist social philosophy developing among Tibetans. Nonetheless, even in the Tibetan case there is recognition of the age-old tension "between personal soteriological goals and the concern for proper ordering of this-worldly life."[60] The resolution, in the Tibetan case, is achieved not from without, through the critique of tradition, but from within, through its exegesis, in such a way that both the personal soteriological element and the element of social action are preserved. Part of the Dalai Lama's task, then, is to draw out for a Buddhist audience the social implications of Buddhist philosophical theory. Here the Dalai Lama is functioning as a homiletician, encouraging Buddhists to action by making clear the practical and social dimensions of doctrine. For example, the Dalai Lama, when asked whether it was better to be in retreat or to be active in the world responded as follows:

> In general, if one can do both, it is best. I think this is the practical way to do it. For the greatest part of the year we have to live in society, we have to lead a good life...but for a few weeks, for two months or three months, to make retreat, to forget other types of worldly business and to concentrate solely on one's practice, I think this is the best way. If, however, someone has a special vocation for the hermetic life, if someone has this talent for living and practicing in isolation...then it may be worthwhile to...put all of one's energies toward spiritual practice. But this is the exception and quite rare. I think that among one million people there may be one or two with this type of talent or vocation.[61]

Hence, for the vast majority of humanity it is a balance between interior cultivation and external work in the social sphere that is considered the ideal life. No amount of social activism can supplant private spiritual practice. Indeed, social activism that is devoid of a proper spiritual/humanitarian foundation is question-able, to say the least. Also, for most people, no amount of meditation can take the place of involvement in the world. In the Tibetan Buddhist case, then, the soterio-logical, other-worldly element is neither abandoned nor redefined. The path of lib-eration is not reduced to social activism. At the same time, the practice of the soteriological dimension does not, except in rare cases, permit one to isolate oneself from the world. In the Tibetan case, the duality and tension between the two realms is resolved without being denied, and this results in a vision of the two realms as complementary.

Sociologically, Buddhism has traditionally conceived of the religious and secular worlds as interdependent but separate—the monastic community teaching and giv-ing guidance to the laity, and the laity providing economic sustenance for monks and nuns. A Buddhist philosophy of social action, however, maintains that the religious and secular ideals should be united *within individuals* through a balance of their activities (each community taking on part of the work of the other), but this is a relatively novel development in the history of Indo-Tibetan Buddhism. The fact that such complementarity is to be achieved at the individual level, however, implies nei-ther the sociological nor the soteriological equality of the two realms. Even for the contemporary Buddhist who follows the path that unites spiritual cultivation and social action, it is the exalted state of buddhahood, achieved through the practice of the doctrine and exemplified in the monastic community, that remains the object of greatest veneration and the highest state of human fulfillment, both for self and for the other. Although responsible engagement in the world is part of the obligations of the contemporary Buddhist, such engagement alone is incapable of bringing about true and permanent human happiness, either for oneself or for the world.

It is worth noting that the social philosophy emerging out of the Tibetan libera-tion movement has not allied itself ideologically with any existing political worldview or form of economic analysis, as have many theologies of liberation in Latin America.[62] There are a variety of reasons for this, but perhaps the chief one is this: the Tibetan liberation movement is not a socioeconomic critique of Tibetan political institutions. Instead, as we have stated, its chief goal is the end of Chinese rule in Tibet. Ideological affiliation has little place in helping the Tibetans to achieve this end. Historically, neither the capitalist West nor the formerly Communist Eastern bloc has gone out of its way to support the Tibetan cause. This has led to a general skepticism on the part of the Tibetan intelligentsia concerning political ideology in general. Of course, in regard to the particular brand of Marxist-Leninist-Maoist thought espoused by the Chinese there is no skepticism on the part of the Tibetans, only abhorrence. This is hardly surprising, given what it has meant for them as a people.

Cultural, historical, and religious differences obviously account for the different ways that Liberation Theology and the Dalai Lama's philosophy have developed. The Dalai Lama's thought on its own undoubtedly emerges as a unique philosophy of social transformation; but the comparative dimension, it seems to me, gives us greater insight into the "hows" and "whys" of this uniqueness. In discussing the Buddhist principles behind the social philosophy emerging from the Tibetan libera-tion movement in the first portion of this chapter my goal has been to demonstrate the continuity of the Dalai Lama's thought with the Buddhist tradition. But there is novelty here as well, and even though that novelty does not manifest itself as a chal-lenge to tradition, it does manifest itself as a reinterpretation of tradition that makes explicit the social implications of Buddhist doctrine. This new message is important not only for Tibetans and for those of us who support them in their struggle to regain their independence but also, it seems to me, for humankind as a whole.

Notes

1. This is a chapter in Christopher S. Queen and Sallie B. King, eds., *Engaged Buddhism: Buddhist Liberation Movements in Asia* (Albany: State University of New York Press, 1966).

2. Taken from Thomas Taylor's Iamblichus' *Life of Pythagoras*, and cited in Whitall N. Perry, *A Treasury of Traditional Wisdom* (San Francisco: Harper & Row, 1986), p. 600.

3. Marvin C. Goldstein, *A History of Modern Tibet: 1913–1951, The Demise of the Lamaist State* (Berkeley, Los Angeles, and London: University of California Press, 1989), p. 769.

4. *Tibet Briefing* (New York: The Office of Tibet, 1991), p. 1; John Avedon, *Tibet Today: Current Conditions and Prospects* (New York: The U. S. Tibet Committee, 1987).

5. John Avedon, "Inside Tibet," *Utne Reader* (April 1989), pp. 34–36.

6. Avedon (1987), p. 15.

7. Michael van Walt van Praag, *Population Transfer and the Survival of the Tibetan Identity* (New York: The U. S. Tibet Committee, 1986).

8. *Tibet Briefing*, pp. 10–11.

9. Given that the generous concessions of the Strasbourg Proposal, which included placing Tibet's foreign policy in the hands of the Chinese (*Tibet Briefing*, p. 15), received no positive Chinese response, the Strasbourg Proposal has since been withdrawn under pressure from Tibetans, both in Tibet and in exile, and is considered no longer binding. (*Tibet Briefing*, p. 17.).

10. Dalai Lama, "Nobel Lecture by the His Holiness Tenzing Gyatso, The Fourteenth Dalai Lama," in *News Tibet*, vol. 23, no. 2 (1989).

11. For an interesting discussion that parallels the Tibetan Buddhist one in some respects see Eric Fromm, *The Art of Loving* (New York and Evanston, Ill.: Harper & Row, 1962), pp. 27–28.

12. Dalai Lama, "The Principle of Universal Responsibility," pamphlet and material gathered from various talks given in Europe (New York: Potala Publications, n.d.), p. 6.

13. Dalai Lama, *Kindnes, Clarity and Insight*, eds. J. Hopkins and E. Nappier (Ithaca, NY: Snow Lion, 1984), p. 62.

14. Ibid., p. 11.

15. Ibid., p. 62.

16. José Cabezón, *H. H. The Dalai Lama, The Bodhgaya Interviews* (Ithaca, NY: Snow Lion, 1988), p. 47.

17. Ibid.

18. Dalai Lama, "Five Point Peace Plan," pamphlet (1987), p. 2.

19. Ibid., p. 1.

20. Dalai Lama (n.d.), p. 2. See also Dalai Lama (1984), pp. 48, 58, 61, where the doctrine is worked out in more detail and illustrated with examples.

21. For an example of the Dalai Lama's discussion of the principle of interdependence in the context of Buddhist philosophical theory, see Dalai Lama, "A Brief Teaching by His Holiness the Fourteenth Dalai Lama," commentary on the *Eight Verse Mind Training* (Los Angeles: Thubten Dhargye Ling, 1979), p. 10.

22. *Bodhicaryavatara* (VII, 94–96); my translation here differs slightly from Stephen Batchelor's, upon which I base it. See Stephen Batchelor, *A Guide to the Bodhisattva's Way of Life by Shantideva* (Dharamsala: Library of Tibetan Works and Archives, 1979), pp. 113–114. For the Sanskrit and Tibetan of these verses, see the Bhattacarya edition (1960), pp. 60–61.
23. Dalai Lama (1984), p. 16.
24. Dalai Lama (n.d.), p. 1.
25. Dalai Lama (1984), p. 11. Compare this to the following passage from Plato's *Symposium.* " 'And what does he gain who possesses the good?' 'Happiness,' I replied; 'there is no difficulty in answering that.' 'Yes,' she said, 'the happy are made happy by the acquisition of good things. Nor is there any need to ask why a man desires happiness; the answer is already final.' " From B. Jowett, trans. *The Works of Plato* (New York: Tudor Publishing Company, n.d.), p. 334.
26. Dalai Lama (1984), p. 11.
27. Dalai Lama (n.d.), p. 2; (1984), pp. 11, 16.
28. Dalai Lama (1984), p. 47.
29. Ibid., p. 59.
30. The difference between the two types of suffering being discussed here has obvious parallels to the distinction between natural and moral evil in Western philosophical discussions of the problem of evil.
31. At the same time, there are many instances in which human diversity is celebrated in the Dalai Lama's writings; see (1984), pp. 49, 60. A distinction needs to be made, therefore, between accepting and celebrating human differences, on the one hand, and using human differences as a basis for creating discord. The differences exist; it is, practically speaking, a question of what we do with them.
32. Sigmund Freud, *Civilization and Its Discontents*, James Strachey, trans. and ed. (New York: W. W. Norton, 1961), p. 57.
33. Cabezón (1988), p. 32.
34. Dalai Lama (n.d.), p. 2.
35. Ibid., p. 5.
36. A more detailed discussion of other Buddhist principles (an understanding of *karma*, the ability to grow from living in adverse situations, etc.) that come into play in the Dalai Lama's own understanding of the present Tibetan situation is to be found in an interview with Daniel Goleman, "The Experience of Change" in *Parabola*, Spring (1990), pp. 8–9.
37. Dalai Lama, *Freedom In Exile.* Autobiography (New York: Harper Collins, 1990), p. 261.
38. Dalai Lama (1984), p. 62.
39. Dalai Lama, *Freedom in Exile*, p. 116.
40. Dalai Lama, *Kindness, Clarity, and Insight*, J. Hopkins and E. Napper, eds. (Ithaca, NY: Snow Lion, 1984), pp. 46–47, 60, 62.
41. Dalai Lama, "Emerging Consciousness for a New Humankind," in Michael von Bruck, ed. *Emerging Consciousness for a New Humankind* (Bangalore: Asian Trading corporation, 1985), p. 3.
42. Dalai Lama (n.d.) p. 3.
43. Dalai Lama (1984), p. 62.
44. For a discussion of this idea in the context of the long-life prayer (*zhabs brten*) literature of Tibetan Buddhism, where the truth of the Buddha's doctrine (especially interdependence), or of the three jewels, is invoked as a way of praying for

the long life of the spiritual master, see my forthcoming article in *Tibetan Literature*, J. I. Cabezón and Roger Jackson, eds.

45. Dalai Lama, "A Prayer of Words of Truth and the Tibetan National Anthem," translated by the Translation Bureau of the Library of Tibetan Works and Archives (Dharamsala: Library of Tibetan Works and Archives, 1950), p. 1.

46. Dalai Lama, *Freedom in Exile*, p. 261.

47. Dalai Lama (1984), p. 64.

48. Ibid., p. 87.

49. Ibid., pp. 15–16.

50. I am not unaware of the fact that there is great divergence of opinion in Liberation Theology in Latin America. For the purposes of this chapter, however, I am allowing myself some pedagogical license and purposely simplifying points that might otherwise lead to major discussions of differences in these various movements. The focus of this chapter is not, after all, Latin American theological polemics but Buddhist social philosophy.

51. Raul Vidales, "Methodological Issues in Liberation Theology," in R. Gibellini, ed., and J. Drury, trans., *Frontiers of Theology in Latin America* (Maryknoll, N. Y.: Orbis Books, 1983), p. 36.

52. Ibid., p. 38.

53. Gustavo Gutiérrez, "Liberation Praxis and Christian Faith," in R. Gibellini and J. Drury, eds., *Frontiers of Theology in Latin America* (Maryknoll, NY: Orbis Books, 1983), p. 18.

54. This tendency in the direction of universality can also be attributed in part to the fact that underlying the Tibetan social philosophy under question are Buddhist principles, which are themselves viewed as having universal applicability.

55. Vincent Harding, *Hope and History: Why We Must Share the Story of the Movement* (Maryknoll, NY: Orbis Books, 1990), p. 10.

56. Gutierrez (1983), p. 10, for example, states that, "because of an upbringing that was ahistorical and focused on abstract principles, Christians were generally insensitive, if not actually hostile, to any scientific reasoning applied to the political realm." See also Joseph Comblin, "What Sort of Service Might Theology Render?" In Gibellini and Drury (1983), p. 62.

57. This is in marked contrast to the theory of the development of a Buddhist social ethic that assumes the kammatic/nibbannic distinction, in which social action belongs in the kammatic, that is, "secular," realm, and is therefore related primarily to the goal of higher rebirth, as opposed to the nibbanic aspect of the religion whose goal is emancipation from all rebirth. In the Tibetan setting, and perhaps more generally in Mahayana Buddhism, the case can convincingly be made that such a distinction is unwarranted. Social action is as much the cause of *nirvana* as monastic discipline is; and vice versa, typically "nibbannic" practices such as wisdom and compassion are as relevant to properly acting within the world as is the concept of *karma*. One of the best treatments of the development of a Buddhist social ethic in a Theravada Buddhist society is to be found in Bardwell Smith, "Toward a Buddhist Anthropology: The Problem of the Secular," in *Journal of the American Academy of Religion*, vol. 36, no. 3 (1968), pp. 203–216.

58. Gutiérrez (1983), p. 16.

59. Raul Vidales, "Methological Issues in Liberation Theology," in Gibellini and Drury (1983), p. 40.

60. Frank Reynolds, "The Two Wheels of Dhamma: A Study of Early Buddhism," in Bardwell Smith, ed., *The Two Wheels of Dhamma: Essays on the Theravada Tradition in India and Ceylon* (Chambersberg, Penn.: AAR Studies in Religion, 1972), p. 62.

61. Cabezón (1988), p. 62.

62. The Dalai Lama has on several occasions in the past spoken out in favor of Marxism in its pure form, but this has been qualified in the following way in his recent autobiography, *Freedom in Exile*: "...The pursuit of Communism has been one of the greatest human experiments of all time, and I do not deny that I myself was very impressed with its ideology at first. The trouble was, as I soon discovered, that although Communism claims to serve 'the people'...'the people' does not mean everyone, only those who hold views that are held by a minority to be 'the people's view'" (Dalai Lama, 1990, p. 268).

That the Dalai Lama's political views are ultimately eclectic, and that he sees advantages and disadvantages in different political ideologies is evidenced by the following passage: "...inasmuch as I have any political allegiance, I suppose I am still half Marxist. I have no argument with Capitalism as long as it is practiced in a humanitarian fashion, but my religious beliefs dispose me far more towards Socialism and Internationalism....Against this, I set the fact that those countries which pursue capitalist policies within a democratic framework are much freer than those which pursue the Communist ideal....Having said that I remain half Marxist; if I were actually to vote in an election it would be for one of the Environmental parties" (Dalai Lama, 1990, pp. 268–269).

EAST ASIA AND THE WEST:
CATCHING UP WITH EACH OTHER[1]

Wm. Theodore de Bary

No real dialogue can take place between East Asia and the West unless both parties are equally and deeply involved, but for all the West's desire to understand East Asians, so far its effort has not been equal to theirs. This may be an odd time to raise the issue, since interest in East Asia had never been higher in the West than it is now, and the achievements, in both economic and cultural terms, of the East Asian peoples are more respected today than ever before. Nevertheless if I return now to the question posed at the beginning whether the West might need to catch up with East Asia—I do so not only in the obvious sense that East Asia has now overtaken us in several economic areas and that America must become more efficient or proficient if it is to compete. I mean rather that we have not yet grasped the deeper meaning of our encounter with East Asia or adjusted to the new reality of the Old World discovered there.

We have long since passed the last frontier of outward, westward expansion (the bounds of the original New World), but we have not realized that our new frontier must be conceived in terms other than further penetration into others' space. Rather we must learn to live with both ourselves and others as East Asians have been doing for centuries—by a deeper, more intensive cultivation of our limited space, which is to say much more of an "inner space" than an open frontier or "outer space." Whatever mission we still have to perform in East or West—be it religious, educational, political, legal, or any other cause one feels called on to take up—must adjust to this reality. Yet the West, facing this new fact of life, the end of the road for its long outward journey, has been as unprepared to accept it as the East Asians were to come out of their world into ours.

To illustrate the point, let me cite the case, not too long ago, of a columnist for the *Wall Street Journal* who adduced the negative example of China in arguing for the aggressive exploration and development of space. In an article entitled "Mandarin Mondale and the U.S. Future in Space," the writer set up Walter Mondale as a modern Mandarin, likening him to the Confucian Chinese of the fifteenth and sixteenth centuries who put a stop to the voyages of Cheng Ho and Chinese maritime exploration, just as, according to this interpretation, Mondale would have put a stop to U.S. space exploration.[2] The author quoted such authorities as the "author-physicist" Arthur Kantrowitz, Joseph Needham, and Jung-pang Lo on behalf of his view that, at this crucial turning point in history, the Chinese went into "a general decline," a "depression of the spirit" that overtook the Chinese "desire to learn" and inhibited "the temper and spirit of the Chinese people." This reversal and decline he attributed,

not altogether incorrectly, to the influence of "the champions of Chinese standpat-
tism: the Confucian bureaucrats."

> For political and cultural reasons, these Mandarin bureaucrats hated the
> "outward bound" policy of the treasure ships and their admirals. In Mr.
> Needham's words: "The Grand Fleet of Treasure Ships swallowed up funds
> which, in the view of all right-thinking bureaucrats, would be much better
> spent on water-conservancy projects for the farmers' needs, or in agrarian
> financing 'ever-normal granaries' and the like." Under their influence,
> Chinese science ossified and, even worse, became divorced from technol-
> ogy. And this, the ongoing partnership of science and nuts-and-bolts tech-
> nology, was what gave Western civilization the edge it has kept to the
> present.[3]

We need not concern ourselves with the political conclusions drawn here, but observe
rather the manner in which the writer dismisses the moral position of the so-called
Confucian bureaucrats:

> To the argument that we can no longer afford large-scale exploration of space,
> I would respond that hindsight makes it clear that the destruction of the Ming
> navy was the real extravagance...As in Ming China, there are those who have
> gained center stage by its suppression. The suppressors in both cases claim
> moral superiority and have too often been able to conceal the magnificent role
> of creative technology in liberating and elevating mankind.

> Three hundred years after Cheng Ho and the great treasure fleets, a Chinese
> ruler did build a rather impressive ship: a full-size barge made of solid marble.
> If our modern Mandarins get to run things, we might have a marble space
> shuttle down in Houston—you know, something to really impress the Russians
> and Japanese.[4]

The article would be of only passing moment were it not that it invoked one of
the most indelible images of dynastic China—the marble pleasure boat in the
Summer Palace near Peking—which virtually all visitors to China are shown as typi-
fying the misplaced values of the traditional order. What I wish to single out is the
easy assumption that the Confucian position too can be disposed of simply by pointing to the same bizarre example. It is an assumption rendered plausible by the view,
dominating the whole article, that the Confucians clearly went wrong, that they
failed to keep up with "the spirit of expansion and enterprise" and were so addicted
to the notion of their moral superiority that they could see no use whatever for science and technology—certainly a vast oversimplification.

I do not wish to argue here either for or against Mondale's supposedly "liberal"
position on "star wars" (a view which, in a more fundamental sense, might be
thought conservative as opposed to expansive). My concern is rather with the question of who is being short-sighted and parochial here and who is being realistic.
Realism, it seems to me, would require us to question seriously a policy of indefinite
expansionism and exploitation of the earth's human and physical resources, and not
just dismiss this thought as already discredited by Chinese history. What is presented
here as a more open and expansive view of the human enterprise may actually be a
narrow, parochial one.

Lest my own view be misunderstood as calling for a limiting of intellectual or scientific horizons, the need I see is rather for a better sense of where we stand, of the home base from which we start in reaching out to take on global challenges. Along with an awareness of new possibilities for learning and growth, and prerequisite to exploring them, we must have a sense of direction, of context, of due process, and of deliberate speed in our use of present resources, both human and physical.

This is no more a conservative view than it is a liberal one, since being conservative as to means does not preclude liberal ends and may indeed be the only practical way to advance them. Nor does it ignore the possibility that real and present dangers to basic human values may even, in some circumstances, call for prophetic vision or radical action. Such options would exist even in circumstances recognized as severely limiting, just as within the limited horizons of the Confucian world there were both liberal and conservative tendencies, both scholarly and prophetic voices. It does, however, mean accepting the idea that freedom may be found elsewhere than in recourse to a great liberality of means, the exploitation of material resources, or the conquest of space. The discovery of true freedom and creativity comes only in limiting contexts, when we are compelled to draw more deeply on inner resources of the human spirit. Indeed, do we not already witness such liberating possibilities in the current popularity of the traditional arts of Asia, whether martial, cultural, or contemplative, the challenge of which is precisely to self-mastery and deeper spiritual creativity in clearly defined contexts?

Similarly in the social order, a more truly open and cosmopolitan—or I should say planetary—outlook might require a more Confucian view of our primary responsibilities. It would have to consider whether our most deep-seated problem in a world of rapid and almost compulsive change may not be the lack of any parochial loyalties in the sense of a responsibility to any given human or earth community. What we need is not new worlds to conquer, star wars and all that, but a new parochialism of the earth or planet. This should start, as the Confucians did, with self-reflection and self-restraint. Conscious of the interrelatedness of all things, and of one's own place in an interdependent world, this view should develop a sense of equal responsibility for oneself and others and of reciprocal support for a life-sustaining environment. It would address the question of what we will *not* do, what choices we will voluntarily forgo, what limitations we will accept out of concern for the welfare of our earth, our fellow man, and the generations to come who will otherwise suffer for our sins of earth pollution, resource exhaustion, genetic disorders, and so on.

In view of our past history, it is natural enough for us to project a future of unlimited expansion into outer space—the "conquest of space" as contemporary conquistadors put it, now that they have given up singing "Onward Christian Soldiers." But as we contemplate such an endless, aimless adventure, we should pause to consider whether it does not, after all, manifest a compulsive drive to control everything but ourselves, lest we stop long enough to discover a great emptiness within. If it is not hubris that propels us to this incredible ambition to dominate, it may well be the lack of any genuine self-satisfaction. Not being at peace with ourselves and failing to come to terms with the world ("taking responsibility for oneself," as the Confucians put it, and for all those actions that affect the lives of other beings), we are driven by an ever-deepening addiction, the vain idea that success and satisfaction must be out there somewhere just over the horizon. Just so, the astronomer Carl Sagan, though at opposite poles politically from the defender of star wars, insists that we set as our national goal the placing of man on Mars, lest we lose the momentum for great achievements—as if no task, no pressing human need closer to our home on earth, could compel our attention or be worthy of our noblest aspirations.

We have lived so long on the "high" of rising expectations, on the "speed" of constantly accelerated, fossil-fueled locomotion, on the stimulation of our jaded appetites by advertising that can sell us only what is souped up as "exciting," "shock-ing," "fantastic," or "out of this world," that it seems normal and natural for a whole society to live on credit cards and wildly unbalanced national budgets, throwing more and more dollars at problems that do not yield to quantitative solutions, even at the risk of runaway inflation and eventual catastrophic collapse.

Some indeed cry out, "Stop the world, I want to get off"; others think of sitting it out in a Zen monastery or in transcendental meditation (recognizing to this extent at least that the East has antidotes, if not anodynes, for such disorders of the spirit). But many more are like the character Monkey in the Chinese novel *Journey to the West*. As the story goes, the Monkey King had ambitions to seize the throne of the Jade Emperor, but the Lord Buddha stopped him. To settle the matter they agreed on a wager. If Monkey could jump off the palm of the Buddha's hand, he would have the throne. "'This Buddha,' Monkey thought to himself, 'is a perfect fool. I can jump a hundred and eight thousand leagues, while his palm cannot be as much as eight inches across. How could I fail to jump clear of it.'"[5]

Monkey leapt with all his might, whizzing by so fast that the Buddha, watching him with the eye of wisdom, saw a mere whirligig shoot along. Then:

> Monkey came at last to five pink pillars, sticking up into the air. "This is the end of the World," said Monkey to himself. "All I have got to do is to go back to Buddha and claim my forfeit. The Throne is mine." "Wait a minute," he said presently, "I'd better just leave a record of some kind, in case I have trouble with Buddha." He plucked a hair and blew on it with magic breath, crying "Change!" It changed at once into a writing brush charged with heavy ink, and at the base of the central pillar he wrote, "The Great Sage Equal to Heaven reached this place." Then to mark his disrespect, he relieved nature at the bottom of the first pillar, and somersaulted back to where he had come from. Standing on Buddha's palm, he said, "Well, I've gone and come back. You can go and tell the Jade Emperor to hand over the Palaces of Heaven." "You stinking ape," said Buddha, "you've been on the palm of my hand all the time." "You're quite mistaken," said Monkey. "I got to the end of the World, where I saw five flesh-coloured pillars sticking up into the sky. I wrote something on one of them. I'll take you there and show you, if you like." "No need for that," said Buddha. "Just look down." Monkey peered down with his fiery, steely eyes, and there at the base of the middle finger of Buddha's hand he saw written the words "The Great Sage Equal to Heaven reached this place," and from the fork between the thumb and first finger came a smell of monkey's urine. It took him some time to get over his astonishment. At last he said, "Impossible, impossible! I wrote that on the pillar sticking up into the sky. How did it get on to Buddha's finger? He's prac-ticing some magic upon me. Let me go back and look." Dear Monkey! He crouched, and was just making ready to spring again, when Buddha turned his head, and pushed Monkey out at the western gate of Heaven.[6]

In the end, Monkey had to give up his world-conquering ambitions and submit to the restraint and direction of the humble, plodding pilgrim Tripitaka in order to achieve enlightenment. I shall forgo the temptation to allegorize here. I do not mean to equate Monkey with the bumptious West or Tripitaka with the wisdom of the East, as if they were antithetical rather than complementary (as the original *Journey* had it). Nor do I wish to moralize about space conquerors carrying their stinking pollution to the ends of the universe (perhaps the more insidious, because less detectable, when it does not stink!). Rather I confine myself to one observation: that no matter how far we hurtle through space, even if there is no one to "throw us out of Heaven," we shall still have to return to Mother Earth and face the unresolved, inescapable problems left behind there.

We may have to look at the situation with the Confucian eyes of Hsia Yüan-chi, the Ming Yung-lo Emperor's fiscal genius, who provided the logistic support for Cheng Ho's voyages. Hsia was open to the thought that these voyages might explore terra incognita and expand China's economic horizons; his was not a closed mind. Yet in the end, weighing the great human costs against the ephemeral returns, he opposed their continuance and carried on his protest to the point of incurring imprisonment, risking indeed even death. How much less would he have acquiesced in the empress dowager's marble boat!

The Confucians faced many of these questions as early as the eleventh century, though not on quite the scale or with the same complexity as we must today. Sung civilization, as we have seen, had reached the point where new technologies could be suitably applied to solving its urgent problems (demographically speaking, be it noted, of modern proportions). Hu Yuan believed that in education the humane values of the Confucian classics were needed to guide the application of the more concentrated political power and sophisticated technology available in his day. Thus his curriculum included classical studies for basic principles ("substance") and technical studies for practical application ("function"). Chu Hsi, for his part, developed the "substance" aspect further in his philosophy of human nature and the moral mind, but most especially in a cosmology that saw man's moral consciousness as coaxial with the life-giving and life-sustaining powers of Heaven-and-Earth.

If as a philosopher Chu Hsi thought it essential to ground his philosophy of human nature in such a cosmology and did not simply assume that man was the measure of all things, as a teacher he thought it no less vital for education to be centered on the self and the home. Working out from that center, as one disciplined and developed one's powers, one could take on ever-expanding tasks and opportunities for humane endeavor.

In this context it is understandable that nineteenth-century neo-Confucians, though impressed by the power and technology of the West and compelled to come to terms with it, still harbored grave, unresolved doubts. How could one pursue the seemingly unlimited development of power and technology without asking what commensurate conception of the moral center would hold these centrifugal forces within bounds or direct them to the humane ends traditionally summed up in "a humanity forming one body with Heaven-and-Earth and all things" (that is, feeling for all things as if they were your own flesh and blood)?

Some East Asians are still looking for an answer, while others have long since ceased even to ask the question. Many simply follow the dominant trend in the West, where increasingly it appears that, in dealing with severe social problems, self-restraint and moral guidance are no longer considered acceptable options. Rather the West's solution often seems to be in impersonal, mechanical means—material inducements, legal sanctions, penal institutions—that have already proven ineffective. The expenditure of more and more money, with less and less attention to the deeper problems of the human spirit, leads only to bankruptcy.

There is of course another side to the "West," which stands in significant contrast to this dominant trend and offers some hope of reversing it. This may best be identified with the environmental movement, which, when it has not lent itself to ulterior, ideological ends, has shown remarkable dynamism as a grassroots effort cutting across the political spectrum. Although it is still far from achieving its larger objectives, what it has already accomplished in a few short decades to reduce air, water, and earth pollution (especially smoking) is a major triumph. That these gains have been made largely by voluntary educational efforts, with a minimum of legal coercion (while more tightly controlled and planned societies have done little), is a great credit to the popular initiative and leadership of the movement in Western democracies.

Ironically, since Oriental philosophies in the form of "nature mysticism" are often seen as a source of inspiration for such movements, we have the apparent paradox of the West, with its cultural and political pluralism, taking over certain aspects of the East Asian tradition, while modern East Asia, industrialized and commercialized almost with a vengeance, lags behind in the struggle to control pollution. In this respect, then, the meeting and mixing of East and West have already progressed to the point where modern East Asia may need to catch up with some of its best traditions, as exemplified by the West.

What may seem even more paradoxical is the official alarm expressed in the People's Republic of China, which is formally committed to a materialist philosophy and is now admittedly pursuing a "pragmatic" policy, over the alleged danger of moral degeneration and spiritual contamination from the West. Some observers would discount this as more truly designed to curb people's pent-up desires for the good things of life and to justify the continued repression of human rights and freedom of thought. One cannot rule this out, certainly, as a subconscious motive. Having defaulted on many of the original promises of the revolution, made to justify the seizure of power by a party dictatorship, its leaders now reach out for new justifications that may appeal to popular prejudices, including an old-fashioned fundamentalist morality. Thus they use the defense of traditional virtue as a cloak for the preservation of their own authority.

Yet it would be a mistake to assume that no more is at issue, or at work, than this. Similar doubts and fears have been expressed over the years, in most East Asian countries, by spokesmen of both right and left, by elements of the establishment and of the opposition to it, by radicals of the Cultural Revolution as well as by more moderate, secular socialists like Lee Kwan-yu of Singapore who broods, as the liberal Nehru once did also, over the moral corruption that "Westernization" seems to bring in its train.

Nor do these apprehensions represent only Asia's stubborn rearguard action against the West. Similar fears beset the West itself. As one particularly apt expression of this sentiment, let me quote in conclusion from an essay written by Lionel Trilling just before his death, in which he tried to diagnose as an American problem what we recognize as a worldwide malaise:

If we consider the roadblocks in the path of a re-establishment of traditional humanistic education, surely none is so effectually obstructing as the tendency of our culture to regard the mere energy of impulse as being in every mental and moral way equivalent and even superior to defined intention. We may remark, as exemplary of this tendency, the fate of an idea that once was salient in Western culture: the idea of "making a life," by which was meant conceiving human existence, one's own or another's, as if it were a work of art upon which one might pass judgment, assessing it by established criteria.

This desire to fashion, to shape, a self and a life has all but gone from a contemporary culture whose emphasis, paradoxically enough, is so much on self…Such limitation, once acceptable, now goes against the cultural grain; it is almost as if the fluidity of the contemporary world demands an analogous limitlessness in our personal perspective. Any doctrine, that of the family, religion, the school, that does not sustain this increasingly felt need for a multiplicity of options and instead offers an ideal of a shaped self, a formed life, has the sign on it of a retrograde and depriving authority, which, it is felt, must be resisted.

For anyone concerned with contemporary education at whatever level, the assimilation that contemporary culture has made between social idealism, even political liberalism, and personal fluidity—a self without the old confinements—is as momentous as it is recalcitrant to correction. Among the factors in the contemporary world which militate against the formulation of an educational ideal related to the humanistic traditions of the past, this seems to me to be the most decisive.[7]

If Trilling seems to agonize here over aberrations of the counterculture in the 1960s, with its drive toward liberation from all constraints of tradition, there may well have been, in the inchoate cross-currents of that age, many whose radicalism was less political than moral and spiritual, and who sought desperately to shape a life, to define a self, precisely at a time when the permissiveness of their elders offered them little real challenge or reliable guidance. The frequent incantation in those days, "Not to decide is to decide," may often have been abused in the absence of persuasive evidence on which to base a decision, but it did not reflect a sense of the "limitlessness of personal perspective," in Trilling's phrase.

In such circumstances tradition would appear to have failed, and young persons, in a generation unmoored to any meaningful past, would be apt to ignore the claims of history. On this point, a decade later in 1986, one of Trilling's successors as Jefferson Lecturer, Leszek Kolakowski, had this to say about the nature of historical self-understanding:

Educated (and even un-educated) people in pre-industrial societies, whose historical learning was very meager, were perhaps more historical—in the sense I mean here—than we are. The historical tradition in which they lived was woven of myths, legends and orally-transmitted stories of which the material accuracy was more often than not dubious. Still it was good enough to give them the feeling of life within a continuous religious, national or tribal community, to provide them with the kind of identity that made life ordered (or "meaningful"). In this sense it was a living thing, and it taught people why, and for what they were responsible, as well as how this responsibility was to be practically taken up…But whoever is interested in, and worrying about, the spiritual fragility of young people cannot deny that the erosion of a historically-defined sense of "belonging" plays havoc with their lives, and threatens their ability to withstand possible trials of the future.[8]

Kolakowski, speaking also to the question of personal rights in the modern world, says that they are defensible "only on the assumption that there is a realm of personal reality that is definable in moral, not biological terms. They have to be vindicated on moral grounds, much as their implementation depends on political conditions."[9]

Confucians would have resisted the dichotomy of moral/ biological here, but what both Trilling and Kolakowski saw as key to the crisis in modern education—a dialogue with the past—was already central to the teaching of Confucius in the sixth century B.C. and remained so in the dialogue conducted by the Confucians down through the ages, in conversation with other traditions and cultures. The Japanese particularly set that dialogue in a multicultural context and kept it open to new influences. In that respect Japanese pluralism, with its genius for consensus formation, best represents the international dimension of East Asian civilization and, despite the great contrast in size between it and the United States, comes closest to our own outgoing impulse to incorporate new experience into a culture still in the process of formation.

I believe that we are entering a new and severely constricted phase of our development that will, contrary to the thrust of modern life so far, compel us to attend first to our inner space—of self-reflection, family intimacy, neighborly concern, and responsibility for our own bioregion—and only then to outer space. If I am right in this, we may have much to learn from both the Buddhist and the neo-Confucian experience, especially from Chu Hsi's effort to define an educational curriculum aimed at the "shaping of a self"—"learning for the sake of one's self," as he put it—as a life formation on which a public philosophy could be grounded.

Chu's model for the curriculum—starting from a personal reading of and confrontation with the classics, followed by study of the major histories, and continuing as a lifelong discussion of value issues and contemporary problems, alongside the technical specialization for which Hu Yuan had recognized a need—is still worthy of consideration today. The "classics" would have to be more broadly representative of major world traditions; the "cosmology" should include what we now know about the larger universe and earth origins; the "history" would need to be extended to include biological and cultural evolution; and the "contemporary problems" would require updating, but in essence Chu's would still be a valid approach. As a pattern for a core curriculum balancing the specialized and vocational training so emphasized today, it would compare well with the requirements in effect at most colleges, and even better with those in many well-advertised institutions that trade heavily on the total flexibility of their approach to learning. Admittedly, however, such a program would have to go beyond the college years. Today a truly humane or liberal education can be conceived only as a lifelong enterprise, starting in the under-graduate years but continuing in graduate or professional school and adult education.

Chu recognized the compelling need for spiritual and moral training alongside the reading and discussion of books. Today we confront crises even more severe than his and threats far more deadly, implicit in the potential of new technologies for both catastrophic destruction and totalitarian control. No educational program will be able to meet these challenges that does not rouse the individual motivations and galvanize the human energies needed to cope with them—in other words, that does not by a virtual religious revolution reach deeply into the resources of the human spirit. Each of the four stages of civilization discussed here was inspired and sustained by such an inner revolution, while at the same time building upon the material and spiritual capital of the preceding age. This, I believe, will be no less true of the next great age of world civilization. No new order can endure that does not draw on the legacies of the past, but no tradition, whether Confucian, Buddhist, or Christian, can survive untransformed in the crucible of global struggle.

Often the study of East Asia is seen as one aspect of a larger program of international education that looks optimistically to new and expanded horizons, to consciousness raising, global awareness, and other grand visions of the future. But as we become more deeply conscious of the global dimensions of our problems, of our responsibility for the damage now being done to the earth, and of the jeopardy in which we have already put future generations, our education, instead of discussing universal values or the "humanities" in the abstract, will need to focus on something more concrete—on the best examples we can find of individual human beings, trying to meet their responsibilities in their own time, who have exercised their human freedom to make crucial decisions and difficult choices in facing such dilemmas. Trilling and Kolakowski worried about the erosion of any sense in modern culture that one can take responsibility for oneself and one's actions. I hope I have suggested here a few cases from the East Asian experience, now part of our common human inheritance, that can help us to recognize ourselves in such situations and suggest how we may begin to shape new selves more adequate to the prodigious challenges of both the present and the future.

NOTES

1. This is the concluding chapter in Wm. Theodore de Bary, *East Asian Civilizations: A Dialogue in Five Stages* (Cambridge, MA: Harvard University Press, 1988).
2. Here I am drawing in part on my response to Paul Cohen's review of *The Liberal Tradition in China*. His review appeared under the title "The Quest of Liberalism in the Chinese Past" in *Philosophy East and West, 35* (July 1985): 305–310. My reply, ibid. (October 1985): 399–412, was entitled: "Confucian Liberalism and Western Parochialisms." Professor Cohen's response to it is in the same issue, pp. 413–417.
3. Jack Kirwan, "Mandarin Mondale and U.S. Future in Space," *Wall Street Journal,* Oct. 23, 1984.
4. Ibid.
5. Arthur Waley, *Monkey* (London: George Allen and Unwin, 1942), p. 75.
6. Ibid., pp. 75–76.
7. Lionel Trilling, "The Uncertain Future of Humanistic Education," *American Scholar* (Winter 1974–75): 56–57.
8. Leszek Kolakowski, "The Idolatry of Politics," *New Republic,* June 16, 1986.
9. Ibid. In saying that Confucians would probably not accept any dichotomy between the moral and biological, I should acknowledge that Kolakowski's real point is more to affirm the moral reality than to set up any antithesis between the two.

SELECTIVE BIBLIOGRAPHY

PART ONE

Seyla Benhabib, *The Claims of Culture: Equality and Diversity in the Global Era* (Princeton, NJ: Princeton University Press, 2002).

James Bohman, *Democracy Across Borders* (Cambridge, MA: MIT Press, 2007).

Elise Boulding, *Building a Global Civic Culture* (Syracuse, NY: Syracuse University Press, 1988).

James Clifford and George Marcus, eds., *Writing Culture: The Poetics and Politics of Ethnography* (Cambridge, MA: Harvard University Press, 1986).

Fred Dallmayr, ed., *Border Crossings: Toward a Comparative Political Theory* (Lanham, MD: Lexington Books, 1999).

Fred Dallmayr, *Dialogue Among Civilizations: Some Exemplary Voices* (New York: Palgrave Macmillan, 2002).

Eliot Deutsch and Ron Bontekoe, eds., *A Companion to World Philosophies* (Malden, MA: Blackwell, 1997).

Eliot Deutsch, ed., *Culture and Modernity: East-West Philosophic Perspectives* (Honolulu: University of Hawaii Press, 1991).

David A. Dilworth, *Philosophy in World Perspective* (New Haven, CT: Yale University Press, 1989).

Johan Galtung, *The True Worlds: A Transnational Perspective* (New York: Free Press, 1980).

Clifford Geertz, *The Interpretation of Cultures: Selected Essays* (New York: Basic Books, 1973).

Amy Gutmann, ed., *Multiculturalism and "The Politics of Recognition"* (Princeton: Princeton University Press, 1992).

Samuel Huntington, *The Clash of Civilizations and the Remaking of World Order* (New York: Simon & Schuster, 1996).

Hwa Yol Jung, ed., *Comparative Political Culture in the Age of Globalization: An Anthology* (Lanham, MD: Lexington Books, 2002).

Alfred J. Lopez, *Posts and Pasts: A Theory of Postcolonialism* (Albany, NY: State University of New York Press, 2001).

Gerald J. Larsen and Eliot Deutsch, eds., *Interpreting Across Boundaries: New Essays in Comparative Philosophy* (Princeton: Princeton University Press, 1988).

George F. McLean and John Kromkowski, eds., *Relations Between Cultures* (Washington, DC: Council for Research in Values and Philosophy, 1991).

F.S.C. Northrop and H. H. Livingston, eds., *Cross-Cultural Understanding: Epistemology and Anthropology* (New York: Harper & Row, 1964).

Bhikhu Parekh, *Rethinking Multiculturalism: Cultural Diversity and Political Theory* (London: Macmillan, 2002).

Anthony J. Parel and Ronald C. Keith, *Comparative Political Philosophy: Studies Under the Upas Tree*, 2nd ed. (Lanham, MD: Lexington Press, 2003).

Edward Said, *Orientalism* (New York: Vintage Books, 1979).

Ninian Smart, *Worldviews: Cross-Cultural Explorations of Human Beliefs* (New York: Scribner's, 1983).

Ninian Smart and B. Srinivasa Murthy, eds., *East-West Encounters in Philosophy and Religion* (London: Sangam, 1997).

Huston Smith, *The World's Religions* (New York: Harper Collier, 1991).

Charles Taylor, "Understanding the Other," in *Philosophical Papers II: Philosophy and the Human Sciences* (Cambridge, UK: Cambridge University Press, 1985), pp. 279–297.

PART TWO

Abdullahi Ahmed An-Naim, *Islam and the Secular State* (Cambridge, MA: Harvard University Press, 2008).

Mohammed Arkoun, *Rethinking Islam: Common Questions, Uncommon Answers* (Boulder, CO: Westview Press, 1994).

Osman Bakar, *Islam and Civilizational Dialogue* (Kuala Lumpur: University of Malaya Press, 1997).

Anthony Black, *A History of Islamic Political Thought: From the Prophet to the Present* (New York: Routledge, 2001).

Michaelle L. Browers, *Democracy and Civil Society in Arab Political Thought* (Syracuse, NY: Syracuse University Press, 2006).

Charles E. Butterworth, ed., *Alfarabi: The Political Writings* (Ithaca, NY: Cornell University Press, 2001).

Charles E. Butterworth and I. William Zartman, eds., *Between the State and Islam* (Cambridge, UK: Cambridge University Press, 2001).

William Chittick, *Faith and Practice of Islam* (Albany, NY: State University of New York Press, 1992).

John Cooper, Ronald Nettler, and Mohamed Mahmoud, eds., *Islam and Modernity: Muslim Intellectuals Respond* (London: Tauris Publ., 2000).

Ahmet Davutoglu, *Civilizational Transformation and the Muslim World* (Kuala Lumpur: Mahir Publications, 1994).

Hamid Enayat, *Modern Islamic Political Thought* (Austin, TX: University of Texas Press, 1982).

Roxanne L. Euben, *Enemy in the Mirror: Islamic Fundamentalism and the Limits of Modern Rationalism* (Princeton: Princeton University Press, 1999).

John L. Esposito, ed., *Voices of Resurgent Islam* (New York: Oxford University Press, 1983).

John L. Esposito and John O. Voll, *Islam and Democracy* (New York: Oxford University Press, 1996).

John L. Esposito and John O. Voll, *Makers of Contemporary Islam* (New York: Oxford University Press, 2001).

Majid Fakhry, *A History of Islamic Philosophy*, 2nd ed. (New York: Columbia University Press, 1983).

Sohail H. Hashmi, ed., *Islamic Political Ethics* (Princeton: Princeton University Press, 2002).

Martin S. Kramer, *Arab Awakening and Islamic Revival* (New Brunswick, NJ: Transaction Publ., 1996).

Elie Kedouri, *Afghani and Abduh* (London: Cass and Col., 1966).

Charles Kurzman, ed., *Liberal Islam: A Source Book* (New York: Oxford University Press, 1998).

Charles Kurzman, ed., *Modernist Islam, 1840–1940* (New York: Oxford University Press, 2002).

Oliver Leaman, *A Brief Introduction to Islamic Philosophy* (Cambridge, UK: Polity Press, 1999).

Oliver Leaman, *Averroes and His Philosophy* (Oxford: Clarendon Press, 1988).

Robert D. Lee, *Overcoming Tradition and Modernity: The Search for Islamic Authenticity* (Boulder, CO: Westview Press, 1997).

Bernard Lewis, *The Political Language of Islam* (Chicago, IL: University of Chicago Press, 1988).

Bernard Lewis, *Islam and the West* (New York: Oxford University Press, 1993).

Muhsin S. Mahdi, *Alfarabi and the Foundations of Islamic Political Philosophy* (Chicago, IL: University of Chicago Press, 2001).

Fatima Mernissi, *Islam and Democracy: Fear of the Modern World* (Reading, MA: Addison-Wesley, 1992).

Sachiko Murata, *The Tao of Islam: A Sourcebook on Gender Relations in Islamic Thought* (Albany, NY: State University of New York Press, 1992).

Seyyid Hossein Nasr, *Knowledge and the Sacred* (Albany, NY: State University of New York Press, 1989).

James P. Piscatori, *Islam in a World of Nation-States* (Cambridge, UK: Cambridge University Press, 1986).

Fazlur Rahman, *Islam and Modernity* (Chicago: University of Chicago Press, 1982).

Nissim Rejwar, *Arabs Face the Modern World* (Gainesville, FL: University Press of Florida, 1998).

Abdulaziz Sachedina, *The Islamic Roots of Democratic Pluralism* (New York: Oxford University Press, 2001).

Annemarie Schimmel, *My Soul is a Woman: The Feminine in Islam* (New York: Continuum, 1999).

Ali Shariati, *Marxism and Other Western Fallacies: An Islamic Critique* (Berkeley, CA: Mizan Press, 1980).

Abdel S. Sidahmed and Anoushiravan Ehteshami, eds., *Islamic Foundamentalism* (Boulder, CO: Westview Press, 1996).

Emmanuel Sivan, *Radical Islam* (New Haven, CT: Yale University Press, 1990).

Abdolkarim Soroush, *Reason, Freedom, and Democracy in Islam* (New York: Oxford University Press, 2000).

Marietta T. Stepaniants, *Sufi Wisdom* (Albany, NY: State University of New York Press, 1994).

W. Montgomery Watt, *The Faith and Practice of Al-Ghazali* (Chicago: Kazi Publications, 1982).

PART THREE

M. J. Akbar, *Nehru: The Making of India* (New York: Viking, 1988).

Philip H. Ashly, *Modern Trends in Hinduism* (New York: Columbia University Press, 1974).

Upendra Baxi and Bhikhu Parekh, eds., *Crisis and Change in Contemporary India* (New Delhi: Sage Publ., 1995).

Roger Boesche, *The First Great Political Realist: Kautilya and His Arthashastra* (Lanham, MD: Lexington Books, 2002).

Paul R. Brass, *The Politics of India Since Independence*, 2nd ed. (Cambridge, UK: Cambridge University Press, 1994).

Fred Dallmayr and Ganesh N. Devy, eds., *Between Tradition and Modernity: India's Search for Identity* (New Delhi: Sage, 1998).

Dennis Dalton, *Mahatma Gandhi: Nonviolent Power in Action* (New York: Columbia University Press, 1993).

M. N. Das, *The Political Philosophy of Jawarhalal Nehru* (New York: Day, 1991).

Margaret Chatterjee, *Gandhi's Religious Thought* (Notre Dame, IN: University of Notre Dame Press, 1983).

Ainslee T. Embree, *Utopias in Conflict: Religion and Nationalism in Modern India* (Berkeley, CA: University of California Press, 1990).

Rajmohan Gandhi, *The Good Boatman: A Portrait of Gandhi* (New York: Penguin, 1997).

Harold A. Gould, *Caste Adaptation in Modernizing Indian Society* (Delhi: Chanakya Publications, 1988).

Wilhelm Halbfass, *India and Europe: An Essay in Understanding* (Albany, NY: State University of New York Press, 1988).

A. L. Herman, *A Brief Introduction to Hinduism* (Boulder, CO: Westview Press, 1991).

Ronald Inden, *Imagining India* (Oxford, UK: Blackwell, 1990).

Daya Krishna, *Indian Philosophy: A Counter Perspective* (Delhi: Oxford University Press, 1991).

T. M. P. Mahadevan, *The Hymns of Shankara* (Delhi: Mortilal Banarsidass, 1980).

J. L. Mehta, *India and the West: The Problem of Understanding* (Chico, CA: Scholars Press, 1985).

V. R. Mehta, *Ideology, Modernization, and Politics in India* (New Delhi: Manohar, 1983).

V. R. Mehta, *Foundations of Indian Political Thought* (New Delhi: Manohar, 1992).

V. R. Mehta and Thomas Pantham, eds., *Political Ideas in Modern India* (New Delhi: Sage, 2006).

J. N. Mohanty, *Classical Indian Philosophy* (Lanham, MD: Rowman and Littlefield, 2002).

B. R. Nanda, *Three Statesmen: Gokhale, Gandhi, and Nehru* (New Delhi: Oxford University Press, 2004).

Ashis Nandy, *Tradition, Tyranny, and Utopias: Essays in the Politics of Awareness* (Delhi: Oxford University Press, 1987).

Ashis Nandy, ed., *Science, Hegemony, and Violence: A Requiem for Modernity* (Delhi: Oxford University Press, 1996).

Thomas Pantham and Kenneth L. Deutsch, eds., *Political Thought in Modern India* (New Delhi: Sage, 1986).

Thomas Pantham, *Political Theories and Social Reconstruction: A Critical Survey of the Literature on India* (New Delhi: Sage, 1995).

Bhikhu Parekh and Thomas Pantham, eds., *Political Discourse: Explorations in Indian and Western Political Thought* (New Delhi: Sage, 1987).

Bhikhu Parekh, *Colonialism, Tradition, and Reform* (New Delhi: Sage, 1989).

Bhikhu Parekh, *Gandhi's Political Philosophy: A Critical Examination* (Notre Dame, IN: University of Notre Dame Press, 1989).

Bhikhu Parekh, *Gandhi* (Oxford: Oxford University Press, 1997).

Anthony J. Parel, ed., *Gandhi: Hind Swaraj and Other Writings* (Cambridge, UK: Cambridge University Press, 1997).

Anthony J. Parel, *Gandhi's Philosophy and the Quest for Harmony* (Cambridge, UK: Cambridge University Press, 2006).

Ganesh Prasad, *Nehru: A Study in Colonial Liberalism* (New Delhi: Sterling, 1976).

Sarvepalli Radhakrishnan, *The Hindu View of Life* (New Delhi: Harper Collins, 1927/1933).

R. Sundara Rajan, *The Primacy of the Political* (New Delhi: Oxford University Press, 1991).

R. D. Ranade, *Mysticism in India* (Albany, NY: State University of New York Press, 1983).

K. L. Seshagiri Rao, *Mahatma Gandhi and Comparative Religion* (Delhi: Motilal Banarsidass, 1990).

Rameshra Roy, *Self and Society: A Study of Gandhian Thought* (New Delhi: Sage, 1984).

Ramakant A. Sinari, *The Structure of Indian Thought* (Delhi: Oxford University Press, 1984).

Glyn Richards, ed., *A Source-Book of Modern Hinduism* (London: Curzon Press, 1985).

Lloyd L. and Susanne H. Rudolph, *The Modernity of Tradition: Political Development in India* (Chicago: University of Chicago Press, 1967).

Lloyd L. and Susanne H. Rudolph, *Postmodern Gandhi and Other Essays* (Chicago, IL: University of Chicago Press, 2006).

Arvind Sharma, *Classical Hindu Thought: An Introduction* (New York: Oxford University Press, 2000).

Arvind Sharma, *Hinduism for Our Time* (New York: Oxford University Press, 1996).

Arvind Sharma, ed., *Hinduism and Secularism, After Ayodhya* (New York: Palgrave, 2001).

D. L. Sheth and Ashis Nandy, eds., *The Multiverse of Democracy* (New Delhi: Sage, 1996).

Ronald Terchek, *Gandhi: Struggling for Autonomy* (Lanham, MD: Rowman & Littlefield, 1998).

Sashi Tharoor, *Nehru: The Inventor of India* (New York: Arcade, 2003).

Heinrich Zimmer, *Philosophies of India*, ed. Joseph Campbell (Princeton, NJ: Princeton University Press, 1969).

Part Four

Masao Abe, *Zen and Western Thought* (Honolulu: University of Hawaii Press, 1985).

Masao Abe, *Zen and Comparative Studies* (Honolulu: University of Hawaii Press, 1997).

Byung-joon Ahn, *Chinese Politics and the Cultural Revolution* (Seattle: University of Washington Press, 1976).

Roger T. Ames, *The Art of Rulership: A Study of Ancient Chinese Political Thought* (Albany, NY: State University of New York Press, 1994).

Daniel A. Bell, *East Meets West: Human Rights and Democracy in East Asia* (Princeton: Princeton University Press, 2000).

Daniel A. Bell, *Beyond Liberal Democracy: Political Thinking for an East Asian Context* (Princeton, NJ: Princeton University Press, 2006).

Daniel A. Bell, *China's New Confucianism* (Princeton, NJ: Princeton University Press, 2008).

Daniel A. Bell, ed., *Confucian Political Ethics* (Princeton, NJ: Princeton University Press, 2008).

Daniel A. Bell and Hahm Chaibong, eds., *Confucianism for the Modern World* (Cambridge, UK: Cambridge University Press, 2003).

John H. Berthrong, *Transformations of the Confucian Way* (Boulder, CO: Westview Press, 1998).

H. Gene Blocker, *Japanese Philosophy* (Albany, NY: State University of New York Press, 2001).

Wing-tsit Chan, *A Source Book in Chinese Philosophy* (Princeton, NJ: Princeton University Press, 1963).

Carsun Chang et al., eds., *The Development of Neo-Confucian Thought*, 2 vols. (New York: Bookman Associates, 1957).

Hao Chang, *Chinese Intellectuals in Crisis: Search for Order and Meaning, 1890–1911* (Berkeley: University of California Press, 1987).

Yung-Ping Chen, *Chinese Political Thought: Mao Tse-tung and Liu Shaochi* (The Hague: Nijhoff, 1966).

Chung-ying Cheng, *New Dimensions of Confucian and Neo-Confucian Philosophy* (Albany, NY: State University of New York Press, 1991).

Wen-Shun Chi, *Ideological Conflicts in Modern China* (New Brunswick, NJ: Transaction Books, 1986).

Min-hong Choe, *A Modern History of Korean Philosophy* (Seoul: Seong Moon Sa, 1980).

Tse-tung Chow, *The May Fourth Movement: Intellectual Revolution in Modern China* (Cambridge, MA: Harvard University Press, 1960).

James W. Coleman, *The New Buddhism* (New York: Oxford University Press, 2001).

Wm. Theodore de Bary, *Neo-Confucian Orthodoxy and the Learning of the Mind-and-Heart* (New York: Columbia University Press, 1981).

Wm. Theodore de Bary, *The Liberal Tradition in China* (New York: Columbia University Press, 1983).

Wm. Theodore de Bary, *East Asian Civilizations: A Dialogue in Five Stages* (Cambridge, MA: Harvard University Press, 1988).

Wm. Theodore de Bary, *The Trouble with Confucianism* (Cambridge, MA: Harvard University Press, 1991).

Wm. Theodore de Bary, *Nobility and Civility: Asian Ideals of Leadership and the Common Good* (Cambridge, MA: Harvard University Press, 2004).

Wm. Theodore de Bary and Tu Wei-ming, eds., *Confucianism and Human Rights* (New York: Columbia University Press, 1998).

Heinrich Dumoulin, ed., *Buddhism in the Modern World* (New York: Macmillan, 1976).

Charles W. Fu and Steven Heine, *Japan in Tradition and Postmodern Perspectives* (Albany, NY: State University of New York Press, 1995).

A. C. Graham, *Disputers of the Tao* (La Salle, IL: Open Court, 1989).

Paul J. Griffith, *On Being Buddha: The Classical Doctrine of Buddhahood* (Albany, NY: State University of New York Press, 1994).

Ruben L. Habito, *Total Liberation: Zen Spirituality and the Social Dimension* (Maryknoll, NY: Orbis Books, 1989).

David L. Hall and Roger T. Ames, *Thinking Through Confucius* (Albany, NJ: State University of New York Press, 1987).

David L. Hall and Roger T. Ames, *Anticipating China: Thinking Through the Narratives of Chinese and Western Culture* (Albany, NY: State University of New York Press, 1995).

David L. Hall and Roger T. Ames, *Democracy of the Dead : Dewey, Confucians, and the Hope for Democracy in China* (LaSalle, IL: Open Court, 1999).

James W. Heisig, *Philosophers of Nothingness: An Essay on the Kyoto School* (Honolulu: University of Hawaii Press, 2001).

Fu-Wu Hou, *Chinese Political Traditions* (Washington, DC: Public Affairs Press, 1965).

Jamie Hubbard and Paul L. Swanson, eds., *Pruning the Bodhi Tree: The Storm over Critical Buddhism* (Honolulu: University of Hawaii Press, 1997).

Hiroshi Ito, *Japanese Politics—An Inside View* (Ithaca, NY: Cornell University Press, 1973).

Joseph R. Levenson, *Modern China: An Interpretive Anthology* (New York: Macmillan, 1970).

Joseph R. Levenson, *Confucian China and Its Modern Fate* (London: Routledge & Kegan Paul, 1965).

Shu-hsien Liu, *Understanding Confucian Philosophy: Classical and Sung-Ming* (Westport, CT: Greenwood Press, 1998).

David R. Loy, *The Great Awakening: A Buddhist Social Theory* (Boston: Wisdom Publications, 2003).

David S. Nivison, *The Ways of Confucianism* (LaSalle, IL: Open Court, 1996).

William S. A. Pott, *Chinese Political Philosophy* (New York: Knopf, 1925).

Henry Rosemont, Jr., *A Chinese Mirror: Moral Reflections on Political Economy and Society* (LaSalle, IL: Open Court, 1991).

Gilbert Rozman, *The East Asian Region: Confucian Heritage and Its Modern Adaptation* (Princeton: Princeton University Press, 1991).

Benjamin I. Schwartz, *The World of Thought in Ancient China* (Cambridge, MA: Harvard University Press, 1985).

Benjamin I. Schwartz, *Communism and China: Ideology in Flux* (Cambridge, MA: Harvard University Press, 1968).

Jonathan Spence, *The Search for Modern China* (New York: Norton, 1990).

Chester C. Tan, *Chinese Political Thought in the Twentieth Century* (Garden City, NY: Doubleday, 1971).

Frederick C. Teiwes, *The End of the Maoist Era* (New York: Sharpe, 2007).

Elbert D. Thomas, *Chinese Political Thought* (New York: Prentice Hall, 1927).

Tu Wei-ming, *Humanity and Self-Cultivation: Essays in Confucian Thought* (Berkeley: Asian Humanities Press, 1979).

Tu Wei-ming, *Way, Learning, and Politics: Essays on the Confucian Intellectual* (Albany, NY: State University of New York Press, 1993).

Tu Wei-ming, ed., *Confucian Traditions in East Asian Modernity* (Cambridge, MA: Harvard University Press, 1996).

Tu Wei-ming, ed., *China in Transformation* (Cambridge, MA: Harvard University Press, 1994).

CONTRIBUTORS

Daniel A. Bell is professor of political philosophy at Tsinghua University in Beijing, China. Among his publications are: *East Meets West: Human Rights and Democracy in East Asia* (2000); *China's New Confucianism* (2008); and *Confucian Political Ethics* (2008).

José I. Cabezón is professor of religion at Iliff School of Theology; among his publications are: *A Dose of Emptiness* (1992); *Buddhism and Language* (1994); and *Tibetan Literature: Studies in Genre* (1996).

Fred Dallmayr is Packey J. Dee Professor in the departments of philosophy and political science at the University of Notre Dame; among his recent publications are: *Dialogue Among Civilizations: Some Exemplary Voices* (2002); *In Search of the Good Life* (2007); and *The Promise of Democracy* (2010).

Youssef M. Choueiri is Reader in Islamic Studies at the University of Manchester, England; among his publications are: *Arab History and the Nation-State* (1989); *and Islamic Fundamentalism* (1997).

William Theodore De Bary is University Professor and Provost Emeritus at Columbia University in New York; among his publications are: *The Trouble with Confucianism* (1991); *Asian Values and Human Rights* (1998); and *Nobility and Civility* (2004).

John L. Esposito is University Professor of religion and international affairs at Georgetown University; among his publications are: *The Contemporary Islamic Revival* (1991); *Islam and Politics* (1998); *The Islamic Threat: Myth or Reality?* (1999); and *The Future of Islam* (2010).

Roxanne L. Euben is professor of political theory at Wellesley College; among her publications are: *Enemy in the Mirror: Islamic Fundamentalism and the Limits of Modern Rationalism* (1999); and *Journeys to the Other Shore* (2006).

Chaibong Hahm is professor of political theory at Yonsei University in Seoul, Korea; among his publications are: *Confucianism for the Modern World* (with Daniel A. Bell, 2003).

Ronald C. Keith is professor of political science at the University of Calgary in Canada; among his publications are: *The Diplomacy of Zhou Enlai* (1989);

China's Struggle for the Rule of Law (1994); and *China as a Rising World Power* (2005).

Ira R. Lapidus is Emeritus Professor of History at the University of California-Berkeley; among his publications are: *Islam, Politics, and Social Movements* (1988); and *A History of Islamic Societies* (2002).

Mushin Mahdi (1926–2007) specialized in medieval Arabic and Islamic philosophy and was Director of the Center for Middle Eastern Studies at Harvard University; among his publications are: *Ibn Khaldun's Philosophy of History* (1964); *The Political Aspects of Islamic Philosophy* (1992); and *Alfarabi and the Foundation of Islamic Political Philosophy* (2001).

Thomas Pantham is Emeritus Professor of political theory at the M.S. University of Baroda, India; among his publications are: *Political Thought in Modern India* (with Kenneth Deutsch, 1986); *Political Theories and Social Reconstruction* (1996); and *Political Ideas in Modern India* (with V.R. Mehta, 2006).

Bhikhu C. Parekh is member of the House of Lords and professor of political theory at the University of Westminster, London; among his publications are: *Gandhi's Political Philosophy: A Critical Examination* (1999); *Rethinking Multiculturalism* (2000); and *A New Politics of Identity* (2008).

Anthony J. Parel is Emeritus Professor of political theory at the University Calgary in Canada; among his publications are: *Hind Swaraj and Other Writings* (1997); *Gandhi, Freedom, and Self-Rule* (2000); and *Gandhi's Philosophy and the Quest for Harmony* (2006).

R.C. Pillai has served as Reader in political science at Deshbandhu College of Delhi University; among his publications are: *Nehru and His Critics* (1986).

A.K. Shah (1922–1994) was professor and head of the department of philosophy at Karnataka University, India; among other publications he edited *Wittgenstein's Lectures on Philosophical Psychology* (1972).

Tu Weiming is the Harvard-Yenching Professor of Chinese history and philosophy at Harvard University; among his publications are: *Way, Learning, and Politics* (1993); *China in Transformation* (1994); and *Confucian Traditions in East Asian Modernity* (1996).

INDEX